To the heroic victory
of the Indo-Chinese people
over U.S. imperialism.

The Political Economy of Imperialism

It s theoretical and polemical treatment
from Mercantilist to Multilateral Imperialism.

Dan Nabudere

Zed Press Ltd., 57 Caledonian Road, London N1 9DN.

Tanzania Publishing House, P.O. Box 2138, Dar es Salaam.

The Political Economy of Imperialism was first published
by Zed Press, 57 Caledonian Road, London, N1, and
Tanzania Publishing House, P.O. Box 2138, Dar es Salaam,
Tanzania, in October, 1977.

Printed by Whitehall Printers
Typeset by Lyn Caldwell
Designed by An Dekker

First Impression, October 1977
Second Impression, June 1978
Third Impression, 1983

ISBN   Hb   0 905762 03 7
       Pb   0 905762 02 9

U.S. Distributor:
Biblio Distribution Center, 81 Adams Drive, Totowa,
New Jersey 07512, U.S.A.

CONTENTS

PREFACE TO THE FIRST EDITION

This effort is the result of an earlier attempt to grapple with the problem of the theory of imperialism. The earlier monograph, the *Political Economy of World Trade and Finance*, was generally unsynthesised, as it was in the form of lecture notes for students who were doing a course in Legal Aspects of International Trade and Investment, as back-ground reading. During the course of the year (1974), it became clear from the discussions with comrades and students that the monograph could be developed into a theory on imperialism.

This work is the result of about two years reading on the subject and is the joint effort of all those who participated in commenting on it. My particular thanks go to Professor Joe L. Kanywanyi, the Dean of the Faculty of Law, who from the very inception of the project encouraged me on with comradely and revolutionary enthusiasm. His rigorous comments on the work as it progressed helped greatly to put it into the shape it has taken in its final form. My thanks also go to Professor Yash Tandon, of the Department of Political Science, University of Dar es Salaam, who also commented on the manuscript as a whole during the period it was under authorship. His scholarly comments helped me to be on guard on various issues. Henry Bernstein, Lecturer in the Department of Sociology, University of Dar es Salaam, commented on the first Part of the manu-script. I thank them all, including the students of the Faculty of Law who attended my classes on International Trade and Investment, whose discussions in seminars with me helped me greatly.

Needless to say, the final responsibility lies with me, but the views expressed here are entirely those of a class and therefore belong to society, of which I am but a product.

Finally I would like to record my appreciation to Ida Bethukile, my wife, and the family who have endured the long hours of silence from me during the period of concentrated study, writing and general preparation for the publication. Their encouragement is very much part of this effort.

D. Wadada Nabudere,
Dar es Salaam,
15th December, 1975.

PREFACE TO THE SECOND EDITION

This edition comes out with a few additional materials which were inadvertently excluded from the first edition. The major addition occurs on page 281. This is the material concerning self-financing of monopoly enterprises under modern conditions which, it is argued in some quarters, had turned today's monopolies away from their reliance on the banks. This 'argument' is refuted in this edition. There is also a slight reformulation in one part of the book (the Conclusion) on the question of political consciousness of the working class which makes the text more in line with Lenin's arguments on this question.

I would like to thank very much Comrade Dick Hensman, who has been so helpful in getting this book into print. This book might otherwise have never seen the light of day, having been brushed aside by the big publishers at first. I regret that my appreciation of this fact did not appear in the first edition due to my oversight. Many thanks also go to Roger van Zwanenberg and Walter Bgoya, the publishers, and to their comrades in the press, who have worked so untiringly under great pressure to get this book out at the time it did.

This book, as was only to be expected, was received well in Marxist-Leninist circles, and very harshly by neo-Marxists and neo-Trotskyists, who have piled abuse upon it. The bourgeoisie and their henchmen have, of course, turned a cold shoulder to it, and this is all they can do, having nothing else to answer back. Nevertheless the petty bourgeoisie of all hues, including the neo-Marxists and neo-Trotskyists, in their castigations only of course speak for the imperialists. Hence the imperialists need not say anything in attack.

We hope that this book will provoke a serious discussion among Marxist-Leninists as a way of improving our analysis of the contemporary situation of peoples' struggles against imperialism.

D. Wadada Nabudere,
Dar es Salaam,
25th May, 1978.

INTRODUCTION

'Political economy is therefore essentially a *historical* science. It deals with material which is historical, that is, constantly changing; it must first investigate the special laws of each individual stage in the evolution of production and exchange, and only when it has completed this investigation will it be able to establish the few quite general laws which hold good for production and exchange in general. At the same time it goes without saying that the laws which are valid for definite modes of production and forms of exchange hold good for all historical periods in which these modes of production and forms of exchange prevail'.

Frederick Engels
(Anti-Duhring)

Lenin's booklet, *Imperialism, the Highest Stage of Capitalism*, which he sub-titled: *A popular outline*, (1) has continued to attract bourgeois and populist attacks because of its scientific exposition and ideological presentation of the position of the working class on the question of modern imperialism. While the bourgeoisie attacked the thesis as 'one-sided' because it explains imperialism from the stand-point of the economic interpretation of history, the petty-bourgeoisie attacked it as 'economistic'. To the bourgeoisie 'economic interpretation' was conceived in its narrow, one-sided, bourgeois sense, as being concerned with the allocation of scarce resources. This conception of imperialism by the bourgeoisie had its roots in idealist philosophy, thus manifesting the incapability of bourgeois economics and politics to conceive social reality in its totality. The populist attack had its roots in the same idealist philosophy, although some of the attackers preferred to call themselves Marxists.

This bourgeois and petty-bourgeois inability to comprehend the phenomenon of imperialism was not surprising. In their treatment of the subject they tried to associate modern imperialism with colonisation as such. The Marxist-Leninist explanation on the contrary has sought to trace the phenomenon of imperialism to its roots in the development of societies. Hence a study of imperialism is for us a study of *historical materialism*, the study of the development of human societies in their essentially contradictory movement. It also involves a study of *dialectical materialism*, which gives us the scientific tools for analysing these contradictory forces

i

in nature and societies. These two aspects constitute modern *materialist philosophy*. The study of imperialism also entails the study of *political economy*, for the development of man and his society is a development by man of his productive forces together with the corresponding production relations and social organisation. All these together help us to isolate laws of social development which then enable us to study the different *modes of production* and the laws of motion specific to them. These three complementary and inter-related aspects of the same body of thought constitute the Marxist-Leninist analysis of modern imperialism; they form both an *ideology* for the proletariat, and a *scientific exposition* of capitalist production at a specific stage of development. Bourgeois ideologists would smile at this statement for to them it is impossible for an ideology to be scientific. This is not surprising, for historically the bourgeoisie could not advance materialistic philosophy to a scientific level. When they emerged as a class, still within the womb of feudalism, they counterposed mechanical science to theology under the guise of 'natural philosophy'. They made a tremendous contribution to the rise of modern science but could not transcend this contribution.

From the Renaissance in the latter half of the fifteenth century, interest in the philosophies of antiquity slowly shattered the dictatorship of the church over men's minds, and with the Reformation, Protestantism became the agent for such change among the Germanic peoples. In Italy there was the work of Leonardo de Vinci who, like all great men of the period, took advantage of the new developments to travel widely, and made valuable scientific observations in his travels. These discoveries pushed scientific knowledge forward. But perhaps the one single development which created a new age in natural science was the great work of Copernicus. From this moment onwards natural science was liberated from theology, although up to this day the church still makes efforts to bring science within its confines. There is no doubt that from this day the bourgeoisie, who increasingly challenged the church, made rapid developments. Beginning with the science of terrestial bodies authenticated by Kepler's discovery of the laws of planetary movement, Newton formulated the general laws of matter. By the first part of the eighteenth century, however, although no doubt great advances had been made, natural science could no longer make any significant break-throughs in the general outlook on nature. this had to wait until the next century, by which time the bourgeoisie were rapidly becoming a reactionary force. No such progress could be made so long as all motion in nature was thought to be restricted by the absolute *immutable laws* that mechanical science had been able to elaborate at the time. All change and all development in nature were denied. As Engels commented: 'Natural science, so revolutionary at the outset, suddenly found itself confronted by an out-and-out conservative nature, in which even today everything was as it had been from the beginning and in which — to the end of the world or for all eternity — everything would remain as it had been since the beginning'. (2)

Science, although it had challenged the church in the earlier phase, still remained deeply enmeshed in theology. 'Everywhere it sought and found the ultimate cause in an impulse from outside that was not to be explained from nature itself'. (3) It is only with philosophers beginning with Kant, Descartes, Dalton, etc., that the idea of the first impulse was done away with, establishing that the earth and the solar system had come into being in the course of time. Further scientific researches confirmed motion in nature linking organic and inorganic bodies through the laws of chemistry. But science, notwithstanding this philosophical development, was still 'predominantly a collecting science', a science of 'finished things'. (4) It could not break out of this limbo to become a true science, concerned not with *collection* but with *systematising*, a science of the origin, development and interconnection of all the processes into *one coherent whole*, until the three great discoveries of the first half of the nineteenth century. The first of these was the discovery of the *cell* as the unit from which the whole plant and animal body develops, multiplies, and differentiates. Then there was the theory of *transformation of energy*, which demonstrated that all forces, heat, radiation, electricity, magnetism and chemical energy, were different manifestations of universal motion. Finally, there was the proof by Darwin that all organic products of nature, including man, were the result of a long process of *evolution* from a few originally unicellular forms, and that these arose from protoplasm or albumen which came into existence by *chemical means.*

With these great discoveries and other developments in natural sciences a point was reached where it was possible to demonstrate the interconnection between the processes in nature. Not only particular spheres but also the interconnection between particular spheres could now be presented in an approximately systematic form to give a comprehensive view of the interconnection in nature, by means of the facts provided by empirical natural science itself. (4) On this basis the *dialectical* interconnection of nature as a 'system of nature' became possible.

By the 1830s the bourgeoisie were denying the very basis for developing such a scientific synthesis of knowledge. Every effort was being made to deny philosophy any role in systematising the sciences. August Comte postulated a 'new positive science' to 'put an end to metaphysical speculation'. In 1836 John Stuart Mill was hitting at the 'mistiness of what we find represented as preliminary and fundamental notions'. To him first principles were in truth *last* principles requiring proof: 'Instead of being fixed points from whence the chain of proof which supports all the rest of science hangs suspended, they are themselves the remotest links of the chain. Though presented as if all other truths were to be deduced from them, they are truths which are last arrived at'. (5) As we all know, this positivist movement unleashed a chain of obscurantism which still bewitches bourgeois sociology today. (6)

In the field of history and social science the positivist positions of Comte and Mill reigned supreme. The French materialists of the eighteenth century, arguing from the science of their age, attributed man's views and feelings to the influence of his *environment*. They regarded all man's psychic activity as transformed *sensations*. (7) It followed that in order to transform man the environment must be changed. This led them into one-sided conclusions about man; at times they held that since the environment is the determinant of man's psychic activity, his views had no influence on his conduct. This French materialist position, in spite of its weaknesses, at least acknowledged that in their historical development men's ideas were determined by the development of the social environment or the history of social relationships. But it could not solve or even state the problem of how and why historical development could be explained in this way. The French materialists ended up with the tautology that men's opinions are determined by their environment and that their environment is determined by opinions. So long as French materialism remained at this level it could not scientifically explain the laws of social development.

Nor could the French historians of the Restoration (1814-30), make a step forward. In line with the dominant concepts of the period they reduced the reality of man's relations in society to the development of political institutions in a given country. Accordingly the character of a people was entirely determined by the character of the government, by its legislation and politics. Guizot and Mignet sought the key to understanding of man's development in the property relations of the dominant interests. According to Mignet the needs of the various classes, and the struggle to satisfy them, determined their politics. But the question of what determined these property relations was unsatisfactorily answered. The answer was seen to lie in the legal institutions. These historians ended up by tracing the origin of institutions and hence of property relations to human nature. As Plekhanov correctly stated:

> 'If man, when he appears in the world, does not bring with him a prepared store of innate "practical ideas", if virtue is respected, not because it is innate in people, but because it is useful as Locke asserted; if the principle of social utility is the highest law as Helvetius said; if man is the measure of things wherever there is a question of mutual human relations — then it is quite natural to draw the conclusion that the nature of man is the viewpoint from which we should assess given relations as being useful or harmful, rational or irrational. It was from this stand-point that writers of the Enlightenment of the eighteenth century discussed both the social order then existing and the reforms which they thought desirable. Human nature was for them the most important argument in their discussions with their opponents'. (8)

Nor did the Utopian socialists of the nineteenth century make any progress. Steeped in eighteenth century idealism of human nature, they sought to formulate perfect systems of legislation which would conform with an ideal social order based on that human nature. They thus repeated the mistakes of the eighteenth and early nineteenth centuries and therefore could not make any new break-throughs in human knowledge. Holding to the wrong theory that the share of social production which falls to the exploiters diminishes with the passage of time, in proof of which they referred to the gradual decline in the level of interest and land rent, they concluded that this tendency will automatically result in the disappearance of the class of exploiters themselves. This utopian law led to other utopian illusions, on the basis of which a plan of social organisation was drawn and demands made for legislation to effect it. When the exploiters declined to pass such legislation the idealists threatened them with 'social revolution', which was in fact never an integral part of their programme and could not be, given their position. Bernstein's Second International revisionism reverted to the same dogma of 'human reason', formulating reformist programmes during the period of capitalist crisis.

The historic mission to complete the scientific struggle ending with Darwin's work lay in the hands of a new class. It was no longer in the class interest of the bourgeoisie to develop philosophy and science to-gether. They had attained what they desired and had abandoned the utilitarian moral philosophy which they had made their own when they dragged the feudal aristocracy to the Bastille. They no longer saw any need for philosophy. Theology and obscurantism were sufficient. All they required were the natural sciences, since the development of capitalist production depended on them. The proletariat which had a new vision of society arising out of the contradiction of capitalist development saw the need for philosophy. But in order to confront the bourgeoisie as a class their philosophy had to be a scientific one arising out of the devel-opments of natural science and philosophy in general. Their ideological representatives, Marx and Engels, were to carry out this mission.

Marxism emerged as the anti-thesis of bourgeois obscurantism. From German *philosophy*, English *political economy*, French *socialism*, Marx and Engels built materialist philosophy, political economy and scientific socialism. The materialist philosophy they built-up was no longer opposed to natural science. On the contrary the two merged into a coherent whole. Marxism brought human knowledge to a point where Engels could finally infuse meaning into Hegel's formulation: *The Truth Is The Whole.* On the other hand bourgeois social 'science' stagnated. Since Adam Smith's *Wealth of Nations*, published in 1776, bourgeois political economy retained simple reproduction as its basic thesis, constituting the rationale behind capitalist production. Ricardo never made any progress in this particular respect. Modern bourgeois economists instead of moving forward stuck to a formulation which represented simple reproduction of feudal com-modity production as the basis of capitalist production and could not grasp the importance of expanded reproduction based on modern machinery. Saddled with this dogma of simple reproduction, bourgeois political economy could not comprehend the laws of motion of capitalist development leading to modern imperialism.

The petty-bourgeoisie, who saw Marxism merely as a method, sought to turn it into a dogma detached from its object, the making of revolution to change existing conditions. Confused by preconceived ideals they tried and still try to turn Marxism-Leninism into a piece of social theory concerned with the reform of existing conditions. From such a position there can be no understanding of imperialism.

Marxist-Leninism does not claim to have absolute knowledge, for that would be nonsensical. On the contrary, it states that, given the scientific tools in our hands at present, we are able to comprehend social reality around us and that with the method of historical and dialectical materialism, and with political economy, imperialism can be analysed scientifically. To be sure, imperialism did not emerge in our life time. It existed in antiquity, under feudalism, and does so under capitalism. Indeed, as Lenin observed:

> 'Colonial policy and imperialism existed before the latest stage of capitalism, and even before capitalism. Rome, founded on slavery, pursued a colonial policy and practiced imperialism. But "general" disquisitions on imperialism, which ignore or put to the background the fundamental difference between socio-economic formations, inevitably turn into the most vapid banality, bragging, like the comparison: "Greater Rome and Greater Britain". Even the capitalist colonial policy of *previous* stages of capitalism is essentially different from the colonial policy of finance capital'. (9)

Thus for us modern imperialism is a stage of development of capitalism at its highest phase, that of monopoly capitalism *based* on finance capital. It was preceded by a mercantilist imperialism, based on *feudal merchant capital*, and by British free trade imperialism based on *industrial and loan capital*. All these are stages of the development of capital, the first within the womb of feudalism, the second in its youth as a system propelled by its own laws of motion, and the third in its moribund, decadent, old age. Therefore there cannot be any misconception as to what imperialism is all about. It has to be analysed in relation to the age and the stage of development of human society, looking at its material base, the productive forces that propel it, and the corresponding property relations and their interaction, producing the ideologies that sustain it.

We try to show in Part One of this work how mercantilist imperialism arises and how it acts as the basis for the development of capitalism. We try to demonstrate the specific nature of this imperialism, which was based on the laws of motion of the feudal mode of production. Here primitive accumulation based on plunder, enslavement of aboriginal peoples, and their entombment in the mines of Latin America opens the possibilities of later developments. This plunder, however, was of a qualitatively different kind from capitalist exploitation. Generally it was based on *trade* of commodities between Europe and the undeveloped areas of the world in which the exchange of commodities could be called *unequal*, being exchange between two different modes of production. As Marx has said, it is only within the sphere of circulation of commodities that merchants capital is possible, not where equivalents are exchanged. The merchant, by inserting himself between producers and consumers, can then cheat in buying cheap in order to sell dear. (10)

The rise of the capitalist mode of production proper puts an end to mercantilist imperialism. We examine these developments in Part Two. Here we notice that the new property relations that come into being in accord with the development of the productive forces lead to very rapid growth. Britain, which was first on the scene with capitalist development, became the only 'workshop of the world'. Her relatively hegemonic position soon led her to advocate a policy of free trade. Actually this policy was the result of the growing need for cheaper food and agricultural products, which were all necessary to improve her profitability in production. This free trade imperialism resulted in Britain's renewed reliance on her colonies, held over from mercantilist imperialism. It also led to the acquisition of new ones although on a small scale. We shall examine the laws of motion specific to the capitalist mode of production and the ideology of free trade imperialism. The Law of Value, and its relation to the Law of the Tendency of the Rate of Profit to Fall, will be shown as cardinal laws in capitalist development. The continuing pressure on profitability, which is but an increasing sharpened struggle between the two classes, eventually leads to concentration of production with the increasing rise of the organic composition of capital. This tendency, which Marx demonstrates, is at the back of modern imperialism as analysed by Lenin, which we examine in Part Three. We try to show that modern imperialism, based on the rise of finance capital, itself a merger and coalescence of industrial and bank capital, has its roots in the *historical fall in the rate of profit* which occurs in the capitalist world in the 1870s. This forms the watershed of free trade imperialism and modern imperialism, an imperialism characterised by the rise of a financial oligarchy which for the first time in history divides the remaining uncolonised world among monopoly concerns and big imperialist states.

In Part Four we analyse multilateral imperialism. This is modern imperialism operating under conditions of narrowing horizons created by the emergence of the socialist system that was marked by the October Revolution. The second World War worsened the contradictions between the imperialist countries, which led to a devastating destruction of the productive forces among vanquished and victors alike. The US which emerged as the strongest power soon dictated a new redivision of the world based on the Open-Door policy. A system of multilateral institutions was worked out under US supervision to anchor this redivision. The dissolution of bilateral colonial markets marked this redivision. The monopolies could now compete in these open neo-colonial markets as long as US hegemony was assured. The rise of the transnational corporate strategy is the direct result of these developments.

We then expose efforts by neo-Marxist revisers to create confusion in the Marxist-Leninist thesis on imperialism. These neo-Marxists theories are shown to be no more than a reformulation of the outworn products of bourgeois economism and Trotskyism. Neo-colonialism under multilateral imperialism is a cornerstone in the imperialist policy in the post war period. Any discussion of multilateral imperialism which did not discuss neo-colonialism would therefore be incomplete. Bourgeois economism is incapable of providing us with any analysis of the question, which is but a reflection of its failure to comprehend imperialism. We examine this phenomenon last in Part Five of the work. For us neo-colonialism, like the colonialism of the previous period, is merely a form of imperialist control and exploitation of backward countries which monopoly capitalism cannot allow to escape its grip. Neo-colonialism is one manifestation of a system of 'rule the world' which the financial oligarchies of the imperialist countries impose on these countries. The neo-colony becomes the base for capital exports and markets for the monopolists. Finance capital secures an overwhelming grip on the neo-colony, thus making it impossible for it to develop its productive forces autonomously. We therefore try to refute the neo-Marxist centre-periphery ideology which treats the relationship between the 'centre' and the 'periphery' as based on 'unequal exchange', in which primitive accumulation continues. We produce evidence of post-war developments to show that the centre-periphery ideology seeks to place the relations between the 'centre' and the 'periphery' at the level of relations between nations and hence smacks of economistic explanations of imperialism. This ideology takes a one-sided view of imperialism which is ahistorical and hence unscientific. The 'centre-periphery' ideology is further shown to blur the class nature of neo-colonial exploitation. Its erroneous theorising thus creates problems for the class struggle both in the 'centre' and the 'periphery', since these ideologists see a hostile relation between the working classes in the two countries. Indeed the whole 'centre' and 'periphery' approach to the study of imperialism is a clear response to D.K. Fieldhouse who in criticising Lenin's work as misleading appealed for this approach in research on the subject. We finally argue that the socialist revolution in the 'centre', and the national democratic revolution on the basis of 'new democracy' in the neo-colony transforming itself into a socialist revolution under the leadership of the proletariat, offer the only solution which will bring imperialism to an end on a world scale.

REFERENCES

1.   V.I. Lenin, *Imperialism, the Highest State of Capitalism — A Popular Outline*, Scientific Socialism Series, (Moscow, 1970).
2.   F. Engels, *Dialectics of Nature*, Progress, (Moscow, 1934-74) p.24.
3.   F. Engels, op. cit. p.25.
4.   F. Engels, *Feuerbach and the End of Classical Germany Philosophy*, *Selected Works*, Progress, (Moscow, 1973), Vol. 3, pp.363-365.
5.   J.S. Mill, in Nagel, *J.S. Mills Philosophy of Scientific Method*, (1950), pp.408-9.
6.   See, for instance Alvin H. Gouldner, *The Coming Crisis in Western Sociology*, Free Press, (New York, 1965).
7.   G. Plekhanov, *The Development of the Monist View of History*, in G. Plekhanov, Selected Philosophical Works, Progress, (Moscow, 1975), p.484.
8.   G. Plekhanov, op. cit. pp.504-5.
9.   V.I. Lenin, *Imperialism*, op. cit.
10.   K. Marx, *Capital*, Progress, (Moscow, 1971), Vol. I. pp.159,161; Vol. III. p.327.

PART ONE

FEUDALISM AND THE RISE OF MERCANTILIST IMPERIALISM

CHAPTER I

'Thus feudal production, to be judged properly, must be considered as a mode of production founded on antagonism. It must be shown how wealth was produced within this antagonism, how the productive forces were developed at the same time as class antagonism, how one of the classes . . . went on growing until the material conditions for its emancipation had attained full maturity. Is this not as good as saying that the mode of production, the relations in which productive forces are developed, are anything but external laws, but that they correspond to a definite development of men and of their forces, and that a change in men's productive forces necessarily brings about a change in their relations of production? As the main thing is not to be deprived of the fruits of civilization, of the acquired productive forces, the traditional forms in which they were produced must be smashed'.

Karl Marx.

With the dissolution of the Roman Empire the scene for the dominant developments of the productive forces in human society shifted to the West. This may seem paradoxical since whilst the Eastern Empire witnessed a relatively peaceful transformation rich in cultural content, the dissolution of the Empire in the West was accompanied by great confusion caused by the barbarian invasions. Between the fifth and ninth centuries, towns and centres of civilisation decayed, disappearing completely in places like Britain because of their alien origin, surviving to some extent in places like Italy, where a long history lay behind them. Although the Franks and Goths in the West and the Slavs in the East maintained a system of trade in luxury goods and slaves, classical culture gradually died out, leaving Constantinople, a christianised Europe able to maintain itself, to guard the classical heritage.

The initial western re-unification efforts under Charlemagne after 800 resulted in the re-establishment of an Empire, but failed to achieve anything like a unified state organisation. The semblance of an army established under the Carolingians disappeared by the 850s; the harassing attacks of the Normans, Magyars, and Saracens were resisted only on the basis of small self-sufficient local defence units. From these units in the country-side, feudal production developed, at first basing itself on 'natural economy' and later, with the rise of the towns, on money rent. This is the origin

1

of the feudal system in Western Europe which began to establish itself around 1000 AD. The earlier imperial public authority based on the fief and salaries collapsed with the death of Charlemagne. If we are to understand how these units later became nation-states with developed economies, and how they came to dominate the trade and the resources of the rest of the world, including those of the erstwhile advanced nations in the East, it is necessary for us to show the conditions which made this possible. Since we are concerned here only with the general movement, we will draw our historical material from centres influencing this general movement. Consequently most of our historical sources will be from England, although material from Western Europe as a whole will be used where available.

One of the chief factors which assisted the early development of Western Europe was the heavy forest soils. Once the technical problem of cutting down the woods and ploughing the heavy soils was overcome, the development of agriculture even on the basis of small communities was possible. The technical innovations that contributed to this advance, at least until the crisis of the fourteenth century, were the use of the iron-plough for tilling, the stiff-harness for traction, the water-mill for mechanical power, marling for soil improvement and the three field system. Based on a new production relation, dynamic agrarian progress emerged.

In the Eastern Empire, on the other hand, because of the arid lands which were liable to erosion and desiccation, such development would only have been possible with organised irrigation, which could only have been undertaken by a governmental organisation. This, however, was precluded by a general decay in governmental institutions at the time. In the West no such government organisation was necessary and hence development did take place, and a new civilisation surpassing the earlier ones in vitality was rapidly built on the basis of fertile and abundant land, worked with serf-labour.

The basic foundations for this type of production were laid within the slave system of property relations. Before the Roman Empire based on the slave-master property relationship disintegrated, elements of the new system had made their appearance in competition with the old. In the fourth century AD, the institution of serfdom made its appearance in Sparta, Thessaly and Crete at the height of the forces of disintegration of the Roman Empire. The reasons for this development lay in the contradictions of the slave-master based property relationships. Unlike the feudal mode of production, slave economy possessed no internal mechanism of self-reproduction of its labour force. The supply depended largely on foreign conquests, and the possibilities of natural reproduction were limited by the fact that slave-masters never encouraged the use of female slaves for lack of ready profitable employment for them. The result was a generally low rate of reproduction. (1) The slackening of Roman conquests towards the end of the Empire, and the substitution of ransom for enslavement reduced the supply of labour to Rome; ransom was necessary to meet the expenses of the warfare state on which the system was based. The recruitment of slaves and the collection of ransom could not proceed at the same time. Either one or the other was possible. Moreover, at about the same time, Roman Law allowed a slave to regain his freedom. In order to do so, the slave was obliged to pay a lump sum of money to his master and he usually remained a client of the slave-master. Later as the system decayed manumission was encouraged instead. (2)

The decrease in the number of slaves which resulted corresponded to an increase of 'free' workers on the farms. These were called *colonii*. The transformation was the inevitable result of the break-up of production based on slavery. It resulted in turn in universal impoverishment and decline of commerce, handicrafts, the arts, and of the population. Towns decayed and large scale agriculture based on slavery ceased to exist. The old large-scale productive farms were replaced with pastures of sheep and oxen since this type of farming required less labour. With the decay of the towns, (as the market shrank), the country estates and horticulture fell into disuse. Small-scale farming was again the only feasible profitable occupation. Estates were parcelled out and leased in small lots to hereditary tenants who paid a fixed sum; or to sharecroppers (*partiarrii*) who received one-sixth or even one-ninth of the year's product for their work. The major part of these lands were distributed to *colonii* who were part of the land could be sold with it. As indicated, these slaves-turned-serfs originated in the dissolution of large slave estates. Slavery was retained by the rich for household luxury. But the freeing of slaves amidst the jungle of extortionate officials, judges, and usurers made them easy prey under the new conditions. Free peasants existed by the side of the *colonii* but the free peasant communities almost invariably placed themselves under the protection and patronage of men of power. This practice became so widespread and gave so much power to these new patrons that the Emperors of the fourth century AD prohibited it. The slave society had driven itself into an insoluble contradiction: slavery no longer paid and it died out, but equally free labour could not exist! As Engels correctly observed: 'The one could no longer, the other could not yet, be the basic form of social production. Only a complete revolution could be of help here'. (3)

The freed slaves who surrendered themselves to patronage were required by the patron to transfer the titles to their lands to him and in return he ensured them the usufruct of their lands for life. This practice, which the latterday feudal and early bourgeois scholars referred to as the origin of the social contract, was resorted to by the Holy Roman Church in the ninth and tenth centuries AD 'for the glory of God' to enlarge its possessions, under the feudal mode.

Thus we see that the main conditions for serfdom were prepared within slave society, although elements of feudalism are also traceable to Germanic origin. Anderson shows that vassalage, the manor, and communal enclaves were of Germanic inheritance. He also maintains that serfdom itself probably descends both from the classical statute of the *colonus* and from the semi-coercive 'commendation' of Germanic clan warriors. (4)

In this way the feudal mode, which as a general system can be placed between the fifth and seventeenth centuries, was taking root and developing. In its first phases slavery co-existed with serfdom. Later slavery disappears. But it is not until the eleventh century that the system appears in its developed form and henceforth leads to a continuous sustained growth, complete with its political and religious superstructure. (5) Its economic basis was feudal landed property, with agricultural production in the main consumed in the locality on the one hand, and scattered domestic handicraft industry, on the other. The village and later the manor were the basic economic units, with serfs sharing out the land and work, and the landlord of the manor appropriating the surplus product of their labour. With better implements than those used in the classical slave system, widespread use of iron, better ploughs, better harness, better looms and the use of labour saving devices like the mill (6), they were able to produce a surplus which was appropriated by the feudal hierarchy of lords, bishops, and kings under the nominal leadership of the Emperor and Pope, leaving a portion for their own consumption.

Feudal payments and services by the enserfed peasantry to the lord, extracted either by the use of force or by custom backed by threat of force provided by an armed body of retainers, constituted the basis of the system and the central contradition which ultimately led to its transformation from about the sixteenth century. The enserfed peasant, unlike the slave, was a direct producer and in possession of both his means of production and the 'material labour conditions' required for the realisation of his labour and the production of his means of subsistence. He worked in agriculture and rural house industries connected with it as an independent producer whereas a slave worked under conditions of labour provided by the master. (7) Under feudalism the surplus was not extracted by economic means but was forced from the producers by 'other measures'; this constitutes the innermost foundation of the feudal state.

Since production was basically for consumption, and since the implements of production were simple individual instruments, the division of labour was rudimentary. The product accordingly was only sufficient for the household or village community and not for a wider market. It is for this reason that the feudal state was decentralised politically — the feudal lord exercised judicial and quasi-judicial functions in relation to a directly dependent population. The rural mode of production was very much determined by the sparse population of the Middle Ages, scattered over a large area.

There were three possible forms of extraction of the surplus open to the feudal lord at different stages of development: in the form of work (or labour rent), in the form of products (rent in kind), or in the form or money

(money rent). At the earliest stages of the Middle Ages in Western Europe surplus was appropriated in the form of labour services. The manorial lands were divided into three types according to use. The first portion consisted of the lands the peasants cultivated to meet their own subsistence needs; the second consisted of the lands on which the peasantry for three days of the week performed their labour service, the product of which went directly to the lord; thirdly there were the common lands, woods, meadows, wastes, pastures, etc., which according to custom remained at the disposal of both the peasants and lords. The peasant's total labour time was divided between his plot (necessary labour) and his master's demesne lands (surplus labour).

Alongside the labour service, rent in kind consisting of agricultural or craft products was also demanded of the peasantry. So long as the surplus retained these forms, trade, money, and capital only existed in the pores of natural economy. The bulk of the producers, the peasantry, hardly ever directly affected the market, since they consumed what they themselves produced, after deducting the surplus product which was partly consumed by the lord. The bulk of the population could not buy the produce of the towns and the trade in these products remained chiefly luxury goods, which in turn severely limited the development of craft production.

With the transformation of the surplus from that of labour rent and rent in kind to money rent the social situation was correspondingly revolutionised. In order to pay his rent the peasant had first to sell the product and pay over to the lord its price. Hence part of the peasant's products had to be produced as commodities, and this transformed the character of the entire mode of production. It lost its independence, its detachment from social connection and set the ground for capitalist accumulation on which we shall say more later. Suffice it to say here that production and consumption in the countryside at this stage developed with the unprecedented expansion of trade. Money penetrated everywhere into the pores of the hitherto 'natural' economy and helped to dissolve and transform the old bonds and relationships.

This 'intrusion' of money into the feudal economy was no accident. It arose out of the need of the feudal lords in the economic circumstances of the period to meet their commitments to the feudal aristocracy above them. This was accentuated by the class struggle taking place on land. Between 1000 and 1250 there was considerable movement by peasants to new lands or colonies aimed against feudal exploitation on demesne lands. As this movement succeeded the peasantry gained considerable freedom which led to increased production. The class struggle went on hand in hand with the developments in the productive forces, and this characterised the rapid movement in the position of classes generally in Western Europe. It is estimated by Duby that between the ninth and thirteenth centuries, average harvest and seed increased from between two and a half to four times and that as a result the portion of the harvest at the disposal of the producer almost doubled; a change comparable to that in the eighteenth and nineteenth centuries. This advance correspondingly gave impetus to other forces. There was a rapid increase in population from 20 million in the whole of Western Europe in 950 to 54 million in 1348, with a rise in life expectancy from 25 in Rome to 35 in feudal England.

Increased contacts with Europe led to diversification in production, with a corresponding dependence on imports of cereals. This expansion led to a serious crisis as the overuse of the soil, the exhaustion of the mines and the increasing extravagance of the nobility started to affect economic life. The financial needs of the lords increased as the money form penetrated further and further into the traditional 'natural economy'. The growth of trade stepped up the pressure on the peasant to supply the surplus for the market. As Dobb has remarked:

> 'The result of this increased pressure was not only to exhaust the goose that laid the golden eggs for the castle, but to provoke from sheer desperation a movement of illegal emigration from the manors: a desertion *en masse* on the part of producers, which was destined to drain the system of its life blood and to prove a series of crises in which feudal economy was to find itself engulfed in the fourteenth and fifteenth centuries.' (9)

In spite of the attempts including use of force to stop this movement, the conditions could not be reversed; change was necessary. Agreements by lords to capture and exchange escaped peasants and the right of hot pursuit in each other's territory proved futile. When these measures failed, competition ensued among the lords to induce peasants back into the fold, which sometimes succeeded. The escaped peasants went to virgin forest lands and rented them from other lords. When it became clear to the lords and the Church that this 'would be profitable to us and our successors' (10) the renting and creation of peasant colonies and communes were encouraged. This arrangement was convenient to the peasant. There were no objectionable labour services to the lords, only a rent in money was paid. The growth of the market and trade in the towns enabled greater specialisation and the peasant had an interest in working harder to enable him to pay off rent and retain a surplus. This development faced the feudal lords with a *fait accompli* and they had to adjust themselves to the changed situation. They became more willing to commute labour services for a money rent, since the lord needed the money badly at times. The development of the market meant, too, that the lord could get his supplies with the income from money rent instead of labour services.

The Black Death, coming in 1348 in the wake of the economic crisis in this period, hastened this process of peasant emancipation. At the same time it set limits to it. Evidence of attempts to intensify serfdom is to be found in England in the *Statute of Labourers*, in the French *Ordonnance* of 1351, as well as in other legislation in Germany, Spain etc. which not only provided for the control of wages but also made service to the master compulsory for all poor persons *whether bond or free* and placed restriction on their free movements. The 'Death', travelling 'like a typhoon', swept the whole of Europe killing off half of the population in some places. It is estimated that London lost 200 people a day and Paris 800 as long as the Death lasted. In France, England, the Low Countries, and Germany between one-third and one-half of the entire population was wiped out. (11) Combined with other plagues which occurred in the same period, the total of casualties has variously been estimated at perhaps two thirds of the population. (11) The effect of this reduction in population was to raise wages due to shortage of labour on land. Many land-lords found themselves unable to pay increased wages out of the money rents. This encouraged peasants to flee and at times resulted in peasant revolts, such as those in West Flanders in 1320, in Northern France in 1358, set in motion with the Grande Jacquerie, and in England in 1381, which were precipitated by a new polltax.

Feudal laws imposed to curtail wages could not halt the movement of history. The old feudal organisation based on 'natural economy' was broken up by the pressure of economic forces that could not be withstood. By the mid-fifteenth century in the greater part of Western Europe, money rents had been substituted for labour services, and peasants produced for the market and moved freely, no longer tied to the feudal bonds of the earlier period. The fact that land was bought, sold, and exchanged freely like a commodity spelled the end of the feudal land-based economy. Feudal tenure was abolished finally under Cromwell's Commonwealth in 1646 in England and in France after the Revolution in 1789. (12)

In Eastern Europe and Asia this rapid movement was lacking. The stability of the internal structure of feudal land property in these countries constituted the decisive factor in checking the autonomous growth of modern capitalism. This stability was due, as Marx pointed out, to the absence of conditions of personal dependence on the nominal land-owner such as existed in Europe. The Asian system was based on direct subordination to a state which stood over the peasant producers as their landlord and simultaneously as sovereign. (13) Under such circumstances there did not develop stronger political and economic pressures than those common to all subjected to that state. The state was the supreme lord and was identifiable with sovereignty which consisted in the ownership of land concentrated on a national scale. Thus although there was private and common *possession* of land, there was no private ownership of it as in Europe. (14) This had a great impact on later development of capitalism in these areas, Japan in particular.

CHAPTER II

We have seen that with the fall of the Roman Empire in the West, the hitherto dominant urban production declined as the towns decayed. The feudal countryside became dominant until the rise of the bourgeoisie, when towns at first based on trade and handicrafts began to engage in manufacturing as a prelude to industrial production. In the Mediterranean, South Italy, Provence, and Catalonia, towns appeared during the eleventh century. These were areas of least destruction at the time of the fall of Rome. In the areas where agriculture had been predominant like the Rhine, the Low Countries, and Lombardy, towns also appeared in the eleventh century, but in Northern France, England, and Germany east of the Rhine, the rise of the town began in the twelfth century. This development arose essentially from the need to create bases for engaging in trade which at first merely trickled through the feudal wall of 'natural economy'. The trickle with the passage of time became a major activity and as trade increased so did the towns.

These new towns are to be distinguished from rural towns where the king's courts were held, places which acted as judicial and military centres, or places where the feudal lord might occasionally allow a market fair to be held. The new towns came to possess a kind of economic and political independence within the feudal system. They were at first set up because the feudal lord benefitted from the dues he collected from visiting merchants. They very soon exerted a significant influence on feudal estates, particularly the smaller ones. Their existence facilitated money dealings hitherto unknown in the feudal countryside.

The trade introduced in the towns promoted greater specialisation of labour and as the town population increased, so did the demand for food to feed them. The money which came in as a medium of exchange in turn reacted on production in the countryside, giving it a greater impetus and thereby creating the basis for a money relationship between the feudal lord and the enserfed peasant. The emergence of money rent in Western Europe, as we have seen earlier, coincided with the rise of the town. The town became a magnetic centre attracting run-away peasants and in periods of declining agriculture encouraged the exodus from the countryside. In time, as the town became entrenched and attained greater freedom from the feudal lord, the knights and other less well-to-do feudal elements found it useful to borrow money and commodities from the town merchant. The relationship between the landed aristocracy and the merchant became warmer. Often the gentry would apprentice their sons to an urban craft or marry a son to a merchant's daughter. Sometimes they would purchase a membership in the urban guild for the son to engage in trade. In the sixteenth century, with the enclosure movement and profitable trade in wool, they sometimes became middlemen themselves and turned into merchants.

The development of guild towns with this independence within the feudal countryside was not a smooth one. The nobility at first insisted on collecting dues. They imposed taxes and labour services and enjoyed monopolies from merchants since the towns existed on their lands. The nobility also wanted to run the courts of justice as they did on their manorial estates. But these privileges only attached to land, based on ownership of the soil. The feudal privileges claimed by the nobility, including administration of the law, were fixed by custom difficult to alter and more suited to a stabler rural economy. But trade was relatively dynamic, impersonal, active and impatient with feudal barriers. The changes in the economy giving rise to trade and towns were already at this stage challenging the *status quo* of these feudal privileges. The merchants formed themselves into associations called 'guilds' or 'hanses', as in Germany, to champion their cause, and win for the towns the freedom necessary for their growth and development. In places this organisation led to fighting and in some continental cities in Flanders and Italy took the form of civil war. In England the struggle went on from the thirteenth to the fourteenth century and in places the merchants were threatened with 'hell fire' and excommunication. Merchants made forcible entry into monastries and imprisoned monks until their demands were met. After centuries of struggle the merchants won freedom from the feudal nobility for their guild towns 'to have a commune and maintain it in perpetuity'.

The freedoms and rights won were of immense historical significance. A charter granted by the king of France to a town called Abbevile contained a wide range of rights and privileges for the merchants in 1370:

> 'We have given and granted them certain privileges, by which it appears, inter alia, that never for what so ever reason or occasion it may be, shall we place, assert, fine or impose nor shall we cause or suffer to be placed, asserted or fixed, imposed on our said town of Abbeville, nor on the other towns of the country of Pinthieu, any impositions, aids, or other subsidies of any kind, if it is not to the profit of the said towns and at their request . . . for which reason we, considering the true love and obedience shown us by the said petitioners, command you and all of you and straitly enjoin that you shall allow all the burgesses, inhabitants of the said town to trade, to sell and to buy, to bring and to take through all the towns, counties and limits of the said county salt and all other merchandise of any kind, without compelling them to pay to us and our men and officers any salt tax, claims, exactions, impositions, or subsidies . . .'
> (15)

This charter in a unique form represents generally the privileges exacted by merchants from the kings in Europe and shows how, with the new money economy, the merchants were becoming close allies of the feudal topnotch.

These privileges soon turned into monopolies. From towns of freedom the merchants soon amassed gigantic monopolistic power. A classic example of this was the Hanseatic League of Germany. This was an organisation of hanses giving it a kind of 'transnational' character. The hanses joined into a union which established trading posts, including fortresses and warehouses, stretching from Holland to Russia. Its organisation included one hundred towns with the consequence that all the trade of Northern Europe with the rest of the world was monopolised by it. It was a kind of state within states and made commercial treaties, protected its merchant fleet with its own warships, and had its own governmental assemblies which made its own laws! This power of the League, however, soon declined with the rise of Dutch competition in the sixteenth century.

Apart from the merchant guild or hanse there arose the feudal town guild which based itself on a form of cooperative property. The property consisted in the labour of each individual who had to be versed in a whole round of tasks connected with his tools, thus becoming a master in the craft. With the accumulation of small capital which mainly consisted of a house and the tools of individual craftsmen the foundations were laid for a craft industry based on the joint labour of the master, journeyman and apprentice. The rapid growth of urban population led to the development of this relation and soon resulted in a feudal hierarchy in the towns similar to that existing in the country. Whereas in the countryside the 'strip-system' of cultivation in agriculture co-existed with cottage industry among the peasants, in towns the separation of industry and commerce, proceded apace especially in the older towns of Italy and Flanders. But production in the craft guild, and in the cottage industry of the country-side, was at first limited by the smallness of the market.

So long as production remained at this level the relationship of master and apprentice was an intimate one, since the master and the apprentice worked side by side. If the apprentice gained sufficient experience and had sufficient funds he started his own craft shop. If he lacked funds, then he stayed on or joined another master and worked for the master as a journey-man for wages. At times efforts by a craftsman to set up a shop were frustrated by the master.

This was the typical arrangement in the Middle Ages. Soon, however, the craftsmen followed the example of merchants who had obtained trade monopolies and formed themselves into associations called craft guilds. All craftsmen, the apprentices and journeymen belonged to the same guild. As production developed and the master accumulated sufficient wealth, he employed more journeymen. This development in time resulted in journeymen forming associations of their own to protect their interests as against the master. The equality that existed between masters, apprentice and journeymen was increasingly undermined. Moreover, the stringent regulations governing the craft guilds also imposed monopolistic practices to protect masters, and associations formed by journeymen ensured that the practice of the craft remained in their hands.

The monopolies preserved the secrets of the craft guilds, but secrets soon leaked just like they do today and harsh laws were imposed to help the craft monopolies. Work had to conform to certain standards and specifications. Disregard of these standards attracted heavy penalties. To ensure their observance, guild supervisors and inspectors made regular tours in which they examined the weights and measures used by members. Specialisation developed under the system to some extent but the limits of this specialisation were set by the restrictive practices of the guild system. Stratification developed between masters and also among journeymen and apprentices. 'Greater' and 'lesser' guilds made their appearance with masters in the lesser guilds at times working as wage earners in the greater ones. In some cases the guild merchant gave up trading in general and dealt in one particular article. In other guilds the wealthy merchants gave up producing and concentrated on trade, becoming exclusive corporations such as the twelve livery companies of London, the six Corps de Metier in Paris and the Arti Maggiori in Florence. The latter were powerful merchant guilds and merchants here formed the aristocracy of the town.

Division of labour soon developed between the guild towns. The immediate consequence was the rise of manufacturing branches of production which had outgrown the guild system. The trade in these manufactures in England and France was first restricted to the home market although the earlier manufacturing which flourished in Italy and Flanders was based on trade between nations. This hastened the investment of merchant capital into the handicraft industry. The concentrating of population in the countryside and the towns provided ready markets for increased production. Moreover, the rising demand for clothing material due to the growth in population, and the growing accumulation and mobilisation of natural capital through accelerated circulation, gave weaving great stimulus. It became the first and the principal manufacture. The increase in demand for luxury goods by the aristocracy which arose as a result of extension of commerce and money provided a further market.

Weaving had started with the peasants but as the demand increased a new class of weavers emerged in the towns mainly in market places outside the guild town since it could be engaged in without considerable skill. With this free manufacture, property relations also changed for it was now possible to inject naturally-derived estate capital, that is capital derived out of the surplus product on land by merchants, in the form of the loans to the individual producers, enabling them to buy raw materials. The intervention of the merchant capitalist enabled these producers to continue with production without the necessity on their part of carrying the products to distant markets for sale. Soon, however, the richer producer who could leave a substitute at home to continue production specialised in trade. Historically this process usually began with the producer/merchant helping to sell a neighbour's product, but later it developed into the merchant buying the product from him and trading in it. This confrontation between the merchant and craftsman in which the merchant became the financier resulted in the subordination of the craftsman to the merchant. The restrictive nature of guilds and higher wages for the journeymen offered by the merchant/producer further hastened the side-tracking of the guilds by the merchant entrepreneurs, who 'put out' raw materials and means of production to the individual craftsmen working at home thus directly creating a relationship of master/wage-earner *de jure*. This took place in Western Europe generally around the sixteenth century. (16) This separation of producers from their means of production by the merchant middlemen, who progressively emerged as the commercial bourgeoisie, led directly to the era of manufacture and joint-stock companies. (17)

Domestic industry remained the chief form of non-agricultural production in Europe for about three hundred years between the sixteenth and eighteenth centuries. As already observed manufacturing was emerging with a new class, the manufacturing bourgeoisie, still operating in the womb of the feudalist system. This was a bridge-head to a new system which was to emerge with the industrial revolution in the form of big industry with the modern bourgeoisie as the anti-feudalist revolutionary class.

The economy and organisation under the system of manufacture meant the assembling under one roof of the workers who worked with the means of production and the raw materials which the entrepreneur provided. But instead of the entrepreneur buying the product, as hitherto was the practice, he paid these workers a wage. This became possible because of the abundance of labour available. Whereas the guild towns had served as refuge for run-away serfs oppressed by the nobility in the countryside, the manufactories (as Marx called them) became places of refuge for the peasants from guild towns which either excluded them or paid them badly. Moreover, around the same period (and particularly in the sixteenth century) there was increased vagabondage caused by the abolition of the feudal bodies of retainers and the disbanding of swollen armies which had flocked to serve the kings against the vassals. There was also surplus labour, owing to the improvement of agriculture and the transformation of great strips of tillage into pasture land, and to the dissolution of monasteries. The rising manufactories natually absorbed this population and paid them low wages, thus creating the surplus value which resulted in further accumulation of capital.

The new system had two advantages for the entrepreneurs. Firstly, it did away with the overhead expenses arising out of the need to maintain large numbers of middlemen to distribute raw materials, collect the finished product etc. Secondly, it put a stop to considerable loss caused by the embezzlement which occurred in domestic industry to compensate for inadequate wages by enabling easy supervision in the manufactory. The direct result was an advance in productivity of labour arising out of improved division of labour, which now became possible by subdividing each craft and each process of production into an infinite number of labour operations, mechanised and simplified as much as possible.

CHAPTER III

Most of the trade in this period of the Middle Ages was limited to a small quantity of luxury products such as spices, silk and salt from the East. It included a small range of products from Europe itself, very much determined by the specialisation and division of labour in individual countries and by small differences in technology. (18) The earlier trade from the East was given great impetus by the Crusades which helped wake Western Europe from its feudal slumber by bringing soldiers and merchants into contact with other cultures. The travelling Crusaders brought back with them products which introduced new tastes among the nobility. All this helped increase the demand for foreign goods.

The Italian cities occupied a central position in this trade since the Crusaders always converged on routes through the Mediterranean; trade was snatched from Moslem hands bringing it under the control of the Italian cities, from where it spread to all corners of Europe. In the North Sea and the Baltic the city of Bruges in Flanders was also a centre of trade in fish, lumber, tallow, skins, leather and feathers, and constituted the main channel for the Russo-Scandinavian world. The trade in goods from the East through Italy and in goods from the North soon found a centre on the plains of Champagne. Here fairs were held at a number of cities particularly Lagny, Provins, Bar-sur-Anbe and Troyes. (19) From these great fairs on the Champagne, the goods spread to England, France, Belgium, Germany and Italy, where periodic fairs were also held. The fairs reflected the sporadic nature of this trade but occasional as they were they laid the basis for the more permanent steady trade of the later period. At any rate they were quite an improvement on the weekly markets of the early Middle Ages, which were small and dealt almost wholly in local goods, most of them agricultural.

Security improved in the feudal countryside, particularly with the 'safe conducts' granted to merchants who travelled peddling their goods, and trade benefitted. A proclamation of 1349 concerning the fairs of Champagne granted such safety in these words:

'All the companies of merchants and also individual merchants, Italians, Transalpines, Florentines, Milanese, Lucchese, Genoese, Venetians, Germans, Provencals and those from other countries who are not of our Kingdom, if they wish to trade here and enjoy the privileges and good customs of the said fairs . . . shall safely come, dwell, and depart, they, their merchandise, and their guides, in the safe conduct of the Fairs, into which we take and receive them from henceforth, together with their merchandise and goods, without their having been subject to seizure, arrest or hinderance by others than the guards of the said fairs'. (20)

These safe conducts enabled foreign merchants to pass unmolested by the robbers who infested the roads, for if this happened, the local merchants were debarred from the fairs, a fact which encouraged the local merchants to ensure safety for the foreign ones. The safe conducts also at times exempted foreign merchants from the road tolls and dues demanded by the feudal nobility. This early trading encouraged the development of money — changing. Special merchants were licenced to engage in financial transactions to assist the trade, which otherwise would have suffered with so many merchants converging from all over the continent.

But all this would not have been possible without prior accumulation of the capital necessary for carrying it on. We have seen that the rise of the craft guilds led to a class of burghers cutting itself off from crafts production and resorting to trading. This was necessary because the surplus which could be realised in the exchange of craft products within the existing patriarchal production arrangements could not create sufficient accumulation for commercial purposes. The activities of the class which gave rise to the accumulation were of three kinds. The first is rooted in Christianity itself. We refer here to the plunder associated with the five Crusades, which were really five expeditions of plunder for the 'love of God', against the Moslems in the Mediterranean area. The second source consisted of the monopoly rights which the merchants obtained from the absolutist monarch, and the third involved the exploitation of some political advantage or of 'scarcely veiled plunder' which Marx called 'primitive accumulation'. In this chapter we shall look at the first two sources and reserve the third for the next chapter.

First the Crusades. This source of accumulation was of greater importance to the Italian city states, but other parties were closely involved to their advantage: for instance the Roman Church, which through the Crusades increased its wealth and extended its power, and the Byzantine Church and Empire which utilized them to contain Moslem power, not to speak of the nobles and the knights who went for the booty and wealth. However it was the city states, accumulating merchant capital, who most benefited.

Venice was well situated to take advantage of these Crusades. Being on a group of islands and at the centre of the eastern trade, having remained tied to Constantinople when Western Europe broke away, her advantages combined to consolidate her lead in the Crusade trade. According to the records of Geoffrey of Villehardouin written about 1209, a treaty was made between the Crusaders and Venice, through the agency of Geoffrey.

In return for 85,000 silver marks of Cologne, Venice agreed to supply the Crusade with transport and food for a year for 4500 knights and their horses, 9000 esquires and 20,000 foot soldiers. In addition Venice was to provide fifty galleys to accompany the Crusade, on condition that one half of the loot and plunder of the Crusade would be given to Venice. The story of the actual sacking sacking of Constantinople has been dramatically described by Steven Runciman:

> 'The sack of Constantinople is unparalleled in history. For nine centuries the great city had been the capital of Christian civiliz- ation. It was filled with works of art that had survived from ancient Greece and with the masterpieces of its own exquisite craftsmen. The Venetians indeed knew the value of such things. Wherever they could they seized treasures and carried them off to adorn [their own] squares and churches and palaces . . . Palaces and hovels alike were entered and wrecked. Even after so much had wantonly perished, the amount of booty was staggering. No one, wrote Villebardouin, could possibly count the gold and silver, the plate and the jewels, the samite and silks and garments of fur, vair, silver- grey and ermine; and he added, on his own learned authority, that never since the world was created had so much been taken in a city. It was all divided according to the treaty; three-eights went to the Crusaders, three-eights to Venetians, and a quarter was reserved for the future Emperor'. (21)

The second source of accumulation arose from monopoly rights which the merchants put to their advantage as soon as they acquired corporate status, thereby protecting themselves from competition. They used this monopoly to turn the terms of exchange to their own advantage in their dealings with the producer and consumer, which Dobb calls 'exploitation through trade'. The secret of this exploitation through trade, as Marx pointed out, lay not in the exportation, of the products of home industries to other countries, but in the promotion of exchange of products with commercially and otherwise economically undeveloped societies; and by the exploitation of both spheres of production — buying cheap in order to sell dear. This was no exchange of equivalents; the exchange relationships were quantitatively arbitrary as a direct result of the primitive conditions of production and exchange markets prevalent at the time. (22) The separation of the raw material from the craftsmen and of the craftsmen from the consumer under the prevailing conditions gave merchant capital its opportunity to expand and exploit. This too furthered the monopoly that the merchants wielded in this process. The accumulation which resulted also partly turned into usury capital, and this promoted the accum- ulation of merchant capital. Here the usurous capitalist accumulated out of onerous and harsh interest rates.

What monopoly rights did these merchant corporations enjoy? First they controlled the market in the guild or town. This included the right to levy market-dues and tolls, which helped the burgesses pay off their *Firma Burgi* to the King as the price for their monopoly charter and privileges. More important, however, was the right exercised by the town authority of determining who could trade in the town. This right was naturally used by the merchants to keep out competition and since they could do this they easily imposed minimum prices. Commodities affected included bread, wine, wood, coal, hides, wool, tallow and candles. Evidence of this regulation is an ordinance of Southampton in England which laid down that 'no simple inhabitant or stranger shall bargain for or buy any kind of merchandise coming to the town before burgesses of the Guild Merchant, so long as a guildsman is present and wishes to bargain for or buy it'. This was a general practice in feudal Western Europe. Moreover, the regulations concerning strangers also prohibited their doing business with the surrounding countryside, a prohibition that enhanced the monopoly and privileges of the local merchants and which opened up wider avenues for their own trade. This monopoly furthered what came to be referred to as the 'urban colonisation' over the surrounding country-side; the power by the town over the countryside was being asserted for the first time since slave-owning Rome. The safe conducts allowed merchants from outside access to the guild town where they sold their merchandise to the merchants who were members of the guild. Thus a writer recording the events of the period points out that:

> 'traders from outside were welcome when they brought with them foreign commodities which the burgher merchants could make a profit on by retailing, or when they purchased for exportation the commodities which the burghers had procured for the purpose from English craftsmen and agriculturists. They were welcome so long as they were ready to serve the interests of the burghers, and when they sought to thrust these on one side they seemed to be violating the very conditions upon which their presence was allowed'. (23)

These monopoly privileges when they were combined with the minute regulations concerning quality and standards of products in the final analysis worked to control competition and constituted what came to be known as staple rights, which were fought for and guarded throughout this period. The question of how many routes led to a town became a crucial political issue of the period, since the more central a guild or town, the more the privileges and profit.

Monopoly privileges which at first were collective rights of all the traders began to be concentrated into the hands of specialised dealers, and the merchant corporation were soon dominated by the richer merchants constituting themselves into 'the patriciate'. This entailed change of the merchant guild from a democratic form into a plutocracy and then into an oligarchy of the rich few, who, in alliance with local nobility, wielded considerable political power in the area. By the fifteenth century, in industries like cloth-making and cloth-finishing, power had passed into the hands of mercers and drapers, who prevented craftsmen from trading in their raw material or finished products except through them. Concentration of monopoly privileges became commonplace in other craft industries like the saddlers, grocers and haberdashers.

This development was important in that it established the hegemony of merchant capital over the smaller naturally derived capital of the craft guilds thus restricting the latter to retail in the local market and made it possible 'where the local market was not the main outlet for their products to subjugate the craftsmen to a close corporation of merchants with whom and on whose terms the producers had no option but to deal.' (24) Thus the craftsmen were cut off from direct link with the outside market at a time when it was beginning to become important, and those who retailed were equally excluded from wholesale trade with merchants who were not burgesses of the city. The richer craftsmen could only, and did where possible, leave crafts for trade as soon as they had accumulated large enough capitals to enable them to participate in the wider markets.

These proceedings were a precondition for participation in the overseas trade that was to be a permanent feature of the seventeenth century. They particularly affected the English whose home market was dominated up to this period by foreign merchants. The staples established in Flanders (The Flemish Hanse) and in the Italian city states had obtained privileges in England, as these foreign merchants were the financiers of the English Crown. Until the English merchants had sufficient finances to lend to their monarchs to pay off expenses incurred mainly in the prosecution of wars, the crown had no alternative but to farm the privileges out to foreigners. By the fourteenth century the English merchants were ready in their Fellowship of the Staple to barter the Crown's loans for monopoly rights in the wool export trade. Among the first to partake in the trade in wool, challenging the Flemish Hanse, were the mercers who set up factors at Bruges, Antwerp, and Bergen. This resulted in bitter trade wars, leading to English ships being attacked and taken as prizes, but eventually the English merchants were allowed to trade at Danzig once a week but only with the burgesses and in no other town of Prussia. Although in 1614 export of English wool was officially prohibited, as a concession to the cloth industry, by the middle of the century a number of joint-trading companies were being set-up to partake in the trade in the North Sea and into the Mediterranean, each possessing privileges in new areas.

What led to this rapid development? The main reason was the eviction of the Flemish Hanse in 1598, marking the end of the period of 'tutelage' when the major part of overseas trade was in the hands of foreign merchants. Venetian control of the English cloth exports ended in London in 1533 and in Southampton in 1587. The Flemish Hanse which had extraterritorial rights in England was deprived of its privilege in 1552 and finally evicted in 1598. 'In a symbolic way this latter event was a sign that England was moving from the periphery towards the centre of a new trading system.' (25)

What gave rise to the 'new trading system'? The rise of 'the Company' was itself a product of this 'new trading system' and had its origin in the 'discoveries' by Vasco de Gama of the India route via the Cape and by Columbus of the Americas. These 'discoveries' led by the Portuguese and the Spanish were centrally concerned with procuring spices and in the course of events it became clear that large quantities of gold and silver could be found in Mexico and Peru. This was at a time when mining in Europe had exhausted all avenues of expansion. The finding of gold and silver at this time was to have immense expansionary impact on trade and vice-versa. In the East Indies the Portuguese stumbled on new riches of oriental quality in spices, precious stones, drugs, perfumes, silks etc. Vasco de Gama's trip was such an immense success for the merchant (26) that it overturned the Mediterranean route. The Venetian cities which acted as the main centre for the Eastern trade declined as a result. This route, however, had already been subjected to Turkish harassment and the new route via the Cape came just in time. The Atlantic opening on the other hand also had a tremendous effect. As Leo Huberman has picturesquely put it:

> 'Now the direction of currents of commerce was changed. Where formerly the geographical position of Venice and South German cities had given them advantage over the countries lying farther West, now those countries on the Atlantic seaboard had the advantage. Venice and the cities which had been tied to it commercially were now off the main road of commerce. What had been the highway of the trade now became the by way. The Atlantic became the new highway, and Portugal, Spain, Holland, England and France rose to commercial prominence.' (27)

International trade could now be spoken of as being beyond Europe and it is here that great riches were made, adding ever more to the growing merchant capital. Mercantile imperialism was being erected on the basis of unequal exchange between various modes of production. Unlike in Europe, where the trade was essentially one of exchange values, the trade with the undeveloped parts of the world was basically exchange for use-values. To quote Marx:

> 'So long as merchants capital promotes the exchange of products between undeveloped societies, commercial profit not only appears as out bargaining and cheating but also largely originates from them. Aside from the fact that it exploits the difference between the price of production of various countries (and in this respect it tends to level and fix the values of commodities), those modes of production bring it about that merchants capital appropriates an overwhelming portion of the surplus product, partly as a mediator between communities which still substantially produce for use-value, or for that matter any sale of products at their value is of secondary importance; and partly, because under these modes of production the principal owners of the surplus-product with whom the merchant dealt . . . represent the consuming wealth and luxury which the merchant seeks to trap . . .' (28)

It is for this reason that merchant capital in this phase stood as 'a system of robbery . . . directly connected with plundering, piracy, kidnapping slaves and colonial conquest'. (28)

In their quest for accumulation the feudal merchants mobilised smaller capitals; joint-stock Companies were a pre-condition for the new trading system. Even piratical expeditions had to be organised on joint-stock lines. Among the first of these Companies to be formed were the Merchant Adventurers. The Russia Company formed in England in 1553 for the monopoly of the Russian trade had the Merchant Adventurers as shareholders. The African Company was formed the same year, a Company whose members were to grow fat on the lucrative enterprise which Nassau senior later described as 'to kidnap or purchase and work to death without compunction' the natives of Africa, and about which 'the English and the Dutch, at that time the wisest and most religious nations of the world . . . had no more scruple . . . than they had about enslaving horses'. (29)

The Eastland Company was formed in 1578 'to enjoy the sole trade through the sound into Norway, Sweden, Poland, Lithuania, Prussia, Finland . . . etc.', with powers 'to make bye-laws and to impose fines, imprisonment etc. on all non-freemen trading to these parts'. In 1592 the Levant Company was formed with Queen Elizabeth among its leading shareholders, leading to the formation in 1600 of the East India Company which had its charter renewed in 1605 in perpetuity by James I. Similar joint-stock Companies were being set up all over Europe, so that by the early seventeenth century there were seven 'East India' Companies, mainly English and Dutch; four 'West India' Companies, mainly organised in Holland, France, Sweden, and Denmark; 'Levant' Companies; 'Africa' Companies; 'Plymouth', 'Virginia' and 'Hudson Bay' Companies etc. Although it is probable that the growth of the Atlantic trade had as its 'main agents . . . the English merchant or small trading partnership rather than the chartered trading Companies', (30) yet without the external economies created by these joint-stock Companies, the small partnership would have had no chance.

The course of European trade in the period just prior to and for a good part of the sixteenth century was dominated by the cloth industry. England at this time was a relatively undeveloped country on the periphery of the European trading system, supplying raw materials, particularly wool, tin, leather, and unfinished clothing to Europe. At the European end the trade was concentrated on Antwerp where the main staples were located. When the flow of trade moved away from the Mediterranean to the Atlantic and the Italian cities declined, Antwerp took their place. Antwerp was free of all trade restrictions, and hence unlike other cities in Europe attracted many merchants with the growth of Indian and Atlantic plunder. The persecution of 'new' Christians in Portugal, many of whom were entrepreneurs and merchants also helped in establishing Antwerp as a commercial centre. Venice lost the spice trade to Portugal and in 1504 the Portuguese merchants transferred their spices staple to Antwerp, thus making it the commercial and financial centre of Europe. There was also the industrial region behind it from which woollens and worsteds from Valenciennes and Tournai, tapestries from Brussels and Oudenarde, iron from Namur, and munitions from the Black Country round Liege came in search of a market. These and other products poured in to strengthen Antwerp's commercial prominence. Moreover, from the accession of Charles V of Spain, it served as the commercial capital of the Spanish Empire. (31)

The importance of Antwerp as the commercial and financial centre of Europe and the growth of merchant capital can be illustrated by the story of one German merchant called Fuggers, who financed most of the wars in the sixteenth century and made fortunes from them. Fuggers began business in the fifteenth century as a merchant dealing in wool and spices. Eventually he established a banking business which loaned money to other merchants, kings and princes and even to the Pope, receiving in return revenues from mines, trading ventures, and crown lands. When loans were not repaid he 'foreclosed' on the mines, estates, and ventures by becoming direct owner of the properties which were pledged as security. According to Huberman, the Fuggers balance sheet of 1646, with a capital of five million gulden, shows debts from the German Emperor, the city of Antwerp, the Kings of England and Portugal and the Queen of the Netherlands.

Fuggers was not alone, however. There were also the Welsers, the Hochstetters, the Haugs and the Imhofs in Germany. There were the Frescobaldis, the Gualterottis and the Strozzis who had replaced the Peruzzis and the Medicis of the previous century in Italy. A comparison below outlining the vast finances of these merchants will indicate the development of merchant and usury capital between the fourteenth and the sixteenth centuries:

1300	—	the Peruzzis	$ 800,000
1400	—	the Medicis	$ 7,500,000
1546	—	the Fuggers	$40,000,000

Another practice which grew up and which gave further impetus to trade was sale by sample, of standard and recognised goods. Soon a credit system suited to the new development was developed by the financiers, to make unnecessary the shipment of large quantities of gold to pay for goods. This worked by, say, English buyers exchanging notes with Italian sellers in lieu of payment in gold or silver coin. Through the agency of the financiers, a central clearing house was created in which these notes were cancelled on a national basis thus inaugurating the modern practice of current transaction accounts. (32)

Amsterdam was the next city to come to the fore. Its rise to pre-eminence at this time was linked to the trade superiority of Dutch merchants: landed property was relatively undeveloped in Holland, and since agricultural production was insufficient the Dutch took to trade and to carrying trade from which vast fortunes were made. Dutch merchants developed Amsterdam as an international trade and financial centre by granting protection to foreign merchants. An English East Indian merchant, Sir Josiah Child, recognised this when he said that: 'Fidelity in their seal (business honesty), encouragement of inventors, whom they reward, while they make the invention public, instead of granting a patent as here, thrift, small ships, low duties, poor-laws, banks, mercantile law, easy admission of burghers, inland navigation, low interest, fisheries, colonies, religious liberty, education' were the factors that made Amsterdam, like Antwerp before her come to the fore as the new centre. But this dominance by the Amsterdam merchants was soon to be challenged by the English.

Dutch, French, and English 'East India' companies set up trading posts in India and China, thus enabling trade with these areas to grow 'more rapidly than trade with America'. The growth of trade reacted on shipping and vice-versa. An example of English tonnages show a growth from 101,000 tons in 1609-15 and 115,000 tons in 1629 to 162 − 200,000 tons in 1660. Growth on the part of English merchants reflected a new development:

> 'This increase in the number of ships and the growth of wealth and expertise of the English merchant class enabled the Dutch dominance of the carrying trade, which was also threatened by the French, to be challenged.' (33)

The Navigation Acts of 1650 and 1651 came just in time to confine trade with the English colonies to English ships. They constituted a declaration of war against Holland, war which actually erupted in 1652. Here, as elsewhere, Law was developing in accordance with commerce and the development of the productive forces as an instrument of the dominant class, protecting the English mercantile system from interference by Dutch and French merchants and helping to wrest seafaring and trade leadership away from the Dutch. Another Navigation Act in 1660, the Staple Act of 1663 and the Plantation Duties Act of 1673 consolidated English power.

The French and the Spanish too tried to establish their own system, but the strong position attained by England restricted them to small areas. Here the English mercantilist policy in protecting markets was concerned with establishing a 'geographical division of labour including the exchange of English manufactures for tropical and semi-tropical products, organised by English merchants and carried out by English ships'. (34) In time this geographical division of labour was not limited to English colonies but soon extended as we shall see, 'in alliance' with Portugal to Portuguese colonies in Brazil, Africa, and Asia, beginning from 1654 onwards.

The English Navigation Act of 1660 completed the legislation on the navigation system by introducing a long schedule of 'enumerated' products such as tobacco, sugar, ginger, cotton, indigo and other diewoods, requiring that these goods, and those to be 'enumerated' in the future, should only be shipped to the European market through an English entrepot. On the other side of the coin, the Act of Frauds of 1662 and the Staple Act of 1663 required European goods to be sent to the colonies through English ports and in English ships. The effect was to give the English merchants a cost advantage which helped to displace the erstwhile leaders, the Dutch, and greatly stimulated the expansion of the English mercantile navy. A number of skirmishes and wars were fought with the Dutch, Spanish and French to get colonies in the West Indies as well as the Americas. Territory after territory was added to the list of British colonies, and although the decline in market conditions between 1685 and 1740 considerably reduced trade in this period, leading to a number of chartered companies being withdrawn, England did much better in colonial and European trade than the other powers.

The time came to remove the competition of Indian textiles; although their import to England had helped England to extend her textile market to Europe this had been at the expense of textile production at home. A long period of protection and national self-sufficiency set in, transforming most tariff structures. In this period of protection, it was colonial trade that propped up the English merchants. Increased volumes of tropical and semi-tropical foodstuffs and raw materials were imported to England for re-export to Europe. While the English cloth industry was being challenged on the European market, England increased her share of re-exports of colonial products from almost nothing in the 1660s to 37 per cent of the export trade in the 1760s. East Indian, American, and African products, including the slave trade, played an increasing role in this direction, strengthening English competitiveness in Europe.

English mercantile imperialism did not only exploit colonial peoples but also had recourse to subjugating other weaker European countries in the quest for the accumulation of merchant capital. The clearest example of this was the relationship developed between English merchant capitalists and their Portuguese equivalents. A recent study has revealed how this relationship bordered on that of informal colonialism. (35)

The English-Portuguese alliance goes back to 1373, when the two countries were united against Castille. At first the two were equal partners but the growth of Spanish power and the eventual Spanish occupation of Portugal in 1580 radically altered the situation. When the Portuguese feudalists regained their independence in 1640 after sixty years of Spanish domination they had become totally dependent on English military support. The English merchants soon ensured that this support was only forthcoming at the price of serious economic concessions. In a series of treaties with England, Portugal's independent development was cut from under her feet. Beginning with the treaty of 1642, Portugal and her African and Indian possessions were opened up to English ships. Special privileges were bestowed on English merchants, including the non-payment of taxes. The treaty stipulated that Portugal had to buy all the ships she needed from England, thus nullifying an earlier treaty with Holland of 1641. Another treaty in 1654, promising 'peace and friendship', confirmed the earlier one and raised the status and privileges of English merchants to treaty level inclusive of judiciary privileges, opening Portuguese colonies for joint exploitation by the two 'friends'. It further stipulated that Portugal had to hire English ships if hers did not suffice.

The effect of these two treaties was to enable England to participate directly in the lucrative slave trade in West Àfrica, and in Brazilian sugar and gold dealings, thus substituting a quadrangular trade for the hitherto triangular one, with England as the centre, and Portugal virtually her commercial vassal. Another treaty signed in 1661 confirmed those of 1642 and 1654 and included a 'secret clause' by which England guaranteed the Portuguese feudalists support against Spain, committing England to the defence of Portuguese colonies against all enemies. The former Portuguese colonies in Dutch hands were transferred to England in return, including Bombay and Tangiers, not to speak of a large dowry of 10 million gold shillings, paid by Catherine of Portugal to England, or of the right to settle four English families in each Brazilian captaincy.

These three treaties resulted in an increase of English merchants in Portugal.

According to C.R. Boxer:

> 'The prosperous English merchants established at Lisbon and Oporto, who could draw on the concentrated mercantile wealth of London, were also able to extend to their Portuguese and through them to their Brazilian-customers longer and more plentiful credit than their foreign competitors were able to do'. (36)

This clearly put the English merchants in a strong position in Portugal. Portuguese efforts in the 1670s to establish manufacturing through a protectionist policy and by encouraging English artisans to immigrate to Portugal to manufacture cloth from local wool, the supply of which was abundant, resulted in a short-lived success for Portuguese merchants. British textile exports to Portugal declined and the English merchants tried to reduce their textile prices in order to beat the ban, but Portuguese textiles still sold more cheaply even then and were able, at least in the short-term, to withstand the competition.

The decline in British exports from £1.2 million in 1760 to £600,000 in 1775 which Boxer ascribes partly to the fall in gold production in Brazil and to crises in the sugar trade, was in fact brought about in the main by the new Pombal policy of protection for Portuguese merchants. Moreover, during the last quarter of the century Portuguese exports showed some improvement, resulting in her export prices rising. But this development also led to increased imports. New discoveries of gold by Portugal strength- ened her drive to regain her market from English control, and it looked as if this policy could consolidate the position of Portuguese manufacturers.

These hopes were, however, shortlived. Relying on the internal class contradictions in Portugal where the merchant class was weak compared to the landed aristocracy and the church, England strengthened the latter who preferred the English 'free trade' system which enabled their wine to be exported to England. The strategy pitted the merchants against the landed aristocracy and set the stage for England to regain control and consolidate it. The newly discovered mines in Brazil, in 1693 — 5 had to be exploited. Using the War of Spanish Succession as cover for its diplomacy, England wrung out of Portuguese feudalists another treaty, the famous Methuen treaty of 1703. This three article treaty permitted the entry of English woollen cloth and woollen manufactures to Portugal, on condition that Portugal's wines be admitted into England at two-thirds of the duties levied on French wine. To quote the Articles:

> Article I:
> His sacred royal majesty of Portugal promises, both in his name and that of his successors, to admit, for ever hereafter, into Portugal, the woollen cloths, and the rest of woollen manufactures of the British, as was accustomed, till they were prohibited by the law; nevertheless upon this condition:
> Article II:
> That is to say, that her sacred royal majesty of Great Britain shall, in her own name, and that of her successors, be obliged, for ever after, to admit the wines of the growth of Portugal into Britain, so that at no time, whether there shall be peace or war between the Kingdoms of Britain and France, anything more shall be demanded for these wines by the name of custom or duty, or whatsoever other title, directly or indirectly whether they shall be imported into Great Britain in pipes or hogsheads, or other casks, than what shall be demanded for the like quantity or measures of French wine, deducting or abating a third part of the custom duty. But if at anytime this deduction or abatement of customs, which is to be made as aforesaid, shall in any manner be attempted and prejudiced it shall be just and lawful for his sacred royal majesty of Portugal, again to prohibit the woollen cloths, and the rest of the British woollen manufactures.
> Article III:
> The most excellent lords the plenipotentiaries promise and take upon themselves, their above-named masters shall ratify this treaty; and within the space of two months the ratification shall be exchanged.

The articles of this treaty are quoted *in extenso* because of the significance of this trade in regard to the theories of comparative advantage in the international division of labour propounded by Adam Smith and David Ricardo based on this experience. Suffice it to say that unknown to the Portuguese, the sacred royal majesty of Great Britain, had in fact since the 1690s reduced duties on Portuguese wine below those imposed on French wine, so that there was no *quid pro quo* nor reciprocity for Portuguese lifting of the ban on English textile imports! The *British Merchant* exposed this lie thus:

> 'We [English] had done this [reducing duties on Portuguese wines] before we were stipulated to do so by our [Methuen] treaty; and it was our interest so to do tho no such treaty had ever been made. We made no alteration in the duties we had already established for the sake of Portugal, tho Portugal took off her Prohibition of many of our Woolen manufactures for our sake, and obliged herself never to prohibit any . . . To talk of our giving an Equivalent is Nonsense, we

have given nothing to Portugal for taking off this Prohibition . . .' (37) Even worse, as soon as English merchants and manufacturers were sure of controlling the Portuguese and Brazilian markets, England equalised the duties on Spanish wines with those of the Portuguese and in 1831 customs duties were fixed at 5s. 6d. on all wines except those from the Cape colony which were only 2s. 9d. The immediate effect of the Methuen treaty was to increase British exports to Portugal by 120 % and Portuguese exports to England by 40 %, in the period 1700 and 1710. Portugal's trade deficit grew in the same period by 235 %. The development brought disaster to the 'infant' Portuguese textile industry. Within a few years of the treaty and ratification British woollen exports quadrupled, eliminating the entire domestic production, (38) thus pushing Portugal full-blast into wine production, increasing it fivefold. The Portuguese entrepreneurs were ruined. After the English manufacturers had developed the textile industry and earned enough to buy the better French wines, their taste changed. Remarking about the effect of this treaty, Sideri has correctly said:

> 'This short and simple treaty achieved two basic things: the market of Portugal and her colonies was legally reopened to English products and, at the same time, an outlet for what was largely a potential Portuguese product was created in England to replace French wines. Thus, by importing Portuguese instead of French wines, England was able to promote her exports, especially of woollens where they were competitive with local products.' (39)

In brief English merchants and manufacturers established a trade relationship with Portugal which encouraged England's manufacturing and at the same time strengthened its bourgeoisie, while the Portuguese merchants and embryonic manufacturing stratum were destroyed, thus retarding the development of the productive forces in Portugal.

Going back to the 'commercial revolution' in general, expanded trade beyond Europe and in Europe itself contributed to Europe's financial strength. The accumulation of merchant capital created a surplus for industrial development, banking and agriculture. But it was a limited source of industrial finance. In particular countries like England merchant wealth strengthened the middle classes and exercised a strong influence on urban development. It sowed the seeds for dissolving the old bonds of feudalism as the monopolistic nature of mercantilist trade became opposed to development of the productive forces. Having been a revolutionary element, creating conditions for bringing about changes in the primitive feudal relationships on land, helping to establish a capitalist element in the form of the yeoman farmer, and creating in the town the embryonic manufacturing class, merchant capital turned conservative and readily merged itself with the feudal landed aristocracy. Instead of investing in manufacturing, the merchants purchased land, went into partnerships in commerce with the aristocracy, married and inter-married in pursuit of titles of gentility, accepted political offices in coalition (e.g. in Italy and other continental countries), and became ministers in the King's Court on the basis of the old feudal state system (e.g. Tudor England). (40) As a consequence they directly influenced and determined the policies of the feudal warfare state.

The determining factors of mercantilist policy, which can be summed up in three R's, restriction, regulation and restraint, naturally harmed the interests of the manufacturing class, which itself arose out of the conditions established by the commercial revolution. The hegemony of the merchants had begun to attract attack as far back as the 1690s. In 1749 Joseph Tucker attacked the policy by which, 'the whole nation must suffer in its commerce and be debarred from trading to more than three-fourths of the Globe to enrich a few rapacious directors . . . (who) get wealthy the very same way by which the public becomes poor'.

The privileges which had been occasional in earlier periods became unbearably systematised in England under James I, concentrating all the trade into the hands of about 200 families. The object was clearly to raise revenue from the merchants. Here, as we have seen, the interests of the feudal state merged with those of the merchants and together they acted as a fetter on the development of manufacturing industry, which through trade they had stimulated and nourished. The movement forward now passed into the hands of the manufacturing stratum, the bourgeoisie in embryo, who were eventually able to unleash the industrial revolution and bring into being a new system of property relations.

Gradually a new type of relationship between worker and employer was created. Whereas in the guilds the patriarchal relationship between journeyman and master existed, in manufacture its place was taken by a money relationship, a new relationship which constituted a new class relation. The manufactory which planted the seeds of the new relationship existed side by side with the feudal monopolies of the Livery Companies and the rapid development of commerce in the next phase of development only helped to bring out the contradiction between the old and the new. But this manufacturing transformation had to await capital accumulation which for a long time was still centred on commerce and landed property.

CHAPTER IV

The merchant capital accumulated during the 'commercial revolution' which we have just examined stimulated manufacturing but did so from the outside. As Marx correctly pointed out, independent merchant capital represented the separation of the circulation process from its extremes, the exchanging producers themselves. The producers became independent of the circulation process just as the merchant capitalist became independent of them. Marx went on to say:

> 'The product becomes a commodity by way of commerce. It is commerce which here turns products into commodities, not the produced commodity which by its movements gives rise to commerce'. (41)

This process was already under way in the second half of the sixteenth century in England, and in the fourteenth and fifteenth century in certain towns in the Mediterranean, Flanders and the Rhine district.

We have already made reference to this development where merchant capital steps in and begins to bend production to its needs. This was important in that it was a move towards the separation of the producers from their means of production, turning them into producers of surplus – value. As Marx said, the process that clears the way for the capitalist system can be no other than the process which takes away from the labourer the possession of his means of production; a process that transforms on the one hand the social means of subsistence and of production into capital, and on the other the immediate producers into wage-labourers. So-called primitive accumulation, therefore, is nothing else than the historical process of divorcing the producer from the means of production, primitive because it forms the pre-historic stage of capital and of the mode of production corresponding with it.

The historic movement outlined above on the one hand appears as the emancipation of the worker from serfdom and from the bondage of the feudal relationships of the guilds, but on the other, and this is the crux of the matter, such emancipation entailed the new bondage of the free seller of labour power to the capitalist.

As we have noticed, by the fourteenth century serfdom had already disappeared in England and in the fifteenth century we had peasant proprietors in its place. The latter part of this century and the first decade of the sixteenth saw the enclosure of lands, mainly motivated by the rise of Flemish wool manufacturing and the corresponding rise of the price of wool. (42) This development was reinforced by the sacking and plunder of the property of the Roman Church during the Reformation. The population of the feudal land holdings of the church and monasteries was hurled into the proletariat and the lands were given away to the rapacious favourites of the King, or sold at nominal prices to speculators, mainly farmers who drove out *en masse* the hereditary sub-tenants and threw their holdings into one. (43) The extent of this robbery of church lands was estimated by Marx at seven-tenths of the whole of England (44) which incidentally shows the extent of feudal church property in England, and at the same time explains the support given to Cromwell by these new property owners in the struggle against Charles I.

This robbery, deprivation, and expropriation of the peasantry intensified with the alienation of Crown estates and the enclosure of communal pastures. As Marx put it:

> 'The spoilation of the Church's property, the fraudulent alienation of the state domains, the robbery of the common lands, the usurpation of feudal and clan property, and its transformation into modern private property under circumstances of reckless terrorism, were just so many idyllic methods of primitive accumulation. They conquered the field for capitalist agriculture, made the soil part and parcel of capital, and created for the town industries the necessary supply of a "free" and outlawed proletariat'. (45)

The robbery of the feudal common lands was sealed with legality in 1689 after the 'glorious Revolution' which overthrew feudal absolutism, by the new owners who abolished all feudal tenure of land. They 'indemnified' the state by taxes on the peasantry and the masses of the people. Thus in England the capitalist farmer grew rich by the agricultural revolution of the sixteenth century at the expense of the impoverished masses who were now employed by the capitalist farmer at low wages and by the merchant manufacturer who also accumulated part of his wealth from the masses of the proletariat. The peasants' former means of nourishment and subsistence were turned into variable capital and some of the raw materials into constant capital; a home market now existed for the new owners of the means of production. Formerly the peasant was almost self-sufficient in the products he produced and partly exchanged. But these were now turned into commodities by the new property owners, who sold them to the expropriated for a portion of their wages.

This development progressively created a division of labour between industry and agriculture, and strategically placed the new property owners in a position to accumulate and thus to make the transformation to modern industry possible. However, primitive accumulation on this basis did not on its own engender the rapid accumulation which enabled the transformation to take place as it actually did. The answer lay elsewhere and here we must look at the external sources of accumulation, both in

terms of English production as a whole and also in terms of sources external
to the unit of production itself.

Marx has remarked that the discovery of gold and silver in America, the
enslavement and the entombment in mines of native populations, the
looting of the East Indies and the turning of Africa into a warren of black-
skin commercial enslavers marked the 'rosy dawn of capitalist production'.
(46) We have, in the last chapter, already examined the 'commercial
revolution' which led to the generation of merchant capital. Most of this
merchant capital in the hands of the merchants was invested in the
circulation of commodities; relatively very little of it filtered into production. Nevertheless, the rapid expansion of world trade on the basis of
merchant capital was of considerable consequence for industrial
development:

> 'The new products imported thence, particularly the masses of gold
> and silver which came under circulation and totally changed the
> position of the classes towards one another, dealing a blow to feudal
> landed property and the workers, the expeditions of adventurers,
> colonisation; and above all the extension of markets into a world
> market, which had now become possible and was daily becoming
> more and more a fact, called forth a new phase of historical
> development'. (47)

The capability to engage in navigation, itself a heritage from earlier
Italian development and the result of wars in the Iberian Peninsula against
the Arabs, led to rapid expansion of maritime and riparian commerce.
Western Europe was relatively poorer in natural resources than the new
areas, hence the drive to procure tropical produce of all kinds (spices, tea,
ivory, indigo, etc.) that could not be obtained nearby; hence also the
effort to import valuable products of oriental skills (high quality cloth,
ornaments, pottery, etc.); and hence finally the wild scramble to bring back
precious metals and stones that were in short supply at home. The resulting
far-flung trade, combined with piracy, outright plunder, slave traffic and
robbery of gold, led to a rapid formation of vast fortunes in the hands of
Western European merchants. (48)

Supremacy over the high seas by Spain and Portugal led to an age of
reconnaissance and division of the world between them. The Portuguese
made contact with Africa, Asia and the far East. The Spaniards concentrated their effort in the Atlantic although Portugal managed to gain
Brazil. The contacts with these areas revealed a great wealth of products.
On the West Coast of Africa, the Portuguese found that the principal
occupations of the inhabitants of the Gold Coast were agriculture, work
in gold, iron and earthenware, fishery, salt-boiling, gold-digging, and
weaving. In the kingdom of the Congo, which the Portuguese did their
best to destroy by treachery, a relatively developed country was found.
According to C.R. Boxer:

> 'The Bantu tribes over whom the King of Congo ruled knew how to
> work metals, including iron and copper, and they were fairly skilled

potters. They wove mats and articles of clothing from raffia tissues of palm cloth. They had domesticated several animals — pigs, sheep, chickens, and in some districts cattle, though they did not use milk, butter, or cheese. Their agricultural instruments were limited to the hoe and the axe.' (49)

In the beginning trade in African products was not carried out on the basis of conquest, but with the discovery of mines in Peru and Mexico by the Portuguese a need for slave-labour was created leading to a new relationship between Western Europe and Africa. Slave trading had started as early as the fifteenth century but it was the discovery of the mines in the sixteenth century which caused its massive expansion. According to Walter Rodney:

'When the Europeans reached the Americas, they recognised its enormous potential in gold and silver and tropical produce. But that potential could not be made a reality without adequate labour supplies. The indigenous Indian population could not withstand new European diseases such as small-pox, nor could they bear the organised toil of slave plantations and slave mines, having barely emerged from the hunting stage . . . Therefore they turned to the nearest continent, Africa, which incidentally had a population accustomed to settled agriculture and disciplined labour in many spheres'. (50)

The Dutch merchants, who had the monopoly of the slave trade, were later joined by the French who shared the profits equally with the Spanish rulers of Mexico and Peru. For this reason Colbert had described the slave-trade as 'recommended for the progress of the national merchant marine'. Under the Treaty of Utrecht by which England concluded the War of Spanish Succession in 1713, English merchants extorted the right to supply Spanish America until 1743 with 4,800 African slaves yearly, for which a special South Sea company was expressly floated. The declared purpose of English involvement in this War was to keep the French Louis XIV and his relatives off the Spanish throne; the other consideration was to prevent the French Guinea Company from keeping the slave *Asiento*. (51) From then on the slave-trade to the Americas was dominated by English merchants and the supremacy over the seas which they established as a result of this slave-trade reacted on navigation and other colonial trade with cummulative and multiplier effects. Even previously, English capital accumulation had benefitted from the colonisation of South America. C.R. Boxer points out that:

'In Portugal itself, the exploitation of Brazil's mineral resources and the great revival of Portuguese trade with that colony enabled the mother country to settle its unfavourable balance of trade with the rest of Europe in gold. Brazilian gold and diamonds also greatly enriched the Crown, the Church and the Court and gave King John V the wherewithal to avoid calling the Cortes and asking them for money during the whole of his reign, 1706-50. This monarch is reported to have said in this connection: "My grandfather feared and owed: my father owed: I neither fear nor owe" '. (52)

There may not have been much in John's neither fearing nor owing. He certainly had onerous debts to pay, notably to England. The balance of trade deficit, as we have seen, was mainly created by English trade with Portugal and, under the unequal treaties of 1642, 1654, 1661 and the Methuen Treaty of 1703, the English trade 'established and codified an international division of labour between the two countries much according to the principle of comparative advantage later (propounded) by Ricardo'. (53)

The last treaty worked towards the inflow of Brazilian gold to Britain through Portugal. The English merchants had become apprehensive about their economy due to the diminishing supplies of gold. This had resulted in a reduction of money in circulation. Having increased by 47-48 % from 1575-1650, it dropped by 11 % in the second half of the seventeenth century. (54) Now, with the treaty of 1703, Portugal provided England with new sources of bullion that were essential for her monetary circulation to keep pace with expanding production and trade, at least for half a century. (55) According to Sideri, Brazilian gold production in the seventeenth century was estimated at £200 million, and in the eighteenth century the amount to reach Portugal was estimated at over £500,000 for the period 1699-1755. Sideri adds that 'Although the total amount of Brazilian gold which flowed to England cannot be ascertained there are good grounds for thinking that between half and three quarters of the gold which entered the Tagus in an average year soon found its way to England'. (56) Boxer quotes figures for the bullion brought by the packet — boats from Lisbon to Falmouth, between 25 March 1740 and 8 June 1741 which value the gold inflow at £447,347; while in the years 1759 and 1760 it totalled £787,290 and £1,085,558 respectively. He adds:

'This certainly underestimates the total bullion flow to England in terms of the first half of the eighteenth century, as warships were used on the scale indicated above and of which many other examples could be given'. (57)

He refers here to the carrying of contraband on British warships since these were exempted from search. Sideri adds that the effect of Portuguese bullion on English monetary circulation can be deduced from estimates of the latter at £9.5 million in 1701, and at 22.5 million guineas in 1773; a 'process whereby the gold standard was established in England'.

This inflow of Portuguese gold reduced the need for paper securities to finance the economic expansion which otherwise 'would probably have been notably slower and even much less stable than it was'. Furthermore, it 'favoured the multilateral growth of the overseas trade' by helping England to settle her deficit trade, and made it possible for the 'East India Company to purchase abroad the silver so essential to trade'. (58) The increased purchasing power resulted in price inflation and higher profits for the merchants and the manufacturers thus adding to the accumulation of capital. Since this price revolution was mainly in foodstuffs, standards of living of ordinary wage earners decreased. But it gave impetus to general business expansion particularly in the latter half of the sixteenth century: 'The inflation [was] reflected in business earnings, in the willingness to invest in commercial undertakings, and in the accumulation of mercantile capital'. (59)

Emphasis has been placed throughout on the slave-trade, on the gold and silver influx which slavery made possible, and in particular on the impact of this primitive accumulation which led to earlier English capitalist development. Mention must be made of the introduction of this Graeco-Roman slavery and its exploitation in the production and export to England (for consumption and re-export to Europe) of sugar, cotton, coffee and cacao, to mention only the main products. The export to the West Indies and to the New World of African slaves for this purpose contributed as much if not more than the inflow of gold and silver into Europe. Henry Brougham estimated that by 1790 there were in the English West Indies ten slaves to one free man, in the French fourteen to one, and in the Dutch twenty-three to one. (60) Between 1680 and 1688 the Royal African Company in which King Charles had shares, paid dividends of 300 per cent on slaves, although only 46,000 of the 70,000 slaves survived the trips over these years. (61) The 'triangular trade' in which this process took place made Bristol bristle with trade and Liverpool 'wax on the fat' of the slave and sugar trade. Eric Williams vividly described this trade in the following terms:

'The triangular trade thereby gave a triple stimulus to British industry. The Negroes were purchased with British manufactures; transported to the plantations, they produced sugar, cotton, indigo, mollases and other tropical products, the processing of which created new industries in England; while the maintenance of the Negroes and their owners on the plantations provided another market for British Industry, New England agriculture and the Newfoundland fisheries. By 1750 there was hardly a trading or a manufacturing town in England which was not in some way connected with the triangular or direct colonial trade. The profits obtained provided one of the main streams of that accumulation of capital in England which financed the industrial revolution.' (62)

The defenders of imperialism have called this conclusion 'clearly exaggeration'.(63) Others have gone so far as suggesting that this development of Europe could have gone on without outside sources of accumulation, although it might have been slower. (64) These apologists of imperialism forget that *whatever might have happened*, Europe did not undertake the industrial revolution without the plunder, enslavement, and entombment of the native peoples of Africa, Asia and Latin America. Many things could have happened without this exploitation, but the fact is that those other things did not happen. The impact on these relatively undeveloped societies created by this exploitation is as important as the development it created in Western Europe and North America.

The plunder of Africa and Latin America was matched by that in the trade with the East. The Portuguese who led the way were soon followed by the Dutch. They established their hegemony over India, Java, and other areas of East Asia. The French and the British were soon following in their footsteps to get at these riches.

In France the development of agriculture and manufactures was greatly benefitting from the slave and colonial exploitation as can be judged from the concern shown by a Bishop Maury. His arguments below were against the proposed abolition of slave trade and the granting of freedom to the French slave colonies, made in the French National Assembly in 1791:

> 'If you were to lose each year more than 200 million livres that you now get from your colonies, if you had not the exclusive trade with your colonies to feed your manufactures, to maintain your navy, to keep your agriculture going, to repay for your imports, to provide for your luxury needs, to advantageously balance your trade with Europe and Asia, then I say it clearly, the Kingdom would be irretrievably lost.' (65)

What is said of England and France can be said for the Spanish, the Dutch and Portuguese whose gold and silver spread all over Europe and particularly to England and France. For although no conclusive figures can be found, various estimates are good indicators of the extent of the exploitation of slave labour and the colonies. Father Rinchon has estimated that France made over half a billion *livres taurnois*. Wiseman has estimated that the British made over £300 million from the labour of slaves in the West Indies alone. Hamilton estimates that over 500 million gold pesos were collected in gold and silver exports from Latin America between 1503 and 1660.

One aspect, of the relations created by the drive for the riches of the East stands out more prominently than any other, and that is the British impact on Indian development. Before the British moved into India, the textile industry of that country was much more highly developed than anything Britain, let alone Europe, could boast of. Up to this time (sixteenth century) all the trade carried on between Europe and Asia, and particularly between India and England was all in favour of India. But this was ruining the balance of trade for England because all the gold was being shipped out to India to pay for calicoes and silks for the English middle class.

The balance of advantage which lay for quite a long time with India, was bound to be changed. William Spence in his book, *Britain Independent of Commerce*, in 1808 wrote to justify what happened. According to him the whole problem was raised by the fact that Britain had to spend specie for Indian textiles since Indians did not wish to import British products. Hence since the wages of Indian labour were very low in comparison to the

British ones, India could undersell the British in every one of their staple manufactures. The only alternative, according to Spence, was to destroy the handicrafts of India. In 1720 a ban was imposed on the importation of Indian textiles, a ban which was not lifted until 1917. The British East India Company in 1702 was given a new lease of life clothed with the authority of the rising power of the merchant middle class, equipped with a new monopoly not created by the Royal grants of old 'but authorised and nationalised by the sanction of Parliament'. (66) In 1784 the Company was given a Board of Control consisting of six members of the privy council thus becoming 'a parastatal'.

The flow of gold and jewels and other forms of tribute became more pronounced after Clive's defeat of the Nawab of Bengal at Plassey in 1757. Treasure flowed in 'on a scale that makes the plunder of the early adventurers look paltry indeed'. (67) This contrasted sharply with the fact that from that point of time no more bullion went to India while imports coming in from India amounted to over £6 million a year. Barrat-Brown estimates that the tribute drained from Bengal to England for fifty years after Plassey may have amounted to £15 million a year (or about £150 million in present terms), 'most of it going not to the company but to establish the private fortunes of its servants'. As to the treasure going to the company itself he estimates the value at £4 million sterling (about £40 million in present terms). (67) Against this should be put the £6 million which Marx estimated went to the companies' employees as gifts from 1757-1766. (68)

These examples of slave trade in Africa, slave labour in South American mines, and the plunder of India are enough to indicate the correlation between European expansion through 'international trade' (basically slave and colonial trade) and the plunder and spoilation of these lands. The Navigation Laws ensured that the colonial trade with the mother country would increase while that with third parties would decrease. In England, Hobsbawn estimates that whereas domestic industries between 1700 and 1750 increased their output by 7 %, export industries did so by 76 %. Cotton manufacture, which was tied to foreign trade since all the raw material had to be imported, was mainly exported to earn gold. By the end of the eighteenth century Britain was exporting two-thirds of its output. This export expansion did not depend on the modest 'natural' rate of growth of Britain's home demand, but rather on:

> 'capturing a series of other countries' export markets, and destroying domestic competition within particular countries, that is by the political or semi-political means of war and colonisation. The country which succeeded in concentrating other people's export market, or even in monopolizing the export markets of a large part of the world in a sufficiently brief period of time, could expand its export industries at a rate which made industrial revolution not only practicable for its entrepreneurs, but sometimes virtually compulsory. And this is what Britain succeeded in doing in the eighteenth century'. (69)

These two 'external' factors of primitive accumulation were dialectically tied up in a 'systematic combination' with the national debt, the mode of taxation, the protectionist system and the over-all system of warfare that enhanced and protected it. The 'internal' factors employing the power of the state, helped hasten the process of transformation of the feudal mode of production into the capitalist one, and, as in England, shortened the transition. (70)

The system of national debt or public credit which was practiced in the earlier period of the Italian city states was an innovation for the new manufacturing class in England and Holland. It was taken up in Holland when capitalist elements there became powerful creditors to the Kings. Amsterdam had become the financial centre of Europe, from its seafarings earnings and the plunder by the Dutch East India company of Java and Malacca. The grain trade, the fisheries and the carrying trade helped consolidate this position. By the seventeenth century Holland was the leading country in Europe and the guilder was the international currency 'before the pound was sovereign'. Amsterdam used the surplus from its colonial plunder to lend to its 'political and commercial rivals', on the basis of 'negotiable public securities binding not only upon the sovereign but upon his state'. (71) It held the key to the international payment system as Antwerp had in the earlier period. The system now developed from a bilateral to a multilateral one with bills of exchange increasingly being used and a constant movement of bullion between England and the Netherlands taking place. Moreover the Amsterdam Exchange Bank which was founded in 1609 was the first bank in Northern Europe which operated exchange and deposit account and it attracted many foreign depositors. The bank did not lend to individuals but made advances to the East India Company in short term loans. In this way by the 1760s Dutch merchants established themselves as stock-holders in the Bank of England and in the English East India Company, which managed about one-seventh of the English 'national debt'.

Profiting from England's own colonial ventures the deposit resources of the Bank of England were growing 'by leaps and bounds' during the closing decades of the eighteenth century. Helped by 'a dozen revolutions' sweeping Western Europe from 1783 to 1815 the English 'financial revolution' swept the money market to London. The emergence of London was inevitable, since England had as we observed been wresting the European and colonial trade away from the Dutch during the eighteenth century. The Bank of England, which was founded in 1694 and which was run by a group of London merchants, became the manager of the 'national debt'. It also received the revenues assigned to the consolidated fund and kept the principal and interest books for the fund holders. It marketed short-term government bills and held them as investment. It issued notes and facilitated the fast turn-over of capital. It also advanced money to the state, on interest, and at the same time it was empowered to coin money out of the same capital and lend it to the public in the form of banknotes. Gradually it became the custodian of the metallic resources of the country and the centre of all commercial activity.

The bank was in league with branch houses outside London who similarly engaged in circulation of notes and the acceptance of bonds based on the 'national debt'. In this way the 'national debt' and the tax-farming by which the merchants were allowed to collect taxes in the countryside or towns on payment of a sum of money became 'the most powerful levers of primitive accumulation'. (72) It also gave rise to joint-stock companies, which dealt in negotiable effects and open selling of shares by auction. At times the bank itself in turn made available funds for investment. Thus the 'national debt', which exceeded £50 million by 1714, had grown to £132 million after the Seven Years War in 1763. (71) It became 'evidence of British wealth' and the main 'agent of its concentration'. Three quarters of the annual government budget in 1783 went to payment of dividends upon this 'national wealth'. As Jenks comments:

> 'Nine million pounds were paid to rentiers when the entire annual turnover of British foreign trade did not exceed thirty-five millions. Hume reports that in his time this enormous claim upon the tax paying ability of the British Isles was held by only seventeen thousand fundholders'. (72)

The 'national debt and wealth' had to be repaid, but it could not be repaid without taxation; so, as the 'wealth' increased, so did the taxes. The modern system of taxation therefore became a necessary complement of the system of national debt. The one reacted on the other in a dialectical relationship. It squeezed the means of subsistence of the masses and hence led to the expropriation of the peasants and artisans and of all the elements of the lower middle class, who now were turned into proletarians. With the rise of capitalism, all roads led to 'proletariatown'. On the other side, however, accumulation took place, which in the end went partly to industrial development.

The expropriation was also heightened by a system of protection, which according to Marx was 'an artificial means of manufacturing manufacturers, or expropriating independent labourers, of capitalising the national means of production and subsistence, of forcibly abbreviating the transition from the medieval to the modern mode of production'. (73) As cloth manufacture developed, the clothiers from time to time obtained protection by the prohibition of export of wool which cheapened the raw material for manufacturers. Also protection was obtained by exemption from export duties on clothing and the prohibition of the importation thereof. The prohibition of the export of bullion had the same effect, namely removing foreign competition.

In France, the system of protection was carried to extremes. A system of patents to protect inventions of new processes was evolved in order to encourage foreign skills. In 1611 Jehan de Bras de Fer was granted such a patent to protect him and his invention, a new kind of mill. The government in France granted him monopoly for twenty-five years. It read:

> 'We have ... permitted that he and his associates ... build and construct mills according to his said invention ... in all the towns and cities of our Kingdom ... We forbid all, of whatever quality or condition they may be, to build mills after the said invention ... whether in whole or in part ... without his express permission and consent, on pain of paying a fine of 10,000 livres and having the said mill confiscated'. (74)

Prizes were also granted to encourage industry. Institutes of technical education were built in France and Bavaria. Subsidies were granted to textile industries by Colbert. Another example of patent protection was in England where one John Lombe was given protection for plans for the mechanisation of silk yarn which he had stolen from an Italian manufacturer. Combe and his brother as a result set-up a vast factory, 400 feet long, which became one of the sights of England, on an island at Derby. Combe died but in fifteen years his brother Thomas made a fortune of £120,000 and was given a knighthood. In 1732 the patent lapsed, but 'a grateful parliament bestowed £14,000 on Thomas and the industry, now open to all ...' (75) Protection was also accorded to the landed nobility and tenant farmers by way of corn laws to protect them from competing foreign grains, which at times ensured availability of food in times of war. Protection was granted to shipping by the Navigation Laws as we have seen, but more importantly by grant of bounties and by duty free importation of tar, pitch, stout timber, etc.

To these 'external' and 'internal' sources of primitive accumulation can be added the 'particular and individual' sources. These too took various forms. For instance the acquisition at low prices of expropriated church and state lands, which were then sold at enhanced prices, put large amounts of money into the pockets of whoever was favoured. There were also cases of 'windfalls', of high rents or gains from usury. These were important elements only to the extent that they contributed to the dispossession of the majority creating the conditions for the industrial transformation; it was the colonial system, slave trade, public debt, heavy taxation and commercial wars that led to the really gigantic increases in accumulation. The ideology of the mercantilist system as a whole was that national wealth was national power which had to be boosted and protected by warfare. For this reason the search for gold, the strengthening of naval power, and the acquisition of colonies all led to war. Gold serviced the navy and the navy fought the wars which kept the colonies within the imperial reach for plunder and more gold. As the empire grew in size, so the military machine, the bureaucracy and the entire state machine expanded, one reacting upon the other.

Wars were fought on order as and when powerful interests were threatened or likely to be threatened. This increased the national debt, hence taxes, and hence expropriations. In the eighteenth century alone England fought no less than seven major wars. Among these were: The Spanish Succession, The Austrian Succession, The Seven Years War, and The War of American Independence. The majority of these were intended to further commercial ends. Britain gained tremendously out of these wars, for they assured her the virtual monopoly of overseas colonial trade and world-wide naval power. Hobsbawn points out:

> '. . . war itself, by crippling Britain's major competitors in Europe, tended to boost exports; peace, if anything, tended to slow them down'. (76)

A classic example of these wars is the Seven Years War between England and France (1756-1763). Pitt had studied statistics of French commerce and industry, which convinced him that France was 'the greatest danger England had to face, and the only rival worth considering in the race for overseas trade'. He put forward two aims which were to dominate English policy, namely supremacy at sea and the capture of French trading posts. For this reason England prepared to attack French possessions in Canada, which was justified on five counts: the conquest would secure the entire trade in fur and fish; the French would be prevented from supplying their West Indian islands with lumber, which would drive up the price of French sugar, to the advantage of English merchants; France would lose the market for her manufactures; French naval armaments would be limited, since she would no longer be able to build ships in America or acquire masts and timber; and finally the expulsion of the French from Canada would give security to British North American colonies. (77) This approach dominated British policy in the prosecution of the war. The merchants gave complete support to the policy and collaborated by giving intelligence reports about the nature, value, and location of French gum, fur, fish and sugar trades in North America, the West Indies, Africa, and India. Although the French later regained some of the territories the policy had its full play. It swelled the English 'national debt' by an extra £60 million and thus added to the expropriation of the poorer middle-classes. It enabled exports of British manufactures to expand as well.

Furthermore, war contributed to the scientific innovation and technological development of the period. The British Navy's demands increased greatly with the wars. Its tonnage increased from 100,000 in 1685 to 325,000 in 1760. So did the demand for guns, which necessitated expansion of iron production. Moreover, government and quasi-government procurements required revolutionary means of supply. It is recorded that Henry Cort, who revolutionised iron manufacture, started out in the 1760s as a Navy agent, anxious to improve the quality of iron production 'in connection with the supply of iron to the Navy'. So too Henry Mandslay, the pioneer of machine tools who began his career in the Woolwich Arsenal, gained the wealth which made his inventions possible from Navy contracts. As we shall see in connection with modern US imperialism, the connection between scientific research and warfare is a fairly close one. This is not an isolated British experience but a phenomenon common to all empire builders. Herbert Butterfield has observed that:

> 'The whole of Western Society was movement, science and technology, industry and agriculture, all helping to carry one another along. But one of the operations of society — war — had probably influenced the general course of things more than is usally recognised. War above all had made it impossible for a king to live of his own, enabling his subjects to develop constitutional machinery, to insist on terms in return for a grant of money. Because of wars, kings were allied with advanced capitalistic developments from the closing centuries of the Middle Ages. The growing demands of governments in the extreme case of war tightened up the whole development of state and produced the intensification . . . of the state. The Bank of England and the national debt emerged during a conflict between England and France, which almost turned into a financial war and brought finance into the very structure of government. In the 17th century armies had been mounting in size, and the need for artillery and for vast number of uniforms had an important effect on the size of economic enterprise'. (78)

CHAPTER V

Feudalism sustained itself ideologically through religion. Property relationships were maintained not only through 'extra economic means', by force, but also through custom and tradition, which were based on religious beliefs; state and church were the necessary superstructure. Pope and Emperor Constantine saw reason in this when he occupied both roles as temporal and spiritual leader. This marriage between church and state continues up to the present day. Whatever survived of Aristotle's 'reason' of slave society was interpreted to suit feudal society. In the Dark Ages this ideology held that at the time of man's fall his nature was vitiated by the original sin; the good side was not fully lost but it became subject to evil predispositions. The former condition of pure nature gave way to greed, passion, and quest for power whereupon the curse of mortality befell humanity as punishment for its corruption. The absolute law of nature which had mirrored the perfect goodness of man was no longer capable of realisation. Therefore, government, property, and the state appeared on the scene to alleviate the deteriorated condition of mankind. These institutions were themselves tainted win sin, but since the church was the guardian of the eternal law of God, it had the unfettered right to interfere with these sinful institutions, for it had unconditional sovereignty over the state. The state is justified as long as it continues to defend the church, to execute its commands, and to preserve order among men by enforcing the worldly law. This was Augustine's interpretation of history from the fifth century which was the basis of feudal ideology until Thomas Aquinas in the thirteenth century when the idea of the state as being a sinful institution was put aside.

So long as the prince was a representative of the Holy Roman Empire this worked well. When the split came in the fifteenth and sixteenth centuries with the Renaissance, the Reformation, and the merchant class backing the princes in their struggle, the princes created their own national churches and religion continued to dominate thought as a weapon for subordination of the masses.

This movement against Rome had its antithesis: the secularisation of thought, the advocacy of mechanical materialism, which began to act as a catalyst for change. 'Natural philosophy' (science) became a new dimension, clearly created by the development of the productive forces: liberation of thought following increasing liberation from feudalism of the new classes. The writings of Machiavelli and Hobbes, although defending absolutism, had in them materialist thought. When the Lockes, Montesquieus and Rousseaus came, the ground for revolt against the old order had progressively been laid. The earlier face of the merchant class, revolutionary in as much as it was in opposition to the feudal countryside, soon gave way to a conservative one. The merchant class had stood against the monopoly of landed feudalism only to establish its own monopoly in trade; however it planted a new seed of antithesis in the manufacturing stratum, which persisted till it was possible to put away the old order. This manufacturing stratum was excluded from the monopolies of colonial trade, but as we shall see it fought these to establish its own monopoly under a new system.

For the merchants, under the system of mercantilist imperialism, feudal power was necessary for the acquisition of gold, greatness and glory. It was assumed in the economic ideological superstructure that the amount of wealth a country commanded was represented by the sum total of its gold and silver. John Harris in *An Essay Upon Money and Coins*, put the case thus: 'Gold and silver, for many reasons, are fittest metals hitherto known for hoarding, they are durable, convertible without damage into any form; of great value in proportion to their bulk, and being the money of the world, they are the readiest exchange for all things, and what most readily and surely command all kinds of services'. It can be seen that the feudalists wanted gold and silver for hoarding. The amount hoarded was an index of a country's wealth. The corollary was that a country with a positive balance of trade was better off in terms of wealth. For this reason laws were from time to time passed to prohibit the export of bullion. Since it was believed that a country could increase its supply of gold by engaging in foreign trade, every country tried to have a net balance in its favour. But this was impossible for all countries and hence the need for war, colonies, protectionism, and monopolies in foreign trade.

Consequently state economic regulation was the *conditio sine qua non* of the perpetration of the feudal property relations and state. For this reason trade was to be so regulated that the import needs of the mother country were met from her colonies; the colonies were in turn prohibited from trading with any other country and manufacture in the colonies was banned to avoid competition with the mother country's industry. Since the colony would be paying for its imports of manufactures by exporting staples like tobacco, sugar, coffee, tea, spices and cotton, no gold would be involved in the exchange. The imports of these products from the colonies could also be re-exported and thereby earn more gold. In this policy it was clear that a merchant engaged in trade with the colonies sought to widen his profit by speculation and by taking advantage of price differences. This necessarily meant that in order to be assured of a margin the merchant needed protection against competitors. This was provided, as we have seen, because the kings relied on merchants for their financial needs, and the kings assured the merchants of this margin by controlling trade to ensure that they bought cheap in the colonies and sold dear at home or in re-export markets. Such was the cradle of primitive accumulation.

This emphasis on trade based on colonial plunder was understandable since productivity at home was still very low. As Dobb has correctly pointed out:

'Until the progress of technique substantially enhanced the productivity of labour, the notion could not arise of a specifically industrial surplus-value, derived from the investment of capital in the employment of wage-labour, as a "natural" economic category, needing no political regulation or monopoly either to create it or to preserve it'. (79)

The eighteenth century quickly produced the ideologists for the manufacturing entrepreneur. David Hume in 1742 questioned the theory that the greater the treasure of precious metals the better for a country. He put forward one of the first views of the bourgeoisie that through the workings of international trade each country with a metalic currency will get the amount of gold which makes its price balance imports with its exports. This was because importation of large quantities of precious metals tended to create inflation and hence reduced the quantities of exports and as a result imports could not be balanced by exports. The country will import more than it will export, but in order to do so it will have to export gold to pay for the imports of the required goods, thereby leading to a drain of gold. This drain will continue until the prices in the country where the inflation existed due to large holdings of gold fell to a level which balances imports and exports. To quote him:

'In every Kingdom into which money begins to flow in greater abundance than formerly, everything takes a new face: labour and industry gain life; the merchant becomes more enterprising, the manufacturer more diligent and skilful and even the farmer follows his plough with greater alacrity and attention . . . It is only in this interval, or intermediate situation, between the acquisition of money and a rise in prices, that the increasing quantity of gold and silver is favourable to industry . . . It is of no manner of consequence with regard to the domestic happiness of a state, whether money be in a greater or less quantity. The good policy . . . consists only in keeping it, if possible still increasing because by that means, he keeps alive a spirit of industry in the nation, and increases the stock of labour in which consists all real power and riches'. (80)

In France state regulation of industry had reached the highest point. Tools and machines had to conform to sizes stipulated and inspectors once in a while called into guilds to check on the implementation thereof. This naturally led to protests by the emergent forces and one of the first notable crusaders in this for the manufacturers was Gournay who coined the phrase *laissez-faire* (or 'let us alone'). This became the cry of the French Physiocrats. These were the school of economists who, beginning from 1757, met regularly under the leadership of Francois Quesnay to discuss economic problems. Most of their publications called for freedom from restrictions, for free trade, for *laissez-faire*. They believed in the 'sacredness' of private property, particularly land. They called for individual liberty so long as it did not injure others. Reflecting the still predominantly agricultural character of the French economy, they approached every problem from the standpoint of its effects on agriculture. They believed that land was the only source of wealth, and labour on land and not in industry was the only productive labour, since it was agriculture which furnished industry with raw materials. Craftsmen's products did not add to wealth. Their product was merely an improvement on the raw material. No wealth was added. It was only agricultural products which added a net wealth (product net).

The value of the analysis of the Physiocrats lay in their demonstrating that wealth was not accumulation but a flow of incomes. Quesnay's simple reproduction tables became the basis for bourgeois economics. Adam Smith regarded the analysis of the Physiocrats as 'the nearest approximation to truth that has yet been published upon the subject of political economy'. Though he regarded their emphasis on land production as narrow and confined, nevertheless he recognised that 'in representing the wealth of nations as consisting not in the unconsumable riches of money, but in the consumable goods annually produced by the labour of society; and in representing perfect liberty as the only effectual expedient for rendering the annual production the greatest possible, its doctrine seems to be in every respect as just as it is generous and liberal'.

The most important case of the new class was, however, put more strongly and perhaps at the right time and right place, by Adam Smith himself. His work, *The Wealth of Nations*, coming out in England at the time it did, 1776, was an event worthy of attention. An industrial revolution was taking place changing the whole structure of society, and it is in this context that Smith argued against feudalist restrictions. On the bullion issue he argued that a country with no mines of its own must undoubtedly draw its gold and silver from foreign countries, in the same manner as one that has no vineyards of its own will its wines. It did not seem necessary, he pointed out, that the attention of the government should be more turned towards the one than towards the other. A country that wants to buy wine will always get the wine which it has occasion for; and a country that wants to buy gold and silver will never be in want of metals. They were both bought for a certain price like all commodities.

He argued that the monopoly of colonial trade, 'like all other mean and malignant expedients of the mercantile system', depressed the industry of all other countries, and chiefly of the colonies, without in the least increasing, but on the contrary diminishing, that of the country in whose favour it was established. It was no accident that the North American colonies declared their independence in the year Smith wrote his book. The

moment was ripe. Smith therefore advocated free trade based on an
international division of labour and specialisation. This specialisation was
to be based on simple structures and is indicative of the type of change
that had already taken place, but was soon to be superceded. In this
structure industry was conceived to be of the nature of handicrafts, not
of mechanical engineering. To him it was 'the skill, dexterity, and judgement' of the workman that was to be responsible for the new order;
machines were only 'labour-saving devices' which facilitated and abridged
labour. The capital stock was savings parsimoniously accumulated out of
the owner's past industry or out of the industry of those from whom he
had legally acquired it either by inheritance or in exchange for the products
of his own labour. Smith saw trade as subsidiary to industry and money
as a vehicle for the distribution of goods, not for hoarding wealth. The
profits earned by the capitalist, in view of his labour theory of value, were
justified on the grounds that they were reasonable remuneration for
productive work done and for the labour-saving use of the property
resulting from the owner's past labour.

In this simple structure, the master and the workman are supposed to
have a mutual interest in turning out the largest and most serviceable output
of goods, prices are competitively determined by the labour-cost of goods,
and the increase in goods produced could only be limited by the extent of
the market. To quote him:

> 'As it is the power of exchanging that gives occasion to the division of
> labour, so the extent of the division must always be limited by the
> extent of that power, or, in other words, by the extent of the
> market. When the market is very small, no person can have any
> encouragement to dedicate himself entirely to one employment, for
> want of the power to exchange all that surplus part of the produce
> of his own labour, which is over and above his consumption, for
> such parts of the produce of other men's labour as he has occasion
> for'. (81)

The case of the bourgeoisie looked quite overwhelming. Increased
productivity comes through the division of labour, which in turn is only
limited by the extent of the market; but with a wider market there is
increased division of labour and hence increased productivity and therefore
the greater is a nation's wealth. Since free trade gives you the widest
markets, it also gives the greatest division of labour and therefore increased
productivity. Free trade is therefore preferable to monopolistic colonial trade.
Smith was not alone, for in 1793 Bentham wrote calling for the 'emancipation' of the colonies. Free competitive trade, it appeared, was inconsistent
with mercantilist imperialism. Capitalism, nourished in feudal conditions,
could no longer operate within its confines. It had to break out and operate
on its own. Marx and Engels scientifically summarised this historical
movement thus:

> 'We see then: the means of production and of exchange, on whose
> foundation the bourgeoisie built itself up, were generated in feudal

society. At a certain stage in the development of these means of production and of exchange, the conditions under which feudal society produced and exchanged, the feudal organisation of agriculture and manufacturing industry, in one word, the feudal relations of property became no longer compatible with the already developed productive forces; they became so many fetters. They had to be burst asunder; they were burst asunder'. (82)

Capitalism arose as a system of new property relations under the hegemony of the bourgeoisie, under its own laws of motion of production, thus negating mercantilist imperialism historically. The new developments were to lead to a new imperialism under free trade.

REFERENCES

1.   P. Anderson, *Passages from Antiquity to Feudalism, and Lineages of the Absolutist State*, New Left Books, (London, 1974), Vol. 1. pp.76-78.
2.   Hornell Hart, *The Techniques of Social Progress*, Henry Holland Co., (New York, 1931), p.410.
3.   Frederick Engels, *The Origin of the Family, Private Property and the State*, in Vol. III of Marx and Engels, *Selected Works*, Progress, (Moscow, 1973), p.310.
4.   P. Anderson, op. cit. Vol. I, pp.130-132.
5.   M. Gibbs, *Feudal Order*, (London, 1949).
6.   J.D. Bernal, *Science in History*, Pelican, (London, 1965), Vol.I.p.288.
7.   Karl Marx, *Capital*, Progress, (Moscow, 1971,) Vol. III, p.791.
8.   Maurice Dobb, *Studies in the Development of Capitalism*, Routledge, Kegan Paul, (London, 1963), p.45.
9.   Maurice Dobb, op. cit. p.46.
10.   Leo Huberman, *Man's Worldly Goods*, Monthly Review, (New York, 1940), p.46.
11.   Leo Huberman, op. cit. p.51, See also Anderson, op. cit. pp.199-201.
12.   Leo Huberman, op. cit. p.54.
13.   H.K. Takahashi, *A Contribution to the Discussion of the Transition from Feudalism to Capitalism*, Symposium, (New York, 1967). Originally published in Economic Review, Tokio, April 1951 Vol. II, pp.128-146.
14.   K. Marx, *Capital*, op. cit. Vol. III. p.791.
15.   Quoted in Leo Huberman, op. cit. pp.33-34.
16.   M. Dobb, op. cit. pp.18-20.
17.   Marx & Engels, *Selected Works*, op. cit. Vol. III. p.56.
18.   K. Glamann, *The Fontana Economic History of Europe*, Vol. II. Editor C.M. Cipolla, Fontana, (London, 1973), Leo Huberman, op. cit.
19.   Leo Huberman, op. cit. p.23, Glamann in Cipolla (ed.), op. cit.
20.   Leo Huberman, op. cit. quoted at p.24.
21.   Steven Runciman, *A History of the Crusades*, Penguin, (London, 1954), Vol. III, p.113.
22.   K. Marx, *Capital*, op. cit. Vol. III. pp.388, 389.
23.   Quoted in M. Dobb, op. cit. p.92.
24.   M. Dobb, op. cit. p.107.
25.   W.E. Minchinton, *The Growth of English Overseas Trade*, Methuen, (London, 1969), p.3.
26.   It is estimated that Gama's trip alone made a profit of 6000%!
27.   Leo Huberman, op. cit. p.92.
28.   K. Marx, *Capital*, op. cit. Vol. III. p.330/1.
29.   Quoted in M. Dobb, op. cit. p.114.
30.   W.E. Minchinton, op. cit. p.3, Glamann, in Cipolla (Ed.) op. cit.
31.   R.H. Tawney, *Religion and the Rise of Capitalism*, Penguin,

(London, 1973), p.83.

32.   Glamann, Parker, in Cipolla (Ed.), op. cit. pp.509-513-589.

33.   W.E. Minchinton, op. cit. p.8.

34.   W.E. Minchinton, op. cit. p.10.

35.   S. Sideri, *Trade and Power: Informal Colonialism in Anglo-Portuguese Relations,*(Rotterdam, 1970). Most of the material hereafter on Anglo-Portuguese trade unless otherwise indicated comes from Sideri's book.

36.   C.R. Boxer, *The Portuguese Sea-borne Empire*, 1415-1825, Pelican, (London, 1969), p.171.

37.   Quoted in Sideri, op. cit. p.43.

38.   Quoted in Sideri, op. cit. p.43, 45.

39.   Quoted in Sideri, op. cit. p.46.

40.   M. Dobb, op. cit. p.120-121.

41.   K. Marx, *Capital*, op. cit. Vol. III, p.328.

42.   K. Marx, *Capital*, op. cit. Vol. I, p.668.

43.   K. Marx, *Capital*, op. cit. Vol. II, p.675.

44.   K. Marx, *A Review of Guizot's Book, 'Why Has the English Revolution been Successful'*, in Marx and Engels, *Articles on Britain*, Progress, (Moscow, 1971), p.89.

45.   K. Marx, *Capital*, op. cit. Vol. I, p.685.

46.   K. Marx, op. cit. p.703.

47.   Marx & Engels, *Selected Works*, Progress, (Moscow, 1973), p.57.

48.   Paul A. Baran, *The Political Economy of Growth*, Monthly Review, (New York, 1968), p.139.

49.   C.R. Boxer, op. cit. p.99.

50.   Walter Rodney, *How Europe Underdeveloped Africa*, Bogle L'Ouverture, (London, 1972), p.87.

51.   J.H. Parry, *The Spanish Seaborne Empire*, Penguin, (London, 1973), p.219.

52.   C.R. Boxer, op. cit. p.159-60.

53.   S. Sideri, op. cit. p.4.

54.   S. Sideri, op. cit. p.48.

55.   S. Sideri, op. cit. p.49.

56.   S. Sideri, op. cit. p.50.

57.   C.R. Boxer, *The Golden Age of Brazil, 1695-1750*, University of California Press, (Berkely, 1972), p.108. Also see H.E.S. Fisher in Minchinton, Ed., op. cit. p.151.

58.   S. Sideri, op. cit. p.51-52.

59.   K. Glamann, In Cipolla (Ed.), op. cit. p.430.

60.   Quoted in Marx, *Capital*, op. cit. Vol. I, p.711 (Footnote 1.)

61.   E. Galeano, *Open Veins of Latin America*, Monthly Reivew, (New York, 1973), p.93.

62.   Eric Williams, *Capitalism and Slavery*, Deutsch, (London, 1972), p.52.

63.   W.E. Minchinton, op. cit. p.47.

64.   D.K. Fieldhouse, *Theory of Capitalist Imperialism*, Longmans, (London, 1967), p.188.

65.   Quoted in W. Rodney, op. cit. p.84.

66.   K. Marx, *The East India Company — Its History and Results*, in Marx & Engels, *Articles on Britain*, Progress, (Moscow, 1971), p.173.

67.   M. Barrat-Brown, *After Imperialism*, Heinemann, (London, 1970), p.41.

68.   K. Marx, *Capital*, op. cit. Vol. I. p.701.

69.   E.J. Hobsbawm, *Industry and Empire*, Penguin, (London, 1969), p.48.

70.   K. Marx, *Capital*, Vol. I. op. cit. Vol. I. p.703.

71.   L. H. Jenks, *The Migration of British Capital*, Knopf, (New York, 1927), p.5-10. All quotes from these pages.

72.   K. Marx, *Capital*, Vol. I. op. cit. Vol. I. p.706.

71.   L.H. Jenks, op. cit. p.13.

72.   L.H. Jenks, op. cit. p.14.

73.   K. Marx, *Capital*, op. cit. Vol. I. p.208.

74.   Leo Hubermann, op. cit. p.128-129.

75.   J.N. Plumb, *England in the Eighteenth Century, (1714-1815)*, Pelican, (London, 1966), p.24.

76.   E.J. Hobsbawm, op. cit. p.50.

77.   H. Plumb, op. cit. p.109-110.

78.   Butterfield, *Scientific American Journal*, Sept. 1960, Article entitled, 'The Scientific Revolution'.

79.   M. Dobb, op. cit. p.200.

80.   D. Hume, *Essays and Treatises on Several Subjects*, (1793), II, p.39-42.

81.   A. Smith, *The Wealth of Nations*, Penguin, (London, 1970), p.121.

82.   Marx & Engels, *Manifesto of the Communist Party*, Selected Works, op. cit. Vol. I. p.113.

PART TWO
COMPETITIVE CAPITALISM
AND FREE TRADE IMPERIALISM

CHAPTER VI

'If the free traders cannot understand how one nation can grow rich at the expense of another, we need not wonder, since these same gentlemen also refuse to understand how within one country one class can enrich itself at the expense of another'.

K. Marx.

The period associated with capitalism as a *system* dates from the successful unleashing of the industrial revolution which enabled profitable experimentation and the development of steam power, the use of coal, the smelting of iron, the rise of engineering, machines and machine tools and the growth of industrial chemistry. These developments, beginning in England in the 1760s, set in motion a new system with new dimensions. The technical improvements did not, however, arise at this period by accident. Experimentation with various techniques had already been attempted. In mining, for instance, improved drainage early in the sixteenth century, resulting from the invention of improved pumps, encouraged the sinking of mines to greater depths, giving rise to big developments in the industry. In the last part of the sixteenth century the first paper and gunpowder mills, the first cannon factories, the first sugar refineries, and the first considerable saltpetre works were introduced into England from abroad, giving rise to investment of large sums in these industries. To this should be added Dudley's patent for making iron with pit coal in 1621, Darby's work at Coalbrookdale also connected with smelting of iron with coal, and Savery's engine of 1698 based on the principle of vacuum created by condensing steam. (1)

The possibilities of expansion in these industries were limited by the division of labour, the extent of the market and the lack of technical improvements that could react on them. The business enterprise was still rudimentary, of the type generally associated with the glamourised hero of the bourgeoisie — Jack of Newbury, who employed several hundred weavers, with a dye-house and filling-mill as his capital. As we have seen the productive forces were still being held back by the monopoly privileges of mercantile imperialism. The developments at this stage were therefore no more than isolated improvements.

With the approach of the eighteenth century the tempo increased. In 1733 there was the invention of Kay's flying shuttle which was of strategic importance. In the same year Wyatt's spinning machine was invented. The earlier Savery's engine which had been improved on by Newcomen's atmospheric pressure device depended on production of steam for its successful operation. At first there was a continuing process stemming from the events discussed in the previous chapters. The primitive accumulation of capital, the contradictions of the feudal state leading to warfare and complications of class positions, and the increasing population of dispossessed peasants providing abundant labour on the free market, all operated to hasten radical change. The earlier class struggles within the feudal ranks resulting in the 1649/1689 bourgeois revolutions created the necessary atmosphere, which was to progressively consolidate with each development.

The first of the great inventions to have a major impact on the economy as a whole and on the other inventions that followed was the jenny invented in 1764 by a weaver, James Hargreaves of Standhill, North Lancashire. This machine introduced the mule moved by hand. Instead of one spindle, as in the ordinary spinning-wheel, it carried sixteen or eighteen spindles manipulated by a single workman; the production of yarn was immediately improved. The demand which was increasing as a result of the cheapened product in turn increased production and productivity. With the increase in demand for yarn, there was an increased demand for weavers and hence there was a rise in wages. This attracted the farming weavers to the industry, who could now earn more this way. The farming weaver's move away from farming turned them into wage earners, alongside the already dispossessed producers. Before, yarn was woven and spun under one roof; now a division of labour took place. Capitalists soon began to set up spinning jennies in big buildings, using water-power to drive them, so that they could cut down on the number of workers and intensify their labour. This enabled the new factory system to develop very rapidly in England.

There was another impact from this single invention. Apart from creating a proletariat of ex-farming weavers, it also gave rise to an agricultural proletariat. The yeoman farmer who had for generations stood relatively stagnant in his production methods soon got thrown out by the new tenant farmer who took over the lands left by the farming weavers. Since the tenants produced more by using capital and labour of others, they could sell cheaper than the yeoman family. Unable to compete, the yeoman farmers were turned into a proletariat for the tenant farmer.

The second major discovery was that of the spinning throstle by Richard Arkwright, a barber of Preston, North Lancashire. Its use was calculated on the basis of motive power, and was based on wholly new principles. Engels called it the most important mechanical discovery after the steam engine of the eighteenth century. By the combination of the jenny and the throstle, Samuel Crompton of Firwood, Lancashire, contrived the mule in 1785; and Arkwright the carding engine. From now on, 'the factory system became the prevailing one for the spinning of cotton'. With modifications, these two latter inventions were also adapted to the spinning of wool and later to flax. These revolutionary improvements were later joined by Dr. Cartwright's power-loom, which was soon easily able to compete with the hand-weaver.

The last major invention was that of the steam engine in 1764 by James Watt. It brought in the most important of the inventions of the century and with improvements was in a position to supply power to spinning by 1785. Engels made the following observations:

> 'With these inventions, since improved from year to year, the victory of machine-work over hand-work in chief branches of English industry was won; and the history of the latter from that time forward simply relates how the hand-workers have been driven by machinery from one position after another. The consequences of this were on the one hand, a rapid fall in price of all manufactured commodities, prosperity of commerce and manufacture, the conquest of nearly all the unrpotected foreign markets, the sudden multiplication of capital and national wealth; on the other hand, a still more rapid multiplication of the proletariat, the destruction of all property - holding and of all security of employment for the working class, demoralisation, political excitement, and all those facts so highly repugnant to Englishmen in comfortable circumstances . . .' (2)

The economic atmosphere of the eighteenth century contributed considerably to this sudden explosion of technical progress. Industry, the rising force, was constantly on the lookout for inventions that could be put to profitable use. Inventions created the need for more inventions as production expanded and the demand for manufactures grew; for instance the discovery of coal smelting was as a result of the growing scarcity of wood-fuel, and Kay's flying shuttle came as a solution to the problem of the width of manufactured material being limited by the length of the weaver's arm.

Let us briefly look at the effect of these inventions on production. According to Engels in the period 1771-1775 less than 5 million pounds of raw cotton from the 'New World' was annually imported into England. In 1785 the exports of British cotton manufactures were worth about £1 million but in 1830 they had risen to £30 million. The population employed in the industry rose from 350,000 in 1788 to 800,000 in 1806, in spite of the labour-saving machinery. In value terms the raw cotton imports rose from £11 million in 1784 to £283 million in 1832. The number of power-looms rose from 2,400 in 1813 to 55,000 in 1829, 85,000 in 1833 and 223,000 in 1850. The number of hand-loom weavers fell from about 250,000 to just over 100,000 by the early 1840s, and by the 1850s there were little more than 50,000 of these 'starving wretches'. (3) The chief centre of all these changes was Lancashire, where it had started.

The changes also brought new activity into areas of production connected with cotton textiles such as dyeing, bleaching and printing. Change came with the application of chlorine in place of atmospheric oxygen for bleaching, with the rapid development of chemistry for dyeing and with the application of a series of mechanical inventions unknown before in printing. The changes which characterised the cotton industry were also manifested in the manufacture of wool, which hitherto had been 'the industry' of the country. The sudden rise of cotton to predominance had also attracted labour to its production, thus pinning down the wool industry. The application of the new inventions to the latter quickly revolutionised production and minimised reliance on a large number of workers. The chief centre of this industry was the West Riding and particularly Bradford which had long wool; other places like Leeds, Halifax, and Huddersfield had short wool, which was used mainly for conversion into hard-spun yarn and cloth. In the West Riding where the long wool was converted into worsted yarns in particular, production increased tremendously with the new methods. Here production in 1738 had been only 75,000 pieces of woollen cloth; in 1817 it had increased to 490,000 pieces. In 1801, 101 million pounds of wool were worked on; in 1835 this had increased to 180 million pounds. This of necessity led to increased breeding of sheep. Similar progress was recorded in the flannel, linen and silk industries.

But epoch-making as these changes were, the real revolution lay in the capital goods industries. The great upsurge of population in industrial centres, the result of increasing proletarianisation, increased demand in urban centres for coal for house heating. The steam-engine came in good time to revolutionise coal production. With it, it was now possible to pump out water from the deepening mines and increase the production of coal to supply the needs of the urban population. The increasing mechanisation of industry created the need for iron and the discovery of coke improved the possibilities of smelting it. Smelting furnaces near the mining areas soon sprang up, larger than before. The production of iron prepared the ground for railway construction, and led to the construction of iron bridges and iron pillars. The smelting of iron also necessitated the increasing production of coke and other products connected with them. Canals were built and roadways were constructed, as the need for easy communication became a necessity for the capitalist.

What were the implications of these developments for the capitalist? There is no doubt that they offered the greatest opportunity to him and his class as a whole. It was the golden historical moment they had struggled for. With the development of the productive forces there grew the new contradiction of capitalist property relations. In slave society the surplus labour produce was the whole product of the slave's labour, less the food the master distributed to the slaves. In the feudal mode, as we have seen, it was the product of the unpaid part of labour-time spent by a peasant serf on the lord's portion of land, the product in kind or the money rent.

Under the new system of social production the capitalist appropriated a portion of the product of *labour sold to him as a commodity*. Through his control of the means of production he paid the worker that portion of the product that was necessary for his subsistence and reproduction (produced in necessary labour-time), and kept for himself the other portion which he appropriated for his own consumption and further accumulation (produced during surplus labour-time). The portion the capitalist appropriates to himself is surplus-value. This form of surplus-value was possible only under the laws of 'free competition' that capitalism set up.

The development of machinery and its application was intended to increase the productivity of labour. This in turn cheapened the commodities, depreciated the cost of labour-power and assured the capitalist an increased surplus-value. Marx called this process the extraction of *relative surplus-value*.

The development of machinery and its application to production resolved the problems that had been posed by the use of simple tools under the earliest form of production in the manufactory system, which necessitated large numbers of workers in the production process. Improved machinery brought together the processes of production inherent in different tools into one machine by the addition of the motor and transmission mechanisms. Development to this stage could not take place until the subject of labour went through a connected series of detailed processes, carried out by a chain of machines of various kinds, one supplementing the other. In earlier forms of production, with a more limited and less mechanised division of labour, any increase in the surplus-value of the capitalist could only be realised by lengthening the working day, in such a way that more time was spent producing that portion for the capitalist (surplus-value) whilst the portion for wages remained the same. This way of increasing the capitalist's 'earnings', is what Marx called the extraction of *absolute surplus-value*.

In the capitalist mode of production this practice became commonplace and initially laws were passed prohibiting the shortening of the working day. Working class struggles against the long working hours resulted in the various Factory Acts from 1833 to 1867 which progressively reduced the working day to 10 hours. The bourgeoisie responded to these reductions with gloom and their ideological spokesmen, the political economists, regarded this interference by their state (which they expected to protect their class interest) as an attack on their natural rights based on freedom of the market. One of them, Nassau senior, argued that the capitalist makes his profit in the 'last hour' and if that last hour was taken away it would ruin industry; this when the working day was fixed at twelve hours.

Marx was quick to refute the bourgeois notion that surplus value could only be increased by lengthening working hours. He observed that under the new system, machinery performed the same operations that were formerly done by workmen. From the moment that the tool proper was taken from man, and fitted into a mechanism, the machine became a mere implement and a basic factor of production. He pointed out that:

> 'As soon as tools had been converted from being manual implements of man into implements of a mechanical apparatus, of a machine, the motive mechanism also acquired an independent form, entirely emancipated from the restraints of human strength. Thereupon the individual machine, that we have hitherto been considering, sinks into a mere factor in production by machinery. One motive was now able to drive many machines at once. The motive mechanism grows with the number of machines that are turned simultaneously, and the transmitting mechanism becomes a wide-spreading apparatus.' (4)

Once machinery was built up to this level, it rooted out the old foundation, and in its place was built a new economic basis corresponding to the new methods of production. The secret, therefore, lay in the use of machinery to intensify the exploitation of the existing or even diminishing labour force by extracting relative surplus-value. But even here the exploitation of this labour required the abundant supply of it. For this reason, although machinery abridged human labour, at the same time increased labour supply was necessary to expand production.

Ricardo understood this and feared that the lack of a sufficiently large proletarian population to supply industry its labour-power would inhibit the expansion of capitalism. Ricardo's worry was unwarranted. Population had increased as a result of the fall in the death-rate late in the eighteenth century and the birth-rate remained high up to the 1830s with brief declines at odd intervals. Moreover there were the starving Irish immigrants, who, having been expropriated by absentee English landlords, were on tap to supplement any shortfall of local supply on the mainland. The repeal of the Laws of Settlement and the partial abandonment of the Speenhamland system after the Napoleonic Wars further ensured abundant supply of labour for the industrial capitalist. Under the Speenhamland system (1705), impoverished labour which had lost its means of subsistence and its means of production in the enclosure movements and other primitive accumulation appropriations, was placed 'on the dole'. The system authorised out-door relief to the poor in all parishes based on changes in the price of bread. This 'bounty on bastardy' tended to reduce labour supply to the urban centres. The 1834 Poor Law, which replaced the system, 'set the seal on unfettered free trade in the labour market'. (5) An abundant supply of labour now enabled the capitalist to pay wages at a level which guaranteed him a large profit. Dobb has commented:

> 'But unless by the dawn of the new century labour had been as plentiful as it was then coming to be, the progress of factory industry once started could not have been so rapid and might have even been halted. There would seem to be fairly general agreement that, whether influenced by the wage-level or not, the technical change of this period had a predominantly labour saving bias: a feature of technical change which probably characterised the whole of the nineteenth century . . . capital accumulation proceeded at a

considerably faster rate than the labour supply was increasing'. (6)

The accumulation made further capital activity possible. The capitalists involved in this development were of humble origin, mainly from the ranks of master craftsmen or yeomen farmers, with a small capital which at times they increased by going into partnership with merchants. The main industrial activities at this stage were clock-making, shoe making, hat-making, and weaving, with which many of the industrialists had acquaintance. For the yeoman farmer, the possession of a piece of land was an additional advantage. The Peels, Wilkinsons, Darbys, Cartwrights, Hargreaves, Cromptons and Arkwrights came from these humble backgrounds. (7) According to Samuel Smiles, of the twenty-eight such successful 'men of invention and industry', fourteen came from the small-property owning class or yeoman farmers, master-weavers, shoe-makers, school masters, etc.; six from the prosperous middle-classes; and only eight had traces of working class origins. (8) These facts have led some bourgeois ideologists to assert that primitive accumulation had little to do with the development of capitalism, that whatever capital was used in early capitalist development was accumulated by 'dint of enterprise and industry' on the part of these humble capitalists.

Whilst it is true that this internal capitalist accumulation contributed to capitalist development at this stage, yet there can be no doubt that such accumulation alone could not have set in motion the financing of inventions and the establishment of a financial system that enabled the capitalists to engage in these capitalist developments. Capitalist development as a system was very much more than the humble enterprise of individual capitalists. The historical developments which we surveyed in the foregoing chapters were all part of the necessary preconditions that enabled the Wilkinsons and other 'captains of industry' to appear and to take advantage of the new conditions.

Be that as it may, the problem of realisation of surplus-value was a central point of departure for the bourgeois political economists of this period. The question of availability of labouring population and the means of subsistence was only of concern because of the so-called 'iron law of wages'. According to Ricardo the 'natural price' of labour depended on the price of food, necessaries and conveniences required for the support of the labourer and his family. As the price of food and other necessaries rose, so the natural price of labour rose and vice-versa. But this natural price had to be distinguished from the 'market price' of labour. According to Ricardo, the latter was the price for which labour was paid according to the laws of supply and demand on the market: it was dear when it was scarce and cheap when it was plentiful. Despite this the market price tended to move to the natural price. This was because Ricardo accepted the Malthusian theory on population by which it was assumed that when the market price of labour was high, (i.e. when the supply of it was scarce), there was a tendency for the family size to increase, since there was more to eat.

This would have the result of bringing the market price of labour down to the natural price, as a result of the increase in the labour supply.

This theory of population, which Marx called the 'dogma of the economists', was based on the law of diminishing returns on land and the law of rent which expressed the bourgeois struggle against the corn-laws. So long as the bourgeois political economists stuck their theory on models based on simple reproduction, this confusion was inevitable. According to the theory, the supply of any commodity was regulated by competition. The capitalists competed in the market to sell their products and this determined prices; labourers competed for employment in a free market and this determined their wages. Capital also competed for outlets of investment, and this too determined its rate of profit or rate of interest. There was no possibility of going wrong!

This type of theorising could not explain much. The rise in wages could never be allowed to destroy the system of production at least at this early stage of development. Marx's contribution lay in his explaining the apparent riddle that confronted the political economists. Whilst he was sure that a scarcity of workers could raise wages, he was also sure that it was not this problem which would result in the collapse of the production and accumulation process under expanded reproduction. The secret lay in the capability by the capitalist to create a 'reserve army of labour' or 'relative surplus population' to check the level of wages paid to workers. Says Marx:

> 'The industrial reserve army, during the periods of stagnation and average prosperity, weighs down the active labour army; during the periods of over production and paroxysm, it holds its pretensions in check. Relative surplus population is therefore the pivot on which the law of demand and supply of labour works. It confines the field of action of this law within the limits absolutely convenient to the activity of exploitation and to the domination of capital'. (9)

The introduction of machinery had a dual purpose. First it enabled the capitalist as we have observed to do away with the necessity to lengthen the working day in order to extract relative-surplus-value. Secondly, it enabled him to minimise his wage-bill and increase his relative surplus-value by keeping wages down. In other words any rise in wages relative to population was counteracted by the reserve army of labour and by each addition of capital in-put.

Ricardo in his chapter 'On Machinery' tried to explain the same thing, but still based himself on the Malthusian theory on population. Marx's contribution lay in his integrating the principle of the reserve army into the general theory of capital accumulation independent of the theory of population, and his remained the only scientific explanation of continued capitalist expansion in spite of the declining birth rates in the 1870s. The system did not come to a halt because of this, although crises arose, but here again, as we shall see, Marx saw crises in capitalist production as a means by which capitalists adjust investment and methods of production to available labour. On this question Sweezy has correctly commented that:

'It is at once apparent that this view of the capitalist process differs radically from the classical theory of economic evolution. The latter is, in principle, unconcerned with changes in methods of production; economic development is viewed exclusively in terms of (gradual) quantitative changes in population, capital, wages, profits, and rent. Social relations remain unaffected; the end product is simply a state of affairs in which all these rates of change equal zero. Since the Marxian view lays stress on changes in methods of production, it implies qualitative change in social organisation and social relations as well as quantitative change in economic variables as such. The way is thus paved for regarding the end product as a revolutionary reconstitution of society rather than a mere state of rest'. (10)

Marx emphasised that by cheapening consumer commodities on which workers spend their wages, machinery also opens the way for cheapening the price of labour itself which assists the capital accumulation process. But whilst machinery assists the capitalist in the accumulation process in this way, it also presents a contradiction. Although machinery (constant capital) provided him with an opportunity to expand production and extract greater surplus-value, it also confronted him with the realisation that as he increased constant capital with a given labour-power (variable capital), the rate of profit on the total capital tended to fall. Marx illustrates this contradiction as follows: Assume a given wage and working day, and variable capital of say 100 (which represents a certain number of labourers). Assume also that £100 are the wages of the 100 labourers for one week. If these labourers perform equal amounts of necessary-labour (for their subsistence) and surplus-labour (for the capitalists), then the value of their total product will be £200; since the necessary labour product would be £100 and surplus-value £100. The rate of surplus-value (s) as compared to necessary labour-value (v) would be $[s] = 100\%$. But this rate of surplus value would express itself in very different rates of profit, depending on the different volumes of constant capital (c) and consequently of the total capital (C), laid out because the rate of profit $(p') = \frac{s}{c}$. (11) The rate of surplus-value as we have seen is 100% .

$$\text{If } c = \ \ 50, \text{ and } v = 100, \text{ then } p' = \frac{100}{150} = 66^{2}/3\%$$

$$\text{If } c = 100, \text{ and } v = 100. \text{ then } p' = \frac{100}{200} = 50\%$$

$$\text{If } c = 200, \text{ and } v = 100, \text{ then } p' = \frac{100}{300} = 33\frac{1}{2}\%$$

$$\text{If } c = 300, \text{ and } v = 100, \text{ then } p' = \frac{100}{400} = 25\%$$

$$\text{If } c = 400, \text{ and } v = 100, \text{ then } p' = \frac{100}{500} = 20\%$$

Thus we see that if a capitalist under the given conditions makes a constant capital in-put (c) of 50 and labour in-put of 100, the rate of profit will be $66 2/3$ %. If on the one hand, he varies the capital in-put and increases it to 400 while leaving the labour in-put unvaried, the rate of profit will fall to 20%, because the material increase of the constant capital implies also an increase albeit not in the same proportion, in its value, and consequently in that of the total capital. (11)

If this change in the composition of capital is generalised and not isolated in individual spheres of production, then the gradual growth of the constant capital in relation to variable capital must necessarily lead to a gradual fall of the general rate of profit so long as the rate of surplus-value, or the intensity of exploitation of labour by capital remain the same. Marx continues:

'This is another way of saying that owing to the distinctive methods of production developing under the capitalist system the same number of labourers . . . operate, work-up and productively consume in the same time span an ever increasing quantity of the means of labour, machinery and fixed capital of all sorts, raw and auxiliary materials — and consequently the constant capital of an ever-increasing value. This continual relative decrease of variable capital vis-a-vis constant capital, and consequently the total capital, is identical with the progressively higher organic composition of the social capital in its average'. (12)

This means that with the progressive development of the productivity of labour the same number of labourers, in the same time (i.e. with less labour) converted an ever-increasing quantity of raw and auxiliary materials into products, thanks to the growing application of machinery and fixed capital in general. What appeared to the capitalist as a contradiction was now *reversed* by the fact that the capitalist was able by this very development to reduce variable capital as constant capital was increased, and thus to counteract the tendency of the rate of profit to fall, and to restore or even raise the rate of surplus-value, since the ratio of the mass of surplus-value to the value of the invested total capital forms the rate of profit. This very fact also tended to change the organic composition of the capital itself by increasing it. For this reason Marx emphasized that rates of profit, or the level of wages, could not be understood unless the organic composition of the different capitals was understood in different epochs and countries.

The above contradiction constituted the basic law of motion of capitalism in that it lay behind the necessity for capitalism to:
a. concentrate the means of production in few hands, and hence explains the rise of monopolies with the crisis of the 1870s onwards;
b. organise labour as social labour, through cooperation, division of labour and the uniting of labour with science and technology;
c. create a world market, that became the very basis of capitalist production.

These helped the capitalist to counteract the contradictory forces that generate the increasing growth of capital, resulting in the tendency of the rate of profit to fall, and instead restored the high rate of surplus-value and hence high rate of profit.

Given machinery, the capitalist was better placed to transfer more and more value from labour to the product which he appropriated. This transfer of value was effected by the fact that instead of the capitalist now paying for labour, he only paid for the labour-power employed on the machine. A limit was thus set on the use of machinery by the relation between the value of the machine and the value of labour-power replaced by it. This development was important for the capitalist since he was now in a position to employ child and female labour, whose wages were fixed below that of a male adult worker because the wage of an adult worker took into account the family's subsistence. By directly employing members of the family, the capitalist now divided the adult male worker's wage between the whole family, increasing his labour force at little cost. This too helped the capitalist to counteract the falling rate of profit.

Machinery also enabled the capitalist to prolong the working day under the changed conditions. Since machinery loses value by depreciation and its life expectancy is reduced by wear and tear, it followed that its value was determined not by the labour utilised in its production but by the time required to produce a cheaper and better one. (13) Therefore the shorter the period taken to reproduce its total value by production, the less was the danger of depreciation; and the longer the working day, the shorter the period necessary. Moreover, the prolongation of the working day allowed production on an extended scale without alteration in the amount of capital laid out on machinery and buildings. Not only was there an increase in surplus-value, but the outlay necessary to obtain it diminished. For this reason the capitalist would try as much as possible to prolong the working day, so that machinery available would not lie idle. This is not the same thing as the prolongation of the worker's working day, which as we saw was progressively shortened. Capitalists observed the laws on the maximum hours of work and yet prolonged the working day through shift or piece-work systems. All this enabled the capitalist to reap greater surplus-value out of available labour and machinery, and hence further helped to combat the falling rate of profit.

Yet another method which the capitalist found handy to counteract the falling rate of profit was the intensification of labour. As soon as it became clear that the working day could not be prolonged beyond a certain limit, the capitalist found a roundabout way of 'not obeying the rules'. He intensified the application of existing or reduced labour to replenish shortened hours. This arose as a result of the increasing familiarity and experience of labour with machinery: the rapidity and intensity of labour with machinery increased as a natural consequence, and in this way a point was soon reached where the extension of the working-day and the intensity of labour excluded one another. It is not for nothing that the bourgeoisie dreamt up ideas of 'scientific management' or Taylorism as the crisis of capitalism increased. Since the workers' wages remained the same, this intensification of labour accounted for more to the capitalist than a mere prolongation of the day.

So long as the capitalist engaged in production at this level using all sorts of manoeuvres to extract surplus-value and accumulate capital with the available market, there was no problem. The process becomes seriously disturbed if the market shrinks, creating problems in production. So we notice that another of the important counteracting forces to the tendency of the rate of profit to fall is expansion of foreign trade and the market. For as Marx pointed out:

> 'To the extent that foreign trade cheapens partly the elements of constant capital, partly the necessities of life for which variable capital is exchanged, it tends to raise the rate of profit by raising the rate of surplus-value and lowering the cost of constant capital'. (14)

CHAPTER VII

So long as production and capital accumulation remained at this level the market did not on the whole pronounce itself as a limiting factor. We have seen that the multiplication of inventions followed each other in a kind of causal cumulative way. Adam Smith's thesis of the market as the factor controlling the extent of the division of labour, and by necessary implication the development of machinery, was strengthened by Ricardo's optimism by which it was assumed that all incomes were spent and hence that consumption depended on production. In other words so long as workers spent their wages on consumption goods and the capitalists and landlords theirs on consumption as well as on productive goods, it was only production which could limit the market.

Marx went on to show that Adam Smith's views on the production and circulation of the aggregate social product was erroneous in that they were based on his division of the price of a commodity into only two parts: wages and surplus-value (which included 'profit' and 'rent'). Based on this division, Smith similarly divided the total social product into the same parts and allocated them as 'revenue' of the classes: workers, capitalists and landlords. It will be noted here that Adam Smith omitted the third component of value, namely constant capital, which he assumed formed part of wages and surplus-value. Marx's recognition of constant capital as the secret of capitalist expanded reproduction is important in the understanding of capitalist production and its market. He pointed out the need to draw a distinction between two kinds of labour: one that produces articles of consumption and another which produces 'useful machines and instruments of trade . . . buildings, etc.', articles that are not for (realisation) had to be resolved by recognising the two forms of consumption: personal and productive.

This recounting is important in laying the ground for the understanding of the problem of realisation and hence the role of foreign trade and imperialism. As we shall see a number of Marxists, and particularly Rosa Luxembourg, completely misconceived Marx's position on capitalist production and accumulation; and hence utilised Marx's reproduction schema in Volume II of *Capital* to establish that it was lack of markets which constituted the basic problem of capitalist accumulation. In his analysis of capitalist reproduction, Marx utilised two schemata: one simple reproduction and the other expanded reproduction. In each of these schemata he used two major departments: the production of the means of production (Department I), and the production of the means of consumption (Department II). In using the schema on simple reproduction, Marx wanted to demonstrate how the capital consumed in production was replaced out of the annual product, and how this movement of replacement intertwined with the consumption of surplus-value by the capitalists and of wages by the labourers.

In this analysis it was assumed that products exchanged at their values and that no 'revolution in the values' of the component parts of the productive capital took place (i.e. no technical change). Although prices diverged from values, this did not affect the movement of the social product as a whole. Nor did the revolutions in value arising from technical change alter anything in the relations between the value-components of the total annual product, provided they were universally and evenly distributed. To the extent that they were partially and unevenly distributed, they represented disturbances which could be understood as such only insofar as they were regarded as *divergences* from unchanged value-relations. But once there was proof of the law of how one part of the value of the annual product replaces constant, and another portion variable capital, a revolution in the value of either the constant or the variable capital could not alter anything in the law. It would merely change the relative magnitudes since other values would have taken the places of the original ones.

Simple reproduction, or reproduction on the same scale, was therefore an abstraction, in as much as the absence of all accumulation or reproduction on an extended scale was an unrealistic assumption in capitalist conditions, and as the conditions of production do not remain exactly the same in different years. The assumption was that a social product of a certain magnitude produces the same quantity of commodity-value this year as last, and supplies the same quantum of wants, although the forms of commodities may change in the process. However, so long as accumulation took place, simple reproduction was always part of it which could therefore be studied by itself, and was an actual factor of accumulation. Any changes in the value of the annual product were merely quantitative aspects of the various elements of reproduction, since we are not here considering the role which they played as reproducing capital or as reproduced revenue in the entire process. Thus for simple reproduction the sum of all the new values reproduced in the course of the year (in both departments) must be equal to the gross value of the product existing in the form of means of consumption. On this basis Marx examines how exchange takes place between the two departments. (15)

In actual fact there could be no simple reproduction in capitalist society. The production of the whole of society cannot remain on the previous scale every year, since accumulation is the basic law of capitalist society. But with the analysis of simple reproduction it is easier to deal with reproduction on an expanding scale. Under expanded reproduction only part of surplus-value is consumed by the capitalists for personal needs, the other part being consumed productively i.e., ploughed back in the form of productive capital for the expansion of production. On the other hand all the wages of the workers are spent on personal consumption. As Lenin pointed out:

> 'Hence, the point of departure in discussing social capital and revenue, or, what is the same thing, the realisation of the product in capitalist society, must be the distinction between two entirely different types of social product: *means of production and articles of consumption.* The former can be consumed only productively the latter only personally. The former can serve *only* as capital, the latter must become revenue, i.e., must be destroyed in consumption by the workers and capitalists. The former go entirely to the capitalists, the latter are shared between the workers and all capitalists'. (16)

Articles of consumption are exchanged for means of production (constant capital) in the two departments. By realising the surplus-value and wages in the industries which produce means of production, this exchange thereby realises the constant capital in the industries which produce articles of consumption. But there remains one part of constant capital which is not realised in this manner, and this constituted Luxembourg's stumbling block, namely that part of constant capital in the department which manufactures means of production. This is partially realised by part of the product going back into production in its natural form (e.g. coal being used in the same industry for production of more coal) and partly by exchange between individual capitalists in the same department (e.g. mutual exchange between coal producers and iron producers in Department I.). It is here that capitalist production acts as its own market: to quote Lenin again:

> 'Production does indeed create a market for itself: production needs means of production, and they constitute a special department of social production, which occupies a certain section of the workers, and produces a special product, realised partly within this department and partly by exchange with the other department, which produces articles of consumption. Accumulation is indeed the excess of production over revenue (articles of consumption). To expand production (to "accumulate" in the categorical meaning of the term) it is first of all necessary to produce means of production, and for this it is consequently necessary to expand that department of social production which manufactures means of production, it is necessary *to draw into it* workers who immediately *present a demand of articles of consumption,* too. Hence, "consumption" develops after "accumulation" or after "production"; strange though it cannot be otherwise in capitalist society'. (16) (Emphasis in original.)

Rosa Luxembourg suggests that Marx does not go further into the problem of accumulation than 'to devise a few models and suggest an analysis'. (17) According to her the whole problem of capitalist production revolves around the question of the market. The capitalist is motivated by profit.

Production only makes sense to the capitalist if it 'fills his pockets with pure income', but this profit must increase. To this end the capitalist uses the fruits of exploitation, not exclusively for luxury consumption but to increase exploitation itself. The largest part of the profits gained are put back into capital and used to expand production. The capital thus mounts up or 'accumulates'. Labour is necessary to this process. Through the reserve army, etc., labour is securely available for exploitation through the wage system; 'a new basic condition of capital accumulation emerges — the possibility of selling the goods produced by the workers to recover, in money, the capitalist's original expenses as well as the surplus-value stolen from the labour force'.

> 'A steadily increasing possibility of selling the commodities is indispensible in order to keep accumulation a continuous process. Capital itself (as we see) creates the basic condition for exploitation. The first volume of Marx's *Capital* analysed and described this process in detail. But what about the opportunities of realising the fruits of this exploitation; what about the markets? What do they depend on? Can capital itself, or its production mechanisms, expand its market according to its needs, in the same way that it adjusts the number of workers according to its demand? Not at all . . . The goods can be sold and the incoming profit turned into money only if goods satisfy the requirements of society. So the continuous expansion of capitalist production, i.e. the continuous accumulation of capital, it linked to the equally continuous growth of social requirements'. (18)

These social requirements on which the accumulation of capital depends are at 'a closer look the accumulation of capital itself'. It is a vicious circle. The problem appears to be solved when production as 'a whole' is examined. According to Luxembourg this is where Marx, in his second volume of *Capital*, attempts to solve this problem. According to her it is not solved by Marx, for he does not explain who is the buyer and consumer of 'that portion of commodities whose sale is only the beginning of accumulation'. This problem which Marx explains in the schema and which Lenin so easily solves, as we have seen, becomes the foundation of Luxembourg's problematic.

Because Luxembourg was unable to comprehend realisation on the basis of expanded reproduction in the two departments of production, she conceived that the best way of getting out of this difficulty was to create a third department. According to her 'there must be more than the two big portions of the social stock of commodities'. If the exploitation of the workers were only to permit a luxurious life for the exploiters, 'we would have a kind of modernised slave system of medieval feudalism, but not the modern rule of capital'. (18) This third department (portion) must consist of the part destined for accumulation, for according to her the other two portions represented in Marx's two departments only contain the stock for the renewal of used means of production and the maintenance of workers.

But how is this third portion realised? Here Luxembourg finds herself confronted with a headache of her own creation; having ruled out the capitalists, workers and petty-bourgeois strata as possible 'consumers' of this portion, she is led to postulate a 'third market'. Capitalists are now forced to find other buyers:

> '. . . who receive their means of purchase from an independent source, and do not get it out of the pocket of the capitalists like labourers or the collaborators of capital, the government officials, officers, clergy and liberal professions. They have to be consumers who receive their means of purchase on the basis of commodity exchange . . . taking place outside of capitalist commodity production. They must be producers, whose means of production are not to be seen as capital, and who belong to neither of the two classes — capitalists or workers — but who still have a need, one way or another, for capitalist commodities'. (19)

This external 'non-capitalist market' can exist within the capitalist country itself in the person of artisans and peasants who are engaged in simple commodity production, but more importantly in 'agrarian' parts of the world outside Europe. Here the capitalists must develop:

> 'right from the start an exchange relationship between capitalist production and the non-capitalist millieu, where capital not only finds the possibility of realising surplus-value in hard cash for further capitalization, but also receives various commodities to extend production, and finally win new proletarianized labour forces disintegrating the non-capitalist forms of production'. (20)

It is quite clear from the above that Luxembourg was putting forth a theory of the 'impossibility' of capitalist realisation within the capitalist country itself. The source of her confusion is her inability to comprehend the production process in the two departments of Marx. Whereas for Marx the two departments represent not only the movement of the total social product, but also the production relation of the two classes involved in the process, for Luxembourg that abstraction is impermissible because it ignores 'the real world', where there are non-capitalist millieux.

For Marx the existence of foreign markets, considered at the level of abstraction in Volume II, does not alter the conflicting relationships of the two classes represented in the schema. Marx nowhere forgets that the law of capitalist production is a law of the world market, and he tried to bring elements of 'the real world' into his analysis of capitalist production in Volume III of *Capital*. It is quite clear, as Bukharin correctly pointed out that Luxembourg confused *realisation with accumulation;* this is why she spoke of realisation of profit when profit itself was the result of realisation. In fact it is surplus-value that undergoes realisation. Again accumulation was confused with the growth of money capital, and her analysis is based on the problems of how money would be raised to buy 'the commodities whose sale is the only beginning of accumulation'. Real accumulated surplus-value in the form of productive capital is ignored. Moreover, she obscurely posed the question of the 'total amount of money capital' and did not see that production of gold was itself capitalist production which was exchanged for means of production and labour-power. (21)

Luxembourg was forced to look elsewhere for a solution to the problem of realisation. Like the Narodniks who looked to the foreign market, she looks for non-capitalist consumers. For Marx the problem of foreign trade is a problem of capitalism as such. A capitalist has to look to foreign markets. He states:

> 'The industrialist always has the world market before him, he compares and must continually compare his cost price with those of the whole world, and not only with those of the home market'. (22)

But even then for Marx the foreign market is not a solution to the problem of realisation *qua* realisation. It is a solution to the production problem, for it is production which determines the market and not the market that determines production. As Lenin correctly pointed out to the Narodniks:

> 'The need for a capitalist country to have a foreign market is not determined at all by the laws of the realisation of the social product (and of surplus-value in particular), but, firstly, by the fact that capitalism makes its appearance only as a result of a widely developed commodity *circulation*, which transcends the limits of the state. It is therefore impossible to conceive a capitalist nation without foreign trade, nor is there any such nation'. (23)

The need for a foreign market arises, Lenin emphasised, not for capitalist production as a whole but for those industries which have outstripped others in accumulation and are threatened with crisis. This crisis arises partly as a result of the disproportional industrial development which is inherent in capitalist development:

> 'If the national capital were distributed *differently*, the same quantity of products could be realised within the country. But for capital to abandon one sphere of industry and pass into another there must be a crisis in that sphere; and what can restrain the capitalists threatened by such a crisis from seeking a foreign market, from seeking subsidies and bonuses to facilitate exports, etc.'. (23)

This push by capital into foreign markets at this stage of development plays a progressive historical role in the backward areas, where it destroys the age-old isolation and seclusion of systems of economy and begins to link all countries of the world in one economy. Thus it is to industries with a high organic composition of capital that foreign trade first becomes a necessity, to cheapen the elements of constant capital and the necessities of life for which variable capital is exchanged, thus helping to raise the rate of profit by raising the rate of surplus-value and lowering the cost of constant capital. In this way the realisation problem is 'solved' for it is realisation at profitable levels that the capitalist is interested in and not realisation at any price, and here the foreign market helps to counteract the tendency of falling profitability. Luxembourg avoids the problem of capitalist crisis by her use of under-consumptionist theories. This problem and others raised by her analysis we reserve for later chapters. How then does Marx's view of the foreign market square up with the historical record as far as English capitalist development is concerned?

The early inventions which were supplying markets and also creating markets for others were soon joined by machine tools 'to beg and to service these new mechanical creatures'. The increasing urban population which entered the labour market also reinforced the demand for these products: textiles were needed for the working population; the demand for food improved agriculture; heating and other industrial requirements increased the demand for coal, iron etc. etc. But as the need for primary commodities increased with growing industry, there was increased need for foreign trade in the new products. The colonies provided the greater part of the market but this levelled off in the early nineteenth century as the new impetus caught on and as Britain established her lead as a free trade 'workshop of the world'. The trade followed the products that the colonies offered. The West Indies took textiles, tools and hardware and in return sold raw cotton, sugar and tobacco. The North of the US took manufactured goods and the South supplied raw cotton. India, whose handloom textile industry was being rapidly destroyed, provided a market for British manufactures including cotton textiles, but emerged as a cotton exporter. Then there was China and Latin America over which as we noted Britain was progressively establishing an 'informal colonialism' having weakened Portugal, Spain and jointly with the other powers, China. We have already noted the overall export figures of cotton textiles. To take a single example illustrating the extent of the expansion of trade with the colonies, India in 1814 took British cotton textiles worth £26,000 and in 1835, £400,000, a quarter of British textile exports. Exports of silk and woollen goods, iron, pottery, glass and paper increased too. Indian exports of cotton goods to England, which stood at £1.3 million in 1814, were reduced to £100,000 in 1832. The trading positions were reversed.

India was not only being turned into a capitalist market, it was being propped-up as a producer of raw materials and food products, for without such production no trade could take place. After 1833 Englishmen were encouraged to acquire land and enter into raw material production. The exports of raw materials leapt up. From 9 million pounds weight in 1813, cotton exports went up to 32 million in 1833 and 88 million in 1844; exports of sheep's wool rose from 3.7 thousand pounds weight in 1833 to 2.7 million in 1844; of linseed from 2,100 bushels in 1833 to 237,000 in 1844. Exports of food grains also went up, principally of wheat and rice, from £858,000 in 1849 to £3.8 million in 1858, £7.9 million in 1877 and £19.3 million in 1914. (24) In Latin America exports were accompanied with the production of sugar, cotton, coffee, tobacco, grains, beef, mutton, and minerals. The trade with the US increased even after independence, mainly in manufactured products from England and primary commodities from the US. Profitable production was being maintained on this basis.

Another factor which provided a market to British industry at profitable levels was war. The Napoleonic Wars acted as a spur to further production in the coal and iron industries for armaments, but also in the cloth industry and agriculture. The army and the navy were important customers and hence a good market. The iron and coal industry was given a rather early boost by the war. Coal production increased from 6 million tons at the end of the eighteenth century to 20 million tons by 1825 and 60 million by the 1850s. Iron production increased from about 600 thousand tons in 1830 to 2 million tons in 1850. As an example of the impetus given to production by the war, £1,573 million was raised by the British government in loans and taxes to meet the direct cost of the war. All this went into industry and production generally. When the war ended the government was raising another £70 million a year, 'largely expended upon the products of British industry and agriculture for delivery to the troops abroad'. (25) The financial aspects of these events put further sums into the 'national debt' to feed the rentiers and the fundholders. Upon this funded wealth there arose the loan-contracting business which the merchant-bankers performed for the government. According to Jenks, 'the loan contracting business led to the (creation) of the stock-exchange'. (26)

As can be seen, the cotton textile industry operated as a lever for industrial expansion in this period. As the US began to create its own capitalist industrial base, production of textiles decreased in England and so too industrial production generally. We will deal a little later in more detail with the problems which led to the production crisis. Just as spinning by machinery made mechanical weaving necessary and both together made the mechanical and chemical revolution that took place in the bleaching, printing and dyeing industries imperative, so did the revolution in cotton-spinning call forth the invention of the gin, for separating the seeds from the cotton fibre. It is at this stage that the production of cotton on the enormous scale then required became possible. More importantly the revolution in the methods of production of industry and agriculture made necessary a revolution in the general conditions and processes of social production, especially in the means of transport and communication.

The means of transport and communication available to the earlier society based on urban crafts and small scale agriculture with subsidiary domestic industries were clearly inadequate to the productive requirements of the manufacturing period. They became unbearable to modern industry with its feverish haste for mass production, its enormous extent, its constant flinging of capital and labour from one sphere of production into another and its newly-created markets over the whole world. They had to be revolutionised: they were. Apart from the vast advances in vessel construction already existing, new means of transport and communication adapted to the modes of production of mechanical industry were developed, such as the river steamers, railways, ocean steamers, and telegraphs.

But to enable this development to take place, huge masses of iron had to be forged, welded, cut, bored and shaped; a task which could only be handled by cyclopean machines, for the construction of which the methods of the manufacturing period were inadequate. Modern industry had to take the machine and with it produce other machines, thus building a technical foundation for itself, revolutionising production in this area by the use of the steam-engine. (27)

The growth of demand for capital goods both at home and abroad and the increasing accumulation of capital which in turn sought profitable investment made it possible for the capitalists to maintain production at higher levels to boost agencies counteracting falling profitability. Opening up of new industries away from those in which the organic composition of capital was very high, made possible the deployment of labour to those industries with low organic composition, while at the same time continuing the revolutionising of the means of production. In the period 1850-1870 industrial output doubled although the number of industrial workers rose by less than half. So too the number of miners rose by less than half although production doubled. Production in iron and steel, machine making, and ship building trebled whereas the number of workers only doubled. Cotton textile output also doubled between 1850-1860 with no increase in the number of workers. (28) Thus more intensification of exploitation of labour was taking place, a development that foreshadowed the crisis that was to occur in the 1870s.

British exports rose by 73% a year between 1840 and 1860, faster than ever before or since, more than in the cotton 'pioneer period' of 1780-1800. This growth benefited mainly the new capital goods industries. In 1840-1844 these formed 11% of the value of the total exports of manufactures, by 1857-1859, 22% and by 1882-1884, 27 %. Between 1840-1843 and 1857-1859 coal exports rose from less than three-quarters of a million pounds to three million; iron and steel exports from three million pounds to over thirteen million, while the exports of cotton rose slowly, though they also doubled. By 1873 they stood respectively at £13.2 million, £37.4 million and £77.4 million. (29)

The railway and steamship transport systems, themselves major markets for British iron, steel and coal exports, added fuel to the opening up of new markets and the expansion of old ones. Between 1830 and 1850, 6,000 miles of railways were opened in Britain; by 1860 the rail network had expanded to 10,000 miles, representing an investment of £150 million. (30) Opportunities were also opened for portfolio investment in European railways. This investment was mainly in the form of loans to governments and it is estimated by Jenks that these absorbed as much as £15 million per year between 1850 and 1875 and had reached £50 million by the 1870s. (31) The Europeans had to produce to repay the loans and their exports to Britain in food, drinks, etc., helped capitalist production there. Between 1856 and 1865, £35 million of rail was shipped abroad and, between 1865 and 1875, £83 million went to the colonies. (32) The push for railway construction in the colonies, whatever other reasons might have been behind the expansion, was clearly big business for British industry. The figures reproduced below show the production of pig-iron, steel and coal (in thousand tons) for the period 1850 to 1880:

	Pig-iron	Steel	Coal
1850	2,250	49	49,000
1880	7,750	1,440	147,000

These developments also laid the basis for expanded colonial production of raw materials and agricultural production.

Taking the US, Argentina, India, Canada and Australia together, the length of railway track in those countries rose from 62,000 miles in 1870 to 262,000 miles in 1900 and thus provided outlets for capital of £600 million in these countries before 1914. (33) This investment in the railways, moreover, went to countries supplying England with food and raw materials in return, which, as we have seen, was of great benefit to the expanding industrial production. When the terms of trade were in favour of countries where the conditions for capitalist development were present, these countries soon laid the basis for their own development, protecting local industry with tariff barriers. Where this was not possible, the countries stagnated under colonial exploitation to serve the metropolitan interests, both in this period and the next.

The period of this intensified industrial growth witnessed the gravest political crisis in Britain and continental Europe. This was a period of social revolution. The rapid rise in urban population increased the disparity of living standards. As we have seen, one of the forces counteracting the tendency of the rate of profit to fall was relative over-population. Marx observed that the relative overpopulation becomes much more apparent in a country where capitalist development is well under way. The abundance of labour made it cheap, and helped to intensify its exploitation, thus assisting the capitalist to increase his capital accumulation. In the case of Britain, the population doubled in the period between 1780 and 1840. It again doubled between 1841 and 1901, while the death rate dropped drastically. This exploding population merely worsened the 'industrial overpopulation' which was being generated independently by the introduction of machinery in production. On the political front, overpopulation aggravated the contradictions between the bourgeoisie and the working class. Working and middle-class pressures for constitutional reform resulted in some concessions by the landed aristocracy still predominant in Parliament. The middle-class won its representation in Parliament in the Great Reform Act of 1832, which led to the strengthening of a *liberal state*, but the bourgeoisie were not prepared to go along with working class pressures for a democratic state which was interpreted to imply social revolution. This break between the classes led to the emergence of the Chartist movement which represented the working class until well into the 1870s when it, too, was betrayed by a labour aristocracy becoming more and more *'embourgeoisified'*. The increasing breach

between the middle and working classes was not surprising since, as Marx
and Engels had pointed out:

> 'The class making a revolution appears from the very start, merely
> because it is opposed to a class, not as a class but as the represent-
> ative of the whole society; it appears as the whole mass of society
> confronting the one ruling class. It can do this because, to start with,
> its interest really is more connected with the common interest of all
> other non-ruling classes, because under the pressure of conditions its
> interest has not yet been able to develop as the particular interest of
> a particular class . . . Every new class, therefore, achieves its hegemony
> only on a broader basis than that of the class ruling previously, in
> return for which the opposition of the non-ruling against the new
> ruling class later develops all the more sharply and profoundly'. (34)

So the bourgeoisie was taking its own position as the new ruling class, but
now poised with its newly acquired class enemy with whom new struggles
emerged as the bourgeoisie consolidated their hold on the state. The
working class at this period, however, was weak, with no proper ideology
and leadership, a problem which was solved in 1848 with Marx's publication
of the *Manifesto of the Communist Party* and in the 1890s with the
appearance of Marxist-led working class parties in the whole of Europe.
But the British 'socialists' opted-out in favour of a social-democratic
Labour Party in 1900, and the betrayal of the working class by the Second
International led the working class back into the ideological fold of the
bourgeoisie in many countries in Europe.

The social upheavals of this period, the seething revolutionary mood of
1830 and 1848, characterised the on-going changes created by a new mode
of production, whilst the bourgeoisie consolidated themselves in the state
machine. Consolidation was achieved partly by smashing the old class
institutions of the feudalists and partly by reform of existing ones. Thus
there were religious reforms, town government reforms, health reforms,
legal reforms, etc. The establishment of the Metropolitan Police office at
Scotland Yard with a force of 1000 was the first step towards an effective
civilian police force under the Home Office. A new Poor Law in 1834
created a new 'work house system' for the control of the poor. In 1835,
the prisons were also reformed. (35) But perhaps one of the most important reforms of bourgeois consolidation were the constitutional reforms
which steadily brought the vote to the working class. As the bourgeoisie
progressively consolidated themselves, they saw that democracy through
'universal suffrage' was a better way to bring the workers within bourgeois
legitimacy and hence made concessions for their representation, but only
gradually. The cabinet became the corner-stone of bourgeois rule. So long
as the bourgeoisie were still in the ascendant and capable of expanding the
productive forces under the ideology of 'free trade', their position was
impregnable, at least for the time being.

CHAPTER VIII

The development of the productive forces in England was soon influencing the development of similar forces in France and later in North America and Germany. Competitive capitalism still allowed progressive development elsewhere. However, England had already attained a hegemonic position in industry and her main problem was to extend her production and to increase the market for her industrial products. The political and commercial policy of Britain, as we shall see, attracted resistance in many quarters. So-called 'National Economists' advocated national protectionism to guard raw materials, markets at home and those acquired all over the world. Unparalleled competition developed among the industrialising nations. Throughout this period Britain still played the leading role in world affairs, but was increasingly being challenged. The question of British free trade imperialism re-opened the ideological positions of the new class. When Adam Smith first set down on paper his thesis on the *Wealth of Nations* in 1776, he was speaking for a system which had already emerged. But just as in all new systems that have smashed an old one, the ideological struggle against the preceding order intensified and continued for a considerable period of time; old classes and their ideas die hard. The ideas put forward by Smith generated widespread debate, which helped to consolidate them. His central message, which opposed mercantilist imperialism, related to the possibilities that 'division of labour' and specialisation had opened up for the growth of the capitalist economy. His theories were, however, concerned with capitalism in its infancy and his ideas on the specialisation of labour were overtaken by machine production.

Smith laid the ground for the bourgeois position on 'free trade', although on other issues he tended to favour the landed gentry, for example on the question of agriculture. On the question of the colonies he insisted that the capital involved in the colonial trade was 'least advantageously situated' and that the capital in the 'carrying trade' was altogether withdrawn from supporting the productive labour of the home country and supported that of a foreign country. (36) Smith felt that home trade supported the greatest amount of labour; whereas foreign trade only gave 'one-half the encouragement to the industry or productive labour of the country'. The distances involved in the colonial trade resulted in less frequent turn-over of the colonial capital employed, besides making it irregular and more uncertain. Moreover, English commerce would benefit from the removal of the restrictions that dogged the colonial trade. England might purchase its tobacco more cheaply than could France as a result of trade restrictions, he noted, but not more cheaply than would be possible under entirely free trade. At every point, he argued, the mercantile system sacrificed the interest of the consumer of goods to that of the producer and the merchant; indeed, 'the home-consumers have been burdened with the whole expense of maintaining the Empire'. It was therefore more profitable to England to grant her colonies independence and to establish a system of free trade with them. (37)

There is no doubt that Smith's views had considerable impact on the later British government decision to recognise the independence of America in 1783. Nonetheless in the nineteenth century a new class of free trade colonialists were to emerge. Henry Brougham the 'Apostle of Free Trade' joined the chorus on the other side. In his *Colonial Policy of European Nations* published in 1803, Brougham anticipated the rapidly piling-up problems of the new capitalist system. These indicated that the British capitalist system had made colonies a necessity for Britain. He did not agree with Smith that colonial trade was less profitable than other trades for the country because of distance and capital turnovers.

> 'Another trade might give quicker returns and employ more British labour, but it did not follow that England would find another source, from whence the commodities might be obtained, or another market to take off her surplus produce'. (38)

The colonies, he argued, provided the type of market which a rapidly expanding British industry required. Colonies provided opportunities for excess labourers from the mother-country. 'The overflowing, or rotten part of the state's population' had 'found a vent in the distant parts of the empire', and members of the middle classes for whom it had been difficult to maintain their status in the colonies, Brougham continued, found this excess labour essential in their efforts to develop outlets for 'super abundant' capital. There was a new and pressing need to increase the employment for capital to keep pace with its increase, otherwise profits at home would be diminished by a glut of capital. He disagreed with the discouragement of manufacturing in the colonies since in his view such restriction was superfluous.

According to Brougham, agriculture was more profitable to colonial pursuit and the ever expanding needs of the colonies for capital would keep the rate of profit on colonial capital higher than at home. He observed even at this early period that Great Britain had already secured 'a general superiority in all three circumstances, particularly of her large capitals in the hands of the few rather than a wide distribution of smaller capitals', a circumstance 'fitted for the colonial trade'.

Perhaps the most outstanding exponent of colonisation was Edward Gibbon Wakefield, who, in his book *England and America*, published in

1833, called for 'systematic colonisation'. Wakefield put forward his views better than his predecessors and actually set up limited liability companies to engage in colonisation. With support in Parliament, various laws were passed to implement his proposals for colonisation in Australia and New Zealand. English society, Wakefield argued, is divided into two broad economic classes: 'owners of capital and owners of labour'. Through empire-building, Britain would solve the contradictions which assailed her economy, an increasing economic polarisation and the misery of the working and middle classes, growing out of the increasingly severe competition among capitalists and the consequent declining rate of profit, and avoid the dangers of revolution and class warfare. (39)

Whilst there can be no doubt that imperialism as Cecil Rhodes pointed out was 'a bread and butter question', and for Wakefield a vent for crisis, it was never to be a final solution. It merely pushed the misery onto the colonial peoples. The present day struggle in the Third World is a clear rejection of this exploitative relationship and victories are being won against it. But the problem Wakefield and his class faced was a real one. The two alternatives open to them were either to 'push out' or perish as a class. Wakefield had finally declared to his fellow bourgeois:

> 'The whole world is before you. Open new channels for the most productive employment of English capital. Let the English buy bread from every people that has bread to sell cheap. Make England, for all that is produced by steam, the Workshop of the World. If, after this, there be capital and people to spare, imitate the ancient Greeks; take a lesson from the Americans, who, as their capital and population increase, find room for both by means of colonisation. (Only in this way can England) escape from that corrupting and irritating state of political economy, which seems to precede the dissolution of empires'. (40)

The growth of the productive forces as we have already seen had unleashed a population 'explosion' in Europe generally. The population in England increased in a brief period of twenty years, when the debate took place, as follows:

1811	12,596,803
1821	14,391,631
1831	18,720,394

Moreover, poor relief increased in the same period from *9s.1d. per capita* in 1801 to only *9s.9d. per capita* in 1831. The encouragement of emigration, which was not the problem under mercantilist colonisation, became imperative. Malthus' agrarian economics and his views on population strengthened this push for colonisation. The establishment of 'natural slavery' in the colonies by more or less forced deportation was justified in the name of God! Wakefield said:

> 'As the goodness of God and the progressive nature of man are unquestionable, and as God has permitted every nation to undergo the state of slavery, so we may be sure that slavery has not been an

evil unmixed with good. Slavery appears to have been the step by
which nations have emerged from poverty and barbarism, and
moved onwards towards wealth and civilisation'. (41)

As the push for colonisation was pursued, the push for 'free trade' by
the manufacturing class was also being waged on another front, by the
Cobdenite Anti-Corn Law League. The two complemented one another.
Indeed for Wakefield the new colonisation drive was to supplement the
existing one. Colonisation was not new and capitalism at this stage was
benefitting from colonial production, but the reformers were calling for
a new type of colonisation fitted to 'free trade' imperialism.

By the 1830s as we have noted the Industrial Revolution in Britain
had taken hold and in the next generation or so Britain was the workshop
of the world. Although other European nations and the US were also set
on the road to industrial development, Britain still had hegemony in
international trade. At this juncture she was producing perhaps two thirds
of the world's coal, one-half its iron, five-sevenths of its steel and about
one-half of the cotton cloth as well as about two-fifths of its hardware. (42)
In these circumstances it is obvious that the representatives of the industrial
classes should have strongly advocated 'free trade', for by cutting down
tariffs among the European trading partners, Britain had nothing to lose
and might gain cheaper food and raw materials.

The debate initiated by the political economists was raging in the whole
country, including Parliament, where these classes had gained admission
by the 1832 Reform Act. Free trade was already taking place in many
products but not yet in corn. The landed aristocracy and tenant producers
whose interests were vested in the production of corn in England fought
for protection of agriculture. The protection tended to raise the price of
food and thus to increase the wage costs of the new bourgeoisie. As
Semmel puts it:

'With the end of wartime demand, . . . with the need to find new
markets for rapidly increasing production, the factory owners,
already feeling hampered by the commercial restrictions of the old
system, became particularly resentful of the corn laws, which they
were convinced, by artificially raising wheat prices in the interest
of agricultural classes, necessitated higher labour costs and thereby
limited the ability of British industries to compete for wider markets,
which, they believed, had to be produced if economic crises were to
be avoided'. (43)

The leading political economist of this period, David Ricardo who, in
his book, *Principles of Political Economy and Taxation*, published in 1817,
had indicated arguments on the same lines, and had stated that the rate of
profit could never be increased except by a fall in wages and that there
could be no permanent fall in wages except as a consequence of a fall in
the price of the necessaries on which wages were expended, concluded his
argument thus:

'If, therefore, by extension of foreign trade, or by improvements in

machinery, the food and necessaries can be brought to market at a
reduced price, profits will rise. If instead of growing our own corn, or
manufacturing the clothing and other necessaries of the labourer,
we can supply ourselves with these commodities at cheaper prices
wages will fall and profits will rise . . .' (44)

Here Ricardo was advocating the ideology of the factory owners, a rather
one-sided ideology; as he was saying this, the Indian textile industry which
sold cheaply to England was being destroyed to eliminate its competition
with British textiles, a destruction which went on even after the era of free
trade. The prohibition on import of Indian textiles to Britain was not
removed until 1917. But the essence of what he was advocating was
objectively in line with the reality of the situation as far as the British
bourgeoisie were concerned. The tendency of the rate of profit to fall at
home could only be reversed by increased supplies of cheap raw and
auxiliary materials, expanding markets, and lower wages, which implied
an intensification of the exploitation of labour. The drive for foreign trade
under the ideology of free trade was a necessary complement.

It was against this background that the Anti-Corn Law League led by
Cobden and Bright, themselves manufacturers, was formed in 1835 with
the aim of getting the British Parliament to repeal the Corn Laws of 1815.
The League were in effect calling for free trade. Seeing a threat in the
setting up of a customs wall under the Zollverein of German States, they
hastened and intensified their pressures.

The main opponents of the League included Disraeli who opposed free
trade on the grounds that all trade concessions must be based on the
principle of reciprocal advantage. Moreover efforts were made in 1825 by
David Hume to prohibit the export of machinery in order to maintain
British manufacturing hegemony. Robert Torrens, agreeing with Hume,
argued that England should not 'give up one exclusive advantage', and
should act 'with a firm hand' to that effect. He also advocated that England
should restrict the export of her cheap coal without which the French
could not operate steam-engines and suggested a duty of 50% on coal
exported to the continent.

This, however, was not the main trend of thought among the bourgeoisie
and the Cobdenite Anti-Corn Law struggle had at least for a time frozen
any further protectionist moves. The Cobdenites who had relied on the
wages argument were soon shocked, however, by the workers' opposition
to their move. The workers retorted that the tax on corn was no more than
three pence per week and yet the wages of the hand-loom weavers had
fallen between 1815 and 1843, from 28s. per week to 5s. and the wages
of the power-loom weavers had done so from 20s. per week to 8s. between
1823 and 1843. Marx reproduced the debate in the form of a dramatic
dialogue:

'How is it that in the course of the last thirty years, while our
industry has undergone the greatest development, our wages have

fallen far more rapidly, in proportion, than the price of corn has gone up? . . . And during the whole of this period that portion of the tax which we paid to the landlord has never exceeded three pence. And, then, in the year 1834, when bread was very cheap and business going very well, what did you tell us? You said, if you are unfortunate, it is because you have too many children, and your marriages are more productive than your labour!' (45)

Whereupon the Cobdenites turned around and said: 'This fallacy of wages is at the bottom of all opposition to the repeal of corn laws'. Cobden, who had all along threatened Peel with 'revolution' unless the Corn Laws were repealed, found the ground cut from under his feet. He now appealed to base national sentiments: 'Great Britain could only be assured of foreign markets if she provided agricultural nations, potential consumers of British hardware and cloth, with a market for their export of food and raw materials'. This latter strategy implied colonies. Here we have a full swing from 'free trade' to 'colonialism for free trade'!

However, when Parliament finally repealed the Corn Laws in 1846, it was already clear that the landed interests had nothing to fear from the change. As Semmell has correctly pointed out:

'By 1846 . . . a substantial part of the landed aristocracy had been converted to free trade: some out of sympathy for the distress, others because of fear of revolution, still others, and not the least part of the aristocratic supporters of corn law abolition fell into this group, because they had sufficiently diversified their interests so that they might readily believe they had much to gain from the growing prosperity of an Industrial England. By marriage and investments, the aristocracy and the gentry had become connected with mercantile and industrial enterprise; moreover, the gentlemen upon whose lands the cities of industrial England were encroaching were anticipating the rising values and rents which must result from industrial development, and others who owned coal, or lead mines were similarly in agreeable situation'. (46)

The repeal of the Corn Laws in 1846 was followed with the further repeal of the Navigation Laws in 1852 a combination which went to fulfill the dreams of the industrial bourgeoisie. Now 'free' international trade could be explained as being to the benefit of all parties.

In order to generalise the ideology of free trade imperialism for the benefit of the British capitalist class, classical political economists paid attention to the theory of comparative cost. The best exponent of the law of comparative costs and advantage was Ricardo. In a passage in his book on political economy, he stated that:

'Under a system of perfectly free commerce, this pursuit of individual advantage is admirably connected with the universal good of the whole. By stimulating industry, by rewarding ingenuity, and by using most efficaciously the peculiar powers bestowed by nature, it distributes labour most effectively and most economically: while by increasing the general mass of productions it diffuses general benefit, and binds together, by one common tie of interest and intercourse

the universal society of nations throughout the civilised World.
It is this principle which determines that wine shall be made in France and Portugal and that hardware and other goods shall be manufactured in England'. (47)

Let us look at the political economy of the theory as a whole, in the context of British-Portuguese relations, to discern reality from myth. British trade clearly placed Britain as a net importer of food and primary products as Table I below shows. Furthermore, as we have observed in Chapter III. British trade with Portugal was based on unequal treaties and not on natural international division of labour between equals. The treaties of 1642, 1654, 1661 and 1703 had sealed Portuguese dependence on England and had destroyed her potential to industrialise. The treaty of 1703 (Methuen Treaty) created a specialisation which in the short run at least was unable to provide products to Portugal at lower prices. The expansion of English textiles under the treaty involved a sacrifice by Portuguese merchants which was intended to preserve 'British-looms and the rents of Great Britain'. British wine imports from Portugal became the means by which British textile production could be expanded. In the process Britain gave up better French wines in order to further her industrialisation process.

'From this time the drinking of Port (Portuguese wine) was regarded as a patriotic duty by the English squire who later, after industrialisation had brought him affluence, reverted to drinking French wine'. (48)

Moreover, the reciprocal privileges that England granted Portugal were innocuous since no Portuguese merchants had sufficient competitive power to utilize the privileges, whilst the 'factories' of the English merchants at Oporto and Lisbon put these privileges to good use, thereby further weakening the Portuguese merchant class. Sideri makes the following point on the effects of the Methuen Treaty:

'Thus, in exchange for her concessions to England, Portugal obtained neither a real reduction of English import duties on wines nor the stabilisation of those duties as (Portugal) had repeatedly demanded. The export of wine cannot be considered to have been very advantageous to Portugal. As we have already seen, trade was largely controlled by English interests which took most of the profits, while the Portuguese had to cope with unfavourable effects created by the expansion of such an "enclave" in which British investment soon reached the million pound mark. A trade "completely" in the hands of English merchants who did not hesitate to mercilessly sacrifice Duoro producers'. (49)

Taking advantage of Portugal's weakness in the face of French invasion during the Napoleonic Wars, Britain skilfully wrung out of Portugal more and more privileges. Contrary to the previous treaty obligations which bound Britain to protect Portugal's independence and that of her colonies, Britain insisted that John V of Portugal, who had fled Portugal to Brazil after the invasion and had stayed there from 1807 to 1821, should open up Brazilian ports to the trade of friendly nations, which meant in effect British trade. A decree was promulgated for this purpose in 1808, with the immediate effect of disorganising Portuguese industry, which as we noted in a previous chapter had begun to pick-up under the Pombal policy of protectionism at the end of the eighteenth century. The decree, by attacking the Brazilian market, further weakened the process of recovery, a fact which led a contemporary Portuguese economist Das Neves, writing in 1810, to complain:

'The magical power of the steam engine, which has revolutionised the mechanical arts within the last few years, has provided the English with the means to produce manufactured goods so cheaply that nobody else can compete with them'. (50)

A seal was put onto the policy which inspired the decree when Britain, again against its treaty commitments, sponsored the idea of the independence of Brazil, which, according to Sideri, 'revealed the exploitative nature of the alliance and the kind of interests that lay behind the support which the British then lavished on Latin American independence movements'. The 1810 Treaty of Commerce was another privilege-creating instrument: according to Article 9, Brazilian sugar, coffee, and other goods similar to those produced by British colonies were denied entry to British markets. Whilst Britain exported to Brazil, she didn't allow Brazilian products in her market. This naturally undermined Brazil's economy, just as the earlier arrangements undermined Portugal's.

In Portugal itself there was a bourgeois revolutionary ferment in the 1820s supported by industrialists, merchants and members of the liberal professions, which resulted in a liberal government. This development was, however, short-lived, as the British intervened, creating a split with the Septemberists representing the progressive wing and Chartists representing landed and wine-exporting interests. British support for the Chartists led to the Septemberist wing being thrown out of power within six years. This was of significance to England since all the measures of industrialisation which had been undertaken by the Septemberist government were reversed.

The result was another Treaty of 1842, which on the face of it introduced the principle of reciprocity and the most favoured-nation clause, spelling out 'complete freedom of trade and navigation for the subjects of the two signatories'. In spite of this treaty, Britain in 1831 unilaterally increased duties on Portuguese wines from 4s. 10d. to 5s. 6d. per gallon thereby bringing them level with those imposed on French wines. This had the effect of raising the average duty paid for the period 1816-1853 on all Portuguese commodities into Britain by 136% of their value, and that on wines by 194%.

In the field of shipping, Britain took an increasing share of the carrying trade: 50% of imports to Portugal were carried in British ships and only 31% in Portuguese ones. Even Portuguese exports went in British ships

(60%) while Portuguese ships only carried 31% of their own products. By the 1850s Portugal remained an agricultural country described by one writer as 'economically speaking a small South American republic that happened to be attached to Europe', but even then suffering from a 'chronic inability to produce sufficient food to supply the domestic market'.

Contrary to Ricardo's assumption of capital immobility, Portugal in the 1850s was dominated by foreign industrial and loan capital. The British investments were estimated in 1807 at abour £10 million at both the Oporto and Lisbon 'factories'. The total amount transferred to Portugal from Britain for the period 1792-1853 was estimated at £9.4 million (15% of all investments transferred by Britain abroad). On the other hand advances by 'way of subsidy between 1798 and 1815 amounted to £8.8 million and the amount borrowed between 1813 and 1853 was estimated at £4.7 million making a total of £13.5 million, a much higher figure. For Britain 'the export of capital served the national interest in the same way as it was served by the export of goods'.

In effect Portugal was used as an 'informal colony' of Britain in the same way as Brazil. Although it adopted the gold standard in 1854, Portugal did not obtain monetary autonomy until 1891. English money was the only legal tender and the Bank of Portugal only issued convertible bank notes. The railways construction out of a British loan which resulted in some revival of industrialisation in the 1850s was soon denounced by the British on the grounds that such development was 'calculated eventually to bring (Portugal) into a state of greater poverty than she is at the present time', and as 'injurious to British trade'.

The Portuguese national debt slowly grew into another channel of exploitation. Britain, for the period 1870-1880, charged an average of 14.5% interest (as against British home average of 5.4% for all foreign bonds and an overall average of 6.1% of all British investments abroad). Of the Portuguese national debt estimated at £19 million, Britain provided half and France one-fifth. Debt-servicing amounted to no less than £550,000 per year to which should be added the trade deficit of £900,000, which went into British coffers. According to Feis, however, the debt became burdensome. From £27.8 million in 1860, it grew to £66.2 millions in 1870, and £97.0 million in 1890. (51) For this reason all inflow to Portugal of precious metals stopped and in 1891 a net outflow of about £5.5 million worth of gold and bullion started and her survival and the maintenance of her own colonial set-up depended on further loans. The outflow continued until 1908. Portugal finally went off the gold standard and her currency was no longer convertible.

Thus Ricardo's theory of comparative advantage based on the experience gained under English/Portuguese trade fails in the light of that very experience, and proves that imperialist exploitation knows no racial nor geographical bounds. What was happening to Portugal was also happening to weaker states in Europe where English industrial interests dominated.

Table I

Import Structure U.K. %

	1814-45	1854-60	1875-1933
Food and Live animals	27.9	31.5	41.2
Primary products	64.4	61.2	41.6
Manufactures	7.7	7.3	17.2
	100.0	100.0	100.0

Source: Werne Schlote: British Overseas Trade from 1700 to the 1930s.

Equipped with an advancing manufacturing industry, Britain had nothing to fear from opening up her market to cheaper food and wine. Indeed, as Table I clearly reveals, British interest in foreign trade was to enable the importation of primary products which represented about two thirds of all her imports. Food imports accounted almost entirely for the other one third, with imports of manufactures occupying a minimal portion. Britain's exports were intended to elicit the above type of trade from foreign countries since these supplied the materials the country needed to cheapen the components of constant capital, and the commodities on which wages were spent. The Table shows that in the period 1875-1933, British hegemony is challenged, as we shall see in the next chapter. Her imports of food increase, while her importation of primary products decline. Her imports of manufactures rise. The monopolistic era of finance capital saw the intensification of the struggle with labour and the rise of trade unionism; hence the increased importation of cheap food. The struggle for the division of the world and the new tariff policy introduced the need for reciprocal arrangements with other monopolies, hence the import of manufactures from Germany and the US. We shall examine the dynamics of these changes in the next chapter.

Whilst the English political economists were thoroughly convinced that 'free trade' was beneficial to all parties, the German and American bourgeoisie, the so-called national school of political economists, had come to more critical conclusions. In their arguments at home on whether or not free trade was beneficial to England, the proponents of free trade in England asserted that an advanced manufacturing country enjoyed a considerable advantage over an agricultural country, and that with free trade an advanced country could maintain such advantage. When the 'national economists' used the same logic in making out a case for the protection of infant local industry in opposition to free trade, the English political economists were shocked at the proposition!

The first 'national economist' to put forward an argument on protectionism was the American Secretary of the Treasury, Alexander Hamilton. In his *Report on Manufactures* to the US Congress in 1791 he pointed out that:

'If the system of perfect liberty to industry and commerce [i.e. free

trade] were the prevailing system of nations, the arguments which
dissuade a country in the predicament of the United States from
zealous pursuit of manufactures would doubtless have greate force
. . . but the system which has been mentioned is far from character-
ising the general policy of nations. In such a position of things the
United States cannot exchange with Europe, on equal terms'. (52)

He pointed out further that an agricultural country was at a disadvan-
tage in trading with a manufacturing country since the foreign demand
for agricultural products was 'rather casual and occasional, than certain or
constant'. Hence the terms of trade were bound to be against her due to
the bulky character of the products and the high costs of transport.
Hamilton was writing before the drive for 'free trade' at the political level
but his arguments were valid for even this later period.

Another outstanding exponent of the idea of protection of infant
industry was a German professor of political economy Friedrich List. In
his book, *National System of Political Economy*, List described England's
Empire of Free Trade as:

'A cosmopolitan country supplying all nations with manufactured
products, and asking in return from each country, its raw materials
and commodities; the arsenal of extensive capital, the universal
banker; regulating, if not controlling the circulating money of the
whole world, and making all nations tributary to her by loans and the
payment of interest'. (53)

He argued that society passes through a series of stages, each of which is
an advance on the preceeding ones, but the state can facilitate the transition from one stage to another. The first stage is the hunting and pastoral
life of early man. The second stage is characterised by agricultural production pure and simple, and the third by agricultural production with
manufacturing. According to List, it is the duty of the statesmen to bring
the country to the last stage as soon as possible. Some countries are so
backward that it is hopeless to try to reach it; others have already reached
it. The system of national protection does not apply to any of these stages.
Free trade on the other hand is the best policy for an undeveloped country
to obtain manufactures that they cannot produce themselves and for a
manufacturing country to gain a market for its products. To overcome the
difficulties of the transition, protective duties for infant industries are
necessary; Germany and the US were in such a situation. England on the
other hand did not need such protection and any such protection in her
case was due to the stupidity of her governing class.

The English political economists did not think much of these arguments
and regarded them as 'unworthy of notice', 'the work of zealous and
unscrupulous advocates', 'extravagant fictions'. However, the arguments
were accepted by John Stuart Mill, particularly in his analysis of the terms
of trade. In an essay written in 1829, *On Unsettled Questions of Political
Economy*, he observed that England drew to herself the largest share of the

gains of international commerce because her exports were in universal demand and were of the kind which increase with a fall in price. 'Countries which export food have the former advantage but not the latter'. (51) He conceded, although later he tried to qualify his views, that tariff protection for infant industry was only necessary 'temporarily'.

The debate was joined by Carey in America. He maintained that the British policy of free trade was aimed at perpetuating the economic subservience of America. He called for solidarity of all agriculturalists against Britain. But, as Marx rightly observed, 'Carey sees the contradictions in the economic relations as soon as they appear on the world market as English relations'. (55) Carey and his friends did not see the problem dialectically and historically. Whereas England developed capitalism under the protective arm of feudal foundations in its 'pure form', in the US, as Marx put it:

> '. . . the bourgeois society did not develop on the foundation of the feudal system, but developed rather from itself; where this society appears not as the surviving result of a centuries-old movement, but rather as the starting point of a new movement; where the state, in contrast to all earlier national formations, was from the beginning subordinate to a bourgeois society, and never could make pretence of being an end-in-itself; where, finally bourgeois society itself, linking up the productive forces of an old word with the enormous natural terrain of a new one, has developed to hitherto unheard-of-dimensions and with unheard-of-freedom of movement, has far outstripped all previous work in the conquest of forces of nature, and where, finally, even the antithesis of bourgeois society itself appears only as a vanishing moment'. (56)

In Germany the Zollverein replaced the fragmented feudal system of protection and helped to establish the basis for reconstruction into a capitalist order already taking root in England and France. Starting with the Prussian tariff of 1818 it incorporated other smaller states into a Unified Customs Union, with a common customs frontier. The idea was to move away from agriculture as the only base of the economy and to establish manufacturing, but to do so by 'keeping out British goods'. (57)

However the 'national economists' were, in the final analysis, struggling for free trade, since protection was 'nothing but a means of establishing large-scale industry . . . that is to say, of making it dependent upon the world market, and from the moment that dependence on the world market is established, there is already more or less dependence upon free trade'. (58) Hence protectionism was a means of helping competition within a country, and objectively and in the last analysis the weapon of a weak bourgeoisie, such as the German one, in its efforts against feudalism. Marx saw the protection advocated by Germany and the US as conservative and free trade as destructive, breaking up old nationalities and pushing the antagonism of the proletariat and the bourgeoisie to the extreme point. In other words free trade hastened social revolution and in 'this revolutionary sense alone', Marx 'voted in favour of free trade'. (59)

CHAPTER IX

The period 1860-1890 has been called the 'Golden Age' of free trade, which is something of an exaggeration. The adoption of the Gold Standard by most European countries facilitated for a time the operation of a single free and multilateral system of world trading around London as the trading and financial centre. This liberalism had been set in motion among other things, by the signing of the Cobden-Chevalier Treaty of 1860 between England and France which incorporated the Most-Favoured-Nation principle into trade policy. This liberalisation was Richard Cobden's crowning achievement. It was also the dialectical result of the general move-ment in the economy of England at this time as we have shown in the last chapter. Under the Treaty all prohibitions to imports were removed and England was to admit at reduced duties French wines and brandies. The French in return were to reduce duties on English goods to 30% as a maximum, till 1864, and thereafter they were to reduce them to 24%. The Treaty was to last ten years. Coal was excluded from the deal, since it was agreed to prohibit its importation on either side.

Although it is true that as a result of this Treaty, France, by signing commercial treaties with other parts of Europe, generalised the concessions made to her by England, and that the other countries further generalised them *inter se*, such effort was short-lived. By 1871, at the end of the Franco-Prussian War, the liberalisation was already cracking as France imposed duties again to raise revenue to pay her war-debts. France was thus the first major country to turn away from free trade after barely a decade. Italy did so in 1878 and Austria followed suit in the same year. Germany also veered around in 1879 and imposed duties because of cheap wheat coming in from the US. As one economist has observed:

'Thus, whereas France after the Cobden-Chevalier Treaty was for a decade to become an agent of free trade on the continent, after 1879 Germany became the nodal point of a protectionist system which was to last and be improved upon until the first World War. In this sense the tariff revision of 1879, marking the end of free trade in Germany was, indeed, a turning point in the tariff history of modern times'. (60)

Although England continued her liberal tariff, maintaining duties on only 15 items, this was soon to change. She had nothing much to gain by such a policy now. Due to increasing competition from the US, France and Germany, by 1930 she too had imposed an imperial preference system. The chicken of the free trade ideology had come home to roost.

In fact such free trade in our view did not exist in 'pure form', even for liberal England. During this period as we have shown, Britain imported from and exported its products to countries with complementary economies, products in which Britain had the advantage in terms of trade. Import products came from areas in which Britain had either formal or informal dominion: wool from Australia, nitrates and copper from Chile, guano from Peru, wine from Portugal, meat and dairy products from New Zealand, wheat and beef from Argentina, and gold and diamonds from South Africa.

Although Britain had moved into capital goods production, textiles still continued to play a significant role in its export trade. Between 1867-1869 textiles still formed 75% of manufactured exports, falling to 51% by the eve of the first World War. Capital goods moved up from 20% to 39% in the same period. As far as cotton piece goods (textiles) were concerned, British trade was with the underdeveloping parts of the world, India leading among them. Trade in these products with Europe and the US, amounting to 60.4% of exports in 1820, had fallen to only 7.1% in 1900, whereas exports to the underdeveloping world soared from 31.8% in 1820 to 86.3% in 1900. Thus colonial production and markets were of crucial importance to British industry at this stage of free trade imperialism.

The pattern of other exports was similar, though not so extreme as in cotton. There was a steady flight from the modern protected and competitive markets into the underdeveloped ones as Britain moved into a new stage of capitalist development: the era of monopoly capitalism, about which we shall say more later. Suffice it to say here that two areas were significant for British industry: India, as pointed out, and Latin America, over which Britain was establishing informal dominion. In 1840 Brazil had taken close to 40% of the cotton goods exports. Later Argentina, which was more or less an informal colony, assumed importance. The East Indies (which were split up into India and Far East) were a crucial market. From 6% of cotton exports after the Napoleonic Wars (1815), these regions absorbed 22% in 1840, 31% in 1850 and 60% by 1873 — India alone taking about 45% at the onset of the Great Depression of 1873. As Hobsbawn has correctly said:

> 'Indeed, in this period of difficulty Asia saved Lancashire, even more decisively than Latin America had done in the early part of the century'. (61)

This is an understatement; it was by destroying Indian textile industry that Lancashire ever came up at all. However it is important to note that at the height of free trade ideology, Britain's textile industry was surviving on 'unfree' colonial trade as well as on dividends. India's general foreign payments to Britain on loan capital and her payments of 'Home Charges' for having the privilege of being administered by Her Majesty's

Government rose from £70 million to £225 million by the end of the century. (62) India was also creating a big surplus in her trade of opium with China, which Britain encouraged during the opium war fought by Britain against China. India alone met over two-fifths of Britain's deficits in trade in this period. This growing reliance by Britain on the formal and informal empire was evidence of a general crisis in the internal economic situation and market, 'a watershed between two stages of capitalism: the earlier vigorous, prosperous, and flushed with adventurous optimism; the later more troubled, more hesitant, and some would say already bearing marks of senility and decay'. (63) The importation of cheaply obtained colonial products very much helped to contain the crisis. But free trade imperialism must be clearly distinguished from the later imperialism which emerged after the crisis. The main distinguishing, characteristics of the earlier phase are:

a. The role of the state in the trade and investment of the capitalists is, in general, minimal.

b. Most enterprises, if not all, are still small and competitive as compared to those of the next period; as a result, they could not exercise any monopoly control over markets and investment.

c. The 'channels of international finance' were still 'democratic'. The centralising power of the Banks had not attained monopoly heights. Hence it was small capitals in the form of loan stock, centralised through the stock exchange, that dominated. As Jenks commented:

    '. . . during the period 1815-1875, "imperialism" was not a prominent factor in the movement of British capital'.

d. Control of capital and production were still separate and trade as such still predominated. 'Tied loans' were not dominant. Moreover, competitive capitalism at this stage was progressive in encouring production overseas which, given the favourable atmosphere, could have led to a number of colonial territories developing fully fledged capitalist economies. Marx was aware of these possibilities regarding India.

e. The need for particular raw materials and strategic materials, although important for the major capitalist countries, at this stage was not crucial. Most of the raw materials of today were still available in Europe and North America, e.g., copper, iron, aluminium, oil. Some were not vital in production (e.g., copper).

f. Tariff policies were still protective in character. Even in the US and Germany they were not as yet 'aggressive', and still played a defensive role.

It had been argued by bourgeois political economists that crises under capitalist production could never occur; and others argued that if crisis did occur it would be because of lack of money. Malthus, who had tried to protect landed interests in his theory on population, maintained in a later publication that continual accumulation by capitalists had a self-defeating logic, since ever increasing accumulation of capital must lead to an excess in production which could not be sold for lack of demand. There must follow a 'glut' and a general overproduction of goods, a shortage of money to pay for the increased production. For Malthus the remedy therefore lay in maintaining the income of landlords who according to him would spend their rents on luxury goods, and hence keep up the level of effective demand.

Ricardo rebuffed Malthus on this question by invoking Say's Law on markets by which there could never be any over-production and lack of market since every sale was invariably followed by a purchase of equal amount. Excess production of a particular commodity can only be temporary, as demand will switch from one commodity to another. Jean-Baptiste Say's thesis (64) put forward in 1803, was an attack on the Mercantilist confusion between money and wealth. It was dominated throughout by the Physiocratic analysis based on simple commodity production which explained production in terms of circular flow, where commodities exchange for commodities and money merely acts as a medium. The implication of this was that as commodities can be bought with other commodites all commodities will be sold so long as they are produced in correct combinations, for all production was meant for purchase. In a word: 'Supply creates its own demand'.

It was this thesis that Ricardo brushed up in his rebuff of Malthus in the following terms:

> 'No man produces but with a view to consume or sell, and he never sells but with an intention to purchase some other commodity which may be useful to him, or which may contribute to further production. By producing then, he necessarily becomes either the consumer of his own goods, or the purchaser and consumer of goods of some other person. Productions are always bought by productions or by services. Money is only a medium by which the exchange is effected'. (65)

So long as bourgeois political economy remained at this level of abstraction, it could never transcend the limits of simple commodity production and exchange. But this simple production belonged to a distant past where production was basically for consumption by a producer, or by an appropriator as in the slave and feudal systems. Such exchanges as took place were not basic to the operation of these systems and merely supplemented the consumption oriented production. In these circumstances over-production could not disturb the system. On the contrary, it was under-production that tended to result in catastrophes.

In capitalist production, on the other hand, this is not the case. We are no longer dealing with simple commodity production C-M-C, but expanded commodity production $M-C-M^1$. Money (M) is converted into commodities (C) by production in order to obtain more $money (M^1)$, and it is this which characterises the capitalist epoch and distinguishes it from the previous ones. Marx criticised Ricardo in the following terms:

> 'This is the childish babble of a Say, but it is not worthy of Ricardo.

In the first place no capitalist produces in order to consume his product. And when speaking of capitalist production it is right to say that : "no man produces with a view to consume his own product", even if he uses portions of his product for industrial consumption. Previously it was forgotten that the product is a commodity. Now even the social division of labour is forgotten. In a situation where men produce for themselves, there are indeed no crises, but neither is there capitalist production. Nor have we even heard that the ancients, with their slave production, ever knew crises, although individual producers among the ancients too did go bankrupt. The first part of the alternative is nonsense. The second as well. A man who has produced does not have the choice of selling or not selling. He must sell. In the crisis there arises the very situation in which he cannot sell or can only sell below the cost price or must even sell at a positive loss. What difference does it make, therefore, to him or to us that he has produced in order to sell? The very question we want to solve is what has thwarted this good intention of his?' (66)

The root of capitalist crisis must therefore be sought, as Marx has said, in the real movement of capitalist production, competition, and credit. This tendency towards crisis is a reflection of a basic contradiction in capitalist production. As we have seen, Marx's reproduction schema and his two departments portray this basic contradiction, a contradiction which is the struggle between the two classes for the proceeds of the product. As we saw in Chapter VIII this struggle leads to falling profitability for the capitalist enterprise in spite of (and because of) efforts to intensify the exploitation of labour through machinery and technology. Once the element of technical change is introduced it is clear that the department producing means of production(Department I), will grow faster than the department producing means of consumption. This revolution in the means of production also calls for a similar revolution in the specialisation of labour. As Lenin stated:

'To increase the productivity of human labour, in for instance the making of some part of a whole product, the production of that part must be specialised, must become a special one concerned with mass production and therefore, permitting (and engendering) the employment of machines'. (67)

The combination of the two revolutions all lead to an effort by the capitalist to replace labour as much as possible in order to increase relative surplus-value. The effect of this is to turn an ever larger share of newly formed capital into the department which produces the means of production. Hence products for personal consumption increasingly occupy an ever-diminishing place in the process of capitalist production. This is a contradiction which is inherent in capitalist production and arises in the production process itself and not in distribution.

To put it another way, a crisis in capitalist production would occur when the expansion of production outruns its average profitability, when the existing conditions of exploitation preclude a further profitable capital expansion or when an increase of accumulation does not increase the mass of surplus value or profit, and when an absolute over-accumulation has occurred and the accumulation process halted. This will occur at a point where the existing capital is at the same time *too small and too large*, when the over production of capital is *too large* with respect to the degree of exploitation and in relation to the existing surplus-value, and *too small* to overcome the lack of surplus-value.

In this connection it is necessary to note that those who have identified themselves with Marx have tended to split themselves into two camps on this question, in the so-called 'breakdown controversy', the two camps being the 'disproportionality' and the 'under-consumptionist' schools. (68) The disproportionality thesis is based on Marx's reproduction schema. This treats of the necessary relationship that must exist between the two principle departments of social production if the process of simple and expanded reproduction is to continue undisturbed. Marx's schema analyses the conditions under which the equilibrium of the reproduction of social capital can be maintained and is a provisional solution to the 'realisation problem'. As we have shown he never took into account technical change and assumed that products exchange at their value. His aim was to show that capitalist crisis does not lie in the circulation process but in the *production* and material process. The Russian Legal Marxists, after Tugan Baranowki, and the German Social Democrats led by Hilferding, Otto Bauer, and Kautsky, took up this thesis and Hilferding and Kaustky held, purely on this basis, that capitalism could never break-down 'if only the proportions were maintained'. This one-sided view ignored the contradiction that falling profitability implied, which Marx addressed himself to in Volume III, of *Capital*, and in his *Theories of Surplus-Value.*

The underconsumptionist thesis, on the other hand, appears as the 'antithesis' of the proportionality theory by holding that capitalism must break down because of the tendency towards limited markets inherent in capitalist development. The main exponent of this thesis is Rosa Luxembourg, who, as we have seen, also misunderstood the reproduction schema. In her view capitalist accumulation was impossible *ab initio* without a 'third market' of non-capitalist consumers and producers. There are many variants within this thesis. Paul Sweezy, for instance, holds that it is 'the inherent *tendency* to expand the capacity to produce consumption goods more rapidly than the demand for consumption goods', which leads to the crisis. He postulates his own 'counteracting forces' to this tendency towards underconsumptionism. According to him, these forces divert the 'surplus' into 'socially unnecessary and wasteful channels'. As we shall see in Part Four, this leads Sweezy into attacking the Marxist Law of the Tendency of the Rate of Profit to Fall, and replacing it with his (and Baran's) law of the tendency of the 'economic surplus' to increase.

The weakness of both these theories is that they look at single aspects of the problem of capitalist production and ignore the central contradiction of the production process as a whole. The disproportionality school abstract the undisturbed accumulation process and abandon the law of falling profitability from the whole question. Grossmann was the first among this group of Marxists to point out this serious weakness in the theory. He showed correctly that capitalist production must lead to increase in the organic composition of capital with the accompanying increase in technical process and production of relative surplus-value. This development, according to him must lead to capitalist break-down due to lack of surplus-value.

Marx, in his refutation of Malthus and others who put forward under-consumptionist theories, had pointed out that the central contradiction in the accumulation process was the discrepancy between material and value production. Overproduction only occurred in relation to profitability, in other words it was the under-production of surplus-value in relation to the growing mass of total capital that led to crisis. Marx, in Part III of *Capital* volume III, and specifically in the *Grundrisse*, regarded the Law of the Tendency of the Rate of Profit to Fall as of *crucial* importance. He said, and we quote *in extenso:*

> 'This is in every respect the most important law of modern political economy, and the most essential for understanding the most difficult relations. It is the most important law from the historical standpoint. It is a law which, despite its simplicity, has never before been grasped and, even less, consciously articulated. Since this decline in the rate of profit is identical in meaning (1) with productive power already produced, and the foundation formed by it for new productions; this simultaneously presupposing an enormous development of scientific powers; (2) with the decline of the part of the capital already produced which must be exchanged for immediate labour, i.e., with the decline in the immediate labour required for the reproduction of an immense value, expressing itself in a great mass of products with low prices, because the total sum of prices is = to the reproduced capital + profit; (3) [with] the dimension of capital generally, including the portion of it which is not fixed Capital; hence intercourse on a magnificent scale, immense sum of exchange operations, large size of market and allsidedness of simultaneous labour; means of communication etc.; presence of the necessary consumption fund to undertake this gigantic process (workers' food, housing etc.); hence it is evident that the material productive power already present, already worked out, existing in the form of fixed capital, together with population etc., *in short all conditions of wealth, ie., the abundant development of the social individual — that the development of the productive forces brought about by the historical development of capital itself, when it reaches a certain point suspends the self-realis-ation of capital, instead of positing it'. (69)*

It is this growing incompatibility between the productive development of society and its hitherto existing relations of production, which expresses itself in bitter contradictions and crises. Marx did not see this crisis as necessarily bringing down the capitalist system. On the contrary, he saw this as a warning to the capitalists to adjust. The capitalist does this by the 'momentous suspension of labour and the annihilation of the great portion of capital' to a point where the process can continue. But this cannot go on indefinitely, since the recurrence of these crises leads to a 'repetition on a higher scale and finally to violent overthrow'. (69)

To put it more precisely, the crisis, while positing an end to the capitalist production and accumulation process, is at the same time the precondition for its continuance on a higher level until collapse. Crisis serves this function in a number of ways. Firstly, by destroying part of the mass of capital or by promoting its devaluation or annihilation by other means. This reduction of use-value and of the means of production will not affect the rate of surplus-value or the mass of surplus-value since these are to be seen in relation to the existing use-value of capital and its existing productive capacity. Secondly, the competition which gave rise to the crisis will be resolved by the restructuring towards greater concentration or monopoly. This helps the capitalist to decrease the value of labour power, which, coupled with the relative surplus population which results from the crisis, will help depress wages and increase the amount of surplus-value. Says Marx:

> 'Since the decline of profit signifies the same as the decrease of the size of the objectified labour which it produces and newly posits, capital will attempt every means of checking the smallness of the relation of living labour to the size of the capital generally, hence also the surplus-value if expressed as profit, relative to the presupposed capital, by reducing the allotment made to necessary labour and by expanding the quantity of surplus labour with regard to the whole labour employed'. (69)

Hence the annihilation, depreciation of capital and the degradation of labour. Thirdly, the introduction of new industries enables new investment to be made in areas of low composition of constant capital in order to yield a high rate of surplus-value. Moreover, the possibility of increasing constant capital enables the capitalist to intensify the exploitation of labour, including prolonging the working day, and hence assures the capitalist of increased surplus-value. Says Marx:

> "The fall [in the rate of profit] likewise is delayed by creation of new branches of production in which more direct labour in relation to capital is needed, or where the productive power of labour is not yet developed, i.e., the productive power of capital. Likewise monopolies'. (69)

How then does this analysis explain the crisis which occurred in the capitalist economy in the historical period we are considering? We have noted how expanding production in England developed with expanding markets at home and overseas. This position was, however, becoming challenged by the emergence of the US and Germany on the world market. Britain had maintained her export position partly with exports of loan capital. Marx had pointed out that a country may experience crisis in the credit system, because of the inability of that country to employ capital 'productively' or 'profitably'.

> 'The English, for example, are forced to lend their capital to other
> countries in order to create a market for their commodities. Over-
> production, the credit system, etc., are means by which capitalist
> production seeks to break through its own barriers and to produce
> over and above its own limits. Capitalist production, on the one
> hand, has this driving force; on the other hand, it only tolerates
> production commensurate with the profitable employment of
> existing capital. Hence crises arise, which simultaneously drive it
> onward and beyond (its own limits) and force it to put on seven-
> league boots, in order to reach a development of the productive
> forces which could only be achieved very slowly within its own
> limits'. (70)

According to Jenks for the twenty years ending in 1874 Britain had
been exporting an annual average 'surplus' of capital of about £15 million.
She had done this in addition to re-investing abroad all the earnings on
foreign investment already made. By the 1850s these amounted to £50
million a year, and 'surplus' capital exports ran well over £30 million.

Within three years of 1874 this trend was reversed. The reason was the
contraction of the loan business to Egypt, Russia, Hungary, Peru, Chile,
Brazil, and other places. The bankruptcy of Spain and the non-payment
of interest on the Turkish debt chilled the investment climate and the
financial difficulties in countries where Britain farmed her capital like
Austria, Latin America and Russia caused an abrupt paralysis of the market
for foreign loans. (71)

This was an abrupt crisis to a well sustained period of British investment
of loan capital; between 1815 and 1875 £500 million had been invested
overseas. This investment it should be remembered was the loan capital of
the rentier class. According to Jenks, this capital 'might otherwise not have
been employed at all'. (72) Thus the export of loan capital to assist the
export of capital goods had enabled Britain to profitably employ its
capital.

From then on there was a drive to increase capital investment at home.
Between 1870 and 1890 there was a considerable investment in technical
improvements and new industries during what came to be known as *the
second industrial revolution*. As capital found its way into the new
industries it stimulated inventions and innovations. What were these inventions? There can be no doubt that the main developments were the discovery
of steel, and the use of electricity, industrial chemistry, and oil. Before the
application of scientific methods steel was for all practical purposes a semi-
precious metal. The Bessemer process, introduced in 1864, opened the way
for the introduction of the open-hearth method in the 1860s. This in turn
led to the 'basic process' developed by Thomas and Gilchrist in 1875 which
made it possible to control the carbon content of steel to within very close
limits. Through the use of alloys it was now possible to obtain tool steel,
armaments, and stainless steel. The outcome was an increase in the

production of steel from an annual average of one million tons in 1874 to twenty seven million tons in 1913. The huge investment which competition in the industry generated had the effect of depressing rates of profit and hence of interest. But more importantly the new technical improvements helped to cut costs of production and to bring about a fall in the prices of iron by 60% and of coal by 40% while steel fell from £12 in 1874 to £4.55 in 1884. (72)

Obviously this considerable cheapening of products should have resulted in an increased relative surplus-value. This did not happen. On the contrary, the period was characterised by increased wages, which no doubt resulted from the increasing trade union organisation of the workers. Moreover the food on which the workers spent their wages was considerably cheapened by wheat imports from the US, a country which had been opened up by the new railway system and by improved ocean transport. This development enhanced real wages, while gains to the capitalist were minimal. Variable capital increased and the increase in constant capital was not rapid enough to enable a higher extraction of surplus-value. The rapid cheapening of constant capital and the increase in variable capital costs did not favour a higher return on investment capital. Moreover, markets in the US and Germany were being closed off behind protective barriers as they could now produce their own steel. The continental and US shift from iron to steel production and the shrinking market were serious blows to British steel manufacturers and many of them 'seriously considered abandoning production in England, and moving their business to Birmingham, Alabama'. (73)

Electricity, a new source of power and light was also revolutionising industry. It made possible the precise controls and complete mechanisation on which modern mass production depends. The discovery in 1886 of the industrial potentialities of electrolysis opened up new possibilities for the refinement of aluminium and generally affected the production of raw materials. One of the countries where electricity made gigantic steps was Germany. Electrical manufacture had existed there since the first electric telegraph in the 1840s. The years from 1860 to 1880 saw the invention (in 1861) and practical adoption (in 1877) of the telephone, the growth of telegraphy and the invention of the dynamo by Wener von Siemens (in 1867) which, after perfection, made the generation of electrical energy in any desired quantity possible and opened up its effective transmission over long distances. These new fields of investment opened up wide avenues for the flow of capital between 1900 and 1902. (74) Fierce competition in the industry created by the new techniques led to a drastic fall in prices. Since profitability could not be maintained, dividends dwindled, and many competitive firms in the industry collapsed. The result was the drawing together of bigger firms into monopolies to limit competition and to restore productivity and profitability. (See next chapter).

The next major invention was in the field of industrial chemistry.

Although chemical processes in metallurgy, tanning and fermentation had been known and used for many centuries, industrial chemistry as such was unknown. In 1860 it became possible to determine the correct number of atoms in a molecule by the recognition of the law that equal volumes of gasses under the same conditions contain the same number of molecules. The concept of structural arrangement of atoms in a molecule became known in 1865 and these new scientific achievements created the basis for new mass production industries including the Solvay-Ammonia Soda process and the catalytic processes for the manufacture of sulphuric acid and ammonia. Like electricity, chemical industry caught on quickly in Germany 'for the old Germany had laid a broad and true foundation of scientific knowledge'. Germany also benefitted from the special geological advantages of large deposits of pure rock salt, potash salts and various other common salts. (75) This industry too could only sustain itself through concentration of production units; 'few industries benefit more by the large scale production which marks the modern chemical manufacture'. (76)

Finally, the oil industry became a major new source for investment. Scientific advances in exploration and refinement of the product constituted a major step in a new direction. The first oil fields which were discovered in Pennsylvania in 1859 were soon being exploited by the Standard Oil Company founded in 1870. From then on petroleum became an important and growing source of power equivalent to coal and electricity as well as being a raw material for a wide range of petrochemicals. The invention of diamond drilling was just the technical advance needed to further this development, making it possible for oil to be used not only for domestic purposes (as kerosene and lubricants) but also in industry and transportation. As in the steel, electric and chemical industries, the new oil companies could only survive the profitability crisis through concentration of production from its early stage. Today 26 of the 50 largest industrial corporations in the US (accounting for over 62% of the total assets of the whole group) are in these four industries; and so are 30 of the 50 largest industrial corporations in the other capitalist countries outside the US (accounting for 73% of the total assets of the group) (77).

The telephone, the gramophone, the bicycle, the wireless, telegraphy, the electric lamp, the combustion engine, mechanised public transport, pneumatic tyres, the typewriter, cheap mass-circulation newsprint, synthetic fibres, artificial silk and synthetic plastics all made their appearance between 1867 and 1881, although the possibility of mass-producing them belonged to a later stage. Moreover, the upshoot of the new developments was an improvement in communications by sea and by land. Metal-built steamships using steel-hulls, steel-boilers, twin screws, and compound engines made sea transport a dominant form of transport in the last twenty years of the century. With the transatlantic cable service established in 1866, the scene was set for a new stage of the monopoly capitalism and imperialism, which we analyse in the next chapter.

However the developments analysed above had no immediate impact in the 1870-1880 period with which we are concerned. On the contrary, in vital sectors like the steel and iron industry, as outlined, the high composition of capital was rapidly leading to declining profitability. When innovations came, they had the effect of further depressing economic conditions, as the drop in prices of production merely led to cut-throat competition for markets among the three now major producers in those industries, bringing about a crisis due to the *historical* fall in the rate of profit in these major industries. In these circumstances it is not surprising that the Royal Commission on Depression of Trade and Industry in England reached the following general conclusion:

> 'We think that . . . over production has been one of the most prominent features of the course of trade during recent years; and that the depression under which we are now suffering may be partially explained by this fact . . . The remarkable feature of the present situation, and that which in our opinion distinguishes it from all previous periods of depression, is the length of time during which this overproduction has continued . . . We are satisfied that in recent years, and more particularly in the years during which the depression of trade has prevailed, the production of commodities generally and the accumulation of capital in this country have been proceeding at a rate more rapid than the increase of population'. (78)

This overproduction of capital which is also seen as overproduction of commodities could not be overcome by expanding the market, in a period of increasing challenge. The expansion of British exports which between 1860 and 1873 had risen by one-third came to an end. By 1876 the exports of British produce shrank (in value) by 25%. Exports to the US alone fell by 50%, and exports of iron and steel by one-third in tonnage and by more than 40% in value. The 1872 peak was not reached again until the turn of the century. (79)

The depression was not restricted to Britain alone. It also struck in Germany and the US; Russia and France which were less deeply industrialised were also affected, although not to the same extent. In Germany iron consumption fell by 50%. For Britain and for the other capitalist states there was clearly emerging a re-arrangement both internally and externally. The small competitive firms and the competition generated by the cheapening of production in major industries, as a result of innovations and inventions of this period, merely made the crisis worse. Thus we observe as early as the 1880s the emergence of associations and combinations formed by industrialists to counteract this competition. In 1884 a market sharing agreement between the British Rail Makers' Association and the German and Belgian Associations was entered into and was extended to the American and French Monopolists in 1904. The purpose was to overcome overproduction by selling above the new costs of production in order to restore profitability. A market became available only at higher monopoly prices. This arrangement became the general feature of a new imperialism much more aggressive than the free trade imperialism we have described.

REFERENCES

1.　M. Dobb, *Studies in the Development of Capitalism*, Routledge, Kegan Paul, (London, 1946) p.139-142.
2.　F. Engels, *The Condition of the Working Class in England*, Progress, (Moscow, 1973), p.46-7.
3.　E.J. Hobsbawn, *Industry and Empire*, Penguin, (London, 1969).
4.　K. Marx, *Capital*, Progress, (Moscow, 1971), Vol. I. p.357.
5.　M. Dobb, op. cit. p.275.
6.　M. Dobb, op. cit. p.277.
7.　M. Dobb, op. cit. p.277/8.
8.　Quoted in M. Dobb, p.278/9.
9.　K. Marx, *Capital*, op. cit. Vol.I. p.701.
10.　P.A. Sweezy, *The Theory of Capitalist Development.*, Monthly Review, (New York, 1942), pp. 93-94.
11.　K. Marx, *Capital*, op. cit. Vol. III. p.212.
12.　K. Marx, *Capital*, op. cit. Vol. I. p.379.
13.　K. Marx, *Capital*, op. cit. Vol. I. p.381.
14.　K. Marx, *Capital*, op. cit. Vol. III. p.239.
15.　K. Marx, *Capital*, op. cit. Vol. II, p.397-399.
16.　V.I. Lenin, *A Characterisation of Economic Romanticism*, in *Collected Works*, Progress, (Moscow), Vol. II. p.152.
17.　R. Luxembourg, *Accumulation of Capital*, Routledge, Kegan Paul, (London, 1951), p.48.
18.　R. Luxembourg, *Accumulation of Capital — An Anti-Critique*, Allen Lane, (London, 1972) p.49-50.
19.　R. Luxembourg, op. cit. p.54.
20.　R. Luxembourg, op. cit. p.57.
21.　Bukharin, *Imperialism and the Accumulation of Capital*, in Tarbuck (ed.) Allen Lane, (London, 1972) pp.196-197.
22.　K. Marx, *Capital*, op. cit. Vol. III, p.398.
23.　V.I. Lenin, *The Development of Capitalism in Russia*, Progress, (Moscow, 1974), pp.65-66.
24.　Palme R. Dutt, *India Today*, Golancz, (London, 1940), p.131-132.
25.　Jenks, *The Migration of British Capital*, Knopf, (New York, 1927), p.17.
26.　Jenks, op. cit. p.19.
27.　Marx, *Capital*, op. cit. Vol. I, p.360-2.
28.　M. Barrat-Brown, *After Imperialism*, Merlin, (London, 1970), p.62.
29.　W. Schlote, *British Overseas Trade 1700-1913*, Blackwell, (Oxford, 1952); p.41-2, in Hobsbawn: op. cit. p.109.
30.　Jenks, op. cit. p.152.
31.　E. J. Hobsbawn, op. cit. p.116.
32.　E. J. Hobsbawn, op. cit. p.332 and 413.
33.　M. Dobb, op. cit. p.270.
34.　Marx & Engels, *The German Ideology*, in *Selected Works*, Progress,

(Moscow, 1973), Vol.I. p.48-49.

35. D. Thompson, *England in the 19th Century*, Penguin, (London, 1967), p.68-72.

36. Bernard Semmel, *Free Trade Imperialism*, Cambridge University Press, (Cambridge, 1970); most of what follows is from this book.

37. Adam Smith, *Wealth of Nations*, Penguin, (London, 1970).

38. N. Brougham, quoted in Semmel op. cit. p.135.

39. B. Semmel, op. cit. p.91.

40. Quoted in Semmel, op. cit. p.91.

41. Quoted in Semmel, op. cit. p.111.

42. E.J. Hobsbawn, op. cit. p.134.

43. B. Semmel, op. cit. p.137.

44. D. Ricardo, *Principles of Political Economy & Taxation*, Pelican, (London, 1971), p.115.

45. K. Marx, *Speech on the Question of Free Trade*. Appendix in *Poverty of Philosophy*, Progress, (Moscow, 1973), pp.180-195.

46. B. Semmel, op. cit. p.139.

47. D. Ricardo, op. cit. p.152.

48. S. Sideri, *Trade and Power*, (Rotterdam, 1970), pp.8-9. Most of the material on this issue is from Sideri, unless otherwise indicated.

49. S. Sideri, op. cit. pp.42-3, 46. For a further discussion see Andre Gundar Frank, *Capitalism and Underdevelopment in Latin America*, Penguin, (London, 1971), chapters III and IV.

50. Quoted in Sideri op. cit. p.47.

51. N. Feis, *Europe, the Worlds Banker*, 1870-1914, Yale University Press, (Yale, 1930), p.41.

52. A. Hamilton, *Report on Manufactures* quoted in Bastable: *Commerce of Nations*, Methuen, (London, 1923), p.129-30.

53. F. List, *National System of Political Economy*, quoted in Semmel, op. cit. p.178.

54. John S. Mill, *On Some Unsettled Questions of Political Economy*, Kelly, (New York, 1971). p.45.

55. K. Marx, *Grundrisse*, Pelican, (London, 1973), p.887.

56. K. Marx, op. cit. p.884.

57. L.C. Knowles, *Economic Development in the Nineteenth Century*, Routledge, (London, 1926), p.259.

58. K. Marx, *Speech on Free Trade*, op. cit. p.194.

59. K. Marx, *Speech on Free Trade*, op. cit. p.194-5

60. G. Curzon, *Multilateral Commercial Diplomacy*, Joseph Michael (London, 1945), p.17.

61. E.J. Hobsbawn, op. cit. p.147.

62. M. Barrat-Brown, op. cit. p.84-5.

63. M. Dobb, op. cit. p.300.

64. J.B. Say, *Treatise on Political Economy*, Kelley, (New York, 1970).

65. D. Ricardo, op. cit. p.274.

REFERENCES

66.   K. Marx, *Theories of Surplus-Value*, Progress, (Moscow, 1969) Part II. pp.502-503.

67.   V.I. Lenin, *On The So-Called Market Question*, in *Collected Works*, op. cit. volume I. p.100.

68.   For a fuller discussion of these camps see Paul A Sweezy, (himself an underconsumptionist): op. cit. pp.190-234 and Ernest Mandel, *Marxist Economic Theory*, Merlin, (London, 1973).

69.   K. Marx, *Grundrisse*, op. cit. pp.745-75.

70.   K. Marx, *Theories of Surplus-Value*, Progress (Moscow, 1969), Part II.

71.   Jenks, op. cit. p.332; Dobb, op. cit. p.35.

72.   M. Dobb, op. cit. p.306.

73.   Jenks, op. cit. p.332.

74.   J.H. Clapham, *Economic Development of France and Germany, 1815-1914*, Cambridge University Press, (Cambridge, 1935), p.306.

75.   J.H. Clapham, op. cit. p.307..

76.   J.H. Clapham, op. cit. p.306.

77.   H. Magdoff, *The Age of Imperialism*, Monthly Review Press, (New York, 1969), p.30.

78.   Quoted in M. Dobb, op. cit. p.307.

79.   M. Dobb, op. cit. p.309.

PART THREE

MONOPOLY CAPITAL
AND MODERN IMPERIALISM

CHAPTER X

'The day of small nations has long passed away; the day of Empires has come'.

Chamberlain (1902)

'Half a century ago, when Marx was writing *Capital*, free competition appeared to the overwhelming majority of economists to be a natural law. Official science tried, by a conspiracy of silence, to kill the work of Marx, who by a theoretical and historical analysis of capitalism had proved that free competition gives rise to the concentration of production, which, in turn, at a certain stage of development, leads to monopoly. Today, monopoly has become a fact . . . and the rise of monopolies, as the result of the concentration of production, is the "general and fundamental law of the present stage of the development of capitalism" '.

Lenin

'I do not exactly know the cause of this sudden revolution, but there it is'.

Lord Salisbury (1891)

The Great Depression described at the end of the last chapter was, as we have seen, the first major manifestation of the contradictions of the capitalist economy. The sole motivation of the capitalist, to realise and accumulate surplus-value from labour under expanding production, inevitably leads to the concentration and centralisation of capital in fewer and fewer hands. This is the same thing as saying that in the process of capitalist production there is a tendency for the organic composition of capital to rise. This arises out of two other tendencies: first, the growth in the constant capital relative to the variable; and secondly the growth in the fixed portion of constant capital (buildings and machines) relative to raw, processed and auxiliary materials. Both of these movements lead to the rise in the average *size* of the productive unit.

Marx differentiated between the two ways in which this growth takes place. Firstly by *concentration;* this occurs when the individual capitalist's appetite to accumulate results in the quantity of capital under his control increasing and making it possible for him to enlarge the scale of his production. Those who do not succeed are eliminated in the competitive process which becomes the very essence of concentration. It is a process which is anti-competition but it never successfully disposes of all competition. Secondly by *centralisation*; capital which is already in existence is combined:

> 'This process differs from the former in this, that it only presupposes a change in the distribution of capital already to hand and functioning; its field of action is therefore not limited by the absolute growth of social wealth, by the absolute limits of accumulation. Capital grows in one place to a huge mass in a single hand because it has in another place been lost by many. This is centralisation proper, as distinct from accumulation and concentration'. (1)

This process is very much hastened by the operation of the economies of large-scale production which also results from the competitive struggle in production. This second way in which centralisation of capital takes place is made possible through the credit system which includes in this sense not only the banks but also financial investment houses and security and stock markets. This does not imply the expropriation of smaller capitalists as such by the larger ones. It consists in the 'amalgamation of a number of capitals which already exist or are in the process of formation . . . by the smoother road of forming stock companies'. Without this centralisation of capital, railway construction would have waited, according to Marx, 'until accumulation should have enabled a few individual capitals to undertake the construction'.

The effects of concentration and centralisation of capital are threefold: (2) first, they lead to socialisation and 'rationalisation' of the labour process within the confines of capitalist production; second, they hasten technical change; and third, they progressively replace competition among a large number of firms by monopolistic or oligopolistic control over production. These developments are not contrived by the capitalists, although in the process of competition it is the shrewdest capitalist who survives; nonetheless from the point of view of the system as a whole, capitalism can have no other outcome.

As we observed in the last chapter innovations were undertaken by the capitalists in the period prior to the depression which resulted in lower prices and profitability. Competition between the smaller units made the situation worse. It was quite natural after this experience that the capitalists should find ways of curtailing competition and ensuring higher profitability, and this consciousness of the dangers of competition was itself the result of the already gathering storm of concentration in the production, ownership and control of major industries.

In the US and Germany this concentration had emerged earlier. Industrial development in Germany went through four rapid stages: spinning by machinery; weaving by machinery; production by the factory system and lastly from factory organisation to combines. (3) This was within a short period of about forty years. In the US as early as 1870 trusts began to appear on the scene, in areas like electricity, the chemical industry and steel where competition against England was possible only on the basis of large units.

Thus the era which has been called the age of free trade is characterised by small-sized firms at one end and concentration of production at the other. One compilation on the history of the 'formation of monopolies' by Herman Levy in 1909 (quoted by Lenin) had this to say:

'Isolated examples of capitalist monopoly could be cited from the period preceding 1860; in these could be discerned the embryo of the forms that are common today; but all this undoubtedly represents a prehistory of the cartels. The real beginning of modern monopoly goes back, at the earliest, to the sixties. The first important period of development of monopoly commenced with the international industrial depression of the seventies and lasted until the beginning of the nineties. If we examine the question on a European scale, we find that the development of free competition reached its apex in the sixties and seventies. It is then that Britain competed the construction of her old-style capitalist organisation'. (4)

It was during the period of the depression of 1873, which ended in 1890 with a short boom, that cartels were resorted to in order to take advantage of the favourable business conditions. But this resulted in rising prices and this first stage ended in a crash. Another period of bad trade ensued for five years, which set the stage for the next phase of cartel formation; since then they have become a key feature of economic life.

In the US concentration was greater. Almost one half of total production was carried on in 1900 by one hundredth of all enterprises. In 1903 the trusts controlled the production of asphalt, lead, petroleum, electric appliances, and agricultural machinery plus a number of industries including chemicals, tobacco and sugar. A report of the Ways and Means Committee of the US House of Representatives in 1913 enumerated 224 consolidations of varying degrees of magnitude. (5)

What were the forms which this concentration of production took and how did these various forms operate? Concentration is attained by various forms of agreements intended to protect, maintain and/or increase the rate of profit. We will consider seven forms of this process. (6)

Gentlemen's agreements: These are voluntary agreements between producers not to sell below certain prices or in certain areas. An example is the agreement by British soap makers in 1901. This form is, however, a weak one and involves the articulation of a common policy among competitors without binding force. Price-regulating associations: These are formal agreements and arrangements of the above. Examples of this are shipping conferences. Pools: These are price agreements sharing out definite markets allocated to each producer. A pool of this kind came into being in the steel-making industry in the US. The American meat packers pool operated for two decades. Such arrangements are dependent on the good will of members and equally unstable.

Cartels, buying or selling syndicates: These are of a more permanent nature than the first three referred to above. The monopolists come to an agreement on the terms of sale, dates of payment, etc.; divide the market among themselves; fix the quantity of goods to be produced; fix prices; and divide profits among the various enterprises. The number of cartels was estimated in Germany at 250 in 1896 and at 385 in 1905 with 12,000 firms participating. There is machinery for disciplining members by a committee. This form may result in merger. Trusts: These are groups to which previously competing companies entrust their shares, receiving certificates in exchange which indicate the proportions of their partici- pation in the joint effort. In the US their number was estimated at 185 in 1900 and 250 in 1905. The Sherman Act of 1890 declared this type of grouping illegal but they continued to operate under different guises.

Holding Company or Konzern: This is a cover under which apparently independent enterprises concentrate financial control through 'a holder'. It remains an instrument commonly used in Germany (Konzern), the US, Belgium and France. The holding company makes it possible to reduce the proportion of capital needed in order to wield effective control over a large number of companies, through various techniques such as 'waterfall' shareholding or cross-share-holding.

Mergers: These are the most 'solid' and lasting form of concentration, in which the legal or financial independence of the constituent companies vanishes. One can draw a distinction between horizontal trusts merging in a single branch of industry such as cigarettes, motor cars, aircraft etc., and vertical trusts merging complimentary groups of firms. The last type of trusts in turn can be divided into: (a) divergent trusts formed from firms which make raw materials and semi-finished or finished products (e.g. US Steel Corporation); (b) convergent trusts which bring together firms making the different raw materials or semi-finished products which go into the making of one finished product (e.g. aircraft); (c) heterogen- eous trusts which have no common bond except that they are under financial control of a single financial oligarchy (e.g. the Lever trust in the 1920s).

Hilferding pointed out in his study that 'combination' firstly, levels out the fluctuations of trade and thereafter assures to the combined enterprise a more stable rate of profit; secondly, has the effect of elimin- ating trade among those units which combine; thirdly, makes possible technical improvements, and consequently, the acquisition of super- profits over and above those obtained by the 'pure' non-combined enterprise; and fourthly, strengthens the position in the competitive struggle of the combined enterprise relative to the 'pure' enterprise during periods of serious depression when the fall in raw material prices does not keep pace with the fall in prices of manufactured goods. (7)

The division of the world by monopolies amongst themselves, as we shall see later, was made possible by international cartel agreements. These were necessary, but did not remove competition entirely. On the contrary, rivalry and undercutting arose and brought the arrangements to a crisis. This was unavoidable and justifiable as long as each monopoly group made a gain. The American cartels and trusts referred to above were used to penetrate Europe, in spite of which international cartel agreements were entered into between the different national cartels. As Raymond Vernon states:

> 'As a result, between 1900 and 1940, international cartel agreements were developed in practically every important processed metal, in most important chemical products, in key pharmaceuticals, and in a variety of miscellaneous manufactures running the alphabetical gamut from alkalis to zinc. The object of these agreements was generally the same as that of similar agreements in the raw materials industry; to take the uncertainties out of the market. Practically all such agreements included some provision for the geographical division of markets among participants. If the product was standardized and price-sensitive, as in the case of alkalis and steel, some arrangements were also made for fixing the prices; if product was technologically difficult and relatively insensitive to price differences, as in the case of advanced chemicals and machinery, there were measures to prevent any participant from stealing a technological march on the others. As a result of arrangements of this sort, US participants generally found their freedom of action curtailed in Europe, Africa and the British Commonwealth; at the same time, US firms usually gained some relief from competition in North America and Latin America'. (8)

The inter-war years merely increased the international cartel arrangements principally because of the excess capacity of plant after the war. As we have seen, this relative increase in constant capital tended to lower the rate of profit for the enterprise. This could only be counteracted, as Marx said, by the 'momentous suspension of labour and the annihilation of the great portion of capital'. Combination at home and cartels overseas could only help to trim this overcapacity. The 'national' industrial concentration of the earlier period (around 1880-1900) created the necessary preconditions for these international arrangements. It would have been difficult for small concerns to drum out an international cartel. It was necessary for companies like Imperial Chemical Industries, IG Farben, Du Pont, Allied Chemical, etc. to take over smaller firms in their different countries before they could talk international monopoly. (9)

Thus the first international cartel came into being in 1896, between US ALCOA and Swiss AG. In 1901 it was expanded to include three new monopolies. But it is after 1918 that cartels on an international scale became a common feature.

As can be seen, these were the first efforts at coordinating international capitalist monopolies. Their success depended on mutual advantage. If mututal advantage ceased to exist, they broke down and international rivalries and undercutting started all over again. The first steel cartel, established in 1926 between the German, Luxembourg, Belgian, Saar, and French monopolies, undertook to order their interests, each country being allocated a production and export quota, on condition that those who exceeded their quota were to be fined. These high hopes were, shattered, however, when the German monopolists suffering from an enormous over-capacity broke the quota requirement. The fines imposed on them exceeded $10 million which was 95% of all the fines incurred by all members. By mid-1931 the cartel had collapsed. (9)

This was followed by another cartel in the sale of bars, rods, structural shapes, etc., between the British, Americans, Czechs, Poles and Austrian monopolies, which under more favourable conditions worked better. Here the exports of each country were determined centrally, and all export sales were made through one organisation. Distributors were licenced and guaranteed a profit and a share of their local market.

In the oil industry the first oil cartel was officially formed in 1928 by Shell, Anglo-Persian (BP), and Standard Oil (New Jersey), who agreed to combine their non-US interests and share each others facilities. They agreed to set common prices, and not to 'steal' each other's customers. They also coordinated their advertising and planning. This cartel arrangement maintained prices at very high levels but it was broken very often and its effectiveness was restricted.

Non-compliance with cartel arrangements sometime resulted in nasty situations for the non-complier. Christopher Tugendhat cites the example of his father and another who started an independent (oil) refinery in Britain, The Manchester Oil Refinery, which was contrary to the interests of the cartel. Shell threatened them with non-supply of crude oil. In their case, however, the situation was saved by an American subsidiary of the same company which agreed to sell them the crude oil. Their problems were not at an end, however: they could not find a market in England. They were again saved by a Belgian subsidiary of Gulf Oil, which agreed to buy their product. (10)

The methods used here were not different from those categorised by a German economist, Kestner, whom Lenin quoted in his pamphlet *Imperialism*. In his book on 'compulsory organisation', Kestner, gave the following methods of bringing to book a non-complier in a cartel: (a) stopping supplies of raw materials; (b) stopping supply of labour by means of 'alliances' between employers and labour unions who agreed to work only for cartelised enterprises; (c) cutting off deliveries; (d) closing of trade outlets; (e) agreements with the buyers, by which the latter undertook only to trade with the cartels; (f) systematic price cutting (to ruin 'outside' firms, i.e., those which refused to submit to the monopolists. Millions were spent in order to sell goods for a certain time below their cost price);

(g) stopping credits; (h) boycott.

As we shall see later in Part IV, cartels and trusts are being superseded but not entirely destroyed by the emergence of transnational corporations, which is a new phase of imperialism led by US monopolists to penetrate the markets and exploit the raw materials of other countries on a larger scale.

But, having looked at the forms and arrangements of concentration and centralisation, it is necessary to go into the changes that take place in the actual process through which expropriation of surplus-value takes place under monopoly capitalism. Under earlier competitive capitalism prices were determined by costs of production under the theory of value. The capitalist's surplus-value was calculated as a cost of production in the form of profit, interest, rent, etc. Under monopoly the prices are distorted and are no longer determined in this way, although the law of value still operates. The capitalist's profit is fixed over and above the costs of production available under a purely competitive model. This is possible because the capitalist is in a monopolistic position and in control of a sector of the industry, whereby he is enabled to restrict supply at will and in this way fix a monopoly price. Since the level of wages is in general at the point calculated to meet the subsistence and reproduction needs of the work force, it follows that it will normally not fall or for long remain below that minimum level. Hence the monopoly capitalists' drive for the extra profit would be directed to other quarters. As Marx has observed:

'The monopoly price of certain commodities would merely transfer a portion of the profit of the other producers of commodities to the commodities with a monopoly price. A local disturbance in the distribution of the surplus-value among the various spheres of production would take place . . . but they would leave the boundaries of the surplus-value itself unaltered. If a commodity with a monopoly price should enter into the necessary consumption of the labourer, it would increase the wages and thereby reduce the surplus-value if the labourer would receive the value of his labour power the same as before. But such a commodity might also depress wages below the value of labour power, of course only to the extent that wages would be higher than the physical minimum of subsistence. In this case the monopoly price would be paid by a deduction from the real wages — and from the profits of the other capitalists'. (11)

This fact has the tendency to further distort and disrupt the general level of prices normal under competitive capitalism.

The tendency to the equalisation of profit rates gives way to the tendency to spreading of monopoly wherever it appears. (12) As soon as monopoly becomes general in the particular industry, the gains of the monopolists are offset by the losses of the smaller capitalists. Thus there is a kind of monopolist equalisation of profit rates, to the extent that the monopolists in other related industries collaborate at this new level. Sweezy illustrates this spreading principle as follows:

'A certain industry, say iron ore production, is monopolised and the price raised, part of the resulting loss is borne by pig-iron producers, who now have an increased incentive to combine both to raise their prices to the steel industry and to bargain for lower prices from the ore industry. In this way combination will spread in concentric circles from any given point of origin, seizing upon those industries where circumstances are favourable to the establishment and maintenance of monopoly conditions'. (13)

This, however, affects all production, even in those areas where monopoly conditions are not present. Hence monopoly equalisation of profit will be an uneven phenomenon and the usual activators of equalisation, mobility of capital and labour, will not operate throughout the whole economy. What prevails is a hierarchy of profit rates, highest in monopoly industries, lowest in small-scale 'competitive' firms. The prices in the small-scale industries must operate within the general level of monopoly prices, although at the lower end of the scale, particularly where monopolies, as is usually the case, dominate key industries which affect most production.

Monopoly also affects the segments into which surplus-value is divided, by reducing their number. This is the result of the increase in accumulation which monopoly brings about. The process, as we shall see, leads to vertical integration of firms under monopoly and thereby does away with other partakers of surplus-value, which manifests itself in the increased costs of distribution. Since merchant capital produces no surplus-value but merely distributes industrial products, it follows that merchant profit is a segment of surplus-value. It follows that since the expansion of the capitalist reproduction process requires a growth in commercial capital, the monopoly capitalists' appetite to increase accumulation will be enhanced by the monopolist directly investing in this sector, thus retaining the merchant's profit and eliminating independent trade.

Another phenomenon which results from monopoly is its tendency to restrict output. Competitive capitalism expands production because of the high profits that can be reaped thanks to youthful capitalism's economies of scale, economies which demand the intensification of labour and an expanding market. Monopoly profit, however, comes in on a negative level. Monopoly contains output in order to reap a monopoly profit. This does not mean that struggle among the monopolies stops once they are assured of this profit. On the contrary, as Engels had the insight to note at a very early stage of his development:

'Every competitor *cannot but* desire to have the monopoly . . . Competition is based on self-interest, and self-interest in turn breeds monopoly. In short, competition passes over into monopoly. On the other hand, monopoly cannot stem the tide of competition — indeed it itself breeds competition; just as a prohibition of imports, for instance, or high tariffs positively breed the competition of smuggling. The contradiction of competition is exactly the same as that of private property. It is in the interest of each to possess everything but in the interest of the whole that each possesses an equal amount. Thus the general and the individual are diametrically opposed to each other. The contradiction of competition is that each cannot but desire the monopoly, whilst the whole as such is bound to lose by monopoly and must therefore remove it'. (14)

The struggle to remove monopoly in this case is resisted by other monopolists and any effort to cut prices in order to monopolise the market is similarly resisted. In the end the monopolists agree to maintain prices but only temporarily. Monopoly has no alternative but to resort to salesmanship and advertisement, and competition becomes more pronounced in these spheres, indeed it becomes an endless and burgeoning activity of monopoly capitalism, all directed to realising surplus-value.

CHAPTER XI

Central to the phenomenon of imperialism is the role of banks. Marx had stated that the banking system, so far as its formal organisation and centralisation is concerned, was 'the most artificial and most developed product turned out by the capitalist mode of production . . . [creating] an immense power . . . over commerce and industry . . . [it] possesses indeed the form of universal book keeping and distribution of means of production on social scale, but solely the form'. (15)

The function of the bank was to serve as middleman in the making of payments, turning inactive money into active, and making a profit in the process. This served the interests of the capitalist very well. But with the appearance of concentration of capital by means of cartels, trusts and syndicates as outlined, the banks *also* took on a new role. Just like all other capitalist enterprises, the banks operated initially in competition with several other small banks. Very soon, however, particularly in periods of crises, the bigger banks began to buy off the smaller ones. As the banking system developed and became concentrated into a small number of establishments, they grew from the role of modest middlemen into powerful monopolies commanding almost the whole of the money capital of all the capitalists and the small sized businesses, and the larger part of the means of production and sources of raw materials in many countries. This concentration took gigantic leaps in all the European countries.

In 1907-1908 the combined deposits of the German joint-stock banks, each having a capital of more than one million marks, amounted to 7,000 million marks; in 1912-13 these had grown to 9,800 million an increase of 25% in five years, and of the 2,800 million increase, 2,750 million was divided among 57 banks, each having a capital of more than 10 million marks. In Great Britain and Ireland in 1910 there were in all 7,151 branches of banks. Four big banks had more than 400 branches each, four had more than 200 branches each and eleven more than 100 each. In France three very big banks extended their operations from 64 branches, with capital of 200 million francs in 1870, to 1,229 branches, with capital of 887 million francs; raising their deposits in the process from 427 million to 4,363 million francs in the same period. (16)

What is important, of course, is the relationship established between the banks and the capitalist class with this concentration of capital. From the

110

operation of carrying the current accounts of a few capitalists, a purely technical and auxiliary operation, the banks extend the relationship into one that they dominate. Here we see a few monopolists using their newly acquired power through their knowledge of the accounts of the individual capitalists, first to ascertain exactly the financial position of the various capitalists, then to control them, and to influence them by restricting or enlarging, facilitating or hindering credits. The banks increasingly assume the role of a stock exchange, in the process becoming the determinant of stock and loan issues.

The concentration of bank capital, just like that of any other capitalist enterprise, proceeded through the various forms already referred to, but the one popularly used was that of bank trusts. Through these trusts and 'holding' companies, big banks were able to control the finances of other smaller banks still in existence.

The inter-connection of banks and industry, a fact very much accentuated by link-ups in boards of directors of banks and big industry, also helped to restrict competition in industry itself. The banks' interest in being repaid and reaping a profit gave them a more than casual interest in the profitability of the enterprises to which they made loans, and since that profitability under conditions of increasing concentration of production and capital became more strained with each passing day, it followed that unless the enterprise was moving in the direction of monopoly, the banks would find it harder to retrieve their loans and profit.

It is not surprising therefore that the banks should have become agents for the encouragement of concentration of production. The more an enterprise became dependent on a bank for its operating capital as well as its capital investment, the more it opened itself to this pressure by the banks, and since small and middle enterprises would have only small capital, it became almost inevitable that the banks would have a considerable say in their affairs. Any indebtedness on the part of an enterprise soon attracted directors representing the banks on the board of directors of the enterprise and further facilitated the process of coalescence of capital.*

In this way, and through the use of the 'holding company', a financial oligarchy emerges, which entirely depends on the manipulation of *finance capital*. Capital invested abroad in railways, in mines and in plantations comes from this oligarchy who control 'the money (finance) market'. They issue out bonds, loans and stocks, take out debentures on industry and business, finance smaller financial houses and back up insurance houses creating an ever interlocking web-like financial empire which merges monopoly banks and monopoly industry.

Marx in the chapter on the role of credit in capitalist production (17) theoretically anticipated this movement when he pointed out that the formation of stock companies, which is facilitated by the credit system and banks, has the effect of transforming the actually funcioning capitalist into 'a mere manager', and administrator of other peoples capital. It

*See appendix for additional paragraphs; p.281.

has also the effect of transforming the owner of capital into 'a mere owner' of money capital, who is now turned into a receiver of interest; his return is a 'mere compensation for owning capital that is now entirely divorced from the function in the actual process of reproduction'. This, according to Marx was the 'abolition of the capitalist mode of production within the capitalist mode of production itself', and hence was a 'self dissolving contradiction' which *prima facie* represents 'a mere phase of transition to a new form of production'. This development establishes a monopoly in certain spheres and thereby requires state interference:

> 'It produces a new financial aristocracy, a new variety of parasites in the shape of promoters, speculators, and simply nominal directors, a whole system of swindling and cheating by means of corporation promotion, stock issuance, and stock speculation. It is private production without the control of private property'. (18)

The growth of monopoly almost coincided with the growth of finance capital. It is for this reason that Lenin treated the separation of ownership of capital and its application as a general characteristic of capitalism. This was certainly true for competitive capitalism and for capitalism approaching monopoly. He stated:

> 'It is characteristic of capitalism in general that the ownership of capital is separated from the application of capital to production, that money capital is separated from industrial or productive capital, and that the rentier, who lives entirely on income obtained from money capital, *is separated from the entrepreneur and from all who are directly concerned in the management of capital.* Imperialism, or the domination of finance capital, is the highest stage of capitalism in which this separation reaches vast proportions. The supremacy of finance capital over all other forms of capital means the predominances of the rentier and of the financial oligarchy; it means that a small number of financially 'powerful' states stand out among all the rest'. (19)

Here the finance oligarchy being the coalescence of bank and industrial monopolists subordinate all other capitalists and through this financial control exploit them by concentrating their earnings or saved profits within the financial system of the oligarchy, who continue to be the financiers of production of such enterprise.

But perhaps one of the most important developments which emerges with finance capital is the shift in emphasis *from the export of goods to export of capital.* Since capitalism inevitably leads to uneven development of individual enterprises, individual branches of industry, and individual countries, it follows that the few rich countries will struggle for outlets for the profitable use of this capital.

The crucial distinction that arises with the new emphasis on export of finance capital, as opposed to earlier exports of loan capital, is that the financial oligarchy now directly utilises this capital in the production abroad of particular products it considers essential to its production process at home. In this same way it opens markets in new areas.

Lenin emphasised the fact that these vast sums of capital are *surplus* in the imperialist countries in the full knowledge of the fact that there exists simultaneously a great need for such capital in the imperialist countries themselves, for the development of agriculture, which is starved of much needed capital, to feed the population cheaply, and for the raising of the standards of living in health, housing and other social services. Such measures, however, would be in contradiction to the essence of capitalism. Capitalism does not produce use-values *qua* use-values, but with a view to their being posited as exchange-values in production with the sole purpose of realising surplus-value. Not to do so would be disastrous for the financial oligarchy. As Marx pointed out:

> 'If capital is sent to foreign countries, it is not done because there is absolutely no employment to be had for it at home. It is done because it can be employed at a higher rate of profit in a foreign country'. (20)

As we have seen, monopoly arose at a time when areas of high returns like the US were beginning to become major competitors in the world market. By 1890, through cartelisation and trusts, the US and Germany had overtaken Britain in the production of steel, and the British share of the European market was contracting. We have already seen how Latin America and India were at this period becoming major producers of raw materials and markets for the British textile industry and other products. The same was true in respect of export of capital.

Whereas before the 1840s the loan capital exports from Britain were in the form of government loans for construction of railways and other public utilities (mostly in the US and Europe), by the 1860s most of the capital was finance capital, in the form of portfolio investments held either by banks or by individual enterprises and individuals. The movement of exports of capital away from the old centres to the new 'colonial' ones was a new feature. Lenin's thesis was that by the 1870s capitalism had gained a new momentum under monopoly and a general movement towards a new imperialism based on finance capital had emerged.

Whereas Empire and Latin American 'informal colonial' investments constituted 46.5% of all Britain's foreign investments in the 1880s, by 1929 they were accounting for 81% of her total foreign investments. Of this the Empire provided 36% in the 1860s and 59% in 1929, whereas Latin America provided opportunity for 10.5% in the 1860s and 22% in 1929. (21) This was clearly a new direction and movement. To argue that Latin America was not part of the Empire is facile and formalistic. Imperialism subjugates all the weak countries or regions whether formally recognised as colonies or not. The case of Portugal which we have tried to outline is instructive in this respect.

In terms of quantities, total British foreign investment between 1870 and 1913 increased from £1,000 million in 1870 to £4,000 million in

1913. (22) Professor A.K. Cairncross has estimated the net export of capital at £2.4 billion which yielded an income to Britain of £4.1 billion. (22) Although many other studies (23) have been undertaken to contest and modify these figures, it still remains true that Britain was able to finance its new investment overseas out of the proceeds of previous investment! These figures do not even include the salaries, pensions and emoluments paid to the British civil servants in the colonies.

Although it must be emphasised that capital exports assumed greater importance than in the previous period under competitive capitalism, one must also note that Britain's capital exports assisted British industry not only in production but also in enlarging her market. According to Professor Caincross:

> 'In the short period . . . an increase in activity abroad, generally associated with increase in foreign investments by Britain, pulled the country out of the pre-1914 slumps by improving the prospects of the export industries. If investment was on the continent, the textile industries gained; if in America or the colonies, the metal industries expanded'. (24)

Professor Caincross did not, however, restrict his assessment of whether foreign investments did or did not pay purely to the level of profit figures. His analysis revealed the 'unquantifiable' benefits which accrued to Britain as a result of its investment activity overseas.

Posing himself the question of whether Britain gained from these investments, he maintained that the gain to British export industries was quite straightforward. There was, as a result of the investment, expansion of buying power in the British markets, increased orders for equipment, with the prospect of additional orders later for replacement and increased sales to consumers. Moreover, he continued, another source of gain lay in the spread of information on profitable openings for investments. Companies promoted in Britain, however controlled, were often staffed by British engineers or British managers who tended to specify British machinery for new construction and equipment for replacement.

> 'Thus the market imperfections which allowed Britain to dominate the business of exports (for industrial purposes at any rate) worked also in the Victorian age to put large sections of the export industry in a semi-monopolistic position'. (25)

But this was not all. Professor Caincross maintains that Britain gained also through the cheapening of imports, and this is where the real service to industry lay, for as we have observed this helped the profitability of the monopolies. In the seven years 1907-1914 Britain provided £600m for the construction of railways in countries supplying her with foodstuffs and raw materials.

> 'At a time when the population was increasing rapidly it was vital that foodstuffs should be obtained as cheaply as possible'. (25)

So quite apart from the fact that the capital investment of £2.4 billion had resulted in an income of £4.1 billion, there were the above additional indirect gains as a result of the investment in this period.

What Professor Caincross describes was clearly reinforced by the administrative and legal regime designed by the British state to meet the demands of monopoly capital. Whereas in the competitive capitalism of free trade imperialism, state intervention was minimal, now the state began to take an active part in assisting monopoly profit. The Colonial Stocks Acts passed by the British Parliament ensured that a good amount of British finance capital would go to the colonies and dominions, where conditions for its profitable employment existed. Under the Act as amended in 1900, all colonial and dominion securities duly registered in the United Kingdom, which observed Treasury orders, were eligible for inclusion among 'Trustee Securities', which status enabled them to become purchasable by trust bodies and other institutions whose choice was restricted. These trust funds were a considerably concentrated form of capital which often found its way to the colonies and dominions.

Under section 2 of the Act, the British Treasury imposed conditions which had to be observed by the borrowing colonial and dominion governments 'to augment the confidence felt by investors'. (24) Firstly, the borrower had to pass legislation in the colony and dominion to provide for the payment out of its revenues any sums adjudged due under a judgement, decree, rule, or order of a court in the United Kingdom. Secondly, the borrower had to ensure that adequate funds existed to satisfy these types of claims. Thirdly, the borrower had to place on record the expressed opinion that any of its legislation 'which appears to the Imperial Government to alter any of the provisions affecting the security to the injury of the investor, or to involve a departure from the original security contract would be disavowed'. (26)

The colonies and dominions where these measures could be enforced had other advantages. As Feis has remarked:

> 'A trust in consanguinity, in British qualities transplanted abroad, bred the conviction that they were the safest outside fields of investment and so widely favoured. Then, too, there was the assurance that a substantial part of such borrowing would be expended in the United Kingdom. For under the British colonial regulations, the borrowing of the colonies not possessing responsible self-government was arranged through Crown Agents . . . Into their care was given the purchasing of colonial governments in foreign markets. In the offices of these agents were drawn the specifications for colonial railways, harbour works, public utility plants, and the contracts for materials signed'. (26)

The same procedures were operated through the office of the Secretary of State for India; it was stated by the Under Secretary of State for India in 1923 that in the past 95 % of the borrowed funds spent abroad by the Indian Government had been on purchases in the United Kingdom. Such was also the case with the self-governing dominions, the largest borrowers

115

of whom retained financial and purchasing agents in London. Adds Feis:

> 'The accepted belief that foreign investment always must stimulate foreign sales after all, rested upon abstract, complex reasoning. In the case of colonial and dominion loans the fact became self-evident. Thus opinion in industrial circles supported the preference conferred by the Colonial Stocks Act'. (26)

A very similar process of concentration and export of capital, with attendant advantages for home industry, went on in Germany and France, (26) although both countries tended to invest more heavily in Europe. The main industrial powers, with the assistance of their national states' guarantees on investment, began an unprecedented expansion into the capital markets of the world. There was no field which was profitable into which finance capital did not find its way, whether it was railways, mines, plantations, steamship lines, banks or foreign securities. In other words the type of fields that, as we shall see in the next chapter, were essential to the development of agricultural and raw material production. As Bukharin observed:

> 'The general direction of the movement is, of course, indicated by the difference in the rates of profit (or rate of interest): the more developed the country, the lower is the rate of profit, the greater is the "over production" of capital, and consequently the lower is the demand for capital and the stronger the expulsion process. Conversely, the higher the rate of profit, the lower the organic composition of capital, the greater is the demand for it and the greater is the attraction'. (27)

Thus it can be seen that the contradiction created by overproduction of capital leads to cartels, trusts and syndicates, to a contradiction between the growth of the productive forces on the one hand, and the limits created by a narrow national economic organisation on the other. This is resolved partly by the internationalisation of economic life. In the words of Hilferding:

> 'The policy of finance capital pursues a three-fold aim: first, the creation of the largest possible economic territory which secondly, must be protected against foreign competition by tariff walls, and thus, thirdly, must become an area of exploitation for the national monopoly companies'. (28)

This opens colonial agrarian regions to the cartels, trusts and syndicates and consequently creates sources of raw materials, sale markets and spheres of capital investment, with the aim of increasing the rate of profit for the monopolies. In the next chapter we examine this new phase of colonisation, in a period of monopoly capitalism; in short, imperialism under the sway of finance capital.

CHAPTER XII

In distinguishing the old imperialism from the new, Lenin stated that the principal feature of the latest stage of capitalism was the domination of monopolist associations of big employers. These were firmly established when *all* the resources of raw materials were captured by one group. He pointed out that colonial possessions alone gave complete guarantee against all contingencies in the struggle against competitors, including cases of the adversary wanting to be protected by a law establishing a state monopoly. He further observed that the more capitalism was developed, the more strongly the shortage of raw materials was felt, the more intense the competition and hunt for sources of raw materials throughout the whole world, and the more desperate the struggle for the acquisition of colonies became. It did not matter that the monopoly did not require the raw materials immediately:

> 'Finance capital is interested not only in the already discovered sources of raw materials but also in potential sources, because present day technical development is extremely rapid, and land which is useless today may be improved tomorrow if new methods are devised . . . and if large amounts of capital are invested . . . Hence the inevitable striving of finance capital to enlarge its sphere of influence and even its actual territory'. (29)

He castigated those who argued like Kautsky that the question of raw materials was not a problem for imperialism, because these could be obtained on the open market, without a 'costly and dangerous' colonial policy, and that the supply of raw materials could be increased simply by improving conditions of agriculture in general. This argument ignores the principal features of the latest stage of capitalism, namely the monopolies:

> 'The free market is becoming more and more a thing of the past; monopolist syndicates and trusts are restricting it every passing day, and "simply" improving conditions in agriculture means improving the conditions of the masses, raising wages and reducing profits. Where, except in the imagination of sentimental reformists, are there any trusts capable of concerning themselves with the conditions of the masses instead of the conquest of colonies'. (29)

Furthermore, the export of finance capital to the colonies was best in that it was easier there to employ monopoly methods to eliminate competitors, to ensure supplies and to secure necessary 'connections'. (29) Finally, Lenin recognised that 'the non-economic superstructure which grows up on the basis of finance capital, its politics and its ideology' also encouraged colonial conquest. Understood in this context, Cecil Rhodes' 'dreams of a British Africa', the 'personality' of Joseph Chamberlain, as well as the struggle of the military brass for retention of India, etc., (30) appear as superstructural features arising out of finance capital, as the ideology and politics of imperialism.

Marx observed that once the common interests of the 'moneyocracy', the 'oligarchy', and the 'millocracy' had conquered India with their armies, turned it into their landed estates and inundated it with their fabrics, the interests of the industrialists had become dependent on the Indian market and it became necessary to create 'fresh productive powers' in India, after having ruined her native industry. He stated:

> 'You cannot continue to inundate a country with your manufactures, unless you enable it to give you some produce in return'. (31)

Under monopoly India was turned into a colony of a new type to which finance capital was exported for the production of surplus-value. This became true of all the colonies, formal or informal. This employment of finance capital in the colonies has a double function which is often forgotten: It obtains higher profits in the colony but also helps to keep the rate of profit relatively higher at home; Dobb emphasises this point:

> 'Not only does it mean that the capital exported . . . is invested at a higher rate of profit than if it had been invested instead at home, but it also creates a tendency for the rate of profit at home . . . to be greater than it otherwise would have been. The latter occurs because the plethora of capital seeking investment in the metropolis is reduced by reason of the profitable colonial outlet, the pressure on the labour market is relieved and the capitalist is able to purchase labour-power at home at a lower price . . . capital thereby gains doubly: by the higher rate of profit it reaps abroad and by the higher 'rate of surplus-value' it can maintain at home'. (32)

In these circumstances the scramble for colonies and spheres of influences towards the last quarter of the nineteenth century and the struggle for redivision in the twentieth hardly appears as an 'accident of history', as some authors have claimed. (33)

According to Hobson, in his work on *Imperialism*, which Lenin relied on, the colonisation process by the chief European powers intensified between 1884-1900. Great Britain acquired 3.7 million square miles of new colonies with a population of 57,000,000 inhabitants. These included places like Baluchistan, Burma, Cyprus, North Borneo, Kuwait, the Sinai peninsula, islands in Australia, New Guinea, the Solomon Islands and the Conga Islands. In Africa she grabbed Egypt, Sudan, East Africa, Somalia, Zanzibar, South Africa, Central Africa, West Africa, etc. France increased her share by acquiring 3.6 million square miles of colonial territory with a population of 36.5 million inhabitants. Writing of French colonisation of this period, a French historian recorded:

> 'Beginning with 1870 we witness an actual colonial regeneration. The Third Republic placed Annam under its protectorate, it extended a French protectorate over Tunis and the Comoro Islands, it occupied Madagascar, it increased its possessions in Sahara, Sudan, Guinea, the Ivory Coast, Dahomey, the Somali Coast, out of proportions and its founded a new France extending from the Atlantic Ocean and Congo to Lake Chad'. (34)

All this plus other areas by the end of the century had brought under French control colonial territory almost twenty times the size of France proper.

Although German imperialism was late in the field, it too made great haste in grabbing its share of the colonial cake. Beginning in 1884, it occupied South Western Africa, Cameroon, Togoland, Tanganyika (East Africa), Guinea and the 'Bismark Archipelago' (a number of islands). In 1897 it seized Kiaochow, sections of Turkey and Asia minor. In all 1 million square miles of colonial territory with a population of 30 million people came into German hands.

Belgium acquired 900,000 square miles with a population of 30 million people, including Leopold's 'personal' colony in the Congo. Portugal too retained and consolidated its hold on 800,000 square miles of African and Asian colonies, with a population of 9 million inhabitants. Russia conquered Central Asia, Manchuria and Mongolia, and with the help of Britain, took Persia.

The US, also craving for a share of the globe, contested for the former Spanish Empire in South America and pursued an Open Door policy in China. Japanese colonialism over China was vigorously resisted and Japan's hunger for colonies explains her siding with Germany in the first World War.

But what was the characteristic feature of this colonialism as opposed to the old imperialism? Lenin emphasised, and this constitutes one of the central theses of his work, that the new colonialism had completed the seizure of the unoccupied territories:

> 'For the first time the world is completely divided up, so that in the future *only* redivision is possible, i.e., territories can only pass from one owner to another, instead of passing as ownerless territory to an 'owner'. Hence we are living in a peculiar epoch of world colonial policy, which is most closely connected with the latest stage in the development of capitalism, with finance capital'. (35)

This development was significant and continues to be so to the present day, for from that moment onwards, it ruled out the possibility of the emergence of a developed capitalist state in any of the colonial, semi-colonial and informally colonial territories under the control of the various European metropolitan 'owners', including to some extent the weakened metropolitan countries like Portugal. These colonial territories henceforth became appendages to the metropolitan home market for manufactured goods, a reservoir of cheaper labour and raw materials and an outlet for the need to export capital. The maintenance of monopoly capitalism at home became dependent on these colonial preserves. Without them there could be no monopoly capitalism.

This analysis of Lenin's has been subjected to a barrage of criticisms since it was written. Barrat-Brown in a recent book described by the publishers as being 'within the Marxist tradition where the author himself stands', summarises the 'challenge' to the Leninist thesis as follows:

"The fact is that expansion of both territory and capital exports occurred simultaneously for Britain in the 1860s and for France in the 1870s-1890s while German territorial expansion *preceded* her capital exports. Moreover, the greater part of British expansion of both territory and capital exports took place before the "monopolistic stage" followed the great depression. There was evidently no turning point in the 1870s, for Britain at least, when competitive capitalism supposedly began to change into monopoly capitalism . . . We must conclude that there was some association in time between export of capital and the process of industrial concentration at the end of the nineteenth century but that colonial expansion mainly preceded both rather than following after, as Lenin suggested . . . Lenin's thesis of a new imperialist stage of capitalism dating from the 1880s, does not fit the facts. This might mainly be because capitalism in Britain had never been anything else than imperialist and newly emerging capitalist nations were bound to follow'. (36)

The arguments summarised by Barrat-Brown do not really deal with the substance of Lenin's thesis. First of all Lenin recognised that capital exports from England and France took place also before the 1870s and that there existed colonies before then. It is for this reason that he distinguished between the old and the new imperialism. He said:

'Colonial policy and imperialism existed before the latest stage of capitalism, and even before capitalism . . . Even the capitalist colonial policy of previous stages of capitalism is essentially different from the colonial policy of finance capital'. (37)

Moreover he recognised that as far as Britain was concerned monopoly came later than in the US and Germany, but he emphasised that nevertheless her free trade policy led to concentration of capital and production although in a different form:

'It is extremely important to note that in free trade Britain, concentration also leads to monopoly, although somewhat later and perhaps in another form'. (38)

The different form which concentration in England took was described by Hermann Levy, on whom Lenin relied for the above statement. Levy in his study of British capitalism had observed that it was 'the size of the enterprise and its high technical level which harbour monopolistic tendency'. This, he explained, was due to the 'great investment of capital per enterprise' which gave rise to increasing demands for new capital and made their launching more difficult. Moreover, Levy emphasised that every new enterprise that wanted to keep pace with the gigantic enterprises that had been formed by concentration would produce such an enormous quantity of surplus goods that it could dispose of them profitably only as a result of an enormous increase in demand, otherwise the surplus would force prices down to a level that would be unprofitable both for the new enterprise and for the monopoly combines. (38)

Furthermore, Lenin had shown that Britain differed from other countries where tariffs facilitated the formation of cartels in that manufacturing associations, cartels and trusts arose in the majority of cases only when the number of the chief competing enterprises had been reduced to 'a couple of dozen or so'. But the 1860s and 1870s, concentration was taking root and the era of monopoly, although coming later to England in the form of cartels, etc., was already on the agenda. Lenin appreciated the absurdity of trying to fix exact dates for the emergence of such epochal developments for he stated:

> 'Needless to say, of course, all boundaries in nature and in society are conventional and changeable; it would be absurd to argue, for example, about the particular year or decade in which imperialism "definitely" became established'. (39)

It follows that the anti-Leninist arguments on this score are merely scholastic and really avoid the substance of the phenomenon of imperialism which clearly had emerged in the 1870s. The Great Depression had enhanced this movement and current. Dobb in his *Studies* states in respect of the 1880s:

> 'Having witnessed the drastic effect of competition in cutting prices and profit-margins, businessmen showed increasing fondness for measures whereby competition could be restricted . . . such as protected or privileged markets and the price and output agreements. This enhanced concern with the dangers of unrestrained competition came at a time when the growing concentration of production, especially in heavy industry, was laying the foundation for greater concentration of ownership and of control of business'. (40)

By the 1880s British industry was participating in the International Railmakers' Agreement for partitioning the export market among the rail monopolies, and the 'fair trade' movement which came up at this period, demanding prohibition of 'dumped' goods, was clearly the voice of monopoly. In his study of the *Commerce of Nations*, Bastable also observed the interdependence of the struggle for colonies among the European powers about this time and the rise of monopoly. Referring to the Great Depression and the Royal Commission's Report already mentioned, he observed that the consequence was a revived demand for protectionist measures:

> 'This was the rise of modern imperialism, which, as is well known pays much attention to the value of colonial possessions and their

use as potential markets. The eighties were the era of colonial expansion by France and Germany, and it is not surprising that this competition in "empire building" should have brought in fuller consciousness of the potential resources of the British Empire. The "fair trade" movement, consequently, emphasized both the value of the colonies and what it regarded as the relative defenselessness of the United Kingdom'. (41)

What Lenin, therefore, observed for Britain was that the period of 'enormous expansion of colonial conquest was between 1860 and 1880' and that it was 'considerable' in the last twenty years of the century. When he refers to the period of the 1860s and 1870s as the one after which the tremendous 'boom' in colonial expansion begins, he is doing so in *a global sense*, in relation to the categorisation at the beginning of his study where he refers to the 1860s-70s as the 'highest stage, the apex of the development of free competition', and not in relation to any particular country. In fact it is a summarisation of the development of capitalist concentration of the major capitalist countries, (42) as a movement.

It is only in this sense that Lenin concluded that 'it is beyond doubt , therefore, that capitalism's transition to the stage of monopoly capitalism to finance capital is *connected* with the intensification of the struggle for the partition of the world'. (43) It is, therefore, sheer sophistry to try to show that as far as England and France are concerned colonisation took place before the monopoly stage. Capitalism was already a world system, and particularly a European and American system and the emergence of any monopolistic tendencies in one or more of these countries was bound to have repercussions on the others, just as the British 'free trade' drive gave rise to protectionist tendencies in the other less developed countries in Europe and in the US.

Moreover, it is short sighted to argue that for Germany colonial expansion preceded capital exports, as if openings for capital exports were only relevant after colonisation. The acquisition of colonies as *potential markets* and potential *outlets for capital as well as potential sources of raw materials*, is as good a reason as any for monopoly capitalism, incipient or developed. Moreover, to top it up by saying that capitalism in Britain or, for that matter, any other country has 'never been anything else than imperialist' is to misconceive Marx and Lenin's thesis which analyses the historical development of capitalism *dialectically* and not *statically*. The capitalism of the 1880s cannot have been the same as that of the 1820s in England. The structure of the economy, as of every other institution based on it, had gone through a development in both quantitative and qualitative terms and it is only in the 1880s that the whole world was, for the first time in the written history of man, divided up among a handful of the richest countries. This would not have been possible without the development of capitalism precedent to that special stage. Again, it has been argued that:

> 'To sustain the Marxist thesis which relates colonial expansion to openings for a surplus capital, as well as for a surplus of goods, it would be necessary to show that the direction of capital exports was to the colonies'. (44)

Here again the fallacy of the argument lies in the lack of understanding of the laws of motion of capitalist development and in particular of the role of the colony in this development. As we have shown, the export of capital or of goods need not take place at any particular time after the acquisition of the colony. It is enough that the acquisitions are potential outlets. Furthermore, the acquisition of colonies does not of necessity *rule-out* the possibilities of investment or markets in other developed capitalist countries, where the return is expectedly higher than in the colonies. Imperialism is not a centre-periphery phenomenon, but a world system.

The investment of capital in, or export of goods to, the other capitalist countries will not be any less imperialistic if those other countries are less developed. Imperialism knows neither geographical nor racial barrier and to present it as *solely* a centre-periphery phenomenon is to display a strange conception of imperialism. Just as imperialism divides up the backward world and subjugates the peoples in these countries to its own needs, so it also subjugates other weaker capitalist states, exploiting them and their resources for the same purpose. It is for this reason that Lenin speaks of 'a number of *transitional* forms of state dependence', and of countries which, 'politically, are formally independent, but in fact, are enmeshed in the net of financial and diplomatic dependence'. (45) That is why semi-colonies and informal colonies like the South American countries were equally subject to exploitation. Lenin quotes a certain Schulze-Gaevernitz who observed: 'South America, and especially Argentina, is so dependent financially on London that it ought to be described as almost a British Commercial Colony'.(45) Lenin particularly cited Portugal as being one of this type of country.

> 'Portugal is an independent sovereign state, but actually for more than two hundred years, since the War of the Spanish Succession (1701-14) it has been a British protectorate. Great Britain has protected Portugal and her colonies in order to fortify her own positions in the fight against her rivals, Spain and France. In return Great Britain has received commercial privileges, preferential conditions for importing goods and especially capital into Portugal and the Portuguese colonies, the right to use the ports and islands of Portugal, her telegraph cables, etc. Relations of this kind have always existed between big and little states, but in the epoch of capitalist imperialism they become a general system, they form part of the sum total of "divide the world" relations and become links in the chain of operations of world finance capital'. (46)

What Lenin said then has been vindicated by studies carried out more recently which confirm the domination and exploitation of Portugal and 'her' colonies by Britain and other more powerful imperialist powers. Sideri and Feis, in their studies already referred to, give evidence of this struggle by Britain, France and Germany to 'divide the world' in Portugal's colonies. To be sure, Germany's designs in Africa, as far as Portuguese colonies went, were dominated by her commercial and financial interests. German cheap goods, cheap freights and cheap credit, part of the monopoly 'dumping' game, had flooded Portuguese and Spanish markets. The total value of German exports to the Iberian peninsula increased constantly from £2 million to £10 million between 1892 and 1911. (47)

We have already discussed Britain's hold on the Portuguese economy. The contradictory interests of the two powers and their desire for a *rapprochement* in 1889 in order for Britain to isolate France in her designs on the Sudan, helped frame the basis for their joint and at times contradictory designs on Portuguese African colonies. Already by 1888 most of the capital used to open up Mozambique was British and in that year a British company, the Mozambique Company, was formed. Although Portugal was 'alarmed at the large number of foreign interests involved in Mozambique', and although it issued a decree in 1889 forbidding any further 'sub-infeudation', within a few months it had to 'swallow its pride' and allow the British company to lease out mining areas.

As a result of her combined obligations to Britain and other imperialist countries, and particularly in relation to the repayments of loans which had by 1891 reached the £130 million mark, of which Britain had supplied over one half, Portugal was obliged in June 1891 to sign a treaty with Britain under which the borders of Mozambique were established and the territory between it and Angola was ceded to Britain. Furthermore, the Zambezi was opened to navigation, and the acquisition of this territory, described as 'imposed in a high-handed way by a strong power upon a weaker one', (48) formed part of Britain's scheme to control the gold discovered in the Transvaal in 1886. It also formed part of the general policy to obtain the region north of Bechuanaland and access to the sea for the British South Africa Company. Sideri correctly remarks:

> 'As in the case of Brazil, England gained the advantages connected with the harbours of Lourenco Marques and Beira without paying for the administration of the territories: In both instances England obtained the minerals and other products of the interior, while Portugal's scarce resources were spent on administering the coastal strips from where those products were shipped to European markets. Only the German presence in Africa "frustrated Rhodes' attempt to buy Delagoa Bay from Portugal", and the Anglo-German rivalry in Europe restrained Great Britain from taking the remaining Portuguese territories'. (49)

On June 23, 1898 Germany put forward proposals for the eventual division of the Portuguese African colonies. This did not materialise but led to an agreement between Britain and Germany. Two conventions resulted from this agreement which were signed between Britain and

Germany on August 30, 1898. These provided, *inter alia*, that the two parties agree to ask each other to share in loans that might be asked by Portugal on the security of the customs or other revenues of the African colonies. In the event of such a loan the British share was to be secured by the customs of the Mozambique Province south of the Zambezi river, and of a designated part of Angloa; the German share was to be secured by the customs of the remainder of the colonies. 'Each was to limit its efforts to obtain new concessions to those sections, the customs revenues of which were assigned to their respective loans'. (50)

In an accompanying secret convention the two powers agreed to oppose the intervention of any third power either by way of loans on security of colonial revenues, by way of lease, cession, or purchase of territory. (50) This was certainly imperialism, within the general system of 'divide the world' relations that had 'become links in the chain of operations of world finance capital' as Lenin described.

The British-German conventions were intended to keep out other powers and as negotiations continued French offers of financial assistance to Portugal were resisted. Keeping out the French, the two proceeded to invest in various railroads and trading ventures in these colonies. But Britain, having obtained Germany's abandonment of the Boers through these conventions and fearing further German expansion in Africa at the expense of the weakened Portugal, leaked news of the secret clause to the Portuguese government, and thus provoked Portuguese rejection of the German offer of a loan in October 1898. Attempts were made by Portugal to raise a loan in Paris, and as the Germans feared French intervention, they sent a fleet to Lisbon in May 1899, which found the British navy already there awaiting them. Sideri concludes:

> 'All this served Great Britain's interests well: Portugal was made to realise that she could no longer play off one power against the other and that she had better accept Britain's terms'. (51)

Having sidetracked her ally in the deal, Britain then made a small loan to Portugal, to 'rescue her from the clutches of France and those of numerous political and financial sharks which hovered around'. (52) She then proceeded to wring another concession from Portugal by a secret declaration in October 1890 re-affirming Britain's 'obligation to preserve' Portugal's integrity, and Portugal's to remain neutral in the event of any South African war.

All this cleared the way for British investment in the Benguela railway, and a ninety-nine year concession for the Lobito-Katanga line, 80% of whose £13 million construction cost came from British financial sources and which was completed only owing to the initiative of her financiers. (51) As Sideri puts it:

> 'The beginning of the 20th century finds the old Anglo-Portuguese alliance firmly re-established, Portugal indebted for about £200 million and the African empire completely under British control'. (53)

Of the total investments in Angola and Mozambique for the period 1870-1936, which amounted to £32 million and £35 million respectively, more than half came from Britain. At the beginning of the twentieth century one quarter of the European population which had settled in the territory assigned to the British-owned Mozambique Company were British subjects. British finance capital also controlled the Delagoa Bay Development Corporation which operated the water works, telephone and tramway at Lourenco Marques and which apparently had large interests in the electrical company and owned much of the land. (53) The situation was very similar in Angola.

Space has been taken to discuss Portugal so as to show that Lenin's analysis of imperialism cannot be left at the superficial level of colonies, that modern imperialism of the era of finance capital and monopoly capitalism subjugates and exploits colonial and weak sovereign states alike and as such is a world system. Today there are many Portugals under US imperialist hegemony.

If monopoly capitalism engenders the division of the world into colonial, semi-colonial, and informal-colonial spheres of exploitation, this exploitation is given more impetus by the new imperialist tariff policy. This policy constituted the basis of the colonial preference system which we referred to in an earlier chapter. Here it is necessary to look into the whole imperialist tariff structure to enable us to see how the imperial preference system worked. Whereas the tariff policy of the period characterised by emergent capitalism was defensive, intended to encourage production in countries which were relatively undeveloped in order to enable them to stand competition in the world market, the new imperialist tariff policy became offensive, aimed at giving protection to those firms which could withstand competition, namely the monopolies. It is in the first sense that the 'national economists', like Frederick List, appealed for protection as a means of 'educating' industry:

'Protection measures can be justified only as a means of encouraging and protecting the home manufacturing power, and only among those nations which are . . . called to secure for themselves a position equal to that of the fore-most agricultural, manufacturing, and trading nations, the great maritime and continental powers'. (54)

Hilferding in his study, *Finance Capital*, adds:

'It is otherwise in the period of capitalist monopolies. Now the mightiest, most-able-to-export industries, about whose capacity to compete on the world market there can be no doubt and for which according to the old theory tariffs should have no interest, demand high protective duties'. (55)

We have already seen how monopoly capitalism, unlike competitive capitalism, aims at 'maximum profits' instead of the 'average profit' that competitive capitalism allows. The new tariff policy enabled monopoly capitalism to reap even more maximum profits by protecting the monopoly home market against competition. This made it possible for the cartels, trusts and syndicates to raise prices in the home market and cut down and restrict supply, which would have been impossible if the home market was opened to foreign products which could compete with the domestic product. Protection enabled the monopoly, after reaping the extra profits, to export similar products at lower prices than those obtaining on the home market and 'dump' them on a foreign market where possible. Thus the protective tariff enabled monopoly capitalism to be 'subsidised' on the foreign market; tariffs became 'offensive' in character, requiring 'defensive' measures of a new type by the state offended against. This resulted in a 'tariff mania' and tariff wars.

Monopoly protective tariffs create a situation which inhibits full utilisation of plant and productive capacity. This also in turn tends to force the newly accumulated capital to seek outlets for investments either in other industries within the country or outside, thus further complicating competition among the monopolies for outlets for capital exports. Here too the monopoly tariff policy finds its place in the colonies. Colonies must be protected against the 'foreigners', and in a way become part of the home market. The protectionist policy was given more impetus by the outbreak of the first imperialist World War. Bastable observes:

> 'It was then found that with regard to a series of articles this country [i.e. Britain] was virtually depending on "enemy sources" of supply, and it was now possible to link the case for protection with the case for self-defence. From this time onwards we get what is now the familiar demand for the protection of "key industries" '. (56)

Thus colonial policy became identifiable with high tariffs. Although a distinction was sometimes made between colonial tariffs in countries with some amount of 'self-government' (non-assimilated), those in countries which were directly administered, (assimilated), and the 'Open-door' tariffs, all colonial tariff on the whole worked towards the same policy.

These tariff policies of the imperialist powers were a general phenomenon of monopoly capitalism. International cartel agreements, 'rationalisation' of production by monopolies and the division of the world did not remove areas of conflict between monopolies as idealists imagined. They merely intensified competition among them. The protective tariffs resulted in heated 'tariff wars'. When these could not solve the contradictions, actual wars by force of arms, 'continued the politics by other means'. Tariff wars broke out between Austria-Hungary and Rumania (1886-1890), Serbia (1906-1911) and Montenegro (1908-1911); between Germany and Russia (1893-1894), Spain (1894-1899), and Canada (1903-1910); between France and Italy (1888-1892), and Switzerland (1893-1895). These were followed with sharper ones in the interwar years, after the first World War had failed to resolve them.

In summarising his thesis Lenin pointed out the five principal features of modern imperialism: (1) the concentration of production and capital had developed to such a high stage that it had created monopolies which played a decisive role in economic life; (2) the merging of bank and industrial capital, and the creation, on the basis of 'finance capital', of a financial oligarchy; (3) the export of capital as distinguished from the export of commodities acquired exceptional importance; (4) the formation of international monopolist capitalist associations which share the world among themselves, and (5) the territorial division of the whole world among the biggest capitalist powers was completed. (57) Of all the explanations of imperialism available at the time Lenin's thesis was the only one that has stood the test of time and, as we try to show in the next chapter, it was increasingly confirmed by the historical experience of the interwar years as well as the period after the second World War, with the rise of multilateral imperialism.

CHAPTER XIII

How do the inter-war years bear out the Leninist thesis? The Great Depression of the 1870s was alleviated between 1896 and 1914 by British reliance on the export of finance capital and capital goods. This shift was markedly in the direction of South America and especially Argentina, Chile and Brazil, as we have seen — areas of British informal colonialism; and to Canada and India. From a total figure for foreign investments of £82 million in 1872, they shrunk to a low £21 million in 1894 and £17 million in 1898. The bicycle, shipbuilding, and electrical construction firms worked towards recovery at home. In 1904 a noticeable recovery in foreign investment set in with the Transvaal Loan of 1903, which was followed by borrowings from Japan and railway issues for Canadian and Argentinian railways. The US, Brazil, Chile, Mexico, Egypt, West and East Africa, India and China all played a part in this revived investment which went mainly in railway and dock construction, public utilities, telegraphs, tramways, mining, plantations, land mortgage companies, banks, insurance, shipping and trading companies. (58) This led to an increase in investment to a figure of £141 million in 1907, 75% higher than 1890, rising to £225 million in 1913. Dobb points out that:

> 'On the eve of the first World War British capital abroad had grown to constitute probably about a third or a quarter of the total holdings of the British capitalist class and current foreign investment may even have slightly exceeded net home investment'. (58)

Of this as already pointed out, about one half was held in British colonies and possessions and the remainder in South and North America. But all this finance was intended to and did stimulate industrial development at home; capital goods exports which stood at £263 million in 1890, but had fallen to £226 in 1895, slightly rose to £282 million in 1900, rising again to £375 in 1906, and in 1910 reached a new high of £430 million. At this stage, unlike during the period before the crisis, capital goods (i.e., iron and steel) constituted more than half the value and 70% in tonnage of the total exports. Dobb quotes Professor Clapham as saying:

> 'The 50% rise in exports between 1901-1903 and 1907 was essentially an investment rise . . . Manufacturers and all who thought like manufacturers gloried in swollen exports: Resources were turned towards foreign investment, rather than to rebuilding of the dirty

towns of Britain, simply because foreign investment seemed more remunerative'. (58)

For partly this reason no investment in new innovative technologies took place. Moreover, towards the end of this period before the war the barter terms of trade began to move against Britain.

In Germany the unification of the country created conditions for expanded industrial development. This was helped by the growth of the electrical and chemical industries in the 1890s as we observed. These two industries, however, could only operate profitably on the basis of monopoly. Their involvement in the international cartel arrangements for the division of markets marked the new imperialism. In the US, railway construction helped to sustain and absorb the capital goods of its heavy industry but trusts and other forms of concentration proceeded with great impetus. Hence 'internal colonialism' had to be supplemented by participation in the colonial scramble.

The outbreak of the first World War had firm roots in the scramble for markets, outlets for capital exports, and sources of cheap raw materials. Lenin quotes one Driault, a historian, who understood the significance of this development. He pointed out in his book that during the past few years, all the free territory of the globe had been occupied by the great powers of Europe and North America. 'This has already brought about several conflicts and shifts of spheres of influence, and these foreshadow more terrible upheavals in the near future'. He added that the nations, which had not yet 'made provision' for themselves stood the risk of never receiving their share and never participating in the tremendous exploitation of the globe 'which will be one of the most essential features of the next century' (the twentieth). Moreover, the relative strength of empires founded in the nineteenth century was 'totally out of proportion to the place occupied in Europe by the nations which founded them'. (59) For this reason Lenin in his thesis foresaw the inevitability of 'repartitions' and 're-divisions'.

Seen in this context, the causes of the first World War become clearer. Although it is difficult to trace all the particular and underlying causes, it is nevertheless clear that the central issues of the war were imperialist considerations in South Eastern Europe, the Near East and the Eastern Mediterranean. These in turn aggravated the rivalry of the two European systems of alliances and hence 'all the problems of the age'. (60) Under this category of 'problems' come the military and political rivalry between Germany and France, brought into sharp relief by the Alsace-Lorraine question; the maritime rivalry between Britain and Germany; and 'the traditional causes of friction on issues of colonial and overseas policy in the Near East, the Far East and in Africa'. (61) The system of imperialist rivalries revolved around particular crises, including the fate of the Danube monarchy and of the peoples of South East Europe, and the future of the

Ottoman Empire.

Although the war was actually triggered off by the oppressed nationalities of the Balkan region in their aspirations for national independence and statehood, the real contradiction soon exploded into the whole question of the redivision of the world. (61) Lenin in his *Report on the International Situation to the Second Congress of the Communist International,* on July 19th, 1920, having briefly surveyed the development of monopoly capital, came to this conclusion:

> The first imperialist war of 1914-18 was the inevitable outcome of this partition of the whole world, of this domination by the capitalist monopolies, of this great power wielded by an insignificant number of very big banks — two, three, four or five in each country. This war was waged for the repartition of the whole world. It was waged in order to decide which of the small groups of the biggest states, the British or the German, was to obtain the opportunity and the right to rob, strangle and exploit the whole world. You know that the war settled this question in favour of the British group. And as a result of this war, all capitalist contradictions have become immeasurably more acute'. (62)

What was the result of this conflict? The world was redivided. Under the Treaty of Versailles the victors, the British and the French, took a lion's share of the colonial empire of Germany. Also, important raw-material producing areas within Germany itself were awarded to Poland, to France, and to Belgium. Germany lost her navy and merchant marine, and her army was reduced in size. Austro-Hungary was broken up into three states. In the Far East, Japan tried to seize colonial territory and was only dislodged by the US and Britain after 'the peace'. The US emerged the sole important beneficiary in the long run in that it was the only country which moved from the position of a debtor nation, which it had been before the war, to that of a creditor nation. The war brought 1,750 million people 'comprising the entire population of the world', under the yoke of the 'top stratum' of the capitalist world.

The seething revolutionary situation throughout Europe constituted the most important side-effect of the imperialist war. The devastation of the war, seen in the context of the time, was staggering. In France 2.7 million people were without housing; 285,000 houses were destroyed and 411,000 damaged; 22,000 factories, 4,800 kilometres of railways, 1,600 kilometres of canals, 59,000 kilometres of roads and 3.3 million hectares of arable land were rendered useless. Germany fell apart and so did the Austro-Hungarian empire, which disintegrated into the three independent states of Austria, Czechoslovakia and Hungary.

The most important 'collapse' was that of Russia, which for the first time in history opened up the possibilities of crushing the hegemony of the bourgeoisie. Led by the Bolshevik party and based on the correct policy of the alliance between the proletariat and the peasantry and other forces, the first stage, that of the bourgeois democratic revolution,

131

was established, leading to the transition to a socialist state under the dictatorship of the proletariat. In Germany, where the situation was very favourable, the leaders of the proletarian parties decided at the most crucial moment to renegue and join forces with the enemy. The interventionist movements in Russia aimed at crushing the successful revolution in the bud, for the Bolsheviks constituted a challenge to imperialism. Their revolution according to the representatives of the bourgeoisie was aimed at making 'the ignorant and incapable mass of humanity dominant in the earth'.

Lloyd George was also worried about the results of the war and the 'peace'. In a letter to his French counterpart Fontainbleau on 25 March 1919, he expressed fear of war breaking out in 'thirty years hence'. He asserted that whereas after the Napoleonic War in 1815 everybody was exhausted, the situation in Germany and elsewhere indicated a continuing state of ferment. The revolution was still in its infancy. 'The supreme figures of the Terror are still in command in Russia'. He continued:

> The whole of Europe is filled with the spirit of revolution. There is everywhere a deep sense not only of discontent, but of anger and revolt amongst the workmen against pre-war conditions. The whole existing order in its political, social and economic aspects is questioned by the masses of the population from one end of Europe to the other . . . Much of this unrest is unhealthy'.

John Maynard Keynes, in a book which Lenin referred to in his Report just quoted, warned the victors: 'what you are doing is madness'. Central Europe, which represented 'the greatest concentration of peoples in the heart of Europe', would explode if humiliating conditions were imposed in the peace. Keynes' central message concerned the fear of revolution. He pointed out that humiliation and starvation would drive Europe into despair and into the arms of communism, thus dragging the rest of the continent 'into the abyss'. (63)

The survival of the October Revolution was a great defeat for the imperialists and its success a victory for the proletariat and all the oppressed peoples of the world. Having condemned the European renegades of the Second International, Lenin correctly concluded in his Report that:

> 'World imperialism shall fall when the revolutionary onslaught of the exploited and oppressed workers in each country, overcoming resistance from petty-bourgeois elements and the influence of the small upper crust of labour aristocrats, merges with the revolutionary onslaught of hundreds of millions of people who have hitherto stood beyond the pale of history, and have been regarded merely as the object of history'.

The period of the interwar years was, for monopoly capitalism, one of reconstruction and development under conditions of increasing monopoly. Superficially there was a 'boom' after 1919 in Britain and other countries, attributable to the desire to replenish depleted stocks. This boom was, however, based on momentary inducements. The collapse of the 'boom' in prices with the arrival of raw materials and foodstuffs which had accumulated in the colonies during the war was merely an expression of the new contradictions of monopoly capitalism.

Import restrictions and prohibitions became the order of the day in central Europe and a conference in 1920 in Brussels which called for free trade had no effect. Each state defended its own market and that of its colonies. For Britain, which had since the Paris Conference in 1916 adopted an anti-dumping and prohibition policy, the Safeguarding of Industries Act of 1921, which was passed 'with a view to the safeguarding of certain special industries and the safeguarding of employment against the effects of the depreciation of foreign currencies and the disposal of imported goods at prices below the cost of production', (64) was a typical expression of the new times. The need to safeguard industries arose from the fact that after the war many countries emerged with basic industries and plant which had not existed before. Hence the fear of unemployment, which, as we have seen, constituted a nightmare for the imperialists because of the explosive social situation. The depreciation of foreign currencies created a new threat; the export of goods 'at prices below cost of production'. This became a characteristic feature of the period.

To begin with, Britain's pound had been over-valued by about 10% at the end of the war. The currency problems arising from this led to Britain's going off the Gold Standard. She returned to the Standard in 1925, in order to bring about 'stabilisation', but this did not last long. Moreover, the new Gold Standard was different from the old one. Firstly, many countries held foreign exchange reserves instead of or in addition to gold. This brought pressure on the pound and the dollar, the currencies in which the countries held their reserves, thus making it necessary for London and New York to hold large gold reserves to cover these holdings. Britain could not maintain this position because of her weakened competitive position and this led to a flight of gold resulting in the second demise of the Gold Standard in 1931. The second weakness of the new Standard was that as a result of the inability of many countries to export their products because of the new tariff incidence, these countries' foreign reserves or gold supporting their Gold Standard were acquired not out of their export surpluses, or even long term borrowing, but on short-term loans in these main centres. This too added to the strain Britain had to bear, since she too was finding it difficult to find export markets to earn her gold.

France, which was one of the countries holding gold and sterling as its reserves, experienced a crisis connected with falling profitability in 1924-26. The export of finance capital which, as we have observed, was a phenomenon characteristic of this period had fateful consequences. The French exported capital, 'selling abroad more than they bought' and holding the difference in foreign exchange. When these holdings were sold to the Bank of France after the latter returned to the Gold Standard, this set in motion a chain-reaction. Arthur Lewis points out:

'In 1928 the Bank of France decided to convert these holdings into gold. There followed a drain of gold from other countries to France, which was aggravated by the under-valuation of the franc giving rise to an export surplus which also was paid for in gold. The gold reserves of the Bank of France increased (in equivalent) from 954 million US dollars at the end of 1927 to 1,633 million at the end of 1929 and 3,257 million at the end of 1932. This put an extra strain on all debtor countries and was one of the factors that eventually caused the system to collapse'. (65)

Once it is realised that this game of over-valuation and under-valuation was the result of the struggle for export markets, and once it is understood that the 'other factors' had to do with international trade, then it is not difficult to see that monopoly was the root cause of the 'collapse of the system'. Devaluations helped to put off for some time the on-coming profitability crisis but they became a general weapon, resulting in competitive devaluations.

To be sure, the problem of currencies was part of the general issue of obstacles to international trade caused by prohibitions and tariffs. A League of Nations calculation of tariff incidence showed that tariffs had increased considerably between 1913 and 1925. (66) As a result of these developments, a number of tariff wars ensued between countries. These led to two conferences in 1927. The first dealt with the tariff problem and the second with prohibitions. Although agreements were reached generally, other countries stood in the way of total solutions. The solutions of the second conference were obstructed by Germany's and Poland's non-ratification, and the first one 'produced recommendations in favour of tariff reductions', which resulted in only slight reductions. According to Lewis:

'Hopes, however, diminished as news of proposed tariff increases in America began to crystallise, from the end of 1928; and the onset of the slump of 1929, followed by the American "biggest ever" Hawley-Smoot tariff in 1930, made agreement impossible: tariff increases after 1929 were bigger than ever'. (67)

For this reason, although the 1929 depression was followed by a steady rise in production in all sectors, this did not lead to increased international trade as would have been expected. Table II overleaf shows this predicament for imperialism.

As a general feature which goes to confirm Lenin's thesis, increase in export of goods, particularly between 1925 and 1929, was assisted by the maintenance of a high level of capital exports. More importantly, investment in raw material and agricultural production soon led to a slump. In capital exports the US stood out as the new lender with Germany as the new borrower. In 1928 the US had invested $1,099 million of which 45% went to Germany, taking advantage of her weakened position. Germany

Table II

Production and Trade, 1929-1937

	1929	1932	1937
Foodstuffs			
World Trade	100	89	93.5
World production	100	100	108
Raw Materials			
World Trade	100	81.5	108
World production	100	74	116
Manufactures			
World Trade	100	59.5	87
World production	100	70	120

Source: A. Lewis, *Economic Survey 1919-1939 p.58*

had debts of $1,007 million in the same period. Britain and France respectively sunk $569 million and $237 million into loans to other countries. (68) Although the total involved in foreign investments was around 6% of the total capital formation of the imperialist countries, the importance of capital movements in the flow of international trade was 'greater than this figure indicates'. (69) Nevertheless this low level of capital exports was evidence of the generally low level of international trade in the period. (70)

The depression of 1929 has been ascribed to the collapse in primary commodity prices, because of their wide ramifications. (71) The fall in these prices checked capitalist confidence, causing them to become more cautious in investment. It also provoked 'a crop of bank failures', thus inducing deflationary effects, checking expansion, encouraging hoarding of currency and discouraging any further investment. This had other effects on other countries. They were forced off the Gold Standard and took measures to curtail their international payments. This in turn resulted in new trade restrictions, thus complicating industrial production under monopoly control. The result was a contraction in lending (foreign and domestic), a fall of prices, a contraction of trade, and then a monetary crisis. (78)

The curtailment of international trade was the inevitable result of the fierce competition for markets leading to a new wave of trade prohibitions and new high tariffs, following the US Hawley-Smoot tariff of 1930. The collapse of the Gold Standard in 1931 for Britain and many other countries and the competitive devaluations that ensued, followed by the US abandonment of the Standard in April 1933, were all bound to result in these trade restrictions. Since most of the debtor countries were relatively weak in the world competitive market and since many were primary producers, reduction in foreign lending by the creditor countries, caused by the run on gold, meant that the debtor countries could not import more than was absolutely necessary since they needed all the foreign exchange they could earn to repay past fixed debts and onerous interest and servicing charges.

Whilst therefore the monopolists were putting up barriers and tariffs for offensive purposes in order to dump their products in weaker foreign markets, the weaker debtor countries were putting up tariffs as defensive weapons against the stronger monopolist groups. Although the strong industrial countries should have benefitted from a fall in prices of primary commodities, nevertheless they also increased their barriers to 'protect their farmers'. Monopolistic competition had tied capitalism in web-like contradictions.

By 1932, as Lewis points out, 'world trade was well tied up'. (72) New efforts to reduce barriers were all hopeless since the fundamental contradiction remained. A tariff truce convention in 1930, in which the 18 major countries of Europe agreed not to raise duties without consulting other parties, was so much empty talk. Two other conferences followed, but perhaps the more important one was the World Economic Conference, held in London in 1933, with a view to reducing tariffs, restoring the Gold Standard, and resuming export of capital in order to revive international trade. The 'experts' had no clear vision and hence 'their general agreement on objectives was matched by equal disagreement on methods'. (79) Failure was therefore a foregone conclusion.

This was bound to be so. All the major capitalist powers were struggling to consolidate their preferential colonial markets. The clearest example in this period was Great Britain. Since her devaluation of the pound sterling in 1931 had failed to produce any new markets, what remained was to improve her market position by bilateral agreements. In 1932 British Commonwealth countries met in Ottawa and agreed on a new preferential system, 'to extend to each other increased import preferences'. But the whole strategy was intended to secure export markets for Britain and hence 'the colonies were instructed to grant preferences to British goods'. (73) This meant, in particular, the exclusion of competitive Japanese textiles from the colonies and dominions.

This was not all. Demands were also made on 'small foreign countries especially dependent on the British market', to increase the proportion of their imports from Britain. (73) This affected Argentina, Denmark, Sweden, Norway, Estonia, Latvia, Finland, Lithuania, and Iceland, who were required to import a minimum of 45% British coal; Estonia was required to import 85% of her coal from Britain. An Export Credit Guarantee Department was set up to assist in the purchase of British goods. (74) This was supplemented by direct assistance by the state to monopolies at home. Here the intention was 'to keep up the rate of profit', in the face of the counteracting forces. Support was given to monopolies in the coal, cotton, iron and steel, railways and shipbuilding industries, as well as to agriculture. The idea was to encourage accumulation by combating competition, 'to discourage the emergence of new and enterprising firms, by protecting by quota the markets of all, irrespective of efficiency'. (74) This tended to restrict new investments in declining industries and main- tain output at the level the market would absorb. All this was consistent with monopoly capitalism as analysed by Marx and Lenin, for as we noted in a previous chapter reduction of constant capital was a short-term solution to profitability crisis.

In Germany similar moves by the monopolists were made to curtail imports by import licensing which was linked with exchange control. In order to ease balance of payments problems banks and industry were required to eliminate interest and dividend payments. A moratorium was imposed. But more importantly, special bilateral arrangements were made with a number of South Eastern European and Latin American countries to improve Germany's export markets. Goods were exchanged on the basis of clearing arrangements. This avoided the need for foreign exchange on transactions. In order to increase the attractiveness of German goods, foreign goods participating in clearing arrangements were bought at above world market prices or at special rates of exchange for the mark fixed below the official rate, and German goods were subsidised to enable them to sell at dumped prices. All these manoeuvres were intended to expand markets: 'to achieve the benefits of devalutation without actually devaluing'. (75)

Nor was the US left out of this struggle for markets. Despite its anti- monopoly legislation passed in the 1890s to 'combat' a spate of combin- ations and trusts, under the New Deal Programme the government encour- aged monopolies. The initial steps which were adopted in 1929 to put up prices in primary commodities produced by US farmers by buying stocks and holding them from the markets under the Federal Farm Relief Board were supplemented by new ones. In spite of this the prices of corn, wheat and cotton in 1933 were at a record low. As Gardner has recorded:

> 'Southern planters warned . . . that they could not survive another
> winter of five-cent cotton; midwest hoggrowers even suggested that
> they should slaughter ten million of their own pigs to create
> scarcity price increases; dairy farmers acted: they poured gallons
> of milk into mud ditches rather than accept further price reductions.
> Roosevelt felt sure that if he waited much longer the nation would
> harvest a revolution'. (75)

The Agricultural Adjustment Act of 1933 introduced the payment of 'benefit payments' in order to restrict acreage planted, and later the policy was turned into one of paying farmers to encourage them not to grow food. As a result the US prices of these commodities rose above world prices and the government had to intervene by subsidising in order to sell surpluses in the outside market. Industry was also assisted in that the National Industrial Recovery Act of 1933 which laid down a code to encourage 'fair competition' was interpreted in such a way, and monopoly capitalism put it to such a use, as to give it a monopolistic twist. The result was that 'recovery' occurred with the raising of industrial prices. Direct government intervention to assist monopoly business to 'recover' from the depression was the order of the day. This spate of monopoly forced Congress to appoint a committee led by Estes Kefauver to 'look into the matter'. The committee discovered that industry was becoming increasingly monopolistic 'over an important sector of the American economy', where 'individual markets are shared by a small number of producers', and that this was becoming a dominant pattern. Kefauver wept over this development:

> 'Every day in our lives monopoly takes its toil. Stealthily it reaches down into our pockets and takes part of our earnings . . . monopoly these days is seldom, if ever, a blatant affair; it lies behind the lines, unobtrusive and unseen . . . Excess prices constitute one important consequence of monopoly . . . Those who hold jobs are affected by monopoly (as rigid high prices affect the volume of sales) . . . This means that productive capacity in the monopolised industry lies idle, and workers face periods of lay off and chronic unemployment . . . Small business is also deeply affected by monopoly. Everyone, at one time or another in his life, has seen economic power throw its weight around . . . The continued increase in industrial concentration in this country has resulted in the diminishing role for small business. This is given dramatic expression in the rising number of failures and bankruptcies in recent years . . . Monopoly can with audacity dip its hand deeply into the public coffers. The very business executives who seize the opportunities monopoly offers to wrest favours from government are among those who attack social measures, such as medical care for the aged, as inflationary. Apparently to some minds government aid to private monopoly is one thing; government aid to improve the living standards of the deprived segments of our population is quite another'. (76)

Kefauver is quoted extensively to show the extent of state-assisted monopoly in this period despite the laws that had been passed to 'combat' it.

In his *Studies*, (77) Dobbs points out five main characteristics of the interwar years, and all confirm this analysis and Kefauver's conclusions.

Firstly, there was an abnormally large gap between price and cost, which resulted in increased accumulation at the expense of wages. Secondly, reductions in demand in particular markets or in markets in general were followed by reduction of output rather than price. Thirdly, there was extensive under-capacity utilisation of plant and equipment which created large unemployment in conditions of market depression. Fourthly, there was a decline in the rate of investment owing to the reluctance of monopolies to expand productive capacity, and also owing to obstacles put in the way of new firms, particularly in monopolised areas. All this assisted the monopoly effort to maintain the rate of profit.

We have noted already that in England the state intervened directly to assist a number of monopolies in textile, coal, iron and steel as well as shipbuilding industries, the intention being in the words of Lewis:

> 'To keep declining industries less efficient than they would other-
> wise have been, and to restrict investment in them'. (78)

This development and policy was itself contradictory since increased
protection of monopolies resulted in large accumulation of capital, which
itself led to the fall in the rate of profit, and to a desire to invest, while
the outlets for investment were limited by the monopoly development
itself. This contradiction could only be 'resolved' by an intensified search
for foreign capital outlets and markets, hence the colonial policy. Dobb's
fifth characteristic, the decline in investment at home, resulted in narrowed
markets at home for heavy industry and unemployment helping to depress
prices in consumption goods and hence their production. All this, too,
suggested a colonial solution.

The new techniques of production adopted in this period also went to
raise the ratio of constant capital to variable capital and actually resulted
in a reduction, in absolute as well as relative terms, in the direct costs of
production by including labour as an integral part of the 'unitary machine
process', thereby converting wages into a kind of over-head cost. (79)
These techniques had the result of producing 'mass consumption' products,
of reduced unit cost. The transformation of the division of labour which
machinery introduced in the previous century had resulted in the subordination of the worker's movements to those of the machine and was now
carried a stage further in that it turned the worker simply into 'a machine-
minder'.

New techniques in actual management of production operations were
dominated by ideas of Taylorism or scientific management. (80) All these
ideas combined to assist monopoly capitalism in maintaining its high
profits in conditions of increasing unemployment, and to increase demand
for the cheaper mass produced goods.

Thus we see that this period, 1880-1939, is characterised by concentration of capital, monopoly, and the division of the entire world among
the powerful capitalist states of Europe. Since monopoly implied struggle
for markets, sources of raw materials and outlets for capital exports, it
also meant that so long as monopoly capitalism continued to be a general
feature of the capitalist economy, the struggle for redivision of these
markets would also be a general feature of the period. This is borne out
by the evidence. The cause of the first World War and the redivision that
resulted from it was clearly connected with this struggle. But the victory
of one group did not remove the basic contradiction of monopoly
capitalism.

The rise of fascism in Germany and Italy was a creature of this struggle.
Without markets, German monopoly capitalism fell to a low ebb. Facism
came in to assist monopoly capitalism by smashing all the bourgeois
individual democratic rights and institutions in order to protect the bourgeoisie as a class against the possibilities of socialist revolution. It also
came in to prepare for war to regain its lost territory and more:

'Those nations which were left out in the first partition of the world, and lost or failed to benefit from the first war of redivision, the nations in which capital had the least opportunity for internal expansion, soon set about preparing for a second division'. (81)

Thus, the invasion of Manchuria in 1931 by Japan, the Italian absorption of Ethiopia in 1933, the push by Japan into China in 1937 and a series of German aggressions in Europe were just initial steps in the preparation and execution of this policy 'by other means'. What happened thereafter and the US push to redivide the world under an 'Open Door' policy after this second imperialist war we shall deal with in the next Part; suffice it to say here that the seeds of the 'new' US policy had been planted in the womb of the 'old' policy, in the creation of preferential colonial markets. When capitalism reemerged it could only continue on the basis of multilateral imperialism, a redivision under US hegemony.

REFERENCES

1. K. Marx, *Capital*, op. cit. Vol.I, p.6.
2. P.A. Sweezy, *The Theory of Capitalist Development*, Monthly Review, (New York, 1942), p.256.
3. L.C. Knowles, *Economic Development in the 19th Century*, Routledge, (London, 1963), p.170.
4. Quoted in Lenin, *Imperialism: The Highest Stage of Capitalism*, (Moscow, 1970), p.21-2.
5. Felix Green, *The Enemy*, Constable, (London, 1972).
6. E. Mandel, *Marxist Economic Theory*, Merlin, (London, 1973), p.22-25.
7. Hilferding, *Finance Capital*, quoted in Lenin, op. cit.
8. R. Vernon, *Sovereignty at Bay*, Penguin, (London, 1971), p.87-9.
9. G.W. Stocking & M.W. Walkins, *Cartels in Action*, Krauf Reprint, (New York, 1975).
10. C. Tugendhat, *The Multinationals*, Penguin, (London, 1971), p.44.
11. K. Marx, *Capital*, op. cit., Vol. III, p.861.
12. P.A. Sweezy, op. cit. p.273, who attributes this observation to Hilferding.
13. P.A. Sweezy, op. cit. p.273.
14. F. Engels, *Outlines of a Critique of Political Economy*, (1843) in Marx, *Economic and Philosophic Manuscripts* of 1844, (Moscow, 1974), p.167, See also Vol. I of Lenin, *Imperialism*, op. cit. pp.84-85, 96.
15. K. Marx, *Capital*, op. cit. Vol. III, p.606.
16. V. I. Lenin, op. cit. p.30-33.
17. K. Marx, *Capital*, op. cit. Vol. III.
18. V.I. Lenin, op. cit. p.46.
19. V.I. Lenin, op. cit. p.58.
20. K. Marx, *Capital*, op. cit. Vol. III. p.95.
21. E.J. Hobsbawn, *Industry and Empire*, Penguin, (London, 1969), p.148.
22. A.K. Caincross, *Home and Foreign Investment*, 1870-1913, (London, 1954), p.180.
23. See for instance Imlah, *Economic Elements in the Pax Britannica*, Harvard University Press, (Harvard, 1956) and Reddaway, *Effects of British Investment Overseas*, Cambridge University Press, (London, 1967).
24. A.K. Caincross, op. cit. p.197.
25. A.K. Caincross, op. cit. Ch. IX.
26. N. Feis, *Europe, the World's Banker, 1870-1914*, Yale University Press, (Yale, 1930), p.93,94,95.
27. N. Bukharin, *Imperialism and World Economy*, Monthly Review, (New York, 1973), p.45.
28. Quoted in Bukharin, op. cit. p.107.
29. V.I. Lenin, op. cit. p.79-81.

30.   References are to M. Barrat-Brown, *After Imperialism*, Merlin, (London, 1970), p.89-91. Also see Arghiri Emmanuel, *Colonialism and Imperialism*, N.L.R. No.73,, 1970.

31.   K. Marx, *The East India Company — Its History and Results*, in Marx and Engels, On Britain, *Selected Works*, Progress (Moscow, 1973), p.180-181.

32.   M. Dobb, *Political Economy and Capitalism*, Greenwood, (Westport, 1972), p.234-35.

33.   A, Emmanuel, 'Colonialism and Imperialism' *NLR*, No. 73, 197.

34.   Quoted in Bukharin, op. cit. p.85.

35.   V.I. Lenin, op. cit. p.74.

36.   M. Barrat-Brown, *The Economics of Imperialism*, Penguin, (London, 1974), p.185-6.

37.   V.I. Lenin, op. cit. p.79.

38.   V.I. Lenin, op. cit. pp.19-20, the quote is also from the same pages.

39.   V.I. Lenin, op. cit. p.86.

40.   M. Dobb, op. cit. p.309.

41.   C.F. Bastable, *Commerce of Nations*, Methuen, (London, 1923),p.62.

42.   V.I. Lenin, op. cit. p.22.

43.   V.I. Lenin, op. cit. p.75.

44.   M. Barrat-Brown, *After . . .* and *Economics*, op. cit. p.186. See also Emmanuel, op. cit.

45.   V.I. Lenin, op. cit. p.82.

46.   V.I. Lenin, op. cit. p.83.

47.   S. Sideri, *Trade and Power*, (Rotterdam, 1970), p.180.

48.   Oliver & Fage, quoted in Sideri, op. cit. p.188.

49.   S. Sideri, op. cit. p.188-9. Reference in the quotation is to F.H. Hinsley, *British Foreign Policy and Colonial Questions, 1895-1904. The Cambridge History of British Empire*, Vol. III. p.495.

50.   H. Feis, op. cit. p.250-252.

51.   S. Sideri, op. cit. p.190.

52.   The expression is ascribed to Salisbury by Sideri, op. cit. p.190.

53.   S. Sideri, op. cit. p.193.

54.   F. List, op. cit.

55.   Hilferding, op. cit.

56.   C.F. Bastable, op. cit. p.64.

57.   V.I. Lenin, *Imperialism*, op. cit. p.86.

58.   M. Dobb, op. cit. pp.314-15.

59.   Quoted in Lenin, op. cit. p.84.

60.   G. Schulz, *Revolutions and Peace Treaties*,   917-1920, Bond, (New York, 1974). p.1.

61.   P. Sweezy, op. cit. p.322.

62.   V.I. Lenin, *Report on the International Situation and the Fundamental Tasks of the Communist International at the Second Congress of the Communist International*, Moscow, in *Selected Works*, (Moscow, 1971), p.450.

63.   J. M. Keynes, *Economic Consequences of the Peace*, quoted in Lenin's *Report* above.

64.   C.F. Bastable, op. cit. p.68.

65.   A. Lewis, *Economic Survey*, 1919-1939, Unwin University Books, (London, 1966), pp.47-48.

66.   See Table V. in A. Lewis, op. cit. p.48 for details of these.

67.   A. Lewis, op. cit. p.49.

68.   A. Lewis, op. cit. p.49.

69.   S. Amin, *Accumulation on a World Scale*, Monthly Review, (New York, 1973), Vol. I. p.102.

70.   A. Lewis, op. cit. p.56, 149-50. M. Dobb, op. cit. p.328-29.

71.   A. Lewis, op. cit. pp.65, 67.

72.   Quotations are from Lewis, op. cit. p.83.

73.   A. Lewis, op. cit. pp.83-85.

74.   A. Lewis, op. cit. p.95.

75.   L.O. Gardner, *Economic Aspects of New Deal Diplomacy*, University of Wisconsin, (Madison, 1964), p.31.

76.   E. Kaufever, *In a Few Hands*, Penguin, (London, 1966), pp.23-25.

77.   M. Dobb, op. cit. p.322-24.

78.   A. Lewis, op. cit. p.87.

79.   M. Dobb, op. cit. p.361, see generally pp.357-386.

80.   For a recent study on this topic see Harry Braverman, *Labour and Monopoly Capital*, Monthly Review, (New York, 1974).

81.   P.A. Sweezy, op. cit. p.323.

PART FOUR

MULTILATERAL IMPERIALISM

CHAPTER XIV

'Eventually Britain's industrial monopoly in the world will be smashed by American competition, but America will not be in a position to take over Britain's heritage as far as world monopoly is concerned. The relatively favourable conditions which prevailed in England between 1848 and 1870 cannot be recreated anywhere'.

Frederick Engels

'The capitalist system is essentially an international system. If it cannot function internationally, it will break down completely'.

Henry Grady (1942) US Assistant Secretary of State.

When Europe emerged from the second World War it was badly torn up with its economies destroyed. Estimates of war damage are various but there is no doubt that Germany, the main aggressor, came out the worst hit. The Europeans altogether lost 40 million people, including 15 million civilians who died in air-raids, land warfare and gas-chambers. American losses, on the other hand, were meagre in comparison: only 0.6% of the combined Allied losses. (1) In the East, Japan was also destroyed. Eastern Europe was added to the socialist sector of the world. Although the Soviet Union came out victorious it lost 30 million people in the War; but its superior social system soon compensated for this.

Britain, the main participant in the war, incurred over $70 billion in debts. It suffered private capital losses of over $8 billion and used up $750 million of gold reserves. To prosecute the war, it sold $6 billion of overseas investments. On the social front the country lost one-third of its housing and incurred a $3.5 billion loss in its merchant shipping. (2)

The US came out of the war the strongest capitalist power. Its GNP rose 100% in five years between 1939 and 1944; what the Allies were losing by waging war, the US was gaining. Thus whereas the US gold reserves were $4 billion in 1932, they rose to $20.6 billion in 1958, as compared to the combined gold and dollar reserves of Britain which rose only slightly from $0.6 billion to $3.1 billion, in the same period. (3) According to Woodruff the US share of world capital exports in 1914 were 6.3%, by 1930 35.3% and 59.1% in 1960. Great Britain's share on the other hand fell from 50.3% to 43.8% and then to 24.5% over the same period. France and Germany lost ground drastically from 39.5% to 11.0% and finally to 5.8%. (4) This, if anything, shows the hegemonic position the US was attaining over its imperialist allies.

Although under her Neutrality Act of 1935, the US had banned the sale of arms to belligerents, this law was soon repealed in 1939, thus allowing her monopolies to reap huge profits. The belligerents were permitted to buy arms provided they paid cash and transported the arms in American ships. US gold imports increased as a result from $1.4 billion in 1936 to $4.7 in 1940. Furthermore under the Lend-Lease Act the US government was allowed to lend, lease or otherwise supply military equipment to any country approved by the President. The Lend-Lease supplies enabled the US monopolies up to 1945 to increase their sales enormously. The profitability of huge monopolies jumped from $3,300 million in 1938 (10.3% of GNP), to $107,400 million 1941-1945 (23.8% of GNP).

The US was quick to seize its chance and emerged as the leading imperialist power in the whole imperialist camp. A new imperialist policy of redivision came to the fore: the 'Open Door' strategy which the US had been pursuing during the interwar years. This new policy was reflected in high monopoly circles. In a publication of the monopolists who stood to gain by this policy it was declared that:

> 'American imperialism can afford to complete the work the British started; instead of salesmen and planters, its representatives can be brains and bulldozers, technicians and machine tools. American imperialism does not need extraterritoriality; it can get on better in Asia if the Tuans and Sahibs stay home'. (5)

This clearly expressed a position of hegemonic self-confidence in which power is exercised through economic control from a distance. The US had seen its immediate competitors shattered. It had nothing to fear from them.

As early as 1939, as soon as it became apparent that war was inevitable, the US started planning its post-war strategy. Secretary of State Hull supervised the drawing up of such a blue-print because 'the President desired to be able later to reach in his basket and to find there whatever he needed in regard to the post-war policy and meanwhile wished to devote himself wholly to ways and means of winning the war'. (6) The rationale behind the US policy was basically to break into the imperial and colonial markets which its allies enjoyed to the detriment of the US. As Richard Gardiner has recalled in a useful book covering this period:

> 'The First World War did much to stimulate American concern with the political importance of non-discrimination. An influential body of literature developed which cited unequal opportunity as one of the major causes of the conflict. Closed trade areas controlled by Imperial powers were held to deny other countries their natural rights to the vital raw materials, markets and investment outlets'. (7)

Moreover a letter written by Williams Culbertson, Acting Chairman of the Tariff Commission, to US Secretary of State Hughes had pointed out that major US export industries had been transformed into mass-producing industries turning out large amounts of products.

> 'These products were particularly vulnerable to the impact of tariff preferences and other forms of discrimination. The US quickly recognised that its growing industrial efficiency might be progressively offset if American products were not guaranteed equal access to foreign markets'.

The main culprit against whom US strategies were aimed was clearly Britain herself, for she controlled the biggest empire, but US strategy required British support to succeed. This support, however, was not difficult to obtain, particularly in view of the impending Loan Agreement which had to be negotiated by Britain with the US. Britain needed the money badly, for her balance of payments was in terrible shape. Whereas her receipts in 1946 amounted to £363 millions, payments in the same year were £527 million, a deficit of some £164 million. Britain had little choice since she needed this loan from the US. Under Article VII of the Lend-Lease Agreement between the US and Britain, the US insisted on non-discrimination as regards importation of goods into Great Britain and on the Most-Favoured-Nation principle which secured access to Empire markets. US Secretary of State Dean Acheson pointed out that Britain could not expect to take aid from the US and then exclude her trade.

Faced with this situation, Keynes, on behalf of Britain, accepted the agreement in return for a $3.75 billion loan; the conditions were that Britain would: (a) pay for imports from the US with dollars or gold after 1947, (b) spend a $930 million credit in the US, (c) refuse all loans to the Commonwealth nations on more favourable terms than the US was granted, and (d) establish the same quotas on goods coming from the Empire as on those coming from the US. Success in this policy is reflected in the optimism of the US monopolists. In a letter from one of them (Robert Wood) to William Clayton, US Assistant Secretary of State, it was stated: 'If you succeed in doing away with the Empire Preference and opening up the Empire to United States Commerce, it may well be that we can afford to pay a couple of billion dollars for the privilege'. (9)

To open up these markets meant interfering with the colonial system. In the proposals for the Atlantic Charter the European powers were required by the US to agree to 'self-determination' of colonial peoples as a guiding principle. Welles, the US Under-Secretary of State had exclaimed:

> 'The age of imperialism is ended. The right of all peoples to their freedom must be recognised . . . The principles of the Atlantic Charter must be guaranteed to the world as a whole — in all oceans and in all continents'. (10)

Point IV of the Charter specifically underlined the whole post-war multilateral policy, and the whole question of markets as follows:

> 'They [i.e. the US and Britain] will endeavour, with due respect for
> their existing obligations, to further the enjoyment by all states,
> great or small, victor or vanquished, *of access, on equal terms*, to
> the trade and to the raw materials of the world which are needed for
> their economic prosperity'.

As we saw in Chapter XIII, the crisis of the interwar years which led
to the second World War was behind these measures. The collapse of the
Gold Standard which was the bulwark of free convertibility of currencies
brought about serious problems in the monetary field. The ensuing
competitive devaluations and exchange controls so radically reduced
international trade that almost all the imperialist countries resorted to
prohibitions and tariff barriers to protect their markets. The British
Imperial Preference System was just one example of such economic
order.

The US set out not only to generalise the 'Open Door' policy in the
Allies' colonial territories, but to do so as champions of 'freedom'! The
strategy of neo-colonialism must be credited to the US at this period,
for it was in its interest to hasten the implementation of neo-colonial
strategy as opposed to a 'classical' colonial one. The crisis that capitalism
faced and which needed solution was the problem of liberalised trade,
and the mobilisation of capital for 'reconstruction'. This could not be
done with the closed markets, closed sources of raw materials and closed
outlets for capital exports that existed in the inter-war years.

The planning of a multilateral system of world production, trade, and
finance was therefore to be achieved by a three-pronged tactical approach;
namely by creating trade, monetary, financial and political institutions.
In the field of trade the objective was not to aim for 'free trade' — for
practice under monopoly had shown this to be a fallacy — but to reduce to
moderate levels the barriers to trade. This was to be followed up by non-
discriminatory policy in trade. In the currency and monetary field, the
strategy envisaged was not the complete elimination of all kinds of exchange
control, on the contrary the aim was to ensure the 'convertibility' of
currencies, at least for non-nationals.

The principle of non-discrimination required the modification of the
Most-Favoured-Nation-Principle to apply to all nations accepting the
arrangement. The economic strategy was aimed at creating fewer obstacles
to movement of capital and payments on current transactions. Trade
flows had to be influenced by relative price considerations rather than by
artificial means to strike a bilateral balance. Purchases had to be made in
cheapest markets and sales in the most lucrative. Such multilateral
strategy, it was assumed, would promote the international division of
labour under the monopoly capitalism of the post-war era and encourage
each country to specialise in the production of those goods in which it
enjoyed 'the greatest comparative advantage'. This would lead to the best
allocation of resources on an international scale.

This post-war imperialist international arrangement, worked out at Bretton Woods and Havana, found its expression in the multilateral institutions which were created for this purpose. The UNO was envisaged to be the new political institution to oversee 'international peace'. Since the US had excluded itself from the League of Nations (which did not stop war taking place in 1939), it took the lead in the creation of the UNO under its close supervision. Under its Organ, the Economic and Social Council (ECOSOC), the first meeting was organised at Havana to set up an International Trade Organisation (ITO). The financial and economic arrangements elaborated at Bretton Woods led to the establishment of the International Monetary Fund (IMF) and the International Bank for Reconstruction and Development (IBRD). Since the arrangements made at Havana for the ITO, resulting in the Havana Charter, were never approved by the US Congress, a temporary arrangement, known as the General Agreement on Trade and Tariffs (GATT), came into force instead. This turned out to be the permanent trade organisation which is still in existence to date. Here it is necessary only to go into the main provisions of these arrangements for the proper understanding of how the multilateral system was to work.

The IMF. This was the first of the so-called *Bretton-Woods System* institutions, through which post-war monopoly capital tried to establish a currency and monetary policy which would make multilateral trade and finance possible. It was launched with a modest $9 billion dollars in gold and foreign exchange. When the socialist states refused to join the institution the amount was reduced to $8 billion. As already explained the collapse of the Gold Standard in 1925 and 1931 created problems in the currency exchange field. Under the earlier system, balance of payments deficits corrected themselves automatically, because the gold to pay the deficit was physically transported to the creditor country, which had the effect of depressing prices of goods and labour. This in turn had the 'desired' effect of making the products of the debtor country cheaper, enabling them to become competitive in the world market and hence to attract capital (gold) and export orders. In this way currencies were made stable in relation to each other.

Monopoly changed all this. In the competition for markets competitive devaluations of currencies and other practices brought international trade almost to a halt. The competitive devaluations also resulted in bilateralism since the poorer countries without the necessary convertible currencies could only import goods through exporting their own goods to the exporting country. Movements of capital were greatly hindered by this development and, as a result, international investment was reduced to almost nothing.

The aim of the *Articles of Agreement* of the IMF were to ensure stability in the international monetary field by promoting international monetary cooperation through a permanent institution which provided the machinery for 'consultation and collaboration' on these matters. In this way it was envisaged to secure the advantages of a Gold Standard without gold — i.e., the dollar was 'as good as gold'. The Fund was further to facilitate the expansion in world trade by maintaining orderly exchange arrangements and by eliminating the competitive exchange depreciation which had characterised the inter-war period. In this way the Fund was to assist in the establishment of *a multilateral system of payments*, develop respect for current transactions between members, and eliminate foreign exchange restrictions.

To this end every member was assigned a quota by the Fund, which could only be altered by a majority of 85% of the total voting power. The allocation gave the US and its major allies over 85% of the quotas and hence over 85% of total voting power. The US as the single major contributor at first was allocated 36% of the total quota. This now stands at 23%. In this way decision-making was tied to the contribution made. The quota had to be paid for in gold and a portion in a member's own currency.

The requirement for non-discrimination in payments on current transactions was provided for in Article VIII and XIV of the Articles of Agreement of the Fund. Article VIII specifically provided that:

> 'No member may, without the approval of the Fund, impose restrictions on the making of payments or transfers for current international transactions, or engage in discriminatory currency arrangements or multiple currency practices'.

This Article was supplemented by the provisions of Article XIV which exempted those members who could not comply with the stringent requirements of Article VIII for a transitional period, during which they were required to do everything possible to move to full convertibility as required by Article VIII. Competitive devaluation was outlawed by constituting the Fund as the determiner of the proper level of exchange rates. Each member was free to establish the 'par value' for its currency in terms of gold in consultation with the Fund. Any change in this value above 10% was to be subject to approval by the Fund.

The Funds current pool of currencies stands at about $29 billion which the Fund can 'sell' to members in balance of payment difficulties, and has acquired since 1971 a power to create Special Drawing Rights (SDR) as 'a supplementary asset' in addition to gold and reserve currencies to increase international liquidity. This huge Fund pool 'has provided in practice a kind of bribe in favour of international multilateral trade, and against nationalist or bilateral solutions to payments difficulties'. (11) The Fund has from its inception been subjected to US global interests together with its main allies against weaker countries in the imperialist exploitation of peoples. Moreover, the US has relied on it considerably, particularly after the 1960s, to solve its deficit problems and hence strengthen its competitive position, financing 10% of its deficit from 1960 to 1967. What is more, the Fund invests most of its resources in US securities thus further strengthening the US financial oligarchy. (12)

The IBRD (The 'World Bank'). This was the second of the *Bretton Woods System* institutions. It was officially established in June 1946, with a subscribed capital of $10 billion, of which only 20% had then been paid. The balance of 80% was to be on call in proportion to each member's subscription. As with the IMF, the main voice behind the Bank was the US. This was inevitable since the dollar was the only usable currency at this time. The US originally subscribed 40% of the capital of the Bank, and consequently her voting strength was 40%. This has now been reduced to 25%.

The central role of the Bank was to be the mobilisation of capital for reconstruction and to stimulate the flow of private investment. It was made quite clear in the official policy of the Bank from the very beginning that its role 'was not so much what the Bank could lend out of its capital as the concept of the Bank as a safe bridge over which private capital could move into the international field'. (13) This capital was at the time US capital, which is why the US insisted that the Bank was 'not created to supersede private banks', in the words of Assistant Secretary of State, Dean Acheson. These demands were re-echoed by the Secretary of the Treasury, Henry Morgenthau:

> 'The chief purpose of the Bank for International Reconstruction and Development is to guarantee private loans made through the usual investment channels. It would make loans only when these could not be floated through the normal channels at reasonable rates'. (14)

It is also for this reason that US banks which had hitherto opposed the creation of the Bank decided to 'back it 100 per cent'. (14) thus removing the main obstacle to its creation.

In its early history the Bank could only raise its money from US banks, by floating bonds on the US money market. It could, therefore, pursue no policies which were unacceptable to US monopoly capital. Its interest rates were to be equivalent or higher than those prevalent in the money markets. Right from the beginning, its loans were to go to 'development' projects which were approved by the Bank officials. Loans and debentures were never to exceed its total assets. This was necessary to ensure repayment to the US monopolies. Moreover, all loan transactions required government guarantee from the borrowing country.

Although the Bank's loans were not supposed to be tied to particular countries' goods, the Bank has encouraged the combination of long-term bilateral development funds alongside the Bank's funds. In this case the Bank does not object to the loan from a particular country being tied to the sale of its goods. Since funds come from the US and other major capitalist countries, non-discrimination entails multilateral *competitive bidding*. Hence the Bank's funds can only be utilised on the basis of international public bidding in which all monopolies have a chance. Moreover, the Bank is not allowed to compete with private Banks, consequently its funds are lent on commercial terms at interest rates ranging from 5 to 7%. This is because, as we have pointed out, it has to borrow its loanable capital and as such it serves the international financial oligarchy. Currently the Bank is largely under the control of the Rockfeller-Chase Manhattan-Standard Oil group. (15)

The Bank's role is to stimulate private capital flow particularly to the Third World countries. The current burdensome indebtedness of these countries is evidence of its 'success'. The creation of the International Finance Corporation (IFC) whose role is to raise and lend funds from private sources to private business enterprises, without the host country's guaranteeing the loan, was intended to facilitate this even further. To create confidence for the investors, the Bank championed the Convention for the Settlement of Investment Disputes with the establishment of an International Centre at the Bank's headquarters in Washington. This convention has been ratified by many Third World countries, in spite of earlier resistance to similar conventions. One writer has tritely observed:

> 'In all these ways Morgenthau's usurious money lenders — far from being driven from the temple of international finance — were brought into new and productive forms of collaboration with national governments'. (16)

The sister organisation, the International Development Association (IDA), was formed to perform the opposite function of raising funds from governments for governments, and these are normally given on 'soft terms', usually for 'social' projects, mainly infrastructure. The real function of the Bank and its affiliated institutions is, apart from enabling the export of capital, the expansion of export and production of goods overseas to reap increasing surplus-value from the Third World neo-colonies. We shall come back to this question in Chapter XXII. It must be pointed out furthermore that these institutions are assisting international monopoly capital in its drive to further concentration and centralisation.

The GATT. The GATT which in reality was a *trade agreement* was set up, in the words of the preamble, to raise standards of living by ensuring full employment and the raising of real incomes and effective demand and by developing full use of resources through expanding production and exchange. To this end the parties agreed to enter into reciprocally and mutually advantageous arrangements directed to the substantial reduction of tariffs and other barriers to trade. (17) The non-discrimination principle was enshrined in the General Most-Favoured-Nation Clause in Article I. This required that there was to be no discrimination between nations, with regard to customs duties and other charges imposed either in connection with the importation or exportation of goods, or on the international transfer of payments for imports and exports. This principle did not apply immediately to preferences in existence of April 10th, 1947, and thereby excluded imperial preferences and other arrangements, to allow a transitional period during which they would be phased out by a diminishing margin of preference in proportion to tariff liberalisation. This was intended to accommodate Britain.

Since the period immediately preceeding the war witnessed a number of barriers to trade, the agreement aimed at the general elimination of quantitative restrictions. Despite this, so many exceptions were included in the agreement that restrictions were finally allowed for agricultural products and for reasons of balance of payments difficulties.(18)

The IMF was made to play a role in this agreement to ensure that quantitative restrictions were not used to defeat the 'free convertibility' provisions of the IMF Articles of Agreement. (19) The 'developing' countries were allowed some use of restrictions to assist 'infant industries' but the provisions were so stringent that most of these new states relied on the balance of payments provision in Article XII instead of Article XVIII.

The Agreement permitted discrimination of a new type which was justified on the grounds that it led to more trade. This was the exception with regard to the formation of customs unions and free trade areas. (20) The formation of these was allowed so long as they encompassed 'substantially all the trade' in the union and so long as the common tariff against third countries was on the whole 'not higher or more restrictive' than the previous corresponding duties of each of the trading partners in the union or free trade area.

This exception, however, made nonsense of the fact that the same Agreement did not approve of the creation of new preferential systems. The exception was justified on the ground that although the 'trade diverting' consequences of a union were to be reckoned with, the 'trade creating' effects were greater; a fact which many found difficult to understand. This provision, it must be understood, was being pushed by the 'integrationists' in Europe and prepared the way for the creation of the European Economic Community and other European institutions. It also meant that new preferences could be formed under the guise of 'free trade areas', which has indeed happened. All this was evidence of the struggle against US redivision of the world under its multilateral strategy, and was partly behind the US congressional rejection of both the Havana Charter and the GATT itself. (21)

Although the US congress ratified neither the ITO Charter nor the GATT, it has been the main spirit behind the operation of the GATT under Presidential powers. Hence the main 'rounds' of negotiations for 'liberalising' international trade have been initiated by the US. These have included the 'Dillon Round', the 'Kennedy Round' and the 'Nixon Ford Round'. All these brought about further reduction in tariffs, but, as experience has shown, reduction in tariffs has had the effect of re-creating non-tariff barriers such as quantitative restrictions, import surcharges, etc. As evidence of this, the US itself has had to impose barriers by way of surcharges against various products including textiles exported by Japan.

This is, indeed, necessary to protect old monopolies in this industry.

CHAPTER XV

The conception of the system of multilateralism was a last ditch attempt to save capitalism on a world scale from the unleashed forces of socialism and national liberation. As already indicated, the end of the first World War saw the birth of the Soviet Union as the first socialist state. The end of the second World War saw the whole of Eastern Europe come into the socialist fold. This was immediately followed by the liberation of China, North Korea, and North Vietnam. By working out the multilateral strategy, US imperialism undertook to underwrite the other capitalist states and provide them with a 'security' cover, both for them-selves and for their neo-colonial puppets, in exchange for which the US was henceforth entitled to an 'Open Door' red carpet under the new umbrella of redivision.

Having been weakened by the imperialist war, imperialist Europe decided on a Common Market in response to the necessity to rebuild and to resist US hegemony in the multilateral framework of imperialist competition. The Europeans, however, realised their own weak position, and for a long time had to accept US supervision and sponsorship in the period immediately after the war. Moreover, they needed the US defence system to stem the advance of socialism.

An official publication of the European Community gives this account:

'In the spring of 1945 the democratic world system which for a century had promised limitless progress towards peace and plenty, lay in ruins. Of the major democratic nations only the United States was intact. Western Europe was torn and exhausted. The Soviet Union emerged victorious and war-weary. Stalin's armies were arrayed across the center of Europe, ready to spring upon the thin remains of European democracy which already was being worried by aggressive communist parties.

To prevent the extinction of European democracy, the United States mounted the Marshall Plan and forged the North Atlantic Treaty Organization (NATO) alliance. These turned the tide. But it became apparent that more than economic and military shoring up from the outside was needed to save Europe over the long pull. Revolutionary changes in the political and economic structure of Europe itself were needed. The nation state system in Europe had bred a century of bloody wars and now it acted as a straitjacket on economic recovery from World War II'. (22)

In this effort to 'unify' Europe a number of 'communities' emerged beginning with the Coal and Steel Community (ECSC) in 1951, and then the Atomic Energy Commission (EURATOM) in 1957. The Common Market emerged with the signing of the Treaty of Rome in 1957 by the 'Six'. The aim of the Common Market was to remove tariff and other barriers to trade and free the movement of capital within the market. A common agricultural policy was also outlined to be achieved on the basis of a programme of gradual implementation. Britain opted out of this market and led the creation of the European Free Trade Area (EFTA) whose convention was signed in Stockholm in 1959, bringing together the 'Seven' into a looser union, which excluded production and trade in agriculture from the aim of their union. The Common Market was later (1972) joined by Britain, Ireland and Norway to form the 'Nine' members of the present European Community, having merged the earlier communities into a single Community under the Treaty of Merger of 1971. Was this perhaps the beginning of the United States of Europe which Winston Churchill so emotionally called for in his Zurich Speech of 16th September, 1946, in which he appealed for French and German reconciliation within the Union? (23)

In his *Slogan of the United States of Europe*, (24) Lenin, in 1915, described this idea in the context of the economic conditions of imperialism, as 'either impossible or reactionary'. He pointed out that:

'A United States of Europe under capitalism is tantamount to an agreement on the partition of the colonies . . . No division can be effected otherwise than in "proportion to strength" . . . Of course *temporary* agreements are possible between capitalists and between states. In this sense a United States of Europe is possible as an agreement between the *European* capitalists . . . but to what end? Only for the purpose of suppressing socialism in Europe, of jointly protecting colonial booty against Japan and America, who have been badly done out of their share by the present partition of colonies, and the increase of whose might during the last fifty years has been immeasurably more rapid than that of backward and monarchist Europe now turning senile'. (24)

This was 1915, but the essential elements of Lenin's argument apply *mutatis mutandis* to the period under consideration. There is no doubt that the Common Market of Europe was a reactionary set-up aimed against socialism in Europe, national liberation in the colonies and general US superiority. There can also be no doubt that it was a *temporary* agreement of European capitalists against the workers of Europe and the workers and peasants of the colonial and neo-colonial Third World. To assert otherwise is to hold that imperialism would have changed its nature within itself out of its wars. The perpetual inter-community struggles by individual countries to protect themselves against others is further proof of the fragile nature of the European Community. Moreover, its policies towards Third World countries demonstrates its aim of domination and exploitation of these countries.

It has been argued by 'neo-Marxists' and other elements that the Community is evidence of the 'changed' situation created by the internationalisation of production, capital and labour. Pierre Jalee in his latest book, (25) for instance, maintains that 'the internal cohesion of the imperialist system itself is a necessity that supersedes all antagonisms'. (26) We do not intend to go into this question at this stage; but reserve it for the conclusion. Suffice it to say here that 'unity' of monopolists in the imperialist system is a contradiction in terms and reality. Whilst monopolies have a common interest in their fight against socialism and national liberation, this is only on the basis of the inherent contradiction of capitalism *manifested* in competition for markets and sources of raw materials. In periods of critical crisis this is resolved through war.

Be that as it may, European integration at this time was subject to US supervision and economic interests which desired to reconstruct Europe only on the basis of the exploitation of Europe. It could not have been otherwise. Any benefits that accrued to Europe were necessary in as much as they strengthened her against the onslaught of socialism. Thus through the Marshall Plan, the US pushed into Western Europe vast direct investments and established a bridgehead inside the European market. In this way it was laying a basis for its transnational corporations to operate inside the market, through the policy of multilateralism.

By 1967 US trade with the EEC earned her a $1.2 billion trade surplus yearly from 1958 through to 1967. In 1969 the EEC bought from the US goods worth $7 billion and sold her only $5.8 billion worth. Whereas US exports to the European Free Trade Area jumped by only 3.9% and to the rest of the world by only 9.7% those to the EEC went up by 13.9%. At the same time EEC exports to the US dropped by 1.4% while those from the rest of the world increased by 8.5%. (27)

As regards capital exports, US direct investments in Europe climbed by 400% in the period 1958 to 1967 from $1.9 billion to more than $9 billion; while US investments in the rest of the world only doubled. This fundamentally reversed the positions as of 1956 when Europe's investments in the US exceeded those of the US in Europe. These direct investments by the US were by transnational corporations. The sales of these corporations inside the EEC amounted to roughly $60 billion a year. What was more important, the corporations, because of their presence in the EEC, were able to tap European capital for local investment, thus using European capital to exploit the working class in Europe.

Europe's response was partly the creation of the European Common Market, but as Servan-Schreiber pointed out in his book *The American Challenge*, (27) this did not stop US penetration of European markets. On the contrary US superiority in science and technology had put it in a dominant position. The creation of the EEC, far from being a barrier, in fact became a contributory factor to the success of the US corporations who took advantage of the increased market inside it. Moreover, the returns on investment were higher in Europe than those in the US, and this was sufficient motivation to operate inside the market by setting up transnational corporations to invest on the spot.

The creation of the EEC was not only significant in terms of putting up barriers against third countries including the US but also in regard to relations with the Third World. The EEC entered into 'free-trade' association agreements with former colonial territories. This neo-colonial arrangement enabled Europe to continue the joint exploitation of the former colonies under the benevolent eye of US imperialism which took advantage of its corporations in the EEC to participate directly in the exploitation of these neo-colonies. This was, of course, quite apart from its own direct dealings with the neo-colonies.

The enlargement of the community with the entry of the UK and the two other European countries has created the conditions for broadening this neo-colonial tie-up to 46 former colonies of the European powers in Africa, the Caribbean and the Pacific (ACP). The recently concluded 'Lome Convention' is the result of this new re-arrangement of the enlarged Europe. The main idea of these association link-ups is to maintain, by such inducements as 'aid and technical assistance' and 'trade preferences', the neo-colonial ties by which Europe is assured of raw material supplies and markets as well as outlets for capital exports.

Although under the post-war multilateral strategy the US has an interest in ensuring that its junior partners have access to these openings as against the socialist countries, it too is interested in them. It is for this reason that President Nixon instructed his representatives in Europe to insist that the EEC drop the idea of obtaining 'reverse preferences' to the exclusion of the US in return for the so-called 'duty free entry' of raw materials and agricultural products from the 46 ACP countries. (28)

In Asia the US had an interest in converting Japan from a defeated nation into a junior partner in the multinational system. At first it subjugated the Japanese capitalists but it later encouraged them by offering support. This was necessary for the global strategy to 'contain communism' in South East Asia and to confront the People's Republic of China. But before entrusting Japan with this role, US imperialism rushed in vast amounts of direct investment and technology to Japan and used it as a stepping stone for the neo-colonial subjugation of South East Asia. Meagre US investments in Japan in the 1950s had by the 1960s grown to sizeable proportions. Thus, of the current estimated foreign investment of $7 billion, the US controls 60-70%. This finance is mainly provided by US controlled banks in Japan. US policy has been to create conditions conducive to Japanese economic growth, with its giant corporations either solely or jointly commanding the heights. For this reason, a greater proportion of the huge military expenditure for the Vietnam war went to Japan than to Vietnam itself, generating vast sums of money for Japanese industry through increased purchasing power in the entire area of South East Asia. (29) This clearly assisted the US imperialist strategy of 'containing communism' in South East Asia, but also acted as a prop to her sagging economy. Table III below shows the extent of this military expenditure.

Table III

US Defence Expenditure in Japan and Vietnam 1964-1969 (\$million)

Year	Japan	Vietnam
1964	321	64
1965	346	188
1966	484	408
1967	538	564
1968	581	558
1969	320	303

Source: Halliday and McCormack: *Japanese Imperialism Today*,p.11.

As a result, the US has gained substantially from its investments in the entire area. Her subordination of Japan in the field of technical tie-ups, patents, and licences has been extreme. Over the two decades 1950-70 Japan has paid out over ten times what it took in on technological royalties. It paid out \$3,175 million to the US monopolies as compared to \$279.2 million it received from the US. Japan has tried to close this gap but only very slowly. The US position, although increasingly challenged still remains hegemonic. (30)

Thus although for the fiscal year 1970, Japan paid out \$506.1 million for imported technologies (17.7% over the 1969 total), its technological exports came to \$69 million — a rise of 27.7% over 1969. A large proportion of her out-payments had to go to the US, since nearly 70% of the 2,563 technical agreements signed by her with foreign interests between 1949 and 1963 were with US companies. (31). In the words of the *Far East Economic Review* quoted by Halliday and McCormack, 'reciprocity in this field is minimal'. (31)

In spite of this, because of the comparative weakness of direct US investments in South East Asia compared with those in other parts of the world (2.3%), US policy is still aimed at strengthening Japan, to help 'tie down reactionary regimes' as well as 'pacifying the area'. This policy was best expressed by President Eisenhower himself when he said:

'One of Japan's greatest opportunities for increased trade lies in a free and developing South East Asia . . . The great need in one country is for raw materials, in the other country for manufactured goods. The two regions complement each other markedly. By strengthening of Vietnam and helping insure the safety of the South Pacific and South East Asia, we gradually develop the great trade potential between this region . . . and highly industrialized Japan to the benefit of both. In this way freedom in the Western Pacific will be greatly strengthend'. (32)

It is clear that US led multilateral imperialism depended on the subjugation of the greater mass of the people of Asia, Latin America and Africa. The second layer of sovereign states like Portugal, Spain and Turkey were tucked in at the bottom of the system to service it. Moreover, countries like Portugal were appended to the NATO alliance for the purpose of strangling the liberation movements in Africa, to the benefit of the powerful imperialist states. The US could only assure itself of the success of this policy of subjugation and exploitation through a warfare machine.

As we have seen the post-war period is characterised by an intensified 'bipolar world' in which the division between the Capitalist World and Socialist World becomes more pronounced. The end of the war saw the destruction of some of the capitalist countries by other capitalist countries. The Soviet defence of Eastern Europe, leading to its integration in the socialist system, together with the addition of the Asian People's Republics to the Socialist World, created panic in the imperialist camp.

US strategy had foreseen as far back as 1920 the dangers that the Soviet Union posed to the imperialist system. In 1938 the adviser to President Roosevelt, W.C. Bullit, had stated: 'Everytime the Soviet Union extends its power over another area or state, the US and Great Britain lose another normal market'. (33) It was clear that the changes that had taken place in the world including those after the second World War had upset this balance of power which had to be maintained if imperialism *as a system* was to survive. This development was emphasised by the US defence department itself in a statement of the post war situation:

'The 20th century has seen the old order disintegrate under the impact of two World Wars, the rise of communism supported by a significant power base in both Europe and Asia, the end of the colonial era leading to the creation of a multitude of weak but strident and nationalistic new nations, and the rapid technological change, particularly the development of nuclear weapons. During the same period the US and the Soviet Union began to emerge as the two leading powers. One long-term implication of these events was that US national interest would require us to accept and discharge the broader responsibilities of a world power. A second implication was that the most pressing of our international interests has become the re-creation of a relatively stable world environment, a new equilibrium to replace the one destroyed by the events of the four decades following World War I'. (34)

To this 'relatively stable environment', there were two threats which had to be met: communism in Europe and Asia, and the liberation movements in the Third World. The warfare machine which was put into force took these threats as the basis for 'free world' military strategy, to protect and maintain within its sphere much of the neo-colonial world for joint exploitation under US supervision and hegemony.

The implementation of the policy of anti-communism required a three pronged approach. (35) Firstly, by rehabilitating the armies of the 'Allies' and incorporating them into a US led alliance; secondly, by setting up a network of military pacts and bases around the perimeter of the socialist camp; and thirdly, by obtaining the arms and men to lend muscle to the network. These objectives were met by setting up the Marshall Plan and by establishing the North Atlantic Treaty Organisation (NATO), as well as getting Japan into the arrangement by signing a peace treaty in 1951. Further NATO was soon supplemented by the setting up of a string of defence pacts around the world. These included the South East Asia Treaty Organisation (SEATO), the Central Treaty Organisation (CENTO or Bhagdad Pact); and a multitude of bilateral treaties for 'mutual defence and assistance' with dozens of puppet states like Turkey, Pakistan, the Philippines, Formosa, Japan, Spain and others. In this way, the US obtained the use of 1,400 foreign bases in more than 31 countries. These bases cost nearly $4 billion and were manned by about one million US soldiers. (36)

To maintain these bases and to supply the military hardware vast sums of money were allocated for recurrent expenditure and for research and development in new weapons. In this latter exercise the US warfare state and big industry had a common interest; the large amounts of money spent on the research and development of weaponry went into the pockets of the huge corporations in military contracts. It has been estimated that of the top 100 Department of Defence (DOD) Contractors in the fiscal year 1971 alone, 39 were also transnational corporations. These were companies like General Dynamics, Lockheed, and General Electric — which alone had over 13 % of the contracts, worth over $4 billion in sales. (37) Moreover, the research which was carried on for military purposes at public expense has from time to time been made available to these corporations for private use to expand overseas markets.

As with all dying imperialism, military demands and defence requirements constitute a larger and larger part of the national cake, to the point where the system can only survive with increasing military expenditure and consumption. US imperialism is no exception in this respect. Professor J.D. Bernal has observed that 'The bitter fact remains that, to a degree unimagined before, physical research in capitalist countries is becoming dominated by military demands. In applications of research the military aspect is even more prominent. The amount devoted to specifically military research and development in the United States and Britain are now many times greater than those spent before the war'. (38) Thus US governmental spending on military research and development rose from £5 million in 1937 to £2,800 million and in Britain from £1.5 million to £246 million, in the same period. (39) These figures are multiplied several times if we take into account the expenditures of the other imperialist states.

Perhaps the most critical area for the imperialist warfare state was the suppression of national liberation movements. There is no doubt that the whole multilateral strategy was aimed at keeping the remainder of the exploited neo-colonial Third World firmly under imperialist control. This has been demonstrated already. The strategy to 'contain communism' was intended to ensure that the neo-colonial reserve was not threatened. The military complex built up in the post-war period and the various tactics used in the Third World were aimed at the realisation of this strategy. Third World agricultural products and industrial raw materials were vital to multilateral imperialism. In fact without such neo-colonial control of these resources there could be no imperialism. Many Western spokesmen emphasised this fact. The fact that the post-war period has been characterised by the need by imperialism to crush any threat to imperialist interests in the Third World constitutes the very history of the period.

In 1966 Robert McNamara, the US War Secretary, reported that in the previous decade alone there had been '149 serious internal insurgencies' in the Third World. Richard Barnet correctly points out in his analysis that the majority of political violence since 1945 has not been between states but *within* states, wars which can be characterised as national liberation wars against imperialism. (40) Modelski records 65 'substantial armed conflicts' in the period 1945-1970 which he calls national wars. (41) In fact, as the US News and World Report put it, these wars have been current perpetually ever since the end of the second World War. The Report states: 'Since the US entered World War II, the pictogram on these pages shows, there have been only three full calendar years — 1956, 1957, and 1959 — in which this country was at peace, with none of its forces involved in foreign conflict situations. American servicemen, planes and ships have intervened in the past 32 years in nearly every corner of the globe, in Europe, Africa, the Middle East, Asia and Latin America'. (42)

These conflicts checkered the whole history of US imperialism since the end of the second World War, and nearly all of them have not been 'internal insurgencies' as McNamara calls them but wars of national liberation. In suppressing these wars, the US has had to resort not only to its war machine, but also to its puppet armies maintained by the petty-bourgeois regimes in the neo-colonies. The principal and objective function of these regimes is to guard, advance and fight for imperialism against the revolutionary forces of national liberation and socialist construction in the neo-colonies. The armies of these puppet states have been trained and equipped with modern NATO weapons and maintained on US and other imperialist official aid. Moreover, this aid has been used by these puppet mini-armies to boost the imperialist weapons industry, to the mutual advantage of the US industrial/military complex and to a lesser extent of the petty-bourgeoisie in the Third World neo-colonies. In this manner the petty-bourgeoisie has played its historical role as true agent of imperialism.

Foreign aid, which has primarily been for military purposes, has grown from year to year. Table IV overleaf shows US economic and military aid to its puppet armies for a period of only 10 years.

161

Table IV

US Economic and Military Aid July, 1 1957 to June 30, 1967.

To:	Billion $	Per cent
Developed countries	7.5	13
'Client' countries	20.7	37
All other underdeveloped countries	27.8	50
	56.0	100

Source: Magdoff, op. cit. p.124. For details of 'client state' see Magdoff, but these are the areas directly involved in the containment policy.

The magnitude of this military aid can be judged from the US appropriations for the single year 1972. In that year forty five countries received aid through a single programme, the Military Assistance Program (MAP), in which $545 million was involved in all. Of this $38 million went in training, the rest in 'supply and operations' which included the procurement of 'weapons and weapons systems. The largest items were vehicles and weapons which took $114 million, ammunition ($109 million) and aircraft ($65 million). According to Lenny Siegel, most of this aid went to 'forward defence' countries, US Allies (en) circling China and the Soviet Union'. Of the total MAP, 68% was appropriated for East Asia and 20% for the near East (including Greece and Turkey), Cambodia ($180 million), South Korea ($150 million) and Turkey ($60 million). (43)

In addition to the MAP, there were other aid programmes. These were the Excess Property Assistance wherein equipment declared 'excess' in the US was 'given away'; in 1969 this involved no less than $54 million. In 1970 a ceiling of $300 million was imposed on this programme. There was also the Service Funded Aid, $2.3 billion in 1972 alone, which was a Vietnam War related aid to countries in Indo-China. The Foreign Military Sales, which were financed by the Import-Export Bank as 'sales' mainly to Germany and Israel were estimated by Senator Fulbright at $750 million a year. The sales for 1971 included $416 million in non-governmental commercial sales, and $1.173 billion in government sales. The 1972 estimates were $2.83 billion.

In addition there was the Security-Supporting Economic Assistance, political-military aid estimated at $583 million for 1972, intended for 'pacification programmes', public safety and currency support to puppet regimes in South East Asia, Israel and Jordan. To this should be added Food for Peace, which ultimately ended up in military procurements. These funds, generated through the sale of US goods, were estimated at

$120 annually over 8 years. The countries involved were mainly South Korea, South Vietnam, Cambodia and Taiwan.

There are several other programmes under which the puppets were and continue to be maintained, e.g. the Ship-Loan Programme for providing ships to puppet 'allies', for which $90 million were allocated in 1972. Military Assistance Advisory Groups and Missions in these countries received $16 million in 1972 and $57 million was spent on the International Military Headquarters. (44)

As already pointed out these 'aid' deals considerably assist the sales effort of the giant corporations. The military aid programme alone provides about $1 billion in sales annually to US manufacturers and gives shipping concerns one-quarter of their total revenue from exports. In 1971, the Defence Department awarded contracts for $175 million to McDonnel-Douglas Corporation for aircraft, $116 million to General Electric for aircraft engines, $61 million to Lockheed for aircraft and maintenance services, $89 million to Belltelicore for helicopters, $10 million to Chrysler for vehicles, etc. (45) Furthermore, 20 of the top 25 DOD contractors for 1971 were on the list of major US suppliers of weapons and equipment for the military assistance, grant aid and sales programme. (46)

CHAPTER XVI

In the period when the first monopolies emerged, during the 1890s, as we outlined in Part Three, we noticed a merging of industrial capital with bank capital, giving rise to finance capital. We also observed that at this stage of development, the export of capital took on a significant role in comparison to export of goods. This was only possible with the concentration of production and the resultant concentration of capital, leading to the division of the world among the major capitalist powers. As we shall see below, the concentration of production and capital in the US and other imperialist countries has continued unabated. Today monopoly capital constitutes the prominent feature of capitalism. In the age of the giant corporation, apologists of the capitalist system still find it difficult to see the concentration that has taken place and still proceeds. But what is most disturbing is the attack on the Marxist-Leninist analysis by the so-called neo-Marxists who, while purporting to interpret developments in the post-war period within the Marxist-Leninist world outlook, unwittingly undermine the very theoretical base they set out to defend. A clear example of this type of analysis is that provided by Baran and Sweezy in their book, *Monopoly Capital*, (47) published in 1966. The authors modestly describe their effort as 'a sketch', an 'essay' having 'no pretence to comprehensiveness'; they set out to 'begin the process of systematically analysing monopoly capitalism on the basis of the experience of the most developed capitalist society'. (48) Despite this modesty they nevertheless make an attack on Marx's Law of the Tendency of the Rate of Profit to Fall which Marx himself, as we pointed out in chapter IX, described as *'the most important law of political economy'*. (49)

According to Baran and Sweezy monopoly capitalism has negated the competitive model on which Marx's law was based. Under the new development, price competition is no longer operative since the intervention of the state in the market place helps monopoly capitalism to reap higher than average profits. Although abandonment of price competition helps monopoly, it does not lead to the 'end of competition'; on the contrary competition 'takes new forms and rages on with increasing intensity'. Nevertheless, oligopolies and monopolies succeed in approximating prices at a monopoly level, and with the never-ceasing efforts to cut costs of production, the conclusion is 'inescapable that surplus must have a strong and persistent tendency to rise'.

According to Baran and Sweezy, cost reduction is so important to monopoly that the monopoly which is in a strong position can precipitate a price-war. Moreover, the capital goods industry furthers the process of cost reduction by always striving to put something new on the market. Competition in this sector tends to compel capitalists to produce products that are 'designed to help (the buyers) increase their profits' and hence reduce their costs. (50) The off-shoot of all this according to the authors is that:

> 'The whole motivation of cost reduction is to increase profits, and the monopolistic structure of markets enables the corporations to appropriate the lion's share of the fruits of increasing productivity directly in the form of higher profits. This means that under monopoly capitalism, declining costs imply continuously widening profit margins. And continuously widening profit margins in turn imply aggregate profits which rise not only absolutely but as share of national product. If we provisionally equate aggregate profits with society's economic surplus, we can formulate as a law of monopoly capitalism that the surplus tends to rise both absolutely and relatively as the system develops.
>
> This law immediately invites a comparison, as it should, with the classical Marxian law of the falling tendency of the rate of profit. . . By substituting the law of rising surplus for the law of falling profit, we are therefore not rejecting or revising a time-honoured theorem of political economy: we are simply taking account of the undoubted fact that the structure of the capitalist economy has undergone a fundamental change since that theorem was formulated. What is most essential about the structural change from competitive to monopoly capitalism finds its theoretical expression in this substitution.' (51)

Although Baran and Sweezy say that in substituting their law of rising surplus for Marx's law they do not necessarily reject 'this time-honoured theorem', their analysis clearly shows that they treat it as being incapable of explaining developments under monopoly capitalism. Moreover, they go further to show how the monopolists faced with this absolutely and relatively increasing 'surplus' decide to 'absorb' it. Since the surplus can either be 'consumed', 'invested' or 'wasted', and since there is under capitalist development a limit to consumption and investment, the only solution left to the monopoly capitalist is (the) 'wasteful' absorption of it in 'the sales effort,' in 'civilian government' and 'military spending'. (52)

If this analysis looks contrived, it is because it does not explain why the monopoly capitalists should strive to accumulate this amazingly increasing surplus in the first place if they have to go to all this trouble to 'absorb' it. What is it that compels them to engage in accumulation? Baran and Sweezy's 'law' cannot explain imperialism, nor does it explain why the monopoly capitalists should fight wars throughout the world to hold on to colonies and neo-colonies. The analysis seems to suggest that monopolists do this in order to absorb the ever increasing surplus!

Moreover, the 'law' cannot even explain why the monopolists face crises. We have to fall back on Keynes for an explanation. It is of course insufficient to explain capitalist accumulation in terms of 'profit motive'. This leaves the question at an ideological level. The bourgeoisie know and acknowledge that they go into business to 'maximise profits', but this is hardly a satisfactory level at which to leave this fundamental question.

It does not help matters to explain away this negation of Marx by suggesting, as Magdoff appears to do, that all that Baran and Sweezy are trying to do is to explain the 'effects' and not the 'causes' of capital exports in relation to the so-called 'economic surplus'. (53) Why in examining this question should they separate effects from causes; is it not a fundamental point of departure for materialist philosophy that things must be looked at in their totality in order to get to their essence as opposed to their mere forms or appearances?

We might leave the matter there were it not for the fact that the concept of 'economic surplus' itself abandons Marx's theory of value, for it is exactly at this point that Baran and Sweezy acutally make a break with the Law of the Tendency of the Rate of Profit to Fall. Magdoff himself rejects this law as an explanation for the rise in capital exports from the imperialist countries, apparently on the ground that it does not account for the export of loan capital, where the 'rates of interest', although 'generally attractive' overseas, are considerably below the 'industrial rate of profit' at home. (54)

This type of analysis really takes us back into the lap of neo-classical economism, where the saver is presumed to determine whether to invest or not depending on the rate of interest. (55) The point is that under monopoly the issue is far more involved. The financial oligarchy decides whether to invest or not depending on profitability in industry which itself is determined by the organic composition of capital in each area of investment. Indeed, Magdoff in his book, the *Age of Imperialism*, when dealing with the 'new imperialism', leaves out of the analysis the Law of the Tendency of the Rate of Profit to Fall and contents himself with the liberalist 'wisdom', that 'there is no simple explanation for all the variations of real economic and political changes, nor is it fruitful to seek one'. (56)

Nor does Jalee take us closer to reality when in his new book, *Imperialism in the Seventies*, he brushes aside the whole controversy over the Law by comforting himself with the less than scientific solution that 'the principle of the general equalisation of profit rates' can be 'reconciled with a rate of profit for monopolies that is higher than the average rate of profit', (57) without showing how. Instead, he merely gives us figures to prove in a Samuelsonian manner that gross profits have risen in France, which only go to prove that the counteracting factors to the tendency of the rate of profit to fall, which Marx pointed out, were operative.

Sweezy lays the ground for the attack on Marx in his earlier book, *The Theory of Capitalist Development*, in which he begins to knock at the

pedestal of Marx's Law. He attacked the law of value when he stated that
'the conclusion is inescapable that in the real world of capitalist production
the law of value is not directly controlling', accepting Bortkiewicz as
having 'grasped the full significance of the law of value and its use'. (58)
He then proceeded to accept Bortkiewicz's formulation of total price as
being different from total value and mystifies the matter by stating that
'no significant theoretical issues are involved in this divergence', (60) when
in fact it eats away the very roots of the law of value enunciated by Marx.

With the above background it becomes obvious why Sweezy adopts
'underconsumptionist' concepts to explain capitalist contradictions.
Indeed, it soon becomes clear that Baran and Sweezy regard the three
'surplus absorbing' agents as the demand creators in the market place:

> 'The stimulation of demand — the creation and expansion of
> markets — thus becomes to an ever greater degree the leitmotif of
> business and governmental policies under monopoly capitalism . . .
> The question for monopoly capitalism is not whether to stimulate
> demand. It must, on pain of death'. (59)

The above reads like a leaf from Keynes. For Baran and Sweezy the
biggest contradiction for monopoly capital is how to find markets and
not how to maintain production at maximum profitable levels, thereby
disregarding Marx's Law as the fundamental explanation of why capitalist accumulation takes place in the way it does.

In this connection it is all the more interesting that whilst Samir Amin
in his recent book, *Accumulation on a World Scale*, accepts the validity of
Marx's Law as the 'essential and permanent expression of the basic
contradiction of the system', he still finds it necessary to defend Baran
and Sweezy's negation of it, on the ground that the 'appearance of potential surplus is the way the downward tendency manifests itself'. He adopts
the same approach when he states:

> 'It is a surplus that has to be absorbed, and it is indeed absorbed, as
> Baran and Sweezy have shown, not by external trade or export of
> capital (which brings about a return flow of profits) but by internal
> modes of absorption, namely by public expenditure and waste'. (61)

Samir Amin's underconsumptionism is further revealed when in another
part of his book he describes the tendency to underconsumptionism as
'the essential law of accumulation' and as leading to extension of markets.
He states:

> 'It is the contradiction between the capacity to produce and the
> capacity to consume, constantly arising and constantly being over-
> come — the essential law of capitalist accumulation — which accounts
> both for the inherent tendency for the extension of markets and
> for the international movement of capital'. (62)

According to Amin these absorbing agents have the status of a law in
counteracting the falling rate of profit, because 'selling costs', military

expenditure, and 'luxury' consumption make it 'possible to spend profits that cannot be re-invested owing to the inadequacy of the rate of profit'. This fact was according to Amin only 'glimpsed by Marx'. (63)

> 'The system cannot function unless surplus-value is wholly expended, whether it be invested, or "squandered". (64)

This is because the contradiction between the capacity of the society to save and the possibility of profitable investment of new capital, 'the outlets for which lie in current consumption', becomes more intense. (64) Samir Amin cannot hide his underconsumptionist theories under the cover of Marx's Law. Like Baran and Sweezy, he opposes Marx's law of value and the Law of the Tendency of the Rate of Profit to Fall and tries to bring in Keynes through the back door. In any case the whole concept of 'wasteful' absorption of 'surplus', far from explaining the essence of monopoly capitalism, mystifies it and brings it within moralist confines, and at best only deals with it at the circulation level. For us the essence of monopoly capitalism has to be grasped in totality at its production level. We tried to demonstrate this fact in Chapter IX.

As we have shown, military expenditure by the bourgeois state does not contradict but merely helps the monopoly capitalist in his accumulation process. There cannot be monopoly capitalism without the bourgeois state, military expenditure, or 'sales effort'. These are all products of capitalist society. Sweezy's 'counteracting forces to the tendency to underconsumption' are extremely contrived. Although Baran and Sweezy recognise the fact that military expenditure favours the monopolists, they do so, as we have seen, in opposition to Marx's Law. Their position then becomes indistinguishable from that held by Kidron in his book *Western Capitalism Since the War*. (65) Kidron's point is that the permanent threat of overproduction under capitalism is to be found underlying the 'mechanism' of 'a permanent arms budget':

> 'Insofar as capital is taxed to sustain expenditure on arms it is deprived of resources that might otherwise go towards further investment; insofar as expenditure on arms is expenditure on a fast -wasting end-product it constitutes a net addition to the market for "end" goods. Since one obvious result of such expenditure is high employment and, as a direct consequence of that, rates of growth amongst the highest ever, the dampening effect of such taxation is not readily apparent. But it is not absent. Were capital left alone to invest its entire pretax profit, the state creating demand as and when necessary, growth rates would be very much higher.
>
> Finally, since arms are a "luxury" in the sense that they are not used, either as instruments of production of other commodities, their production has no effect on profit rates overall . . .' (65)

As pointed out in Chapter IX, it is not the lack of purchasing power which causes the capitalist crises and hence overproduction. Capital is 'overproduced' only in relation to a level of profitability. Moreover, it is *capital* and not goods that are 'overproduced'. Goods are 'overproduced' if capital is overproduced. In fact, as Marx pointed out, such overproduction occurs generally during periods of rising wages since the capitalist appropriates a lesser share of the product at that level of accumulation which fact tends to create unfavourable pressure on profitability. What the under-consumptionists are really putting forward under the guise of 'Marxism' are Keynesian theories of 'effective demand'. Kidron clearly confuses Marx's organic composition of capital, which has the social relationship built into it, and the Keynesian capital-labour ratio which explains marginal productivity of labour, a Keynesian theory which merely attempts to analyse the problem of the availability of investment outlets in relation to so-called 'effective demand'.

The central question remains: how does Marx's Law explain military expenditure in terms of the capitalist accumulation process? As we have noted, the whole misconception of underconsumptionism springs from the fact that military spending is regarded as 'luxury' and hence 'wasteful'. For Marx luxury investment, among other things, plays a part in the accumulation process and hence in determining profitability and the organic composition, and it does so in so far as it affects either the *amount* of surplus-value or the ratio of variable capital to constant capital and to the total capital. He states:

> 'The amount of surplus-value is determined in two ways. [First] by the rate of surplus-value, that is, the surplus-labour (absolute or relative) of the individual workers. Secondly, by the number of workers simultaneously employed. In so far therefore as increasing productivity in the luxury industries reduces the *number of workers* which a certain quantity of capital employs, it reduces the *amount of surplus-value*, hence all circumstances remaining unchanged, it reduces also the *rate of profit*. The same thing occurs if the number of workers is reduced or remains the same, but the capital laid out on machinery and raw materials is increased; in other words, it occurs wherever there is any diminution in the ratio of variable capital to the total capital which [according to the assumption] is not balanced or partially offset by a reduction in wages. But since the rate of profit in this sphere enters into the equalisation process of the general rate of profit just as much as that in any other sphere, increased productivity in the luxury industry would, in the case under consideration, bring about a fall in the general rate of profit'. (66)

The opposite would be the case if increased productivity in the luxury industry was due not to improvements carried out in the industry itself, but in those branches of industry which provide it with constant capital. In this case the rate of profit would rise in the luxury industry. Therefore, apart from the absolute lengthening of the working day, increased productivity in the luxury industry can affect only the number of workers employed and hence the reduction in the amount of surplus-value and consequently the reduction in the rate of profit, even if no increase in constant capital takes place. (66) Marx neither 'ignored existing leaks' nor was he 'hewing the system from brute rock' as Kidron maintains. On the contrary, Marx's incisive analysis of luxury goods enables us to comprehend the reality.

The upshoot of this analysis is to dispose of the arguments based on Sweezy's reformulation of Borkiewicz and on the separation of the process of circulation from its roots in production. We can similarly disregard Kidron's attempt to imply by 'luxury goods' a sector of the capitalist production 'outside' the whole system, consequently constituting neither instruments of production nor means of subsistence, with the implication that the production of such goods do not enter into the capitalist accumulation process affecting profitability of monopoly and other capitalist enterprises. So long as 'luxury' production uses up surplus-value, it has to affect the rate of profit on total capital, by assisting capital to shift to those industries in which the rate of profit is higher.

The intervention of the state in the economy through various forms of public expenditure and arms production in particular assisted monopoly capitalism in increasing the productivity of labour. The state engaged in its normal function of creating the stable conditions of class oppression that are essential to monopoly capital, and financed the so-called 'wasteful production', which in any case is part and parcel of monopoly capitalism. More importantly, it thereby made possible a growing profitability for monopoly enterprises. Were this not so, the system, given its inherent contradictions and in particular the class contradictions, would have faced an irreversible crisis. As it is, continuing centralisation and concentration of capital with state assistance is evidence of the obvious fact that monopoly capitalism is moribund and can sustain itself only through intensified class oppression. Nor is imperialism and its oppressive arm, neo-colonialism, to be separated from this 'wasteful' production. It is because of this state 'waste' that expanded world production and markets can be maintained, without it monopoly capital would already be an item in the museum of world history.

We have already pointed to the contribution that research and development makes to monopoly capital. This, of course, is the same process of making labour more productive and hence assisting the profitability of monopoly capital. Kidron acknowledges this, when he recognises that 'spin-offs' from this research find their way into private industry. He states:

> 'Military research has been crucial in developing civilian products like air navigation systems, transport aircraft, computers, drugs, diesel locomotives from submarine diesels, reinforced glass and so on. Long production runs for military purposes have brought other products such as solar cells, and infra-red detectors down to mass price-ranges. Military use has perfected techniques of general use, such as gas turbines, hydraulic transmission, ultrasonic welding and a host of others'. (67)

He goes on to quote at length an OECD report to the same effect.

Another way in which state expenditure assists monopoly and

concentration is the size of the orders that government makes to industry. We quoted evidence of this military industrial interest in arms production. This can also be seen from the figures that Kidron gives from a United Nations study as to the extent of estimated average military demand by the imperialist countries for some 'internationally traded' materials for 1958 and 1959: 8.6% of world output of oil, 3% of crude rubber, 15.2% of copper, 10.3% of nickel, 9.6% of tin, 9.4% of leads and zinc, 7.5% of molybdenum, 6.8% of bauxite, 5.1% of iron ore, 2.7% of manganese and 2.3% of chromite. (67)

He cites evidence that three quarters of all arms business goes to the one hundred largest corporations in the US and that in Britain the eighteen largest companies, with 10,000 workers or more each, were responsible for 75.2% of all arms production. (68) This helps to show how these large corporations have reaped super-profits to assist them in the accumulation process. Barrat Brown shows that in the US 20% of large corporation profits came from military contracts in the early 1960s, rising with the escalation of the Vietnam War. In the mid 1960s, with 30% of profits coming from foreign investment, the two sources accounted for 50 % of all their profits. This evidence shows that the so-called 'wasteful' state expenditure helps monopolies, not merely by 'absorbing' the surplus but by increasing the productivity of labour through research and other activities which ultimately benefit monopoly.

The point made by Kidron about taxes and state expenditure needs to be examined. Kidron in the long passage quoted earlier appears to suggest that the use of taxes on arms as 'end products', in as much as the taxes come out of capital, has a 'dampening effect on the mass of capital that would otherwise have to find outlets for investment'. He is actually attempting to show that such intervention doesn't enter into the profit rates. We have shown that this is false. But even if one were to treat this question purely at the 'economic' level in-as-much as such taxation and state spending would affect capital formation, Kidron's argument would not hold, as, indeed, he himself seems to suggest by implication in the part of the book from which we derive our second quote. If the state finances its 'luxury' expenditure either from present taxes or future taxes (from loans and deficit spending), and although such state-induced 'end production' may be 'unproductive' from the point of view of capitalism as a whole, in the sense that products bought by the state do not function as capital and, therefore do not produce surplus-value, the monopoly capitalist so producing for the state will clearly be reaping surplus-value from the labour working for his enterprise. Such surplus-value almost invariably will come out of the already produced surplus-value from taxes and its significance lies in its effect on monopoly capitalism as a whole.

Here lies the whole crux of the matter. When state intervention goes beyond its function as a coercive arm of the bourgeoisie and directly helps

171

the profitability of the enterprise as well as furthering the concentration and centralisation of capital (an act which is induced by the earlier crisis) it creates new crises and makes the pre-existing one worse. In this way state expenditure on arms production, bureaucracy and other 'unproductive' areas gives fuel to the inflationary process already inherent in the economy, and acts as a weapon against the gains the workers have made as well as reducing the money value of accumulated debts. This inflating by deflating does not help the monopoly capitalist in the long run and in fact it constitutes the real central crisis in bourgeois economic ideology.

If we are to accept Alvin Hansen's estimation that in the post-war period US military expenditure 'played twice as powerful a role as private investment', and also a UN report on disarmament which estimated military expenditure at something like 60% of domestic fixed capital formation, then the extent of the on-going crises can be grasped (if we remove expenditure derived solely out of taxes). The armaments industry plus the proliferation of unproductive service industries created, from a currency standpoint, an increasing purchasing power, without creating on the market a corresponding additional supply of *goods* as counter-value. Even when this increased purchasing power brings about the re-employment of previously idle machinery and men, it causes inflation eventually. The incomes of the workers and the profits of the companies reappear on the market as demand for consumer goods and capital goods, without the production of these goods having been increased.

Although it is possible to speculate that such inflation could have been avoided by financing this additional purchasing power from taxes (and thus reducing the incomes of those who pay taxes), such a situation is unknown in the post-war period. It is increasingly met from the *public debt* (bonds, Treasury certificates, etc.). *TIME Magazine*, a mouth-piece of big capital, recognises this problem and exposes some slight glimpse of the cause. Writing on the recent inflationary spiral, it stated in a cover story of April 8, 1974:

> 'Although Americans are particularly chastened by their spiraling inflation, having so long considered themselves immune from it, what is happening in the US is only one manifestation of a larger, more virulent strain of worldwide inflation. Like some medieval plague inflation today is sweeping across national borders to infect almost every country at the same time. And the consequences of the international spiral go far beyond economics: they include a sharpening of class divisions and a shaking of values, as inflation rewards speculators while penalising thrift. The ultimate threat is that inflation will eventually weaken confidence in democratic governments and institutions and prepare the way for sharp violent shifts to the radical right or left. At present that seems vague, but political leaders do not dismiss it'.

The paper continues that compounding the alarm and further weakening faith in governments 'is the uncomfortable feelings that no one quite

knows what to do about inflation'; the experts themselves are not immune
from this despair. In the US John Dunlop, head of the Cost of Living
Council, asserts 'I don't believe it is clear that mankind today knows how
to control inflation'. *Time* blames the problem of inflation incorrectly on
Lyndon Johnson but correctly on war:

> 'Lyndon Johnson started the current round of inflation in the US by
> fighting an expensive war in Vietnam without raising anywhere
> near enough taxes to pay for it'.

This 'war effort' which was in the 'national interest' namely in the
interest of monopoly capital cannot be blamed on individuals in a bourgeois
state. The panic and general gloom in the ideological superstructure was
not restricted to *Time*. *Newsweek*, another mass weekly international
news magazine, in an issue of March 25, 1974 reported a generally known
fact of crisis in bourgeois economics:

> 'The implication is clear: the old economics models have become
> obsolete and so have old solutions. Unfortunately, however,
> relatively few economists and politicians are willing to admit that
> fact. Instead most cling to their beliefs that Richard Nixon could
> be acclaimed for declaring that he is a Keynesian. John Maynard
> Keynes, after all, based his judgements on the economic structure
> of the 1920s and 1930s, a world that hardly resembles today's post-
> industrial societies. It seems clear that the remedies that worked in
> predominantly industrial societies cannot be expected to work in
> the same way in societies where more people work in service
> industries than in production jobs. Specifically, the traditional
> reliance on increased productivity to contain inflation clearly is
> inadequate in a post-industrial society. How, for example, does a
> launderette operator increase his productivity?'

Samuelson also confessed that the old belief that 'cost/wage/push'
created inflation does not stand to test. The bitter truth is that bourgeois
economics is lost in its inherent obscurantism. Writing over one hundred
years ago, Marx clearly saw their problem. He pointed out:

> 'The economists explain to us the process of production under given
> conditions; what they do not explain to us, however, is how these
> conditions themselves are being produced, i.e. the historical move-
> ment that brings them into being'. (69)

This brings us to the next point argued by Baran and Sweezy about the
'sales effort' being an absorbing agent of the 'economic surplus' under
monopoly, 'which otherwise would have not been produced'. Renewing
their attack on Marx they state and we quote:

> 'What prevented both the classics and Marx from being more
> concerned with the problem of the adequacy of modes of surplus
> absorption was perhaps their profound conviction that the central
> dilemma of capitalism was summed up in what Marx called 'the
> falling tendency of the rate of profit' . . . When we pass from an
> analysis of a competitive system to that of a monopolistic system,
> a radical change in thinking is called for. With the law of rising
> surplus replacing the law of the falling tendency of the rate of profit,

and with normal modes of surplus utilization patently unable to absorb a rising surplus, the question of other modes of surplus utilization assumes crucial importance . . . One of these alternative modes of utilization we call the sales effort. Conceptually, it is identical with Marx's expenses of circulation. But in the epoch of monopoly capitalism, it has come to play a role, both 'quantitatively and qualitatively', beyond anything Marx ever dreamed of'. (70)

This long passage, profound as it sounds, is no more than Keynes under 'Marxist guise'. Keynes proper emerges when the co-authors in another part of their book, after quoting a New York banker who prescribes a medicinal solution to monopoly by advocating a 'use-value' production, state:

'What indeed would happen to a market continually plagued by insufficient demand? And what would happen to an economic system suffering from chronic underconsumption, under-investment, and under-employment? For the economic importance of advertising lies not primarily in causing a re-allocation of consumers' expenditures among different commodities but in its effect on the magnitude of aggregate effective demand and thus on the level of income and employment'. (71)

Thus it turns out that what we are expected to understand is that advertising is a way of creating 'effective demand' in an 'underconsuming', 'under-investing' society and not apparently a way of absorbing the economic surplus, which by their definition is supposedly a more embracing term than Marx's concept of surplus-value. Their concept of 'economic surplus' is defined as: 'the difference between what a society produces and the costs of producing it'. (72) But this confusion does not end here. The co-authors have other views as to why the sales effort is important to monopoly capital. In another part of the book, they state:

'What has actually happened is that advertising has turned into an indispensable tool for a large sector of corporate business. Competitively employed, it has become an integral part of the corporations' profit maximization policy and serves at the same time as a formidable wall protecting monopolistic position'. (73)

At this stage it would appear that profitablity and not absorption of the surplus is the consideration and that perhaps Marx's 'time-honoured theorem' might have something to do with it! If thus far the evidence does not reveal the eclectic (and hence petty-bourgeois) character of the analysis, it is because it would require quoting extensively from the chapter and neighbouring chapters to do that. We must strike a note of caution here. We should not be understood to be saying that the co-authors do not grapple with the question of profitability in monopoly enterprise; on the contrary they try to do so but in our view purely from the underconsumption and under-investment point of view, which as we have demonstrated cannot satisfactorily explain the almost permanently recurring crisis which is characteristic of the post-war period. In order to show that Marx's Law explains the present day 'sales effort', it is necessary for us to trace the historical roots of the problem.

In Chapter IX it was shown that monopoly results in the reduction of the segments into which surplus-value is divided. This is part of the phenomenon of concentration that the profitability crisis brings about. It is part of the process of the vertical integration of the firm under this process of concentration and is the natural result of competition in the earlier 'pure forms'. The rationale behind it is to reduce the partakers of surplus-value and increase the profitability of the firm by retaining the merchant or middle man profit and eliminating independent trade. This development is also consistent with the need to take advantage of economies of scale that the new monopoly enterprise offers in the circulation of the commodities.

Graham Bannock points out the shift of emphasis developing in the interwar years from production to distribution. (74) He further notes that in markets dominated by a small number of large corporations, both price and product competition decline. Such products as are on offer resemble one another, and scope for consumer choice diminishes. The competition that remains is mainly in the form of packaging, advertising and other forms of sales promotion. Whereas in the period before the 1960s marketing laid emphasis on practical issues like 'what are the customers' needs' and the role of marketing managers at this time was to go all out to satisfy the needs of the consumer, after 1966, L.W. Rodger observes a change in the marketing management function, which is clearly in line with the new strategy:

> 'Marketing is the management function which organises and directs all those business activities involved in assessing and converting customer purchasing-power into effective demand for a specific product or services and in moving the product or service to the final customer or user so as to achieve the profit target or other objectives set by the company'. (75)

Here we notice that it is no longer the 'customer's needs' that matter to the marketing manager, but the company's profit target, and the marketing manager's function is to *assess and convert* the customers purchasing power into *effective demand* to meet those company objectives. This Keynesian explanation is quite acceptable to Baran and Sweezy in their analysis. (76) But the point at issue here is really not *surplus absorption* but *surplus-value realisation.* This haste to realise the surplus-value is understandable since an increased turn-over of goods increases the annual profit to the commercial bourgeoisie by reducing the circulation period of commodities and the rotation period of circulating capital and contributes on the whole to the lowering of prices by the industrial capitalist. This is even more so where this role is fulfilled by the monopoly.

Under these circumstances it is understandable why advertising assumes such frightening proportions. *Fortune Magazine*, spokesman of US big business, confessed to this, when it reported:

> 'The American citizen lives in a state of siege from dawn to bed-time. Nearly everything he sees, hears, touches, tastes and smells is an attempt to sell him something. To break through his protective shell the advertisers must continually shock, tease, tickle or irritate him, or wear him down by the drip-drip-drip or Chinese water-torture method of endless repetition'.

This interlocking contradiction for monopoly capitalism, overproduction under conditions of under-capacity plant utilisation, creates an irremediable conjunction of shrinking markets and increasing exploitation of labour and consumers under the monopoly capitalism of the post-war period.

Thus whether it be state expenditure on the military and the bureaucracy, or 'sales effort', all are the result of competition leading to monopoly capitalism. The crisis that monopoly capitalism seeks to resolve can only be dealt with by increased military spending and intensification of the state machine. This is necessary to suppress the class struggle both in the imperialist centre and in the neo-colonial hinterland. The qualitative aspects of the state machine cannot be detached from the quantitative ones of surplus-value realisation. The increased sales effort is the very organic result of concentration and monopoly. All these developments cannot be explained other than on the basis of Marx's Law of the Tendency of the Rate of Profit to Fall. Whereas for Keynes and his followers, overt or covert, over-production can be resolved by increasing 'effective demand' and stimulating investment outlets, for Marx overproduction is only relative to the productivity of labour and conditions of exploitation. It exists when the mass of surplus-value is inadequate in relation to total capital, the organic composition of which includes both the constant (and technical) capital together with the variable capital. The crisis that arises can only, according to Marx, be resolved by expanding *profitable* production and accumulation.

Moreover the rise of monopolies cannot do away with the law of value, because this law is the basis of the production relations under the capitalist mode of production. So long as capitalism continues to exist as a system based on the production relationship between the bourgeoisie and the proletariat, the law of value operates, albeit in a different form. The law still remains the criteria on which bourgeois exploitation of labour is measured. When we say that the monopoly bourgeoisie fix prices *above* costs of production we imply that the bourgeoisie use this law as a criterion for so fixing those prices. Furthermore the fact that the law of value is increasingly under attack in this way is a reflection of the increasing socialisation of production in conditions of increasing private appropriation of the product. It is a reflection of the fact that monopoly capitalism is becoming increasingly moribund and parasitic, and the time is ripe for removing the contradiction between social production and private appropriation of the product. Indeed as Lenin said, under these conditions monopoly capitalism and hence imperialism signals the 'eve of the socialist revolution'. This law of Marx's also explains other developments in the post-war period connected with the profitability crisis.

To begin with, concentration and centralisation of capital has continued unabated in the post-war period. As we observed in Chapter VIII, this need arose historically with the first great capitalist depression of the 1870s and the great movement towards concentration was lent fire to by the 'second industrial revolution'. This concentration helped to restructure the capitalist firm as a move against competition. In the post-war period when competition is basically between monopolies both at home and in overseas markets, concentration of capital becomes a vital weapon for ensuring the profitability of a firm. (77) This as we shall see in the next chapter becomes a necessity for participation in the overseas market.

The best illustrative example of this concentration and centralisation of capital in the post-war period is the situation in the US. The concentration and expansion of US capital without which the US cannot maintain its lead has been facilitated by the banks. Multilateral agencies like the World Bank and its affiliates such as the IDA and IFC, as well as national institutions like the US Import-Export Investment Bank, are important channels. But of more importance are the US commercial banks. This is evidenced by the fact that the biggest growth in US banking, according to *Fortune Magazine*, is not in the US but overseas, thus 'creating the first truly international network of banks'. (78) In fact this is so true that today any popular international magazine is always full of such advertisements as: 'This is your bank' or 'our-man-on-the-spot — The Bank of America world wide service'! The one reproduced below is characteristic:

> 'Not far from Kuala Lumpur, Malaysia, grow valuable red merenti trees. Helping this lumber get to markets around the world is our-man-on-the-spot there . . . For lumber concerns around the world, Bank of America is a primary source of every kind of routine financing and assistance . . . For example, we can handle receivables and payables, equipment leasing, search out new customers and new sources of supply, and arrange for foreign exchange management through our International Finance Centers in London, Singapore and Panama. And because we are a global network, your international transactions are handled swiftly and effectively'.

This advertisement expresses in a nutshell the role of banks in US monopoly capitalism. They are a source of *primary* financing in every kind of routine activity. They handle even investment in *production* of trees and their marketing the world over, including finding customers. They even help to beat the 'foreign exchange man' in Kuala Lumpur or wherever he may be! Their role fits in with Lenin's analysis of the role of banks in the export of capital during the early twentieth century. Today that role is even more pronounced: they directly engage in financial and industrial activities overseas.

If further evidence were to be required of the increasing role of banks as a means of concentrating capital and hence production, the US News & World Report of 25 March 1974 is worth referring to. Writing under the heading, *Are The Nations Banks Getting Too Powerful*, the magazine reported that: 'buying billions of stock in the nation's industries, branching into all sorts of business, opening offices around the world — that's the picture of big US banks that is arousing concern in the government and elsewhere'. For instance, the paper reported, the Bank of America 'has literally spread across the nation, and around the world with more than 1,000 offices. It recently acquired General Acceptance Corporation, giving it another 317 finance-company loan offices in the East and Middle West.'

The magazine reported that the National City Corporation, 'only second to Bank America in assets', has more than 500 domestic and foreign offices. They engage in activities 'from finance to insurance, from computer services and management advice to armoured cars'. Statistics showed that the trust departments of the big banks holding pension funds, etc. used them to control industrial concerns. For instance, Morgan Guaranty, with the biggest trustee department, had close to $23.6 billion under 'investment management'. Of these, employee benefit funds totalled $16 billion, i.e. more than 70% and growing at $859 million per year. They have full discretion as to how these funds are invested.

Also according to the report 'interlocking directorships' are the order of the day. A survey of 49 banks in 10 major cities found more than 8,000 cases involving 6,500 firms, in which bank officials served as directors of other companies and vice-versa. For instance of the 23 directors of the Central Penn Company, 16 were also directors of 19 banks. Among the 30 top stockholders with an aggregate of 22% of the company's stock were 17 bank trust departments. Many of these banks had made loans to this 'ailing corporation'. Some of the directors involved in both loans and trust stock-holdings were those with interlocking directorship. The assets of the 15 US banks in Table V overleaf make the budgets of most petty-bourgeois 'banana republics' a laughing stock!

We must now look at US investments overseas, and its significance in the creation of the transnational corporation. There is no doubt that monopoly capital in these circumstances aims at internationalising exploitation by the transnational monopolies. As George S. Moore, president of the First National City Bank said, this increased financial activity points toward an 'international interdependence' unprecedented since the emergence of the nation-state:

> 'With the dollar (as) the leading international currency and the United States the World's largest exporter and importer of goods, services, and capital, it is only natural that the US banks gird themselves to play the same relative role in international finance that the great British financial institutions played in the nineteenth century'. (79)

Table V

15 Biggest US Banks Total Assets (including loans, cash, securities, property and other assets).

1.	Bank America	$49.4 billion
2.	First National City	$44.0 billion
3.	Chase Manhatten	$36.8 billion
4.	J.P. Morgan & Coy	$20.4 billion
5.	Manufactures Hanover	$19.9 billion
6.	Chemical N.Y.	$18.6 billion
7.	Bankers Trust N.Y.	$18.5 billion
8.	Western Bank Corporation	$17.9 billion
9.	Continental [Illinois]	$16.9 billion
10.	First Chicago	$15.6 billion
11.	Securities Pacific	$13.5 billion
12.	Marine Midland Banks	$13.0 billion
13.	Wells Fargo & Co.	$11.8 billion
14.	Charter N.Y.	$ 9.7 billion
15.	Mellon National	$ 9.6 billion

Source: U.S. News & World Report, 25th March, 1974. p.72.

Table VI

US Bank Capital from 1900 to 1960 (Assets and Controlled Capital $Million)

	1900	1929	1960
Commercial Banks (loan depts)	10,000	66,000	58,000
Commercial Banks (trust depts)	3,000	30,000	105,000
Investment Banks and brokerage houses	600	10,000	8,000
Life Insurance Companies	1,700	18,000	120,000
Property and Casualty Insurance Companies	500	5,000	30,000
Savings Banks	2,400	10,000	41,000
Loans and Savings Associations	500	7,000	72,000
Investment Companies	—	3,000	19,000
Private Pension Funds	—	500	29,000
	18,700	149,500	682,000

Source: Menshikov: 1969/73: 144

A recent publication by S. Menshikov, (80) about the structure of the US financial oligarchy, confirms that concentration and centralisation of bank capital is a general trend inherent in all types of banking institutions in the

US. About 43% of all bank capital in the US is concentrated in the 102 biggest bank companies; which constitute about 0.4% of all the banking institutions. Most of them are mammoth commercial banks and life insurance companies. The lowest level of concentration is among the loan and savings institutions where 50 of the biggest companies have only 18% of the assets.

He showed that in the last sixty years, the growth of US bank capital has multiplied more than 36 times; and that in the thirty years 1930-60 it went up by 680%. Table VI overleaf illustrates this. It also shows the systematically progressing tendency toward specialisation of bank institutions.*

Perhaps the power of finance capital is nowhere more reflected than in its imperialistic exploitation of weaker peoples, both colonial and sovereign. This is why Lenin's point about finance capital meaning that a small number of financially 'powerful' states stand out among all the rest becomes significant. Here the banks and industry run together. Magdoff points out that US banks enter foreign markets in three ways as finance capitalists:

a.   By use of foreign banks as correspondent banks, which handle overseas transactions for them; these may be supplemented by setting up offices in selected foreign cities. Such activity is, however, limited.

b.   By setting up branches which carry on full banking activities as they would in the US, adapting themselves as much as possible to the banking laws of the host country.

c.   By setting up subsidiary corporations. These buy into foreign-owned banks, set-up bank and finance companies abroad and invest in all kinds of non-banking activities which according to US law they could not normally do in the US . (81)

Table VII below shows the number of branches of US banks established in foreign countries up to 1967.

Table VII

Number of US Bank Branches Outside The United States

	1918	1939	1950	1955	1960	1967
Latin America	31	47	49	56	55	134
Europe	26	16	15	17	19	59
Africa	0	0	0	4	1	4
Near East	0	0	0	0	4	7
Far East	0	18	19	20	23	63
US Territories Overseas and Trust Territories	4	8	12	14	22	31
	61	89	95	111	126	299

Source: Magdoff: op. cit. p.75.

*Due to an earlier omission this part of the book has been supplemented and the reader is referred to the addendum at page 281.

The 1918 figures include 11 branches nationalised by the Soviet government and those for 1960 exclude 21 branches nationalised by the Cuban government in 1960. Paul Volcker, the Under Secretary responsible for monetary affairs in the US Treasury, and 'the intellectual force behind the Nixon administration's thinking on these issues', estimated that there were 400 such bank branches and subsidiaries by 1970, an increase of 100 within three years:

'The growth in the number of US banks with offices in Brussels is one reflection of a world-wide phenomenon. The number of branches and subsidiaries throughout the world of such foreign banks has reached some four hundred — quadrupling in the past fifteen years . . . The rise of the multinational corporations, with vast amounts of liquid funds at their disposal and close banking contracts in a variety of key markets, is another dimension . . . Large and closely-integrated markets mean that funds will move quickly and react in volume to relatively small incentives. Thus questions are posed, both for the independence of national policies and for the international monetary system'. (82)

As we have seen the other vehicles which US banks use to penetrate overseas markets are the *bank subsidiaries*. In 1919 an amendment to the Federal Reserve Act (The Edge Act) was made to enable US banks to set up subsidiaries overseas, to penetrate countries where local laws prohibited branch banks and to enable banks to engage in a wide range of foreign financial and investment activities (including non-financial activities), which US domestic banks were prohibited to engage in under US law. Subsidiaries, however, did not take root until the US was well established as a leader in capital export — i.e., until after 1950. Thus, whereas, in 1929 there were 18 US subsidiaries overseas, these had shrunk to a bare 2 in 1945 due to the problems created by the currency crisis of the 1930s, the depression and war. In 1956 there were 7 and in 1967 they numbered 52. Magdoff observes:

'The contrasting developments of the 1950s and 1960s is an instructive illustration of the changes in foreign finance that have accompanied the new position of the US in its political, military, and economic operations. In this latest period, these subsidiary corporations have mushroomed into an effective and persuasive instrument, and by all signs are still on the increase'. (83)

In any case US leadership in the imperialist world would have been impossible without the capability to command finance capital. Gyorgy Goncol has correctly observed:

'Superior competitive power and superior capital go hand in hand, they mutually reinforce each other. The decline of the economic supremacy of Britain was marked and accompanied by both a lessening of competitive power in the world market and by the constant weakening of the international capital position of Britain. The rise of the United States was marked and accompanied by a distinct strengthening of American competitive power in the world

181

market and an unparalleled strengthening of the international capital position of the USA. [Hence] the capital position is of primordial importance. When all is said and done, in the international accounts it is the creditor-debtor relation that really counts.' (84)

Capital exports and their servicing are bound to pre-determine the balances of trade and balances of payments in both the capital exporting and the capital importing countries. Indeed, financial dictatorship has usually belonged, in the course of history, to that country which played the dominating role at any given moment in world trade and world economy. In the period when the Phoenician and Greek traders were dominant in the Mediterranean, a very great role was played by the Greek and Phoenician talent. The florin ruled when Italian merchant capital dominated the Mediterranean; and the mercantile role of Spain brought the piastre to the forefront. Holland too ruled not only with its fleet, its cloth and its trade generally, but also with its guilden. As the centre of the world moved to England, so the British pound became dominant. Finally American economic supremacy necessarily led to the ascendency of the dollar; for quite a while it was regarded as good as gold.

Even purely from an individual corporation's standpoint, trade must be supported by direct investment. John J. Powers, President and Chief Executive of Chas. Pfizer & Co., a leading chemical and pharmaceutical multinational, said in a speech:

'To compete effectively for a good share of any major market requires direct investment in the market place in the form of sales offices and warehouses and at least packaging and assembly plants, if not basic production units. *It is not possible for a mere exporter [of goods] to become a major long-term factor in a market in this second half of the twentieth century'*. [Emphasis added]. (85)

This conclusion should now be apparent and confirmed by experience since US affiliate sales now account for over twice the US based exports, clearly indicating the importance of such investment to the US competitive position in world trade. The motto for US imperialism is clearly: invest in order to trade.

US subsidiaries have been and continue to be used to buy up minority or controlling interests in overseas banks. They are also used to obtain ownership of industrial and service undertakings such as those described by the Bank of America in the advertisement above. They directly invest in industry in all corners of the world, in textiles, steel mills, paper mills and equipment leasing companies, quite apart from raw material production.

The role of the dollar has been of crucial importance to multilateral imperialism in the post-war period. US led multilateral imperialism was unlike its British predecessor in that the US was forced to assume unique responsibilities for the preservation of capitalism. On the one hand, capitalism had to preserve itself against socialist advance, and on the other to hold on to its colonial domination by a neo-colonial redivision under multilateralism. This entailed the US not only financing Europe's capitalist recovery to avoid social revolution there, but at the same time policing Europe and the neo-colonial Third World. The advantageous position which British imperialism occupied in the eighteenth and nineteenth centuries was not available to US imperialism. The US could only maintain its leadership by actually coughing up the resources their allies and Third World puppets needed to maintain themselves under a global security cover. This created a serious financial position for US imperialism.

Whereas the US at the end of 1938 had $11 billion dollars in *gold assets* as compared to $0.5 billion in *dollar assets* (just above 5% of the gold assets), at the end of 1967 it had $26.9 billion dollars in *gold assets* as compared to $15.7 in *dollar assets* (a significant 58% of the gold assets). Under US law, the US government was becoming more indebted to dollar holders in terms of gold — a situation which was made worse by the US war against Vietnam. The US, in other words, was falling more and more into deficit in terms of its trade with its allies and Third World countries as its gold position weakened. Whereas Britain in the inter-war period could rely on its 'invisible trade' to balance its deficit on 'visible trade', the US could not; Engel's observation of 1886 (see headnote to this part) was being fulfilled by actual experience. In 1967 the US balance of payments stood as shown in Table VIII below.

Table VIII

US Balance of Payments 1967

Purpose	Money Received (billion dollars)	Money going out (billion dollars)
Balance on export and imports	$7.9	
Private and Govt. remittance		$1.2
Military expenditure net		$3.1
Military assistance & economic aid		$4.0
Private capital investment		$3.5
	$7.9	$11.8

Source: Magdoff, op. cit. p.104

The table reveals a deficit in the order of $3.9 billion. As can be seen the deficit was caused by a) military expenditure in Vietnam and elsewhere; b) military assistance and aid; c) US investment abroad in industry and finance. US reserves moved from $21.8 billion in gold in 1955 to $10 billion in 1968 whereas dollar assets held by foreign countries increased from $11.7 billion to $31.5 billion in the same period. The US financial position was being undermined by its own objective contradictory situation as an imperialist power.

The only way the US could cope with this contradiction was by 'heating her economy' through inflationary policies and through devaluation of the dollar. However, this tended to limit its activities outside the US, forcing withdrawal from Vietnam, a situation that led to total defeat for imperialism in Cambodia and Vietnam among other things. Although the US had many military allies, these were at the same time struggling against it in their dealings in trade and finance. This central contradiction of imperialism cannot be resolved by resolutions to be 'united'. Capitalist monopoly groups in the US and in Europe still continue to compete for markets and outlets for financial exports leading to 'vertical cohesion and division of labour' with the Third World as we shall see. The transnational corporation cannot remove this basic contradiction. So long as this struggle for markets and raw material bases continues to be a feature of imperialism (which it must) the problem will remain.

CHAPTER XVII

As we have shown, monopoly arises historically out of capitalist crises of over-production in relation to the level of profitability acceptable to the capitalist. This is caused by the tendency towards a fall in profitability in capitalist enterprise which is excerbated by competition. The crisis can only be resolved by restructuring the organic composition of capital, with a tendency to further intensifying the exploitation of labour. But since competition brings about the conditions leading to the profitability crisis, it has to be combated as part of the restructuring of the capital composition. This essentially means concentrating capital and hence production in order to reap a higher than average profit in order to compensate for the *historical* fall in profitability in the enterprise. As this becomes a general feature of production, a new age of capitalism is arrived at, which Lenin called the highest stage of capitalism: imperialism.

Monopoly capitalism, the new, restructured capitalism, had its own problems. The rise of the cartels, the syndicates, and the trusts, were the visible expression of its contradiction. Concomitant with monopoly capitalism was a world market, characterised by the struggle for exclusive colonial access by each of the capitalist monopoly groups in each nation. Each national monopolistic bourgeoisie had its own demarcated national market plus a territorially demarcated colonial enclave from which it excluded the others by force of arms. With tariff and other barriers protecting the market, the sources of raw and auxiliary materials, and the outlets for capital exports, the colonial system was perfected. Efforts to gain entry into these colonial preserves necessitated a repatriation or redivision by force of arms. The result of this was the two imperialist World Wars.

To be sure, the whole international monopoly system, under international cartel agreements, suited the situation, but as we have seen it soon led to a breakdown of the world trade system, with the consequence that rivalry and war became the only solution in the short term. In Chapter X, we quoted a long passage from Raymond Vernon, in which he showed this tendency. Hugh Stephenson also observes:

> 'It was the search for . . . "rationalisation" that created the great cartels and trusts of the past. But the group of really giant international corporations is in a much stronger position than a

> traditional cartel. For experience of cartels, however formal, is that in the end they always disintegrate. There is always some one who thinks that he can do better by breaking out of the club'. (86)

In any case these arrangements all collapsed and the interwar years were characterised by tariff wars and general economic chaos.

The upshoot of all this was the US led multilateral imperialist strategy which we outlined in Chapter XIV. Under this strategy, redivision was undertaken and survival was only possible by severe competition in the neo-colonial hinterland, under the Open Door policy. Since the two wars had aggravated the capitalist crisis, further concentration of capital and production was the only solution open for any enterprise that sought to compete in the multilateral market. This concentration was itself a feature of the growing organic composition of capital, expressing the same tendency towards falling profitability as that caused by the scientific and technological innovation which occurred in the post-war period. The Law of the Tendency of the Rate of Profit to Fall was clearly at the back of this increased concentration and centralisation of capital. Under these conditions a transnational corporate strategy fitted the situation, and it is therefore not surprising that US corporations were first in the field, followed by the British. The situation was not all that contrived. Capitalists reacted to a real material situation which they had to resolve through this strategy.

The new giant corporations that arose represented a more developed stage in the concentration of production and circulation of both goods and capital. Whereas a *simple cartel* divided the market between independent monopolists, a *syndicate* organised the centralised sale of their output, a *trust* gathered under a single management the sale of goods; a *concern* managed simultaneous enterprises of various sectors by way of production integration, and a *cartel of trusts* divided markets at an immeasurably higher level, the *transnational corporation* combined all these forms of monopolisation and thus raised it to a qualitatively higher level. Whereas during the interwar years trade and investment were at their lowest ebb as evidenced by the trade and investment figures already referred to, with the re-arrangement concomitant with the development of direct investment which replaced portfolio investment, trade and capital were restored. In 1914 90 % of all international capital movements took the form of portfolio investments by individuals and financial oligarchies; today 75 % of capital outflows are in the form of direct investment entailing control of ventures.

Some writers have drawn parallels between the new transnational corporations and the earlier mercantilist internationals (Firms like the Medici of Florence, Genoa and Venice in the thirteenth century, the Grosse Ravensburggesellschaft in fifteenth century Germany, and the Fuggers in Augsburg); however, these 'internationals' were family businesses operating in two or three countries under the very different conditions of feudalist Europe. The transnational corporation of today is really a new phase of international business organisation which can only be properly understood in the context of the development of the capitalist system. Thus failure by cartels, trusts, and syndicates to achieve monopoly on a permanent basis and to respond effectively *in the long run* to the inherent tendency for capital to concentrate was the immediate point of departure for the creation of a new strategy fitted to the new situation of the post-war period.

The rise of the European Common Market which erected a common external tariff against all third countries except those 'associated', was another importance factor. It compelled other monopoly capitalists, particularly the US monopoly groups, to find ways of beating the restrictions by operating inside the restricted markets. William Lever, the founder of the soap empire, had in 1902 anticipated this development and in fact explained the reasons behind the establishment of foreign business in other countries in this period when he said:

> 'The question of erecting works in another country is dependent upon the tariff or duty. The amount of duties we pay on soap imported into Holland and Belgium is considerable, and it only requires that these shall rise to such a point that we could afford to pay a separate plant to make soap to enable us to see our way to erect works in these countries. When the duty exceeds the cost of separate managers and separate plants then it will be an economy to erect works in the country that our customers can be more cheaply supplied from them'. (87)

William Lever's soap empire is now the Unilever transnational corporation, which still operates on these lines, for the same reasons.

The evolution of the monopoly corporations has tended to pass through a number of stages which are generally characteristic of their strategies in general. The initial stage is export-oriented emphasis on production for export and home consumption. The overseas operations are centralised in the home country and overseas business is viewed as subordinate and of secondary importance in corporate strategy. This is the stage in which most big corporations doing business overseas find themselves. Many never go beyond this stage and are sometimes displaced by the stronger ones which go international. In the second stage the big corporation becomes more internationally oriented. It begins to place greater emphasis on its international business in achieving its corporate strategy. It grants greater autonomy and control to its foreign affiliates but retains a greater degree of finance control, through a foreign division under a Vice-President. The cartel system manifests itself during these two stages and particularly under the second. In its third stage the transnational corporation proper emerges. It no longer distinguishes between overseas and domestic operations. Domestic operations are subordinated and fully integrated with the global strategy. It begins to entertain international ownership and control.

These static observations generally correspond to the dynamics of the firm's internal development. When a capitalist enterprise comes into being it tends to pass through three corresponding historical stages based on the life-cycle of a product. (88) The first is characterised by low volume of production for the home market, with high prices protected by licence agreements, patents and tariffs. This represents the early stages of capitalist development, in its competitive phase. The second is the development of the technology of production methods. Here we notice an increase in volume in production which lowers costs and prices, which in turn leads to expanded market through export, expansion of the domestic market and the creation of a skilled management. It is during the transfer from the first to the second stage of the cycle that the pressure to go international builds up. As can be seen this stage tallies with early monopoly.

In the first stage through initial development, pilot plants, and the first full-scale production lines, the existing demand must keep ahead of capacity and support a high-price selling strategy. Moving into the second stage the pressing requirements for capital, managerial talents, and expanding markets all make it logical to think in terms of transferring the new technology through subsidiaries or joint ventures into sophisticated industrial countries, as a strategy for capturing production facilities and markets. This is the prelude to the third and final stage, in which agreements, licences, patents, and high tariffs no longer feature. Technology becomes standardised and generally becomes open to other international monopolies in other countries. Concentration of industry into a few international groups becomes pronounced. Mass production keeps costs down. There is increased investment in production, and larger overseas markets become a necessity to the survival of the firm. Availability of finance becomes the standard, and foreign assets and overseas profits contribute a substantial part of the overall profits and assets. Stable monopoly prices and stable monopoly shares of large markets become essential. Competition becomes anathema but inevitable all the same. This last stage of growth tallies with the multilateral imperialist stage, when the transnationals vie with one another in cut throat competition for the world market.

The main characteristic identifying a transnational corporation is its central direction. In spite of increasing concentration of production, the problem of markets becomes more pronounced. With increased size and widespread location operations are coordinated from the centre. The plan is drawn up at the headquarters and the activities of the subsidiaries are tightly integrated with each other. Losses in a particular subsidiary may be necessary to prevent a rival moving into the market. The availability of good international communications, air service, telephone, teleprinter and telex service as well as computers, become vital to the transnational corporation.

Most transnational corporations are open about their motives. They point out that corporations go transnational to preserve and expand markets in areas protected by trade barriers; to provide consumers with the goods produced in the home country; to take advantage of economies of scale at comparatively lower prices than by export; to search for raw materials and cheap labour if this will contribute to 'general efficiency'; and to obtain knowledge cheaply by calling on local expertise. The transnational corporation, however, must always seek to obtain profits greater than 'average profits'. In order for a company to go overseas it must be in a position to make higher profits there than it can in the domestic market. This is the central motive for the transnational corporation which determines the criteria for its investment decisions.

What are these criteria? They will differ with each concrete situation, but it is generally true to say that most transnationals will investigate the size of the market, investment climate, costs, (production, transportation and resource factors), profitability, payback period, and the average rate of return. As far as the market is concerned, the corporation will try to determine the present and prospective growth of demand and their share of this market. They would naturally consider whether the market is large enough and growing, whether they can attain sufficient sales for economical production and a satisfactory level of profits. To help them come to such conclusion they will analyse a country's gross national and domestic product, the rate of growth of gross national product, per capita and family income, population and its distribution, industrial production, production of specific sectors of industry, and levels and trends in consumption, imports and exports. (89)

To determine the investment climate, the corporation will analyse the impact of various factors such as political 'stability', nationalism and government policies such as receptivity and special incentives to foreign investors, including tax concessions and low-interest loans; and whether there are laws restricting repatriation of earnings, high tariffs, import and exchange restrictions, etc. High tariffs and import restrictions, as already pointed out, may attract investors as they help to keep out competition if the company has to establish a local plant. The analysis of transport costs, taxes, production costs and costs of production factors such as wages and rents will help the company determine whether it is worthwhile investing. 'When goods are expensive to transport per unit and sources of supply are fairly distant, a good basis may exist for local production'. (90) The analysis of labour costs will consider the levels of skills available, the productivity of labour, possible costs of training labour, costs of fringe benefits, and likely problems in dealing with labour unions. They will also consider the availability of technical know-how and of engineers, scientists and especially local management which can be obtained cheaply.

The company wishing to 'go international' will most importantly project profits on alternative investment possibilities over their life, based on carefully stated assumptions; with an eye on the pay-back period, they may evaluate the projects by use of an 'average rate of return' on the investment. Using this criterion, companies will favour investments or more correctly will look for investment projects with the most rapid pay-back of the total capital expenditure. This enhances the profitability of the investment. Dymsza quotes examples of companies which use this criterion (based on interviews):

> 'A major machinery company aims for a pay-back [period] of four years *or less* on many overseas investments. Mennen International considers the pay-back [period] very important in foreign investment decisions and strives for a *quick return on a high-risk investment and settles for a slower return on less risky venture*. Pfizer International looks for a quick pay-back [period] on risky investments. A diversified chemical company requires a pay off [of] between three and eight years depending upon risk involved and opportunities for growth'. (91)

A close examination of US direct investment and the direct investment of the European and Japanese monopolies testifies to the above. Investments in Europe, Canada, Japan and the US earn around 6-8 % whereas those in the Third World — Asia (32 %), Africa (29 %) and Latin America (14 %) — average around 25 %. Charles P. Kindleberger, an ideologue for the transnational corporation, states:

> 'It will be seen that earnings are higher on foreign investment and on foreign sales than in the United States, whether for Otis Elevator, Du Pont, Gillette, Corn Products Refining, Standard Oil Company of New Jersey, or whatever. This trend would be much greater were it not for the existence of defensive investment [i.e., investments to defend existing markets, D.W.N.] in which the return is less than the average at home'. (92)

Thus there can be no mystification of the question of where imperialist capital gains the greatest returns; the answer is in the Third World. Arguments that this cannot be so, since the major part of the direct investments of the major capitalist countries takes place amongst themselves can be fairly well answered by the fact that such profitable investment in the imperialist countries is dependent on the investments in the Third World neo-colonies, since production in the centre is dependent on raw materials from these countries. As we shall see shortly neo-Marxist arguments that these vast returns constitute 'exports of capital' from the periphery to the centre are also false.

A company wishing to operate overseas as a transnational corporation has to concern itself with problems connected with ownership. The countries in which it operates may insist on a joint venture with the host government, as the best means of securing its interest. If this is the case the corporation will have a number of alternative choices as to the type of venture. It may consider any one of the following to be the most suitable:

(a) an association between it and host country investors; (b) an association between it and local government agencies; or (c) an association between it and a number of local and foreign enterprises. In whatever event it may have a 50 % ownership, majority ownership or minority ownership depending on the particular situation.

When a transnational corporation considers a joint venture desirable it obviously is considering various factors it can call upon in its favour. Firstly, it will go into a joint venture in order to raise local finance and reduce risk from devaluation of currency and inflation. Secondly, it will benefit by obtaining the best of the local management skills which are critically scarce in many countries. Thirdly, the local partner may provide positive tangible contributions such as assured sources of raw materials, trained labour force, marketing opportunities, and an established system of distribution. Fourthly, the transnational corporation by this tactic will be identified with local interests and avoid nationalistic resentments against the foreign enterprise. In this way it will be better placed to obtain government approvals, local currency loans, tax incentives, assurance of imports of raw materials and components and other benefits. Fifthly, joint ventures may be a way of converting licencing and technology arrangements into overseas manufacturing, and a means of acquiring some companies abroad. (93) Finally, the joint venture strategy has been a convenient way of establishing overseas production in new national markets while limiting capital investment, utilising local capital and reducing risks. (94)

Whatever proportion the transnational corporation may take in the ownership of joint ventures, it clearly will be in a better position to exercise *control* over the enterprise through the licence and patent agreements whereby the corporation sells to the joint venture the essential technology and management skills. Moreover, technical know-how and management in these circumstances can in many cases (in Third World countries particularly) only be supplied by the transnational corporation. Hence many joint ventures particularly those with minority shares will sell management and technical know-how under management contracts through which the transnational exercises considerable financial, production, and marketing control. In other words exports of technology are tied up with capital exports all with the same aim: to control production and defend markets. The corporation will also control management training, in which it will considerably slow down the training of local personnel. Moreover, it can put off training on cost/benefit grounds and instead resort to capital intensive methods of production which are suited to its technology. Fees paid to the transnational corporation for such contracts are on gross income basis and according to Peter Gabriel they are a better means of getting around growing nationalism, getting a high return on their investment at the same time. (95)

The most significant of the resources at its disposal and the one which keeps the transnational ahead are the science-based and/or management technologies. These are its real dynamic assets with which it dominates the international scene. It is for this reason that transnationals that have diverted a good portion of their finances into Research and Development (R & D) are the only ones likely to participate in the multilateral international market. As Raymond Vernon has said:

> 'As a result of the increasing complexity of industrial innovation, the process came to be associated with the existence of large and complex organisations with commitments of considerable sums of money over long periods of time'. (96)

An example as to how far large transnational corporations may go to finance their R & D in order to keep ahead is the case of IBM; in the single year 1972, IBM spent $676 million, 'equal to half the corporation's net earnings' on R & D alone, in addition to education and training. (97) Behrman has observed that the tendency is towards the centralisation of research and development, which is in line with the concentration of production practiced by transnational corporations.

Britain maintained its lead over the whole world through the development of its productive forces during the scientific revolution of the eighteenth and nineteenth centuries. It lost the lead when its colonial empire, which sheltered it from greater innovation and scientific research, began to crumble. The colonial system produced more efficient administrators and officers than scientists. The latecomers in industrialisation — the Americans, Germans and the French — had to 'innovate or perish'. To compete with the British and with each other, their products needed to be substantially better since they began from a weaker position. (98) The scientific and technological struggle in the post-war period has become a struggle for survival on the international scene. In the race to research and develop technology, the size of the enterprise is of great significance. Moreover, access to military research facilities are assured to those with economic power, namely the financial oligarchy. The US lead in the post-war period was a result of her sizeable investment in scientific research. By the 1930s the US was producing 30 % of the world's scientific literature and great emphasis was laid on scientific education. Scientific research, too, was much more linked to the requirements of industry than elsewhere in the other capitalist countries. A study covering the origins of five major US innovations during the 1950s indicated that the Universities accounted for three quarters of the scientific events that laid the basis for industrial innovations and that half of these events occurred outside the US. Obviously the US was in a position to technologically exploit the research initiated in Europe. (99)

In the post-war period — particularly in the mid-nineteen sixties — the US was spending fifteen times more on R & D than Germany, ten times more than the UK and three times more than Western Europe combined. Moreover, of this expenditure, two thirds was being financed from public funds. (100) Put in figures, the current estimates of expenditure on R & D by the US, Western Europe, and Japan are as follows:

Country	Amount	% of GNP
USA	£5,000 million	2.0
UK	610 "	1.6
West Germany	510 "	1.2
France	420 "	1.2
Japan	300 "	0.8

Of the above amounts the portion of industrial R & D financed by government were: US 54 %, France 37 %, UK 32 %.

Even in a country like the US, which boasts so much about free enterprise, huge finances from taxes go to bolster up the giant monopolies. The aerospace industry alone took one-third of the government finances for research and development:

'This unique injection of tax-payers' money made it possible for American companies to dominate the world aerospace and electronic industries for two decades. The fact, ideologically unpalatable as it may be to some, is that it is only possible to sustain industrial activity in these high-cost industries by increasing government involvement'. (101)

In this way, as already pointed out, defence requirements and innovation for monopoly industry go hand in hand. Putting a man on the moon cost the American tax-payer $23,000 million (most of it going to the aerospace corporations), an expenditure which the US 'free enterprise' system on its own could never have found. Nevertheless, the research generated in the process was very useful for monopoly industry.

Another measurement of a country's R & D effort is the number of patent applications that have been lodged and accepted for protection. Most patent laws exclude theoretical ideas and scientific principles for patents. In the UK 31,686 patents were registered in 1950. These increased to 62,101 in 1970, of which 90 % related to manufacturing industry; over the whole period 1950-70 the rate of growth of patent applications was the same as the rate of growth of manufacturing output at constant prices. (102) The strong position already attained by the US in the field has meant that most of the patents registered in Europe are US owned, from which the US reaps considerable returns. As another study points out:

'Already the flow of know-how, in terms of the licencing of patents on certain manufacturing processes and products in countries other than those in which the patent was first taken out is flowing strongly from the US to Britain and Europe, implying that it is becoming increasingly necessary for European firms to buy their science abroad whilst the flow of scientists is running in the other direction'. (103)

Thus in 1961 the US paid $63 million for technological know-how from abroad but received more than $577 million for its own technology sold abroad. Again in 1965 the US filed more than 100,000 patents applications in foreign countries, as opposed to only 22,000 filed by foreign countries in the US in the same year.

A transnational corporation will initiate research when this fits the overall global strategy of the corporation. The development of technologically based innovations is hastened in the imperialist states since the cost of such research where incurred can be swallowed up in the price of the product; because of large work markets and the volume of production they are able to recover costs through the extraction of surplus-value from all over the world. A 'national market' under capitalism, however large, cannot in the present era of multilateral world markets sustain a technological industry. The advantage clearly lies with the imperialist countries because of their control over the multilateral world markets, which are vital for maintaining the profitability of monopoly enterprises. It is for this reason that the transnational corporation emphasises global strategy in innovation systems which tie together research centres, production plant and markets located throughout the world. Professor Root has worked out a model of a transnational corporation in which its headquarters:

> 'plans, directs, coordinates and controls innovational subsystems located throughout the world. Each innovational subsystem is managed at the regional and subsidiary levels . . . Flow of information of many kinds — market research, production and marketing programs — connect the different subsystems to form one global system guided by a single global management centre;' (104)

In this system (see Figure A), the monopolies reserve to themselves the technologically oriented industries as a form of monopoly control of production while the neo-colonial hinterland receives parts of technology as part of capital exports; the Third World's role in the overall global strategy is as supplier of raw materials, and as an outlet for capital. This phenomenon is little understood by the 'neo-Marxist' critics of Lenin's thesis, who assert that exports of technology under the 'new imperialism' have supplanted capital exports of the 'old imperialism' of Lenin's era. We shall revert to this question in Chapter XXI.

Now let us have a look at transnational corporations in operation. The main difference between monopoly capitalism as it manifested itself in the colonial period before the wars and today's monopoly capitalism lies in part in the type of ventures that they entered into in the colonies and semi-colonies. Whereas in the earlier period there was a concentrated investment in mining, plantation estates and other extractive industries, the contemporary transnational corporations, while maintaining their hold on these raw material ventures, are also going into manufacturing and import substitution industry. The transnationals are also extending their operations inside the borders of the other developed countries and in this way find outlets for capital exports and markets inside these countries. This

FIGURE A
FIG. 2.3 International Headquarters Company Organisation Structure

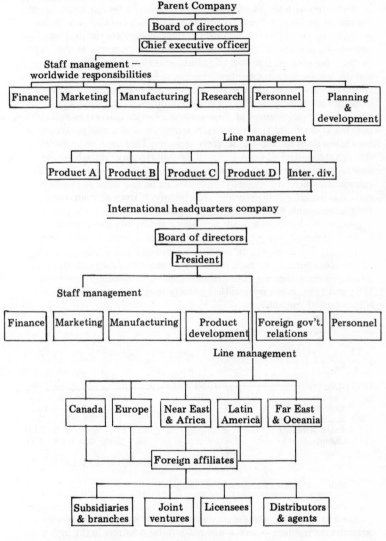

Source: William A. Dymsza 1973:27 [FIG.2.3]

development has increased the role of subsidiaries, particularly of US subsidiaries, engaging in direct manufacturing outside the borders of their countries of origin. To a major extent this has replaced direct export 'trade' as the main vehicle of economic relations between the industrial countries and with the Third World neo-colonies. Under this arrangement the greater part of this 'trade' is between subsidiaries of the same monopolies. In this way US transnational corporations subject the peoples of the weaker imperialist powers and exploit them in the same way as they subject all exploited peoples. The vast US investments in countries like Canada and the UK are in such a category.

In their operations overseas the transnational corporations still invest in raw material ventures in Third World countries. This is necessary to keep a hold on the sources of these materials and on markets as well as on investment channels. This is so even in situations where host governments have taken steps to 'nationalise' these ventures. They are able to do this through the control of finance capital, technology, and know-how. We now notice, however, a new strategy fitted to the new situation whereby enterprises which had originally concentrated on raw material production end up as manufacturing ventures. The history of Unilever is an interesting illustration of this development. From a plantation enterprise it grew into a transnational involved in manufacturing a variety of products: crude oil enterprises turned into petrochemicals producers; copper mines turned into metal fabricators, etc. In this way the number of US manufacturing subsidiaries operating overseas increased considerably. As Table IX below shows, US manufacturing subsidiaries increased tremendously between 1901 and 1967. It can be seen that globally they more than trebled between 1950 and 1967.

Table IX

Numbers of US manufacturing subsidiaries overseas by area 1901-1967

Area	1901	1913	1919	1929	1939	1950	1959	1967
Canada	6	30	61	137	169	225	330	443
Europe & UK	37	72	84	226	335	363	677	1438
Southern Dominion	1	3	8	25	69	99	184	361
Latin America	3	10	20	56	114	259	572	950
Other	0	1	7	23	28	42	128	454
	47	116	180	467	715	988	1891	3646

Source: Vernon Raymond, op. cit. p.68

The financing of the transnational corporation's activities in foreign countries is organised in such a way as to utilise resources in the host countries. The myth that the transnational corporation provides finance from its parent base to its subsidiaries and hence passes on an advantage to the countries where it operates should only deceive the convert to bourgeois obscurantism. Most US direct investment funds are generated abroad. For instance, a study made in 1968 shows that US transnationals financed roughly 40 % of their overseas operations from the cash flow generated where they operated, 33 % from external sources abroad and only 25 % through capital transfers from the US. Christopher Tugendhat adds:

'There is no doubt that since the imposition of tighter controls on capital outflows from the US by the US government the proportion derived from foreign sources has increased still further'. (105)

British companies are in an even better position to rely on foreign generated surplus since the exchange control regulations are tighter in the UK than in the US. As a result British transnationals have had to rely more on their subsidiaries meeting their own capital needs. Between 1964 and 1969 they financed at least 65 % and sometimes nearly 70 % of their foreign investments from the unremitted profits of their foreign subsidiaries. This is bound to be the case since the centralised control of transnational corporation ensures that the parent company will decide where it should borrow large amounts locally, where it should feed in funds from outside, and where it should keep a subsidiary short of cash. This they are able to do through a process known as transfer pricing of which we will say more below.

Transnationals are in a position to manage larger capitals than are revealed by their books. Vernon Raymond has observed of the 1969 US direct investment figure of $71 billion:

'Though this figure is impressive, extrapolations based on the reports of a sample of large companies indicates that in 1967, when the Department of Commerce figure was only $59 billion, the US parents were managing about $116 billion of overseas assets through their positions of control; that about $55 billion of the $110 billion were relatively liquid; and that these liquid assets exceed the short-term liabilities of the subsidiaries by $20 billion or so'. (106)

If we take a single year as representative of the general trend, transnational investments of US corporations normally reap a more than 'average profit' on their investments, a fact which is now generally recognized. Table X overleaf shows US investments by continent and the net outflow to the US of earnings as well as the rate of profitability for the year 1968. This table clearly reveals that the US monopoly capitalist's motivation in exporting capital is to make more than average profit on the basis of *low risk: low return; high risk: high return.* Although the table only reveals the average for Third World countries as a whole, it obscures higher rates of return in particular regions, which have been as high as 32 % in Asia (1968), and 29 % in Africa (1968). The average for all these countries is considerable in relation to those in the metropolitan centres.

Table X

Earnings on US Direct Foreign Private Investment by Area and Sector, 1959 and 1969.

	Reported Earnings (millions of dollars during year)	Value of Investment (millions of dollars at year end)	Rate of Earnings (%)
1959			
Total investment	3,255	29,735	11.0
Underdeveloped countries	1,615	11,536	14.0
Developed countries	1,640	18.199	9.0
Mining and smelting	315	2,858	11.0
Petroleum	1,185	10.423	11.4
Manufacturing	1,129	9,692	11.6
Other sectors	626	6,762	—
1969			
Total investment	7,955	70,763	11.3
Underdeveloped countries	3,747	20,000	18.7
Developed countries	4,208	50,763	8.3
Mining and smelting	844	5,635	15.0
Petroleum	2,494	19,985	12.5
Manufacturing	3,185	29,450	10.8
Other sectors	1,432	15,693	9.2

Source: US Dept. of Commerce, Survey of Current Business (Sept. 1960 and Oct. 1970).

Associated with financing is the question of the transfer of the financial resources generated by transnationals between the parent company and the subsidiaries overseas or between subsidiaries. In their effort to move their profits and capital across national boundaries, the transnational corporations are prompted by various considerations. Among these the most important are taxes; home and host-country attitudes and regulations; international and local competitive prices; anti-dumping requirements; customs duties; import quotas; licensing and other restrictions; local inflation and the possibility of currency devaluation (and revaluation); restrictions on repatriation of earnings; local content and design requirements; anti-trust or restriction-to-trade laws etc.

The capital movements are motivated basically by the desire of the transnational corporations to protect their objective interest. The emergence of the transnational is in itself a challenge to the narrow nationalism of the nation-state. Hence the barriers that nation-states erect in defence of 'national interest' are seen by the transnational as futile and pointless, as instinctive reactions of 'peasants, populists, mercantilists, xenophobes and infants' who 'want to eat their cake and have it too'. In the course of their activities dividends, royalties, interest payments, loans and other capital transfers, payment for goods and services as well as payments for technology, are transferred across national boundaries. As one managing director of a transnational said:

> 'We would not knowingly break the rules anywhere; we always employ one set of experts to tell us what they are, and another set to tell us how to get round them. It is the job of governments to make rules, and ours to find the loopholes'. (107)

The nation-state was fitted to regulating the activities of national companies, or international companies operating under some degree of cartel arrangement. The transnational, with a centralised headquarters pursuing a global interest with the objectives of minimising exchange risks, maximising tax avoidance, maintaining high profits with which to pay high dividends and accumulate capital, is a different kettle of fish. Let us look at the type of activity that transfer pricing entails. The transnationals have to deal with the problem of currency devaluations or with nationalisation or tax policies of the host countries. Many transnationals believe that the best way to guard against these dangers is not to allow their subsidiaries to accumulate any surplus cash out of their earnings. Depending on where these dangers exist and where they do not exist, the transnational corporations will move their funds from points of danger to safe horizons. (108) The five main methods open to them are as follows:

Firstly, sharply raising dividend payments to their shareholders. In 1964 and 1965, when the devaluation of the British pound seemed imminent, the survey conducted by Brooke and Remmers referred to already found that 30 % of the 115 foreign-owned subsidiaries in Britain covered by the survey which had not paid any dividends during the past three to four years did so immediately. 25 of the 115 remitted over 100 % of their earnings which meant dipping into accumulated profits. Some sent all their retained earnings, and one whose profits had been running at about £700,000 a year, paid a dividend of £3 million to its parent in 1964 alone!

Secondly, insisting that the subsidiary should bring forward its royalty and interest payments, and its contributions to general group expenditure, such as head office and research costs. In Britain a US subsidiary was ordered — by its parent company — to pay all outgoing service and royalty accounts immediately, whilst its nine sister subsidiaries were told to delay their payments to it. In the case of some Swiss-owned subsidiaries in Britain it was found that nine such subsidiaries consistently showed a very high proportion of capital debts owing to their parent, the suggestion being that from the point of view of overall taxation, Swiss companies preferred to get money out of British subsidiaries in the form of interest payments on loans, or as royalty payments, rather than in the more usual form of dividends paid out of profits.

Thirdly, manipulating the transfer prices in sales between subsidiaries. The headquarters management of the parent company will insist that the subsidiary in country X, should pay promptly for all imports from other subsidiaries while giving extended credit to those to which it exports. This happened in the 1964-65-67 devaluation crisis in Britain already referred to.

The manipulation of the transfer price may also mean *varying the prices paid by the subsidiaries to each other in their transactions.* If the headquarters of the parent company wishes to run down its reserves in country X, or counteract the effects of exchange control regulations or restrictions on export royalties and interest payments, it can instruct its subsidiaries to increase the prices at which they sell to the country X subsidiary, while at the same time reducing the price at which that subsidiary sells to the others. As illustration of this, Tugendhat gives the example of Mexico which tried to cut down imports and encourage industrialisation by forcing US car companies to manufacture their components locally; the US companies retaliated by increasing the prices on components which they were still allowed to import, to pay for 'losses' suffered by prohibition on importation on other components. As we shall see in Chapter XXI, such practices are widely reported in the neo-colonial world. Another example, in Britain, is the La Roche group which was referred to the Monopolies Commission when a *prima facie* case of over-pricing was discovered. This was a Swiss company exporting drugs in bulk to Britain where tablets and capsules were made. The *prima facie* case was that, while the manufacturing, packaging and selling costs of Librium were £1.70 for 1,000 tablets, the retail price for the same quantity was £10!

The transnationals justify their frequent changes in prices on the grounds of 'tax planning':

> 'This can mean anything from systematic avoidance to ensuring that the same profits are not taxed twice over by two governments, or taking advantage of an anomaly in the international system'. (109)

Many other considerations are involved in manipulating transfer prices. One reason may be not to show large profits in a particular country which could generate pressure from the host government or customers to reduce prices. Another may be to avoid trade union pressure for increased wages on the basis of increased productivity. Another technique in transfer pricing is to move profits to areas where tax liabilities are low. In this case goods are under-invoiced to a low tax country, where the local subsidiary, without even taking delivery, re-exports them at a higher price to where they are actually needed. Here the first and last subsidiaries make losses, which are offset by the higher profits in the low tax country. Many transnational corporations also use the services of Copenhagen free port to assist their subsidiaries. By exporting them to the Danish subsidiary, products can be re-exported at higher prices to third countries on another invoice without going through Danish customs, and the goods do not even have to touch Danish soil. The Danish subsidiary earns its profit between the two prices by merely writing invoices. Denmark gains by the tax on Danish income.

Some transnational corporations endeavour to arrange the flows of goods and services through their subsidiaries in such a way that the highest tax liabilities are incurred in the countries with the lowest rates of taxes. Dymsza quotes an electrical equipment manufacturer who establishes transfer prices for goods and services supplied to overseas affiliates to obtain the most favourable overall tax treatment:

> 'It sells raw materials and components at the lowest possible prices in countries where the tax rate is lower than the US. It levies charges for technical, marketing, and managerial services and central administration to the extent it can in higher tax countries. It also charges higher prices for goods and services in countries where it confronts high political risk, possible currency devaluation and trouble in repatriation of earnings'. (110)

Fourthly, making use of the foreign exchange markets. The transnationals can switch their surplus funds from one country to another, and sell short those they do not like in the hope that when the time comes to hand over the money they have realised from such sales a devaluation will have taken place. John Webb, Vice-President of USM Corporation which manufactures shoe making machinery, explained this technique in this way:

> 'One of our Danish subsidiaries had excess cash which it lent to another Danish subsidiary that was receiving goods from the Swedish subsidiary. The Danish pre-paid its account with the Swedish subsidiary, and this money financed the movement of Swedish products into the Finnish subsidiary. What did this maneouvre accomplish? If Finland had been required to pay for the goods, it would have had to borrow at fifteen per cent, the going Finnish rate. If the Swedish subsidiary had financed it, it would have had to borrow at about nine per cent. But cash in Denmark was worth only five or six per cent. Moreover, Danish currency was weak in relation to Swedish; by speeding up payments to Sweden we not only obtained cheaper credit, we hedged our position in Danish Kroner as well'. (111)

Fifthly, but by no means least important, developing the technique of the holding company as part of its integrated organisation. This technique is useful for all sorts of purposes, including tax avoidance. Transnationals have found that holding companies in such places as Netherlands, Luxembourg, Canada, or Switzerland offer considerable benefits for particular kinds of business. Quite apart from tax minimisation, the technique is useful in the area of centralised financial control. It is cheaper and easier for a transnational like Standard Oil (New Jersey) to channel its European financing operations through a holding company in Luxembourg. Du Pont does its financial coordination through its European office in Switzerland. Pirelli (Italian) also uses its Basle office in Switzerland as a holding company. This link enabled it to survive effects of the war.

> 'The existence of such holding companies is sufficiently extensive in the case of Switzerland, Canada and Panama to distort significantly the official figures for international investment flows. Estimates for investment in other countries from these three sources include substantial volume that is in fact the activity of an international holding company, operating from such a base for some tactical reason'. (112)

The main advantage of the technique is that it can be used to delay payment of taxes by the parent company. By channelling profits through a holding company in a third country, it is possible to introduce a substantial time-lag between making a profit and the final payment of a tax on it. 'A tax payment delayed is money saved', since with high interest rates a handsome income can be gained by merely lending it or investing it. It also makes it easier to set losses against profits to reduce tax liability.

To sum up this chapter, the transnational strategy ensures to the financial oligarchy full control over a good portion of the world's raw materials and agricultural products. The export of finance capital in the form of direct investment is intended to take monopolistic advantage of a technological or product advantage to control the raw material base and the market in the product. The world-wide patent system is suited to this monopolistic control. With production of value under its control, with power to centralise and command savings and smaller capitals all over the capitalist and neo-colonial world, the financial oligarchy can be seen as the rulers and oppressors of the working people both in the 'centre' and in the neo-colonial hinterland. Its power to move huge funds across national boundaries to avoid exchange losses, its use of transfer pricing mechanisms to avert dangers of devaluation, taxation and labour disputes, its production of components in different countries according to whether the advantages of labour-intensive or capital-intensive techniques are predominant all compound the power of the financial oligarchy over nation-states.

CHAPTER XVIII

The above survey covers the main developments in the imperialist camp in the post-war period. It remains briefly to say something about the multilateral strategy in practice in this period. Thus, whereas US imperialism emerged from the war as the strongest in the imperialist camp with a strong currency, and with its GNP having doubled in the five years between 1939 and 1944, this position has progressively deteriorated. In the twenty years 1950-1970 the growth in the world's gross product increased 2.7 times, with industrial production increasing 2.8 times and volume of exports 3.8. This growth was shared with the EEC and Japan, who increased their share at the expense of the US. The growth of US capital exports to Europe and Japan has been matched by Europe's increased investment in the Third World, although US direct investments still lead. The participation of Europe, Japan and the Soviet Union in production and trade has been considerable. The EEC and Japanese annual average rates of growth of GDP surpassed those of the US in the period 1950-68; the EEC grew 5.3 %, Japan 9.9 % and that of the US 3.7 %. EEC exports doubled between 1948 and 1968, overall US share of developed countries exports fell from 34 % to 20 % between 1949 and 1968, whereas Europe's rose from 19 % in 1948 to 46 % in 1968.

In the field of foreign investment and international reserves, the EEC and Japan have moved from the position of mere net importers of capital to that of capital exporters as well in this period, particularly after 1960. Between 1964 and 1969 the flows of direct investment from Western European countries to Third World countries increased by 55 % and from Japan by 267 % while US relative direct investments to the Third World increased by 28 %. (113)

The Western European countries investment increases were as follows:

West Germany	161 %
Holland	235 %
Italy	162 %
UK	106 %
France	200 % (?)

As far as reserves in the world monetary system are concerned, there has been a relative redistribution, with the US hegemonic position correspondingly reduced. Whereas in 1949 the US had three-quarters of the world's gold and almost half of the total monetary reserves, by 1969, due to the outflow for war-mongering averaging $4 billion annually, its gold reserves were reduced by 50 % to 30 % of the world's total. Its total gold and foreign exchange reserves decreased to a mere 21 %.

As opposed to this weakening position, the share of Western Europe in the world's total rose from 11 % in 1949 to 37 % in 1969, almost double the US share. (113) Table XI from the GATT *Annual* for 1973 shows the detailed trade position of the imperialist countries *inter-se* as well as with its Third World hinterland and the socialist camp for the years 1960, 1965 to 1972.

The above analyses should not, however, conceal the fact that what appear as exports of many of the other imperialist countries is US trade generated by its transnational corporations. Under this strategy over 40 % of Canada's exports were US transnational exports operating there in 1970; 20 % of UK exports in 1970 were accounted for in the same way. It is also to be noted that, of the 10 largest exporters in the UK, two (Ford and Texaco) are US transnational corporations. In 1970 10 % of EEC exports were from the US transational corporations and in France two of the ten largest exporters were US owned (Chrysler, IBM).

The impact of these widespread manufacturing subsidiary sales has been to lessen US direct exports. For this reason US merchandise exports have shrunk more noticeably whilst the sales of its manufacturing subsidiaries and affiliates overseas have increased more markedly. In the period 1951-71 US exports rose 4.3 times, whereas the sales of her affiliates abroad expanded 7 times. The result was that by 1971 US transnational sales on the world market exceeded US direct exports by 4 times as against 2.4 times in 1950. The sales of the other capitalist countries were behind in this respect. In all, the sales of all transnational affiliates of all capitalist monopolies are estimated at $330,000 million as compared to $312,000 million of direct exports. Moreover, a big portion of the direct exports of merchandise are transfers between the subsidiaries in different parts of the world. Thus it is estimated by the British Board of Trade that 22 % of the total British exports in value in 1966 were 'transactions between related concerns', which were sales by branches of transnational corporations, British and foreign owned, to affiliates abroad. In the case of US controlled corporations the research showed that most sales were to sister companies. These accounted for 56 % of their total exports; 27 % of exports by British controlled corporations were to affiliates. Similar research in the US in 1964 showed that 25 % of all US exports were from US based corporations to their affiliates abroad. In 1965 a study covering 320 companies with combined exports amounting to $8,500 million revealed that more than 50 % of their overseas sales were to affiliates. (114) Raymond Vernon adds: 'If one were also to include the exports of goods produced by US parents that were shipped indirectly through middlemen, the relative importance of such enterprises would even be greater'. (113)

Table XI

Network of Total International Trade 1960, 1965 to 1972 (Million dollars f.o.b.)

Destination / Origin	Year	Industrial areas Value	%	Devel. areas Value	%	Eastern trading areas Value	%	Total world Value	%
	1960	54.43	42.5	20.93	16.3	2.89	2.3	81.80	63.8
	1965	87.61	46.9	25.53	13.7	4.70	2.5	123.09	65.9
	1966	97.42	47.8	28.01	13.8	5.61	2.8	135.95	66.8
Industrial areas	1967	103.57	48.3	28.33	13.2	6.02	2.8	143.31	66.9
	1968	117.90	49.3	31.71	13.3	6.34	2.7	161.51	67.5
	1969	138.42	50.7	35.01	12.8	6.95	2.5	186.43	68.3
	1970	160.59	51.5	39.93	12.8	8.16	2.6	215.84	69.2
	1971	179.92	51.7	44.74	12.9	8.89	2.6	241.26	69.4
	1972	217.00	52.6	50.10	12.1	11.70	2.8	286.00	69.3
	1960	19.21	15.0	6.26	4.9	1.23	1.0	27.45	21.4
	1965	25.41	13.6	7.73	4.1	2.41	1.3	36.43	19.5
	1966	27.38	13.4	8.04	3.9	2.36	1.2	38.63	19.0
	1967	28.66	13.4	8.21	3.8	2.17	1.0	39.98	18.7
Developing areas	1968	31.95	13.4	9.13	3.8	2.27	0.9	44.35	18.5
	1969	35.45	13.0	10.32	3.8	2.64	1.0	49.52	18.1
	1970	39.97	12.8	11.09	3.6	3.15	1.0	55.45	17.8
	1971	44.92	12.9	12.78	3.7	3.27	0.9	62.18	17.9
	1972	53.40	12.9	15.60	3.8	3.40	0.8	73.80	17.9
	1960	2.79	2.2	1.34	1.0	10.85	8.5	15.02	11.7
	1965	4.65	2.5	3.21	1.7	13.82	7.4	21.73	11.6
	1966	5.58	2.7	3.62	1.8	13.96	6.9	23.20	11.4
	1967	5.90	2.8	3.80	1.8	15.14	7.1	24.89	11.6
Eastern trading areas	1968	6.18	2.6	4.05	1.7	16.69	7.0	26.98	11.3
	1969	6.96	2.5	4.58	1.7	18.14	6.6	29.74	10.9
	1970	7.74	2.5	5.14	1.6	19.95	6.4	32.89	10.5
	1971	8.79	2.5	5.18	1.5	21.88	6.3	35.91	10.3
	1972	10.10	2.4	6.00	1.5	26.20	6.3	42.40	10.3
	1960	79.32	61.9	29.18	22.8	15.15	11.8	128.00	100.0
	1965	121.63	65.2	37.30	10.00	21.26	11.4	186.70	100.0
	1966	134.75	66.2	40.68	20.0	22.08	10.8	203.60	100.0
	1967	142.53	66.5	41.56	19.4	23.59	11.0	214.40	100.0
Total world	1968	160.78	67.2	46.03	19.2	25.53	10.7	239.30	100.0
	1969	186.25	68.2	51.16	18.7	27.97	10.2	272.90	100.0
	1970	213.87	68.5	57.63	18.5	31.60	10.1	312.00	100.0
	1971	239.45	68.5	64.56	18.6	34.31	9.9	347.80	100.0
	1972	288.10	69.8	73.80	17.9	41.60	10.1	412.80	100.0

Source: GATT: International Trade 1973

This phenomenon further demonstrates the increasing concentration of production and capital, which is the sole means by which a transnational corporation can maintain its profitability amidst the intensified competition in the world market by monopolies. Table XII shows the relative positions within this phenomenon. In all about 30 % of the exports of all the world capitalist exports are from US transnational corporations.

Table XII

Share of the American Transnational Corporations' Affiliates in the Export of Some Countries

	1966		1970	
	$'000 million	%	$'000 million	%
Canada	3.3	35	6.8	42
Latin America	4.3	40	4.7	36
Great Britain	2.66	19	3.4	17
EEC countries including:	4.5	9	8.6	10
France	0.8	7	1.6	9
FRG	1.4	7	2.7	8
Other West European countries	2.5	13	4.4	15
Japan	0.08	1	0.35	2
Asia and Africa (without Japan)	4.6	18	10.0	27
Australia and New Zealand	0.34	6	0.76	9

Source: Implications of Multinational Firms for World Trade,
(New York, 1973).

Concentration of capital has already reached remarkable levels; Tugendhat points out with alarm that:

'It was estimated in 1967 that forty per cent of all US direct investments in France, West Germany, and Britain belonged to Standard Oil (New Jersey), General Motors, and Ford. Altogether two thirds of the total existing US investment in Western Europe in that year was held by twenty companies'. (116)

The activities of these US transnational giants have gone on within the purview of the present day international economic relationships and constitute the very basis of international diplomacy. The bourgeois state is nothing but a board of directors for these monopolies. Thorstein Veblen was saying the same thing in different words when he wrote:

'Under the modern situation, as it has taken shape since the industrial revolution, business competition has become international, covering the range of what is called the world market. In this international competition the machinery and policy of the state are in a peculiar degree drawn into the service of the larger business interests; so that both in commerce and industrial enterprise, the businessmen of one nation are pitted against those of another and swing the forces of the state, legislative, diplomatic, and military, against one another in the strategic game of pecuniary advantage'. (117)

The latest phase of the development of monopoly capitalism — the transnational corporation — has been evolving and expanding. This monopoly was made possible to a great extent by the machinery of the bourgeois state itself, which now feigns ignorance. It is a reality which the present day bourgeois state in its effort to balance off one monopoly interest against another has to reckon with. Thus a United Nations Committee of 'Eminent Persons', which conducted an enquiry into the activities of the transnational corporations 'grudgingly' recommended the creation of a permanent commission that would 'seek to harmonise the global companies' activities with the economic plans of developing nations and help develop a 'code of conduct' for relations between the companies and governments'. (118)

This clearly shows the objective power of the transnational corporation and the subordinate position of the nation-state as its superstructure. The neo-colonial state is of course a real outpost of the transnational and the 'economic plans' are nothing but field activities which have to conform to the transnational's global strategy and not vice-versa! This is the reality of the present day economic order. In the next part we examine neo-colonialism within this post-war multilateral imperialism.

REFERENCES

1. Felix Green, *The Enemy*, Cape, (London, 1970).
2. Felix Green, op. cit. p.194.
3. Robert Triffin, *The Dollar Crisis*, Yale University Press, (Yale, 1961), p.61.
4. Woodruff, *The Impact of the Western Man*, p.150, quoted in Magdoff, *The Age of Imperialism*, Monthly Review (New York).
5. *Fortune Magazine*, Vol. XXV, May 1942, pp.59-63.
6. Harley A. Notter, quoted in Richard Gardner, *Sterling Dollar Diplomacy*, McGraw-Hill, (University of Wisconsin, 1969), p.15.
7. Richard Gardner, op. cit. pp.17-18.
8. L.C. Gardner, *Economic Aspects of New Deal Diplomacy*, University of Wisconsin, (Madison, 1964), pp.272-291.
9. Quoted in L.C. Gardner, op. cit. p.290.
10. Quoted in Richard Gardner, op. cit. p.24.
11. Cheryl Payer, *The Debt Trap. The IMF and the Third World*, Penguin, (London, 1974), p.24.
12. Cheryl Payer, op. cit. p.217-221.
13. Quoted in Bruse Nissen; see note 14 below.
14. Bruce Nissen in Steve Weissman (Editor), *The Trojan Horse*, Ramparts Press, (New York, 1974), p.45.
15. J. Halliday & G. McCormack, *Japanese Imperialism Today*, Penguin, (London, 1973), p.51.
16. Richard Gardner, op. cit. p.17.
17. Text of the *General Agreement on Tariffs and Trade*, (Geneva, 1969).
18. Articles XI-XIII of the GATT.
19. Articles XIV-XV of the GATT.
20. Article XXIV of the GATT.
21. The Havana Charter was the original legal document which was to be the legal basis of the International Trade Organisation (ITO), but which aborted due to US opposition. For a fuller discussion see C. Wilcox, *A Charter for World Trade*, Arno, (New York, 1972).
22. The United States and the European Community. Pamphlet of the E.C. (New York, 1972).
23. Mahotiere, *Towards One Europe*, Penguin, (London, 1974).
24. Lenin, *Selected Works*, Vol. I p.662-665.
25. P. Jalee, *Imperialism in the Seventies*, Third Press, (New York, 1974).
26. P. Jalee, op. cit. p.193.
27. Servan-Schreiber, *The American Challenge*, Penguin, (London, 1969).
28. Telex Africa, Newsletter from Brussels dated, October, 1974.
29. J. Halliday & G. McCormack, *Japanese Imperialism Today*, Penguin, (London, 1973), p.11.
30. J. Halliday & G. McCormack, op. cit. p.12.
31. J. Halliday & G. McCormack, op. cit. p.13.

32. H. Magdoff, *The Age of Imperialism*, Monthly Review, (New York, 1969), p.53.

33. Quoted in L.C. Gardner, op. cit. p.261.

34. Quoted in Magdoff, op. cit. p.116.

35. P.A. Baran & P.A. Sweezy, *Monopoly Capital*, Penguin, (London, 1966), p.189.

36. P.A. Baran & P.A. Sweezy, op. cit. p.63.

37. Jonathan F. Holloway, *International Studies Quarterly-Journal*, Vol. 16, no.14. December 1972, p.491.

38. J.D. Bernal, *Science in History*, Penguin, (1965), Vol. IV, p.846.

39. J.D. Bernal, op. cit. p.847.

40. Richard J. Barnet, *Intervention and Revolution*, Paladin, (London, 1972), p.15.

41. Modelski, in Journal at note 37.

42. US News & World Report, February 12, 1975. pp.24-25.

43. Lenon Siegal, in Steve Weissman (Editor) *The Trojan Horse*, Ramparts, (New York, 1974), p.204.

44. Lenon Seigal, in Steve Weissman (Editor) op. cit. p.204.

45. Wall Journal, 1971.

46. J.A. Holloway, see note 37.

47. See for instance an obvious example of Paul A. Samuelson who in his 1973 mass produced book *Economics* still sticks to this,

48. P.A. Baran & P.A. Sweezy, *Monopoly Capital*, Penguin, (London, 1966). p.15.

49. K. Marx, *Grundrisse*, Penguin, (London, 1973), p.748.

50. P.A. Baran & P.A. Sweezy, op. cit. pp.63-79.

51. P.A. Baran & P.A. Sweezy, op. cit. pp.80-87.

52. P.A. Baran & P.A. Sweezy, op. cit. chapters 5-7.

53. H. Magdoff, in Roger Owen and Bob Sutcliftee (Editors), *Studies in the Theory of Imperialism*, Longman, (London, 1972), p.147 note 3.

54. H. Magdoff, op. cit. p.155.

55. Samir Amin, *Accumulation on a World Scale*, Monthly Review, (New York, 1973), Vol.1, p.105.

56. H. Magdoff, *Age . . .* op. cit. p.39.

57. P. Jalee, *Imperialism . . .* op. cit. p.125.

58. P.A. Sweezy, *Theory of Capitalist Development*, Monthly Review (New York, 1942), p.70, 104.

59. P.A. Baran & P.A. Sweezy, op. cit. pp.115-116.

60. P.A. Baran & P.A. Sweezy, op. cit. p.122.

61. Samir Amin, *Accumulation on a World Scale*, Monthly Review, (1973), p.116-133.

62. Samir Amin, op. cit. p.91.

63. Samir Amin, op. cit. p.16.

64. Samir Amin, op. cit. p.192.

65. M. Kidron, *Western Capitalism Since the War*, Penguin,(London,

1968), Chapter 3.

66. K. Marx, *Theories of Surplus-Value*, Progress, (Moscow, 1969), Vol. III pp.349-351.

67. M. Kidron, op. cit. p.55.

68. M. Kidron, op. cit. pp.52-53.

69. K. Marx, Proverty of Philosophy, Progress, (Moscow, 1973), p.9.

70. P.A. Baran & P.A. Sweezy, op. cit. pp.118-119.

71. P.A. Baran & P.A. Sweezy, op. cit. p.128.

72. P.A. Baran & P.A. Sweezy, op. cit. p.23.

73. P.A. Baran & P.A. Sweezy, op. cit. pp.123-124.

74. G. Bannock, *The Juggernault*, Penguin, (London, 1973), p.72.

75. Quoted in Bannock, op. cit. p.73.

76. P.A. Baran & P.A. Sweezy, op. cit. p.125.

77. J.H. Dunning, *Capital Movements in the Twentieth Century* in J.H. Dunning (Ed.) *International Investment*, Penguin, (London, 1972), p.81.

78. Jeremy Main, in *Fortune Magazine*, Dec. 1967, p.143.

79. G.S. Moore, *The National Banking Review*, quoted in Magdoff, op. cit.

80. S. Menshikov, *Millionaires and Managers*, Progress Publishers, (Moscow, 1969).

81. H. Magdoff, *Age* . . . op. cit. p.72.

82. Quoted in H. Stephenson, *The Coming Clash*, Weidenfeld and Nicholson, (London, 1972), pp.128-126.

83. H. Magdoff, *Age* . . . op. cit. p.78.

84. G. Göncöl, in F. Tamas, *Studies in International Economics*, Akdemai Kiaolo (Budapest, 1966), p.9-62.

85. John J. Powers, Speech *The Multinational*, New York, 27th Nov.1967.

86. H. Stephenson, op. cit. p.150.

87. J.H. Dunning, Quoted in C. Tugendhat, *The Multinationals*, Penguin, (London, 1971), p.38.

88. Quoted in Tugendhat, op. cit. p.34.

89. W.A. Dymsza, *The Multinational Business Strategy*, McGraw-Hill, (New York, 1972), pp.189-204.

90. W.A. Dymsza, op. cit. p.205.

91. W.A. Dymsza, op. cit. pp.195-196.

92. C.P. Kindleberger, *International Economics*, 5th Ed. Irwin, (London, 1973), p.254.

93. Polk, Meister and Veit, *US Production Abroad and The Balance of Payments*, (Seminar).

94. W.A. Dymsza, op. cit. pp.206-207.

95. Quoted in Dymsza, op. cit. p.219.

96. R. Vernon, *Quarterly Journal of Economics*, Vol. XXIV, p.96.

97. Summary of written and oral statement given by Gilbert Jones and Jacques Maisonrouge of IBM, before the hearings of the UN Group of Eminent Persons on the study of the *Impact of Multinational Corporations on Development and on International Relations: Summary of the Hearings.*

UN Document ST/ESA/15 p.66.

98. Hilary & Steven Rose, *Science and Society*, Penguin, (1969), pp.24-25.

99. Hilary & Steven Rose, op. cit. p.200. See also R. Vernon, op. cit. p.95.

100. K. Norris & J. Vaizey, *The Economics of Research and Technology*, 1973, Chapter 2. See also R. Vernon, op. cit. p.94.

101. H. Stephenson, op. cit. pp.33-34.

102. Norris & Vaizey, op. cit. p.34.

103. Hilary & Steven Rose, op. cit. p.202.

104. Quoted in Dymsza, op. cit. p.142.

105. C. Tugendhat, op. cit. p.184.

106. R. Vernon, op. cit. p.25.

107. Quoted in Tugendhat, op. cit. p.163.

108. We are indebted to Christopher Tugendhat for the material on the issue of transfer pricing in his Chapter 10.

109. C. Tugendhat, op. cit.

110. W.A. Dymsza, op. cit. p.161.

111. *Fortune Magazine*, 15 September, 1958 quoted in Tugendhat, op. cit.

112. H. Stephenson, op. cit. p.134.

113. A. Pinto & Knaral, *ISER* Vol. 22, No.1, March 1973, p.144.

114. *Survey of Current Business*, May 1969.

115. R. Vernon, op. cit. p.25.

116. C. Tugendhat, op. cit. p.54.

117. T. Veblen, *Economic Theory and the Business Enterprise*, Kelly, (New York, 1965), p.293.

118. *Sunday Post*, Nairobi, 24th June, 1974.

PART FIVE

NEO-COLONIALISM UNDER MULTILATERAL IMPERIALISM

CHAPTER XIX

'Like the historian *Raumer,* the petty-bourgeois is composed On The One Hand and On The Other Hand. This is so in his economic interests and *therefore* in his politics, in his scientific, religious and artistic views. It is so in his morals, in everything. He is a living contradiction. If, like Proudhon, he is in addition a gifted man, he will soon learn to play with his contradictions and develop them according to circumstances into striking, ostentatious, now scandalous or now brilliant paradoxes. Charlatanism in science and accomodation in politics are inseparable from such a point of view. There remains only one governing motive, the *vanity* of the subject, and the only question for him, as for all vain people is the success of the moment, the attention of the day'.

Karl Marx

The imperialist redivison of the world after the second World War was based on the Open Door policy, in which the financial oligarchies of the imperialist countries battled against each other in the open fields of the historic colonial enclaves and preserves of each of the financial and industrial groups.

The origins of this strategy are not hard to find, as we have shown. The world of imperialism was no longer one of expanding markets and frontiers. On the contrary, it was one of shrinking horizons. The completion of the division of the world was increasingly being challenged and an increasing part of the colonial world liberated due to the contradictions that imperialism itself set in motion. The October Revolution had ushered in a new era. For the first time in history a socialist state, representing the international proletariat and the oppressed peoples of the world, gave notice to imperialism that its days were numbered. For the first time the slogan was to be 'workers of all countries *and all oppressed peoples, unite*'! The proletariat was gaining new allies, a fact that arose out of the contradictions of capitalist development as pursued under monopoly capitalism.

In the Soviet Peace Decree of 1917, this changed situation was given expression when the Soviet Union called for peace without indemnities or annexations. It also called for the liberation of the territories annexed by force, the withdrawal of troops from occupied territories, and the complete restoration of the independence of the peoples who had lost it in the course of the war; the Soviet Union called for plebiscites on the political future of national groups who wished to break away from one of the existing states of which they formed parts, and further demanded the democratic rights of national minorities. What is of crucial importance is that the Decree called for the application of the same principles to the colonial peoples and the right of all colonial peoples to independence and self-determination. It condemned secret diplomacy and demanded open popular diplomacy.

It was these revolutionary demands, 'well thought out, morally sound and announced for propaganda purposes,' (1) which greatly embarrassed the imperialists. Whilst the older European powers were reluctant to recognise the Bolshevik 'challenge' or to make a gesture of renunciation of their annexations and colonies, Wilson, the US President, took the challenge seriously and came out with his Fourteen Points, a kind of 'counter-manifesto' in which he too rejected secret diplomacy and endorsed the principle of self-determination, but 'did so equivocally with regard to colonial territories outside Europe'. (2)

> 'These lofty principles were broadly accepted by the other capitalist powers, under US pressure, but despite these verbal commitments [they] were disregarded and over-ridden in the actual settlement at Versailles. The principle of self-determination (the crux of the international programme of Wilson's liberalism) was indeed openly violated by Wilson himself in his invervention against the Bolshevik revolution shortly after the declaration'. (2)

The events of the next war brought to the US the realisation that her expanded production in key sectors required new markets. With the general offensive by the Soviet Union, particularly after the war when Eastern Europe was no longer under the control of imperialism, imperialism was faced with the need to preserve what remained of its power. The new policy was to intensify the idea of the self-determination of all peoples in order to give a progressive stance to imperialism and remove the initiative from the Soviets. The US could lose nothing by pursuing such a policy, which actually strengthened her economy. It is in this sense that the US multilateral strategy which called for the abolition of colonial preference markets must be seen and it is from these proceedings, which arise out of imperialism, that the whole neo-colonial strategy springs.

But there was a more fundamental reason why imperialism felt the need to put forward this new policy. The avowed problem of 'communist subversion' in Europe and more particularly in the neo-colonial hinterland need not have been a problem for imperialism if in fact it stood for freedom and democracy as it claimed to. The fear of 'communist subversion' had organic roots within imperialism itself and that is why imperialism became so sensitive about it. The imperialists were fully aware that the model of 'democracy' and 'freedom' they sought to impose on the Third World was far from having the same consequences for economic development in the neo-colonies as that achieved by the bourgeoisie of Europe, America and Japan in their own countries.

Whereas in Europe the bourgeoisie triumphed over feudalism and absolutism with the mass support of the oppressed peasantry, the conditions for creating this type of bourgeois revolution did not exist in the colonies. Whereas in Europe the change from feudalism led rapidly to economic development and emancipation of the peasantry from feudal exploitation (only to face new exploitation in another form: wage labour) such economic development and emancipation of the peasant masses in the colonies and semi-colonies was impossible under imperialism.

Imperialism cannot allow the complete transformation of pre-capitalist societies, but on the contrary exists on the basis of hindering their transformation and thus subjects them to the needs of monopoly capitalism. Whereas capitalism in its youth gave rise to development even in some of the old colonies held over by the bourgeoisie from the feudalists, the path to such development in a newly acquired colony or one passing over from the earlier colonialism after 1880 was blocked.

This was the era when capitalism reached its highest stage of development, a stage when capitalism, in its crisis brought about by 'overproduction', could only survive, at least in the short run, through concentration of production, the expansion of markets, and the securing of sources of vital raw materials to help keep the organic composition of capital at profitable levels. The result was the emergence of monopolies (cartels, trusts and syndicates) in the period after 1880; the scramble for colonial possessions in the period 1880-1900; and, for the first time, the division of the entire world of 'unoccupied' territories among these monopolies of Europe, America and Japan.

Under these newly changed circumstances, it became clear that so long as imperialism held sway over these colonial and semi-colonial territories, the classical bourgeois road to development was blocked for them. It was blocked precisely by the contradictory development of capitalism in Europe, America and Japan, wherein monopoly capitalism could only survive on the basis of global exploitation. Capitalism itself was in this contradictory process developing further the international working class by creating a working class, however small, in all these countries. This class then arose in the colonies and neo-colonies as a vanguard of the struggle against imperialism since the historical conditions in the neo-colonial world demanded a liquidation of imperialism, if development of the productive forces was to take place.

Moreover, the successful socialist revolution in the Soviet Union in October 1917, offered new hope for the proletariat of the imperialist countries as well as the proletariat and peasantry of the colonial and semi-colonial peoples. It was now possible and historically necessary not only to overthrow imperialism, but to do so on the basis of socialism. The possibilities of revolutionary changes in the backward colonial and semi-colonial countries were opened up. It was in this sense that Stalin in 1918 advanced the following position based on the correct summarisation of the question by the Bolsheviks:

'The great world-wide significance of the October Revolution chiefly consists in the fact that: 1. It has widened the scope of the national question and converted it from the particular question of combating national oppression in Europe into the general question of emancipating the oppressed peoples, colonies and semi-colonies from imperialism'. (3)

This meant that the colonial question had become part and parcel of the national question. More importantly, however, it had become part of the proletarian struggle. It is here that Mao Tse-Tung's thesis *On New Democracy* in 1940 takes on meaning.

'From this it can be seen that there are two kinds of world revolution, the first belonging to the bourgeois or capitalist category. The era of this kind of world revolution is long past, having come to an end as far back as 1914 when the first imperialist world war broke out, and more particularly in 1917, when the October Revolution took place.

The second kind, namely the proletarian-socialist world revolution, thereupon began. This revolution has the proletariat of the capitalist countries as its main force and the oppressed peoples of the colonies and semi-colonies as its allies. No matter what class, parties or individuals in an oppressed nation join the revolution, and no matter whether they themselves are conscious of the point or understand it, so long as they oppose imperialism, their revolution becomes part of the proletarian-socialist world revolution and they become its allies'. (4)

In order to divert the revolutionary struggles which threatened imperialism, the idea of 'self-determination' of colonial territories featured in the US post-war policy. This 'solution' forced on imperialism was inherently anti-nationalist and anti-socialist, since the national question was linked up with the socialist revolution. The 'self-determination' that imperialism offered did not solve this question but merely put it off. Imperialism could adopt this strategy by relying on internal class forces in the neo-colony. It now had class allies in these colonies and semi-colonies. But these classes were weak. Its strategy therefore included the military programme for propping-up its weak petty-bourgeois and 'national bourgeois' class allies.

This analysis gives us a proper historical perspective in which to view the neo-colonial problem, and it gives us a proper and sounder foundation for resolving the theoretical issues raised by the post war imperialist policy which have baffled even those who call themselves Marxists. Looked at from the standpoint of dialectical and historical materialism and not in a mechanical way the mechanics and the essence of neo-colonialism are easily comprehended.

215

The introduction of capitalist relations and competition in the colonies created a social base for neo-colonial class formation. With the exports of capital for production in the colony a 'national bourgeoisie' emerged which in reality was only a petty-bourgeoisie serving the process of colonial production. This stratum had two components. The first was engaged in small production on land and circulation of commodities; the other was engaged in commercial and civil services. A middle class, a small professional cadre, the most prominent being the lawyers and medical doctors, emerged as colonialism consolidated. Also with the consolidation of colonialism a small commercial petty-bourgeoisie took root in metropolitan enterprises. When the struggle for national independence began, this phenomenon presented an opportunity for imperialism to transfer some amount of political autonomy to this stratum while retaining control of the economy through the colonial structure of property relations. The neo-colonial 'state' that emerged is a contradiction in itself. It had its origin in the colonial state itself, which was created by imperialism to oppress the people of the colony and to facilitate the extraction of surplus-value through colonial production. It had emerged not as an autonomous unit but as an arbitrary entity carved out by the metropolitan powers in their scramble for whatever remained of the uncolonised world in the nineteenth century. It cut across ethnic entities and was established as an artificial heterogenous body with institutions introduced and imposed from outside. Whereas the bourgeoisie in Europe and Japan emerged as a class out of the internal development of those societies, the colonial petty-bourgeoisie are a creation of international monopoly capital, and dependent upon it. So long as the petty-bourgeoisie maintain this reliance on imperialism, they cannot complete the national democratic revolution.

Who are the perpetrators of neo-colonialism? These are, of course, the US, the European and the Japanese imperialists. There is no doubt that part of US imperialism's post-war multilateral strategy was concerned with the collective interest of the imperialist camp as a whole. Whilst it used its strong position to penetrate all parts of the world, it also had an interest in preserving the capitalist system on a world scale. If the whole of Europe had fallen to the socialist camp there is no doubt that US imperialism would have been threatened at the base, since Europe controlled most of the colonial Third World. This point is well put by Rupert Emerson, in a paper to the American Assembly, in 1963, in which he stated:

> 'A communist take over in any African country would be a dangerous opening wedge for entry into a continent that has hitherto been held as an inviolate preserve for the free world. To the crowded Europe, Africa holds the promise of a frontier land still susceptible of great expansion, both as a market and as a source of unexplored industrial potential. Its riches in strategic and other minerals are impressive. In industrial diamonds, colombium, cobalt, chromium and berylium, Africa either heads the list of world producers or stands close to the

top. It is a significant producer of tin, manganese, copper, antimony; and its reserves of iron ore and bauxite are just beginning to be tapped. The uranium of the Congo and South Africa has contributed to the unfolding of the atomic age. The French discovery of oil in the Sahara has enhanced the importance of Algeria, and Libya has also come into new riches. To this mineral wealth, Africa adds through its agriculture a variety of foodstuffs and industrial materials such as cocoa, coffee, tea, vegetable oil, cotton and pyrethrum.

The United States has a direct interest in many of these products, but it is probably of less importance to assure its own access to Africa's resources and markets than to make sure that its European allies are not cut off from them'. (5)

This statement is corroborated by President Eisenhower's statement already referred to in Chapter XIV as to the role of Japan in Asia for imperialism.

Having said this it is necessary to point out that many people have concluded that the US interest in the neo-colonial Third World is not based on *economic* grounds since her exports of goods and capital constitutes a minor fraction of her GNP. This contention is correct to the extent that the figures quoted show a relatively lower rate of investment when compared, say, to Europe or Canada. But the figures do not show the qualitative aspects of the relationship between the figures and the real interest. These investments give the US considerable control over raw material resources, particularly through technological leadership; Magdoff has correctly analysed these statistics, and comparing the value of US exports and the sales of its subsidiaries overseas with the value of its total internal production of moveable goods, namely agricultural products, minerals, manufactures and shipping, he comes to the conclusion that foreign markets account for two-fifths of the internal production, which clearly shows the importance of this sector. (6)

It is generally recognised that the greater part of US investments in Third World countries is currently in fuels and mining, as well as manufacturing. The fact that other resources are not being tapped now does not, however, mean that US imperialism has no interest in them. On the contrary, they are reserved for future exploitation. This is in strict accordance with the nature of imperialism. It is for this reason, among others, that the US was prepared to put up $760 billion dollars to prosecute one war alone in Vietnam, to ensure that the imperialist market and the outlets for capital exports did not shrink.

Moreover, since most US investments are in extractive industries, the amounts involved need not be large, given the cheapness of labour, rent and other costs. Even where manufacturing is involved the costs of production are lower. The control that such investment and transfer of skills entails is, however, crucial to US global interest. Magdoff makes a cardinal point when he points out that:

'The economic control, and hence the political control when dealing with foreign sources of raw material supplies, is of paramount importance to the monopoly organised mass production industries in the home country. In industries, such as steel, aluminium, and oil, the ability to control the source of raw materials is essential to the control over the markets and prices of the final products, and serves as an effective safety factor in protecting the large investment in the manufacture and distribution of the final product. The resulting frustration of competition takes on two forms. First, when price and distribution of the raw material are controlled, the competitor's freedom of action is restricted; he cannot live very long without a dependable source of raw materials at a practical cost. Second, by gobbling up as much of the world's resources of this material as is feasible, a power group can forestall a weaker competitor from becoming more independent as well as discourage possible new competition. How convenient that a limited number of US oil companies control two-thirds of the 'free world's' oil'! (7)

This potentiality of the market, and the importance of raw materials for future exploitation is not lost sight of by the monopolies. Indeed it is always at the back of their investment policy, as we saw. Every monopoly tries to defend its potentiality in these areas. In an address to American businessmen on November 5, 1962, Dean Rusk was to the point on this issue unlike those who would like to obscure the reality of US imperialism. He stated:

'And these latter investments [i.e., $2.5 billion in Asia, and $1.1 billion in Africa], like the $8.2 billion in Latin America, are largely in the production of oils and ores. Admittedly, in many instances, the returns may be slower and less certain. In some countries the risks, both political and economic, may be prohibitive. Yet American firms who participate in development in its early stages have the prospect of securing ground floor positions in great markets of the future'. (8)

He advised the companies 'to keep the essential American skills in the plant while leaving our flag off the roof'! (9)

Table XIII overleaf shows US investments by area and industry. The relatively lower level of investments in the Third World does not mean a lessening of control. On the contrary there has been increased public loans and credits as we shall see later. Moreover as we have already pointed out the actual volume of capital exported do not tell the whole story of the need for imperialism to maintain control of the Third World hinterland. Such considerations as potential future use, security of imperialist interests globally etc., enter the picture.

Thus US aid, grants and military assistance are aimed as a political weapon at securing the above global strategy. US loans, grants, military and technical assistance amount to $115 billion between the end of second World War and 1968. By the end of 1972 according to Clifford, a US spokesman, Vietnam alone took $760 billion dollars. All this, apart from serving US political global ends, also provided a tremendous boost to

Table XIII

% Distribution of Direct (US) Investment by Area and Industry, 1964.

Industry	All Areas	Canada	Europe	Latin America	Africa	Asia	Oceania
Mining	8.0%	12.1%	0.4%	12.6%	21.9%	1.1%	6.3%
Petroleum	32.4	23.4	25.6	35.9	51.0	51.0	28.1
Manufacturing	38.0	44.8	54.3	24.3	13.8	17.5	53.1
Public utilities	4.6	3.3	0.4	5.8	0.1	1.8	0.1
Trade	8.4	5.8	12.2	10.7	5.7	7.8	5.5
Other	8.6	10.6	7.1	10.7	7.5	6.0	5.9
Total	100.0	100.0	100.0	100.0	100.0	100.0	100.0

Source: Magdoff, op. cit. p.194

its economy. Thus according to statistics given by President Kennedy, over 80 % of the foreign aid programme was spent on US products. The exchange transactions are thus done in the US. The government pays to industry for what the puppets require and industry ships it off, with US shipping also gaining in the process.

Japan also plays a significant role in the global strategy which ensures neo-colonialism, in its role as junior partner to the US in South-East Asia. Being weak in the area, and being relatively unfamiliar with the region, the US preferred to deal with it through a partner. The partner was equally to be subjected to some kind of political and economic control (having been a vanquished power) and in this way US hegemony in Asia and the Far East would be assured. Thus the subordination of Japan in the process of subordinating Asia and the Far East became an important consideration in the post-war strategy. The breaking out of the Korean War helped the incorporation of Japan into this strategy which had already begun to take root. The entry of the US into the Vietnam war further hastened the realisation of this policy.

Thus with the stimulant of the Vietnamese war, war 'reparations' and 'aid', Japanese imperialism strengthened itself in the entire area and other parts of the world. Its investments and aid were mainly aimed at assuring for itself the raw materials it needs badly due to its geographical position. As a result, a lot of capital exports go into the exploitation of fuel, minerals, etc. It imports 100 % of its uranium, nickel and bauxite requirements, 99.7 % of its crude oil, 87 % of its iron ore, 78.5 % of its coal, 75.6 % of its copper, and 54.6 % of its lead. Its foreign investments in these fields in early 1974 amounted to $2.273 million in minerals, $478 million in oil, $226 million in iron ore and $335 million in copper. Investments in manufactures on the other hand had grown to $1.752

million in Africa, Asia and Latin America, of which Asia alone accounted for $772 million.

Japanese 'aid' on the other hand has doubled between 1964 and 1975. This 'aid', as well as direct investments, assists Japanese imperialism in its search for raw materials and markets. As Tunku Abdul Rahman, Prime Minister of Malaysia, said at Expo '70';

> 'Although Japan furnishes loans, it takes back with its other hand, as if by magic, almost twice the amount that it provides'. (10)

Table XIV below shows Japanese investments up to 1967 by region and by type. These show that Japan has a global interest in many neo-colonial Third World countries. Its interest as an imperialist power under US hegemony is, therefore, considerable. The table shows that 70 % of her investments are in raw material production in Third World countries, 4 % in Europe and 29 % in the US, in which US monopolies themselves have interest.

Table XIV

Japanese Overseas Investments by Area and Type 1951 to 1967 (Unit US $1,000)

Area	Portfolio Investments	Loans	Direct Overseas Investments	Total
Asia	122,750	143,297	923	266,970
Central & South America	205,954	162,637	3,397	371,988
Middle East	2,280	—	237,926	240,206
Africa	12,844	4,656	167	17,667
North America	232,654	137,938	30,755	401,347
Europe	25,222	30,643	96	55,961
Oceania	13,134	25,769	—	38,903
Total	614,838	504,940	273,264	1,393,042

Source: Herman Kahn

Europe, having been the 'owner' of most of the colonial world, features prominently in this neo-colonial strategy. As we have seen the multilateral system which US imperialism spelt out to her allies entailed a new arrangement. This strategy had its advantages and disadvantages to the different parties. For one thing, for the victors with colonies, it meant encroachment on their markets, outlets for capital exports and sources of raw materials by others; and for the vanquished, it gave the opportunity of access to the markets they had lost during the war. For these reasons the

Treaty of Rome setting up the European Common Market contained provision for a neo-colonial strategy as far as Europe's African colonies were concerned. A chapter of the treaty was devoted to the question of 'association' of the former African colonies to the European Economic Community (EEC). The neo-colonial character of this arrangement with the EEC was perhaps put squarely by Dr. Allardt, the Director-General of the Overseas Territories and Countries, when he described it as 'a new form of European presence in Africa'.

Under these associations the European monopolies have maintained their links with their former colonies and continued, under a different form of political relationships, the grip of the monopolies in production and over these markets. The various agreements and conventions that have been entered into between the EEC and their former colonies have all served this purpose. The recent Lome Convention merely helped to bring together 46 African, Caribbean, and Pacific countries (ACP) under new arrangement of the enlarged European Community, to continue the exploitation of these countries. The new Convention, while purporting to do away with the 'reverse preferences' by which the products of the European monopolies received 'duty free entry' in return for so-called 'markets' for products of the 46 ACP states, in fact merely multilateralised the neo-colonial ties to other monopolies in the US and Japan. Whereas the old Conventions excluded these two imperialist groups, the new Convention opens up to them the same advantages and privileges the Europeans enjoyed in these neo-colonial countries. Thus exploitation of the Third World countries continues unabated under conditions of multilateral imperialism.

The main feature of the *internal development* in the neo-colonies under the new strategy was the social *class transformation* of the colonial territory. As we have seen, under colonial production there emerged a stratum serving colonial interests and benefitting under it by being given a portion of the surplus-value. Depending on the social structure existing before colonialism, various strata emerged. Those immediately of service to monopoly capital and thriving thereon were the merchants. These acted as wholesalers, or retailers of consumer goods produced by mono-poly capitalists in the metropolis; they purchased locally-produced cash crops and passed them on to the metropolitan monopolies. A section of this stratum became 'comprador', while a section went into petty capitalist industrial enterprise. In some countries where industrial capital had made it possible there developed a national industrial bourgeoisie (e.g., India, Brazil). But with the rise of finance capital this bourgeoisie became dependent on international monopoly capital. The result was that such 'national bourgeoisies' could not develop the productive forces in these countries on their own and consequently ended up serving the monopoly interests of the financial oligarchies.

In some countries, feudal landowners and *latifundia* dominated the countryside, serving the interests of international monopoly capital and exploiting low-waged labour. In many areas the peasant population continued to engage in cash crop production for the monopolies while maintaining a subsistence sector for its own survival. In the colonial plantations, mines, and factories a working class emerged, albeit in many cases with one foot on the land. It is from this class that returns of the highest rate were made by monopoly capital.

This 'development' created both an opportunity for the monopoly capitalist to continue his exploitation, and at the same time confronted him with a contradiction in that it aroused political consciousness on the part of the exploited people and soon led to nationalist movements, a fact which the monopoly capitalist soon took account of by introducing a process of decolonisation, thereby continuing exploitation under the neo-colonial strategy. A class structure created by colonial capitalist production relations helped the monopoly capitalist to set up neo-colonial states with a section of the petty-bourgeoisie and 'comprador bourgeoisie' as their governing representatives; monopoly capitalism ensured that these bourgeoisies and petty-bourgeoisies had to rely on international monopoly capital to sustain themselves both economically and politically. This strategy gave the bourgeoisie and petty-bourgeoisie a semblance of independence, and relying increasingly on populism to maintain support from small producers and workers, these classes played out their true role as agents of monopoly capital. Increasing exploitation of the working masses by monopoly capital intensified the contradiction between the people and imperialism in the neo-colony, thus creating favourable conditions for a more thorough-going struggle against it.

CHAPTER XX

We noted in the Introduction that D.K. Fieldhouse, in concluding that Lenin's thesis of imperialism was 'misleading', suggested that the investigation of imperialism should be 'as much concerned with the periphery — with the world in which colonisation occured — as with Europe'. The idea was to find out from the investigation of each periphery why colonisation of that periphery took place.

> 'By no means all colonial acquisitions resulted from crises at the perimeter, and where the peripheral approach fails, the historian must turn back to Europe for his explanation. Yet the effort of studying the periphery is not wasted, for it ensures that the historian is doing his job properly. Instead of starting with a general hypothesis and leaping from there to a general explanation, he is forced to begin with specific and detailed study and then to pace out the way to a broader hypothesis step by step. Treated in this pedantic way imperialism ceases to be a mystical force and becomes the sum of so many established facts. At the same time it is transferred from the speculative field of the historicist and becomes part of the proper study of the historian'. (11)

The misconception of imperialism as history in the narrow sense of bourgeois compartmentalisation separated from its material basis is what D.K. Fieldhouse was advocating. In this way imperialism could be studied on the basis of historical 'case studies' in which a 'non-doctrinal' approach to a specific field would then reveal the 'facts'. This method clearly does not lead the investigator into a study of imperialism as a historical product of the socially active man but ends up in pure empiricism.

Fieldhouse's method is revealed by his own analysis when he collects together documentation of different people and scattered views of various aspects of 'imperialism'. Fieldhouse's own analysis of the material fails to come to grips with Lenin's thesis. We have already examined these arguments in Chapter XII above. What interests us here is the appeal made by Fieldhouse for the study of the 'centre' and 'periphery' as separate areas in order to provide a theory of imperialism. As we try to show here the appeal was not without response.

Recently a number of neo-Marxist theoreticians have embarked on the study of the periphery as a distinct subject. In many of these studies a certain amount of awareness is exhibited of the interrelationship between the two, (centre and periphery) yet the emphasis given to narrow analysis of the separate areas has tended to create a distorted and, indeed, an anti-Marxist-Leninist picture of monopoly capitalism and imperialism. We have made reference to the work of Baran and Sweezy, *Monopoly Capital*, in which, on the strength of Marx's study of *Capital* based on England, they try to establish 'a theoretical model of a monopoly capitalist system . . . based on study of the United States, which is today as far ahead of other countries in terms of capitalist development as Britain was in the nine-teenth century'. (12) Samir Amin, who is described in some quarters as a 'Third World theoretician', sets out to demonstrate, in *Accumulation on a World Scale*, that Marx, while providing 'the necessary equipment for the theory of accumulation on world scale', does not provide the theory itself. Amin refers to Lenin's work *Imperialism* as a study of 'the centre', which Baran and Sweezy 'brought up to date', but which 'did not study the transformations in the periphery in connection with those in the centre'. Hence 'everything in the field remains to be done'. Before we deal in breadth with Samir Amin's work, we must at this stage deal with the work of Arghiri Emmanuel which has caused quite a stir in Marxist circles. His book falls in the same category as Amin's.

In his *Unequal Exchange*, which he sub-titles: *A Study of the Imperialism of Trade*, Emmanuel sets out to demonstrate the inequality in the exchange of commodities between the centre and the periphery. Emmanuel's thesis in this book cannot be understood in isolation from his views on imperialism. It is in his critique of Lenin's study of imperialism that his eclecticism is revealed. In the article already referred to, which appeared in the *New Left Review*, Emmanuel tries to demonstrate that the concept of 'financial' imperialism, which is according to him 'supposed to be different from the mercantalist imperialism of the 17th and 18th centuries', was 'put to a severe trial' by the breaking up of the huge colonial empires which had taken centuries to build, 'without proportionate violence and without any marked impoverishment of the great imperial parent states, or any reduction in their capacity to exploit the rest of the world'. Moreover, the concept of neo-colonialism is to him 'unsatisfactory' since it was 'devised for argument's sake, in the face of an unexpected situation'. (13) In any case, according to Emmanuel, the concept fails to 'save the traditional theory' of imperialism, put forward by Lenin, whose work is described as 'a marginal work which never had any scientific pretensions, and which was written rapidly in the difficult conditions of exile with no other documentary to hand but the Bern library'. (14)

From this eclectic position, Emmanuel sees colonialism as an 'accident of history', for 'whatever the motivating forces behind this adventure, the advanced capitalist world did not receive any *supplementary* benefit from the direct administration of these territories'. (15) The evidence for this statement is Emmanuel's arguments on export of capital and the returns

on them. According to him the latter were greater than the exports of
capital and thus could not have been the motivation behind the exports
of 'surplus' capital! Geoffrey Pilling has correctly pointed out how
Emmanuel's data misrepresents Lenin. (16)

As has been shown, the monopolists do not export capital solely to
earn interest and dividends on them; it is the pressure of the falling rate
of profit which forces them to engage in production in the neo-colonies
to extract surplus-value. What is ignored by Emmanuel is that, according
to Lenin, colonies were not merely places for the export of capital, but,
more importantly, the reservoir of cheap labour for the production of
agricultural products and raw materials, all of which help the capitalist,
as Pilling correctly reminds us, to maintain 'the momentum of extended
reproduction of capital, in both the metropolitan countries and in the
colonial and semi-colonial areas'. (17)

This is the framework in which Emmanuel sets out to prove 'unequal
exchange'. As can be seen from the above analysis, imperialism in the
Marxist-Leninist sense does not exist. Monopoly capital is not the highest
stage of capitalism. There is no qualitative difference between mercantilist
imperialism and what he calls 'financial imperialism'. 'All imperialisms are
in the last analysis mercantile in character'. (18) The colonial countries,
according to Emmanuel, were liberated and neo-colonialism is a myth as
is the Marxist-Leninist concept of imperialism. In this schema of
Emmanuel's the neo-colonial areas of the Third World are nations engaged
in trade exchange in which they are exploited through the *imperialism of
trade* and not through the imperialism of finance capital. According to
him there are two types of unequal exchange that exist in the relationship between the centre and the Third World. The first is what Emmanuel
describes as unequal exchange in the 'general sense', which is merely a
formula for the calculation of the 'prices of production' which Marx uses
in Book III, and is based on the organic composition of capitals of different
industries, which Emmanuel adopts for countries. The second he calls
unequal exchange in the 'strict sense', based on wage differentials instead
of the organic compositions of capital. Emmanuel concentrates his
analysis on the second type of unequal exchange.

But what is the mechanism through which this unequal exchange is
perpetrated? According to Emmanuel, it is through *prices*. He defines
unequal exchange as:

> 'The proportion between equilibrium prices that is established
> through the equalisation of profits between regions in which the
> rate of surplus-value is "institutionally" different — the term
> "institutionally" meaning that these rates are, for whatever
> reason, safeguarded from competitive equalisation on the factors'
> market and are independent of relative prices'. (19)

The basis of this inequality lies in the different levels of wages and
these do not 'vary in dependence upon prices'; on the contrary 'prices

that vary in dependence upon wages' are an independent variable. (20) A country with lower wages — regardless of the technical composition of capital — loses in exchange with a country with higher wages. Whilst trade and investment assures the developed country 'a first and second transfer of value' from the poorer foreign country, and in turn helps to further raise wages in the former, the latter 'continues to be grounded at the level of elementary physiological subsistence'.

> 'By transferring, through non-equivalent exports, a large part of its surplus to the rich countries, it deprives itself of the means of accumulation and growth. The narrowness and stagnancy of the market discourage capital, which flees from it, so that, despite the low organic composition and the low wages a substantial proportion of labour force is unable to find employment'. (21)

As a result of these 'unequal' relationships, 'wealth begets wealth' and 'poverty begets poverty'. According to Emmanuel 'once a country has got ahead, through some historical accident, even if this be merely that a harsher climate has given men additional needs, this country starts to make other countries pay for its high wage level through unequal exchange'! (22)

Marx's law of value is distorted and then thrown out of Emmanuel's analysis. He tries to draw a distinction between Marx's law of value (labour theory of value) as presented in Volume I and Volume III of *Capital*. In Volume I Marx assumed the same organic composition of capital for simplicity of analysis in order to arrive at the law of value as explaining production and exchange under capitalism. In Volume III he reconciled this law to the different compositions of capital in different branches of production and the resulting differences in rates of profit; the formation of a general rate of profit (i.e., the average rate of profit); and the transformation of the values of commodities into prices of production. Emmanuel concludes that Marx's price of production is equivalent to his 'equilibrium prices'. *'Prices of production are equilibrium prices because they are the only mechanism capable of ensuring the equalisation of profits'.* (23) This, as we shall see, is a mystification. This vulgarisation of the law of value is a matter which is not new to neo-Marxists. As we pointed out earlier, Sweezy tried to marry Marx's law of value with Borkiewicz's method because he found Marx's analysis 'logically unsatis-factory' for Marx went 'only half way in transforming values into prices'. (24)

As Geoffrey Pilling has shown, and as we tried to show in Chapter VII, Marx's contribution to political economy lay in his demonstrating that it was labour power that the worker sold and not his labour since labour has no value, but is only a measure of it. The price of labour power is its value, just as the value of each commodity is its price. Pilling convincingly shows how Emmanuel's value springs *from distribution rather than from production*, for Emmanuel himself states that: 'it is the quantitatives and rewards of these factors that determine prices,' and again: 'once we assume the existence of private ownership it is not value that leads to exchange, but exchange that necessarily results in value'. Yet for Marx the expression of value lies in its actual reality as a *social relation* which is to be located in capitalist production itself, and not in its exchange. Exchange value is only a form of this value and not its essence.

Again, we saw that Emmanuel regards wages as the determinant of relative prices. This of course is un-Marxist and is against the theory of the law of value, and since for Emmanuel wages are an independent variable, he finds himself at a 'dead-end'. The wage is no longer the value of labour power which is in turn determined by the socially necessary labour time required to produce the means of subsistence of the worker and his family but the quantity of subsistence. Pilling emphasises this point, which is at the back of Emmanuel's thesis. He points out that this value of labour power depends upon the productivity of labour and the *changes* in it, not merely in agriculture, but throughout the economy. Improvements in labour productivity in the tractor industry, for example, will tend to reduce the value of wheat and hence, under normal circumstances, the value of labour power in all sectors. Emmanuel would not accept the above analysis 'for to do so would force him back into the investigation of the social relations of production in all countries, which in turn call seriously into question his division of the world into rich and poor countries'. (25)

Marx is clear on the question of how wages are arrived at in different countries. This is historically determined by the productiveness of labour which itself is fettered by physical conditions. 'The fewer the number of natural wants imperatively calling for satisfaction, and the greater the natural fertility of the soil and the favourableness of climate, so much less is the labour time necessary for the maintenance and reproduction of the producer. So much greater therefore can be the excess of his labour for others over his labour for himself'. (26) But such favourable conditions give the possibility not the reality of producing a surplus-product. Whereas nations applying capital to labour under different historical and physical conditions can exchange products expressed in different prices, determined on this basis and on the intensity with which labour is applied, the question for most of the neo-colonial countries is different. It is not wages as such (through prices) that are the centrepiece of the relationship between them and the imperialist centres, but the actual domination by finance capital of production in the neo-colony. Thus low wages are themselves the expression of this domination, inasmuch as monopoly capital benefits through the preservation of these backward conditions.

Emmanuel's thesis as with those of other neo-Marxists is clearly under-consumptionist and Keynesian. This is revealed in statements like: 'since the prime problem for capitalism is not to produce but to sell, capital moves toward countries and regions where there are extensive outlets and expanding markets, that is where the population's standard of living is high'. And again: 'We begin with the end, with consumption, by creating a market actual or potential which is sufficiently large. In this way capital is attracted, and the corresponding consumer goods are produced . . . What has especially shocked people in my thesis is this idea that excessive unproductive consumption may not only impoverish but even enrich a capitalist country'. (27) This should have put on guard any serious Marxist-Leninist that Emmanuel is peddling neo-classical and Keynesian economics under the guise of Marxism.

Before we conclude with Emmanuel let us examine the other thesis put across by Samir Amin in his book already referred to, *Accumulation on a World Scale*. Amin accepts Emmanuel's thesis and raises arguments similar to those advanced by him. Amin like all neo-Marxists begins by misrepresenting Marx and by creating uncertainty about Lenin. All these proceedings are intended to prepare his readers to accept his analysis as an original contribution, and this marks the negative note on which Amin embarks on his task.

To begin with, India is a subject on which Marx is often misrepresented. Amin starts at this 'weak point'. According to Amin, Marx did not work out nor did he study the problem of accumulation on a world scale. 'If he had, he would not have written that British domination of India would revolutionise the mode of production there'. (28) Talking about the terms of trade being 'equal' before 1880 and the 'pause' that ensued between the industrial revolution and the conquest of the world (1880-1890), in which the 'old forms' of exploitation were replaced by the 'new forms' he states: 'In my view, it was this pause that was responsible for Marx's lack of attention to our problem: he thought India would become a capitalist country like Britain, and so the colonial question eluded his thinking'. (28)

Returning to the question in a more substantial manner, he demonstrates how determined he is to quote Marx out of context in order to establish his thesis. Introducing his views on the monetarisation of the 'periphery' and the formation of 'indigenous capital' as being the 'absolute law', and on the direction of investments of 'dominant foreign capital' which rules out the possibility of indigenous capital competing with the dominant one, he states: 'It is because he was not very closely concerned with these problems that Marx was able to state, in his too-brief writings on the subject, that colonial rule would probably establish a capitalist economy in India — meaning a complete capitalist economy'. (29)

As if this misrepresentation was not enough, Amin goes further to 'prove' that Marx considered that 'no power would for long be able to hinder local development of capitalism *on the European model*', (emphasis in Amin's original). He then refers to Marx's article on *The Future Results of British Rule in India* which Marx wrote in 1853 as being 'extremely clear on this point: the plundering of India by the British aristocracy and merchant capital will be followed by industrialisation carried out by the industrial bourgeoisie of the metropolitan country: the railways will give rise to autocentric industries'. (29) He continues: 'Marx is, indeed, so certain of this that he feared lest a developed bourgeois East may become the essential force preventing victory of the socialist revolution in Europe'. Amin is so fascinated by his own case that he sees no reason to indicate that Marx had a proviso to this optimism which Amin so much wants to magnify beyond its significance.

To be sure, Marx, in the article referred to by Amin, made it clear that such development of 'modern industry' in India could not take place nor could the 'Hindoos' reap the benefits thereof until the bourgeoisie in England had been 'supplanted by the industrial proletariat' or till the Hindoos themselves had shaken off colonial rule. In other words, Marx is *clear* on the point that 'modern industry', in its 'European model' sense, could come to India only when there was socialism in Britain or when India had regained her independence. We would be reading Marx too literally if we were to say that in the article in question Marx 'categorically' states that the railway will be a forerunner of modern industry or that his proviso only refers to the *enjoyment* of the fruits of such modern industry. A reading of the entire article clearly shows that Marx meant that it is the Indian bourgeoisie's struggle for independence that would have assured this. Amin cannot show that such development would have been impossible. On the contrary the evidence he produces between pages 83 and 87 of his first volume proves that this would have happened, since the terms of trade in primary products were in favour of the colonial territories before 1880. Instead, Amin describes Marx's analysis as a 'mistake': 'Hardly had the period characterised by the policy of mercantile capitalism drawn to its close, in Marx's day, than capitalism was about to enter into its imperialist, monopoly stage — which Marx did not know'. (30) But this does not qualify Marx's analysis of the conditions of this period as being mistaken. Former colonial territories, e.g., America, Australia, Canada, are known to have developed into capitalist economies in the period Marx referred to, and there was nothing to stop India doing so if the Hindoo bourgeoisie had been strong enough to throw off British colonialism. Indeed, Marx's letter to Engels, to which Amin refers out of context, and an earlier letter by Engels to Marx in 1852, are significant for their incisive insights into the rejuvenating effect capitalist expansion in India, China, Japan and California were having on European capitalism. This is what Marx meant in the letter quoted by Amin when he expressed his fear of imminent revolution on the continent being 'crushed in this small corner, since the movement of bourgeois society is still ascendant on far wider area'. Palme Dutt grasped this point which Marx and Engels were making when in his book, *India Today*, he observed:

> 'Here, in this understanding of the significance of the extra-European expansion of capitalism for the perspective of the development of capitalism and the socialist revolution in Europe, lay the key thought

which Marx had grasped in the eighteen-fifties, but which the main
body of European Socialism has only slowly begun to realise in the
recent period'. (31)

The series of articles on India which Marx wrote in 1853 were among the
'most fertile of his writings, and the starting-point of a mode in thought
on the questions covered' concludes Palme Dutt.

Marx's insights, as early as the 1850s, on the question of extra-European
expansion of capitalist markets foreshadowed Lenin's analysis of imperialism. Moreover, the fact that monopoly capitalism henceforth ruled out
capitalist development in India as, indeed, elsewhere in the colonial and
semi-colonial world is a well known fact, and herein lies the value of
Lenin's work, a fact which Marx need not have 'known'. Indeed our
analysis in Chapter IX shows that it is Marx who provided us with the tools
for comprehending the phenomenon of monopoly which is at the back of
imperialism. We have shown that Marx 'knew' that concentration of
production and capital led to monopoly. This is the theoretical lead which
Lenin grasped before setting himself the task of analysing imperialism.

Turning to Lenin's work *Imperialism*, Amin tries to create doubts about
its scientificity. He starts by stating that 'little progress has been made
since Lenin's *Imperialism*' on the study of accumulation on a world scale;
Marx, of course, according to Amin, did not study the problem. He goes
on to say: 'Lenin examined the problem as that of imperialism, but in a
limited context, namely, the new forms of accumulation on a world scale
that appeared on the basis of the formation of monopolies in the capitalist
centre . . . Lenin perceived one moment in this process, that of the new
specialisation based on export of capital to colonies'. (32)

Now anybody familiar with Lenin's work cannot come to the conclusion that it was concerned solely with monopolies in the centre, nor
that the new specialisation was conceived by Lenin solely as being based
on export of capital to the colonies. Our study in Part Three shows that
this way of representing Lenin's thesis on imperialism is highly mistaken;
but, for Amin, it is a necessary precondition for the economistic analysis
which he tries to introduce under the guise of Marxism.

Armed with this camouflaged attack on Marx and Lenin, one would
expect that Amin would then provide us with a comprehensive theory
of accumulation on a world scale and improve on the work of Marx and
Lenin. What we find emerging, however, is an eclectic-cum-economistic
analysis of the 'centre' and the 'periphery' with no clear concept of
imperialism to improve on Lenin apart from the 'brilliant paradoxes' in
which he floats away into a neo-classical-Keynesian explanation of
imperialism.

Indeed Amin puts the approach to his analysis quite clearly. He states:
'Undoubtedly, the fundamental concepts produced by Marxist
analysis constitutes the necessary equipment needed for a theory

of accumulation on a world scale. This, however, is all that can be said for the theory itself has not yet been created . . . Criticism of university economics has been very useful, for it is through such criticism that these elements have emerged, as in the matter of unequal exchange. This encourages us to persevere in the same direction, to appreciate everything that the criticism of present-day economics can contribute to enriching our thought. After all Marx's own *Capital* assumed just this form. Marx worked out his own concepts from a critique of Ricardo'. (33)

Having laid his general approach to the analysis of the relations between the centre and the periphery purely on the basis of 'criticism of university economics', and starting off in this so-called Marx-like manner, he spells out his strategy. He states:

'It will then be necessary to understand that the concept social formation must be carefully distinguished from that of the *mode of production*, particularly when asking why, at the centre, the capitalist mode of production tends to become the only one (the formation tending to merge ideally with the mode of production), whereas in the periphery this does not occur'. (33)

This argument opens up Amin's basic concepts which in no way differ from those of Emmanuel and the Keynesian economists on imperialism. For Amin, the formation of the monopolies in the centre are linked with 'unequal exchange'. Although Amin recognised that the pre-mono-poly forms of the international division of labour are different from that of imperialism, he finds no difficulty in somersaulting by concluding thus:

'Nevertheless both of these stages of international specialisation depend upon mechanisms of *primitive accumulation* for the benefit of the centre; these mechanisms cannot be grasped only in the context of analysis confined to the capitalist mode of production'. (34)

This latter point is elaborated on by Amin when he identifies Marx's *Capital* as the theory not of socio-economic formations but of the *capitalist mode of production*. Consequently Marx 'does not provide us' with the theory of accumulation on a world scale. Marx's theory according to Amin on this question (of 'unequal exchange') appears only in connection with *primitive accumulation*, which Marx considered to be the *prehistory* of the capitalist mode of production:

'But this prehistory is not over and done with: it goes on through extension of capitalism on the world scale. Parallel with the mechanism of accumulation characteristic of the capitalist mode of production, namely expanded reproduction, a mechanism of primitive accumulation continues to operate and to be character-istic of relations between the centre and the periphery of the world capitalist system'. (35)

This apparent *continuation of accumulation on a world scale* characteristic of the prehistory of capitalism becomes the cornerstone of Amin's thesis.

Whereas imperialism enabled the geographical domain of capitalism to be extended through colonial conquest, this conquest brought different social formations into 'mutual contact' in new forms, that is, those of 'central' capitalism and 'periphery' capitalism. The process of primitive accumulation, according to Amin, in contrast to normal expanded reproduction, is unequal exchange in the sense of exchange of products of unequal value, and hence the reward for these products is unequal. Rosa Luxembourg is credited for being the first Marxist to point out the 'present-day mechanisms' of primitive accumulation — of plunder of the Third World. (36) Here Amin's concept of unequal exchange is built into his concept of social formations. The fact that the capitalist mode of production operates amidst *different* social-formations is made the basis of neo-colonial exploitation, and Marx's theory of expanded reproduction is excluded from the analysis. This is because although the trade carried on between the industrial revolution and the 1880-1890s was 'equal' in that 'equal' products exchanged at their value (or prices of production 'in the Marxist sense'), in the 'pause' that followed the rise of monopoly, capitalism re-established 'unequal exchange'. Again, he continues:

> 'At the start, in the contact freshly established between centre and periphery, if real wages (or real rewards of labour) are more or less equal, the centre, whose productivity is higher, is able to export, whereas the periphery is not competitive in any sphere: real costs are higher there in all branches of production and the periphery can export nothing, except the exotic agricultural produce or crude minerals (provided the cost of transport is not too high) that have no equivalent in the centre, because these are the only fields in which "natural advantage" means anything'. (37)

It is here that Amin tries to bring this relationship within the perview of the pre-capitalist trade relations between the centre and the periphery. Here his 'theoretical model' stands or falls. 'It was in this way', he explains, 'that international exchange began: with exotic products followed by the products of mining activity, which was to call for investment of foreign capital on a scale previously unheard of'. (37) The ruin of the crafts arising from this early relationship created an imbalance in the periphery between the supply of labour and the demand for it, creating the conditions for 'reducing the reward of labour in the periphery', and it is here that given a certain productivity in the centre and the periphery, the lower level of wages in the periphery makes it possible for a higher rate of profit to be earned there. (38) This 'aggression' by the capitalist mode of production from outside, against these social formations, 'constitutes the essence of the problem of their transition to formations of peripheral capitalism' and explains the 'hidden transfers of value' due to unequal exchange. (39)

These positions of Emmanuel and Amin are beset with serious theoretical and methodological difficulties. Firstly, the Marxist method of political economy itself is put into question. Secondly, the scientific concept of historical materialism that is consequent upon such method is also brought into dispute. Their misconceptions lie in their being unable to accept the Marxist theory of the mode of production with its laws of motion as explaining the exploitation of the neo-colonial hinterland. Whereas Engels tells us that the laws which are valid for definite modes of production and forms of exchange hold good for all historical periods in which these modes of production and modes of exchange prevail, and that the mode of production and exchange in a definite historical society, and the historical conditions which have given birth to this society, determine the mode of distribution, (40) this is apparently rejected on the ground that production in different social formations cannot be explained solely on the basis of the laws of motion of modes of production. This distinction between the mode of production and the social formation is not made explicit. In substance they are made to appear to be parallel to one another. The fact that the mode holds 'economic' sway over the formation is recognised in form only, but it is not borne out in the analysis. (41)

As we have seen, Amin credits Rosa Luxembourg with having recognised the phenomenon of unequal exchange through the process of primitive accumulation, which Marx regarded as the *prehistory* of capitalism. As is already known, Luxembourg conceived imperialism as 'the political expression of the accumulation of capital in its competitive struggle for what remains still open of the non-capitalist environment'. (42) This conception was based on her being unable to comprehend Marx's reproduction schema in Volume II of *Capital*. It was her difficulty in seeing how constant capital could be realised in the two departments that forced her to find 'a third non-capitalist market' in the periphery. This position of Luxembourg's, as we have seen, tended to centre the problem of capitalist production in the market and provided fertile ground for underconsumptionist theories. Her one-sided approach to the question of imperialism inevitably led her to emphasise one aspect of the phenomenon of imperialism forgetting that it was dialectically connected with falling profitability in production. (43) Most neo-Marxist writers with their economistic approach have tended to join Luxembourg on this question, and it is therefore not surprising that they too arrive at the underconsumptionist thesis of imperialism which has nothing in common with the Marxist-Leninist thesis.

As we have shown, Amin adopts this underconsumptionist thesis throughout his analysis. We have also demonstrated that Emmanuel follows the same path. Indeed such a position is not far from the Keynesian position which regards present day imperialism as 'mercantilist'. Schumpeter, also a neo-classical economist, maintained that primitive accumulation continued to account for later capitalist accumulation, which process continues through the capitalist era. (44)

Primitive accumulation, as we observed in Chapter IV. played a role at a specific stage of development in the rise of capitalism under conditions of production and exchange belonging to the feudal mode of production. Marx drew a distinction between capitalist accumulation, which operated under the laws of motion specific to the capitalist mode of production, and its 'prehistoric' predecessor, primitive accumulation, which operated under the specific conditions of the feudal mode of production. This distinction is not merely semantic; it is a scientific one. The difference in the two accumulations lay in what type of *surplus* was appropriated under each mode of production, and under what relations of production this was done. Marx emphasised that feudal merchants' capital arose out of *differences in prices* of commodities produced under two distinct modes of production. Exchange-values of commodity production were exchanged for use-values of accumulated wealth of the ruling class in backward, underdeveloped, semi-feudal states (of the Asiatic mode). In Chapter XX of *Capital* Volume III, entitled *Historical Facts about Merchant's Capital*, Marx drew this distinction. We have already taken a long quotation from this chapter in our earlier Chapter III, and it is perhaps apt at this stage to refer to parts of it.

> 'Aside from the fact that it (merchant capital) exploits the differences between prices of production of various countries, those modes of production bring it about that merchants' capital appropriates an overwhelming portion of surplus product, partly as mediator between communities which substantially produce for use value . . . and partly because under those modes of production the principal owners of the surplus product . . . represent the consuming wealth and luxury . . .'. (45)

It is for this reason that Marx regarded this sytem as based on robbery connected with plunder and slave trade. This was 'unequal exchange' and cannot be compared with capitalist accumulation under the capitalist mode of production, which is based on *capitalist production* and not *trade* as such, where the aim of production is the extraction of *surplus-value*.

A similar erroneous position to that of Emmanuel and Amin is adopted by Gundar Frank in his *Capitalism and Underdevelopment in Latin America*, and in a later book, *Latin America, Underdevelopment or Revolution*, in which he goes to the other extreme and argues that the underdevelopment of Chile and Brazil is a result of four centuries of 'capitalist development' and the 'internal contradiction of capital itself'. He argues that these contradictions are the expropriation of the 'economic surplus', the polarisation of the capitalist system into metropolitan centre and peripheral satellites, and the continuity of the fundamental structure of the capitalist system throughout the history of its expansion and transformation.

Marx's analysis of capital and its tendency to concentrate is used by

Frank to explain the Peru of 1736 as 'a paradox of trade and a contradiction of riches — thriving on what ruins others and being ruined by what
makes others thrive'. Frank also believes the same process to be operative
everywhere in Mexico, Peru, the India of Clive, the Central Africa of
Rhodes, and the China of the 'Open Door' period. Quite clearly Frank,
like Emmanuel and Amin, confuses 'mercantile capitalism' and monopoly
capitalism, which manifested their monopoly features under two distinct
modes of production. For Marx feudal monopoly is the thesis, competition the anti-thesis and modern monopoly the synthesis. In other words
modern monopoly is the negation of feudal monopoly. (46)

In our view the development of capitalism to a monopoly stage, and
the extension of capitalist relations in the colonial countries under the
hegemony of capital, also introduced the laws of motion of the capitalist
mode of production in these countries. The relations of production that
were established became a function of the capitalist mode which became
the dominant one, and the hitherto existing modes of production and
social formation were subjugated and made 'answerable' to the dominant
capitalist mode on a world scale. This did not imply that all the forms
of production relations of the old modes were immediately destroyed.
On the contrary, those that suited the new capitalist property relations
were preserved to serve it, their original essence having been destroyed
by capital. It is in this sense that Marx in the *Grundrisse* states:

> 'Bourgeois society is the most developed and most complex historic
> organisation of production. The categories which express its relations,
> the comprehension of its structure, thereby also allows insights into
> the structure and relations of production of all vanished social
> formations out of whose ruins and elements it built itself up,
> whose partly still unconquered remnants are carried along within
> it ... The bourgeois society thus supplies the key to the ancient
> ... Further, since bourgeois society is itself only a contradictory
> form of development, relations derived from earlier forms will
> often be found within it only in an entirely stunted form ...
> They can contain them in a developed form ... or caricatured
> form, but always with an essential difference'. (47)

The 'social formations' of Amin's peripheral capitalism are such
stunted, developed and/or caricatured forms of monopoly capitalist subordination of the earlier modes of production and social formations. But
the key to their understanding does not lie in Amin's theory of social
formations but in the understanding of the overall laws of motion of the
capitalist mode of production. The essential nature of relations between
the 'centre' and the 'periphery' cannot therefore be sought in the trade
relations in which 'unequal exchange' is presumed to be the main contradiction, nor in the relations between 'rich' and 'poor countries'; it must be
sought in the production relations between the bourgeoisie and the
working class across national borders as well as in the subjugation of the
peasantry in all areas dominated by capital and subjected to capitalist

exploitation.

The whole concept of 'poor nations' is populist claptrap. Poor nations in the sense of neo-colonies do not exist except as extensions of metropolitan capitalist production under multilateral imperialism. Therein lies the whole problem of the national democratic revolution which is still on the agenda in these countries. The trick which Emmanuel and Amin use in regarding wages through prices as regulators of this relationship, as if it were a trading one between autonomous parties, is unacceptable. In our view and as we have shown elsewhere in these pages, it is unscientific to talk of exchange through trade where the financial oligarchies of the imperialist countries have the power to centralise all capital in the neo-colony and apply it to dominate production. For this reason to talk of 'unequal exchange' is to say that there is unequal exchange between the elements of finance capital itself.

Emmanuel and Amin's analysis presupposes the existence of 'national capital' in the periphery which produces on its own account. This misconception arises for Amin and Emmanuel because they have *no concept of finance capital*. For us the objectified power of finance capital in the neo-colony, which turns any 'national capital' there into finance capital for the purpose of production required by monopolies, is the basis of capitalist accumulation in the neo-colony. Thus finance capital exploits labour in the centre as it does in the periphery. It does so by taking advantage of generally backward conditions in the periphery, and in the centre it does so by intensifying exploitation through increased use of better machinery. Low wages in the periphery and relatively higher wages in the centre are functions determined by finance capital in relation to the conditions in each area, and cannot be viewed separately from it. Thus lack of 'national capital' in the colony accounts for the dependent capitalist development that the neo-Marxists decry in moralistic and sentimentalist fuming and fretting. In our view Lenin correctly summarises the historic experience and rejects the concept of unequal exchange in the following passage:

> 'There was formerly an economic distinction between the colonies and the European peoples — at least, the majority of the latter — the colonies having been drawn into *commodity* exchange but not into capitalist *production*. Imperialism changed this. Imperialism, is among other things, the export of *capital*. Capitalist production is being transplanted to the colonies at an ever increasing rate. They cannot be extricated from dependence on European finance capital ... In commodity-producing society, no independent development, or development of any sort whatsoever, is possible without capital. Europe and the dependent nations have both *their own* capital and easy access to it on a wide range of terms. The colonies have no capital of *their own*, or none to speak of, and under finance capital no colony can obtain any except on terms of political subordination.' (48)

This in our view disposes of the arguments of the centre-peripherists.

The historical record clearly shows that multilateral imperialism has intensified the exploitation of the neo-colonial world through increased capital exports, and thereby increased the political subordination of these countries to the financial oligarchies of the imperialist countries.

Indeed in our view the theory of unequal exchange is characteristic of the moralistic arguments of the Utopian (Ricardian) Socialists of the 1840s, which Marx so scientifically combated in 1846 in the *Poverty of Philosophy*. The Hodgskins, William Thompsons, and John Brays tried to explain profit on capital as the result of superior bargaining power, lack of competition and 'unequal exchange' between capital and labour. Dr. Duhring had also tried to argue the same point in his 'theory of force', wherein force was seen as the *cause* of exploitation. Engels' polemic (Anti-Duhring) against Dr. Duhring disposed of these arguments. For Marx capitalist exploitation had to be explained, and a way out had to be found, on the basis of the correct understanding of how surplus-value was created. To him such exploitation was possible on the basis of competition and exchange of equivalents. To quote him:

> ' To explain the *general nature of profits,* you must start from the theorem that, on the average, commodities are *sold at their real values, and that profits are derived from selling them at their values.* If you cannot explain profit upon this supposition, you cannot explain it at all'. (49)

Marx insisted in drawing a distinction between labour and labour-power precisely because it enabled him to show scientifically how inequality and non-equivalence took place within 'equivalent exchange'. Lenin emphasised the same thing when he said:

> 'Surplus-value cannot arise out of commodity circulation, for the latter knows only exchange of equivalents; neither can it arise out of price increases, for the mutual losses and gains of buyers and sellers would equalise one another, whereas what we have here is not an individual phenomenon but a mass, average and social phenomenon. To obtain surplus-value, the owner 'must . . . find . . . in the market a commodity, whose use-value possesses the peculiar property of being a source of value' — a commodity whose process of consumption is at the same time a process of creation of value. Such a commodity exists — human labour power'. (50)

It is in this manner that the monopolist bourgeoisie can, in the words of Marx, 'take part in the exploitation of the total working class by the totality of capital . . . for assuming all other conditions . . . to be given, the average rate of profit depends on the intensity of exploitation of the sum total of labour by the sum of capital'. Lenin's concept of finance capital enables us to comprehend this 'sum of capital' on world scale. On this world scale the rate of surplus-value depends upon the proportion of the labour force that is needed to produce subsistence for that labour force.

By this method the phenomenon of the 'centre' and the 'periphery' as 'things-in-themselves' struggling in the market place for exchange of non-equivalents disappears. This Marxist-Leninist approach also explains to us why countries like Portugal, Spain, etc., in the centre remain stunted or caricatured social formations within this world-wide exploitative system. Portugal, according to Amin's analysis, would rank as a 'centre', due to the fact that it 'owned' the periphery. Yet we know that Portugal was a 'periphery' in a hierarchy of domination. Its 'centre' was as much subjected to exploitation by the more powerful monopolies as its periphery as we saw in Part Three. Portugal's exploitation of its periphery was subjected to domination. This does not mean that Portugal did not dominate its 'periphery'. It did, and relied on it for the bulk of its food. But the point is that it too was forced to export labour and to open up its periphery to stronger centres. Foreign finance capital dominated all the vital sectors of Portugal as well as its colonies. (51)

The whole centre-periphery ideology plays into the hands of the populist 'national bourgeoisie' and petty-bourgeoisie. The populists who have for years been making noises in the GATT, the UNCTAD, and the UNO that they are being cheated as Third World countries in international markets find their ideology ready-made for them by the Emmanuels and Amins. The struggle of the neo-colonial peoples is directed by this ideology towards trade councils and negotiations on 'terms of trade' and 'exchange rates'; and away from class struggle. Emmanuel would appear to advise the populists to improve productivity, raise wages; prices will then go up, and you will be on the way to development into a 'centre'! Amin unwittingly exposes this case by showing that productivity in the export sectors responsible for the unequal exchange is actually high and that this sector accounts for 75% of exports from the periphery. (52) Emmanuel advises Third World countries to tax exports and 'transfer this excess surplus-value to the (neo-colonial) state, and diversify production from export sectors to replace import sectors'. (53) No political preconditions are postulated in any serious theoretical way for this exercise. Thus Emmanual and Amin provide the populists with the 'theory' they need for reformist programmes.

The neo-Marxist theory would also seem to support arguments that have been made by a number of academic 'Marxists' that 'underdevelopment' is a myth, and that 'empirical observation suggests that the prospects of successful capitalist economic development of a significant number of major underdeveloped countries are quite good'. (54) Indeed, George Lichtheim in his new book, *Imperialism*, accuses 'Maoists' and Trotskyists, of being responsible for this myth which holds that 'capitalism, by its nature, cannot promote the full industrialisation of its former colonies'. (55) This is apparently because Lenin 'made a mistake' in identifying capitalism with imperialism. We are not told why this myth perpetuates itself in the face of the reality of capitalist development in the colony. For Lichtheim 'taken in the abstract, there appears no reason why a major industrial country — whether capitalist or socialist — should not assume the temporary burden of helping to modernise backward areas'.

Quite clearly philanthrophy is the limit here! For Lichtheim the alternative is to raise oneself by ones own bootstraps, like Japan! The fact that Japan was not a colony is not taken note of and no lesson is drawn except to say that Japan is now a 'major market for Western exports'! (56) Lichtheim advises the US and the West generally to make 'the necessary means available' for this development since, after all, this is the only way in which the productive forces of the Third World countries can be developed to the point where these countries become 'worth-while partners in international exchange'. The West and the US, it should be remembered, have been doing exactly that since 1945 with large aid and private investment programmes, and the results are there for all to see.

Bill Warren's arguments, in an article in *NLR*, look sophisticated but are actually banal, betraying a sorry understanding of the essence of multilateral imperialism and neo-colonialism. According to Warren considerable industrialisation has taken place in the Third World countries. This has mainly been due to the lessening of the ties of dependence in these countries, leading to a development of 'national capitalism'. For this reason Warren comes to the conclusion that 'imperialism declines as capitalism grows' in the neo-colony. This has risen from imperialism itself: 'The international system of inequality and exploitation called imperialism created the conditions for the destruction of this system by the spread of capitalist social relations and productive forces throughout the non-capitalist world'. (57)

While Lenin in his thesis referred to the export of capital as influencing and accelerating the development of capitalism in the colonies, this part of Lenin's thesis has tended to be exaggerated by those who, while claiming to be Marxists, have in actuality taken a hostile stance vis-a-vis the Marxist-Leninist thesis on imperialism. Lenin's thesis must be read as a whole. There is no doubt that imperialism does introduce capitalist relations in the colony (and in this way creates conditions for socialist construction), but this is far from saying that imperialism creates the conditions for a bourgeois revolution of the old type. This is why in his thesis on the national question and the self-determination of nations he draws a distinction between the old and new revolutions, a distinction which Stalin and Mao-Tse-Tung developed further. (58) In the next chapter, Warren's banalities and those of the other centre-periphery ideologists will be shown to have no basis.

Geoffrey Kay, who has recently attempted to explain 'Development and Underdevelopment', although critical of Emmanuel, still retains his place within the centre-periphery ideology. According to Kay, exploitation of the colonies and the neo-colonies of today is accomplished through the medium of merchant capital. Merchant capital emerges as the *specifica differentia* of nineteenth century underdevelopment in two forms. At one and the same time it was the only form of capital, 'but not the only form of capital'. This is because in the colony it remained the only form of capital present, while within the world economy as a whole it 'became an aspect of industrial capital'. (59) As industrial capital, it manifests itself in the colonies and the neo-colonies as merchant capital concerned not only with trade, for which it forms the sole and independent capital, but also with the exploitation of the producers of raw materials. This latter mission merchant capital carries out on behalf of industrial capital firstly because not only are the raw materials indispensable to the productive process, but acquired cheaply, they offer a direct means of maintaining the rate of profit and offsetting any tendency for it to fall. (60) Further-more, according to Kay, merchant capital serves to acquire a reliable and cheap supply of means of consumption, again maintaining the rate of profits, since wages are relatively lower in the colonies. Thirdly, the colony and neo-colony presented industrial capital with a vast potential market in which it could not only realise the surplus-value extracted from the proletariat in the developed world, but also augment it with the 'surplus product' of the non-capitalist world appropriated through unequal exchange, by selling commodities in the markets of the underdeveloped world at prices that exceed their value. This unequal exchange is also enhanced by the further unequal exchange 'in the other direction', in which merchant capital buys raw materials and food below their values.

The enterprises established in the colony and neo-colony by this industrial capital-cum-merchant capital are regarded by Kay as being both capitalist and non-capitalist:

> 'In some ways it would be wrong not to recognise these undertakings as capitalist, for they possess all its formal qualities. On the other hand they have certain features which suggest that it would not be completely correct to treat them in this way'.

Kay avoids the problem of dialectically synthesising this contradiction and retains the eclectic approach. While he is prepared to criticise as neo-classical all economists who have portrayed the relationship as based on *dependence* of the *metropole* on the *satellite*, he is at the same time prepared to see them as having made 'an important discovery' for in 'contradistinction to the classical Marxist view that capital breaks down all non-capitalist modes of production and creates a world after its own image', i.e. a developed world, 'they have shown that capital, despite its corrosive effects, has bolstered up archaic political forms through a series of alliances with powerful elements in precapitalist orders'. (62)

Kay attacks Emmanuel's thesis solely on the ground that Emmanuel wrongly bases himself on the concept that the workers of the centre benefit from the exploitation of peoples of the periphery. At the same time Kay accepts Emmanuel's thesis that unequal exchange takes place between the centre and the periphery. This is so in spite of the fact that he criticises Emmanuel for substituting countries for branches of production in the schemes of transformation. His justification for his version of the unequal exchange thesis is that:

> 'This is because a great many of the economic ties between the developed and the underdeveloped countries, more in the past than today, are mediated through merchant capital'. (63)

Consequently for Kay as for Emmanuel unequal exchange, ('mediated' for Kay through the agency of 'merchant capital'), takes place on the basis that the periphery sell their commodities below value and buy those of the centre above value. Thus through his own ahistorical road he arrives at the same conclusion as Emmanuel. It could not be otherwise, for Emmanuel and Kay converge on one essential issue; for them *finance capital* and *modern imperialism* do not exist. Indeed, in Kay's book concerned with a *Marxist Analysis of Development and Underdevelopment*, Lenin's work *Imperialism* does not appear in the bibliography. The concept of imperialism is nowhere treated except with occasional reference to 'Empires'. The concept of *finance capital* is absent as well. Indeed, for Kay, finance capital is to be referred to as 'circulating capital'. (64)

CHAPTER XXI

We observed in Chapters IX-XI that monopoly capital divides the world in order to find outlets for the export of finance capital, to obtain access to sources of raw materials and to find dumping markets for its cheap goods. In all these spheres finance capital is the sole motivator. In finding outlets for the export of capital, the financial oligarchy regards such capital as 'surplus' only in the sense that it can only be profitably utilised in colonies and not because there is 'too much' of it in the metropole. The idea of a glut of capital does not belong to Marx but to the bourgeois classical and other economists of the nineteenth century.

As we have seen the question of cheap food and cheap raw and auxiliary materials became a paramount issue for monopoly capitalism, hence the push for colonies. Since these products could not be obtained cheaply in the 'centre' they had to be obtained in the colonies. In the metropole monopoly ownership of land assured the monopoly landlords absolute and differential rent which did not enter into the industrial capitalist equalisation of the rate of profit, thereby inhibited increasing capital investment in land. Moreover, this fact helped to push up wages which made raw material production expensive where it was possible.

The financial oligarchy overcame this by 'owning' land directly in the colonies where there were no capitalist monopoly land owners. In most of Africa land was largely unoccupied because of the slave trade and its cost was almost nil. In other areas where there were feudal and semi-feudal landlords, these were easily subjected to the laws of motion of the capitalist mode of production, albeit in a stunted form, and in their weakened position these landlords were easily subjected to the financial oligarchy's control through various mechanisms taking advantage of the backward characteristics of the social formation.

But, most important of all, the supply of *cheap labour* was superabundant, in the sense that it could be turned away from subsistence production into wage labour. This could be achieved only by establishing a colonial state with a coercive arm which through various measures pushed the resisting peasantry into enforced labour. With this super-abundant labour supply, which could subsist partly on the products from their landholdings, wages were necessarily low, since the value of labour was fixed by its subsistence and reproduction costs. Here peasant subsistence

242

economy could assist the financial oligarchy in keeping the value of labour-power down.

This was the secret of colonial exploitation. It continues in changed circumstances under neo-colonialism. In the era of multilateral imperialism, the financial oligarchy exercises this exploitation through the power of the finance capital which it exports to these countries. Although the neo-colony can avail itself of socialist aid, which is of some significance, such aid is normally used in setting up state enterprises in the neo-colony and thus ends up helping the monopolies in their exploitative dealings. Under these circumstances neo-colonial exploitation has become a fact of 'national independence'. The neo-colony remains a monopoly preserve of the financial oligarchy of the entire imperialist world.

Attention has been drawn to the fact that in the post-war period there is a discernible decline in the production of agricultural products in favour of minerals and oil production. This has been attributed in some quarters to the structural changes brought about by the 'scientific and technological revolution' engendered by the 'competition between the two world systems'. As we have observed, these technological developments have been used as a monopoly weapon for the control of sources of raw materials and markets by the transnational monopolies. It is only these monopolies with a technological lead in some fields which are able to compete for the control of industrial raw materials and strategic materials, all necessary for profitable investment in home industries.

Although it is true that production of a number of agricultural products has declined, e.g., logs, leather, skins and wool, due to scientific improvements resulting in savings in use of these materials and the invention of synthetic substitutes, their production is not negligible. (65) On the one hand, a number of monopolies such as Unilever and Nestles are involved in the production of food products such as edible oils, cocoa, coffee, bananas, etc., all important in helping keep wages down. On the other hand, substances like rubber continue to be important agricultural products for the industrialised West.

The shift in the importance of oil and mineral products is noticeable in the post-war period as witnessed by inter-monopoly struggle for control of the sources to these materials. This is evidenced by the fact that oil production in the imperialist world increased considerably from 829 million tons in 1960 to 1,880 million tons in 1970. Production increased by 45 % in the capitalist countries whilst that in Third World countries went up by 300 %. This shows the considerable importance to imperialist industry of this product.

Oil, apart from its use as a petroleum product, has also been an important raw material for the manufacture of chemical products such as plastics and artificial fibres. Large investments have been made in this field leading to rapid production of chemical products in the 1960s. For instance the synthetic material Kiana took Du Pont 20 years to develop with a large investment of 75 million dollars. As a result of these developments it is estimated that by 1975 there will be an increase of 40 % in the range of plastics produced in the US as compared to the 1965 level, of 35 % for petrochemicals and of 30 % for synthetic fibres.

Japan has also rapidly developed a petrochemical industry which is completely dependent on imported oil from Africa, Asia, and Latin America. Estimated production of ethylene was expected to double between 1968 and 1975, while plastics production would go up 150-175%. Output of synthetic rubber is expected to rise by 120 % and that of synthetic fibre is expected to do so by 200 % in the same period. Synthetic paper and synthetic protein from oil is also expected to be produced in Japan. (67) The Third World countries with proven reserves of 75 % of world oil are therefore crucial to imperialist global strategy.

Minerals like aluminium and copper are vital materials for the electrical engineering, electronics, aircraft and aerospace industries. The production of aluminium in 1972 amounted to 9 million tons. Copper production rose considerably. US production of refined copper went up by 20.5 %, while Britain's rose by 16.8 % and Japan's by 14.6 %. As a result of the developments in these industries, there has been a corresponding increase in the demand for refractory metals like vanadium, nobium, tantalum, molybdenum, tungsten, selenium, zirconium, etc.

The requirements for iron ores and for manganese, chromium, cobalt, and tin for the steel industry are also important to the monopolies. The high grade ores can only be found in the Third World countries and it is there that production at low costs is possible. It is anticipated that by 1980 about 50 % of the iron ore requirements of the US will come from outside and by the year 2000 75 %, mainly, of course, from the neo-colonial hinterland. (68)

Of more crucial importance are the sources of strategic materials which are to be found in the neo-colonial world. The importance of these materials lies in their use for the warfare state. Magdoff points out that in the lists maintained by the Department of Defence, 62 of these materials are regarded as being of critical strategic importance, and that of these 52 can only be obtained abroad, three quarters of them from the Third World countries. (69) Most of these materials are needed for use in jet engines, gas turbines, nuclear reactors, etc. The jet engine alone requires up to six of these materials; tungsten, nickel, chromium, molybdenum, and cobalt. The development of nuclear industry is also dependent on a number of strategic materials which can mainly be found in Africa. These are uranium, thorium and lithium. Table XV overleaf shows the relative positions of these raw materials and Africa's estimated reserves as a proportion of the whole capitalist world reserves.

What makes the struggle for the control of these resources crucial is that apart from the immediate needs of the military and industry, the US particularly insists on stockpiling those which are in short supply. The

Table XV

Estimated Reserves of Mineral Raw Materials in 1971

Mineral	Unit	All capitalist and developing countries	Africa	Africa's proportion (%)
Oil	million tons	72,708.00	7,828.7	11.0
Gas	000 million m^3	32,948.6	5,462.0	17.0
Coal	million tons	2,694,544.00	88,156.0	4.0
Iron ore	—	212,397.00	30,825.0	12.0
Manganese	—	984.00	403.2	41.0
Copper	—	253.20	95.7	39.0
Zinc	—	129.80	7.1	6.0
Chromites	—	1,050.20	1,161.5	80.9
Graphite	—	158.60	23.7	15.0
Cobalt	—	2.40	2.0	87.0
Bauxites	—	9,682.00	3,350.0	30.0
Asbestos	—	93.50	13.7	14.0
Titanium	—	659.50	401.5	60.8
Tin	—	5.90	0.3	19.0
Lead	—	49.90	4.4	5.5
Antimony	—	1.56	0.34	21.5
Niobium	thousand tons	9,692.00	1,975.0	20.3
Tantalum	—	69.40	57.9	83.0
Beryllium	—	521.00	68.0	13.0
Lithium	million tons	18.40	2.7	15.0
Uranium	thousand tons	587.00	251.8	31.6
Phosphates	million tons	44,498.20	26,028.8	60.0

Source: E.A. Tarabrin, *The New Scramble for Africa*, (Moscow, 1974)

demand for uranium, for instance, has increased due to the fact that the future source of electric power is likely to be atomic power stations. It has been estimated that the total capacity of these plants will increase from 27 million kilowatts in 1969 to 345 million kilowatts by 1980 in the capitalist world.

The importance of these and other raw materials to the US economy, for instance, can be judged from the fact that the US yearly exports of about 30,000 million dollars are equalled by her imports of raw materials to the same value. The role of a single material like aluminium can also be judged from the fact that it accounts for 3,900 tons of the total output of 22,900 million tons by the US metallurgical industry.

As already pointed out, the location of these industries in the colonial and neo-colonial world is of crucial importance to the US not because they happen to be located there, but because products can be obtained cheaply, the rent paid is low (in terms of royalties) and labour is cheap. These factors are crucially important in enabling the monopolists to maintain a high rate of profitability in industry at home.

It must also be emphasised here that, contrary to Jalee's view, a change in the needs of monopolies for particular raw materials does not at all mean that imperialism is changing as a result. When Lenin in his analysis of imperialism showed that imperialism in pushing out into the colonies did so partly in search of particular raw materials he did not mean that those were the only products that imperialism was interested in. Indeed, he emphasised that the colonies were also important as potential sources of other materials due to 'rapid technical developments'. Jalee unduly exaggerates this change when he points out that Lenin and Bukharin gave 'pride of place to agricultural raw materials' and only 'second rate consideration' to minerals. Lenin stated in his analysis that imperialism's interest in agricultural raw materials 'also applies to prospecting for new minerals'. This in our view, belies Jalee's conclusion that 'a significant change has occurred since the time Lenin and Bukharin dealt with the problem'. (70) The change in emphasis from agricultural raw materials to oil and minerals is merely a shift from one type of materials to another brought about by the technical development in the productive forces. It does not follow that monopolies no longer have need for agricultural materials. Indeed we have shown that they still invest in their production in a considerable way.

The struggle against monopolies of the neo-colonial states for the control of raw material wealth has become legend. Various 'nationalisation measures' have been taken against certain monopolies, which are important developments, but these cannot in the short-run adversely affect the interests of imperialism. Nationalisation *per se* cannot alter the production relations. What happens at best is that the joint ventures are turned into state monopolies, which is not unknown in the imperialist 'centre'. Indeed, there is evidence, as we have shown in Chapter XVII, that such 'nationalisations' are encouraged by the monopolies themselves in order to stem nationalistic tendencies. Jalee lets himself be taken in by these manoeuvres when he wrongly concludes that opposition of this kind by Third World countries necessarily harms the interests of the monopolies. (71) This opposition can only bear fruit when imperialism is completely defeated in the Third World countries.

Whilst one must not underestimate the long-term implications of this contradiction between the peoples of the neo-colonial countries and imperialism, these struggles nevertheless remain within the sphere of bargaining for higher prices; when secured these give rise to huge money returns, as the Middle East experience with petrodollars is showing, but the returns end up back in imperialist banks and investments. The fact that these huge money reserves can only bring about marginal improvement in the lives of the people is proof beyond doubt of the impossibility of capitalist development for the Third World countries under present day conditions. This is because imperialist monopolies have taken up all investment outlets and monopolised all the markets. Nor could these funds be invested in agriculture and other sectors for the benefit of the masses without creating conflict with monopoly interests.

The struggle for the 'control' by neo-colonial states of their raw materials must therefore be seen as a nuisance to imperialism, which imperialism ultimately manages to turn to its advantage. Raymond Vernon recognises this point when he states:

> 'Strong initiatives on the part of the governments of less-developed countries to control key factors in the exploitation of their raw materials are likely to continue. And as they do, the capacity of host governments to participate in management will increase. It is another question, however, whether the host countries will feel that their "dependence" on the outside has declined simply because their management role has increased. As long as the product requires marketing in foreign countries, "dependence" will presumably continue in some form". (72)

It should be added that so long as the monopolies are in control of the technologies and skills necessary for the exploitation of these materials, imperialist control will follow as a matter of course. Also connected with this problem is the question of direct monopoly investments by sector and country. The direction of imperialist investment in the Third World countries measured by the extent of direct investment in each sector has led some to conclude that certain sectors are no longer necessary or vital to imperialism. If we take US direct investments alone for 1970, the picture comes out as follows: Canada 29.2 %; Europe (UK inclusive) 31.3 %; Latin America 18.8 %; Asia 7.2 %; Africa 4.5 %; and Australia 4.2 %. In Table XIII it was shown that in 1964 US direct investments in the Third World went almost entirely into mining and petroleum, with a little more in manufacturing and trade in Latin America. For Africa the investment was 51 % in petroleum and 21.9 % in mining; in Asia it was 65 % in petroleum alone and 17.5 % in manufacturing; and in Latin America the proportion was a little more balanced: petroleum 35.9 %, manufacturing 24.3 %, mining 12.6 %, and 10 % in trade. By region in Africa over a half of this investment was in South Africa (mining), Zaire (mining) and Libya (petroleum). In Latin America most of the investment went to three countries: Brazil, Mexico and Argentina.

The amount invested in manufacturing although less as compared to mining and petroleum has in fact increased in volume. This increased investment in manufacturing must, however, be examined in detail to see the type of activity that US investment is interested in. Moreover, the relative decline in imperialist direct investment in the Third World countries between the period before the war and the early part of the post-war period should not blind us to the fact that large amounts of capital have been advanced for the purposes of assisting the export of goods by way of credits and short-term loans.

Thus although direct investment as such decreased between 1960 and 1969 from 33 to 28 %, this was counterbalanced by credit capital from private as well as multilateral and government institutions in the form of loans and guaranteed export credits, whose share increased from 11 to 27 % and from 5 to 14 % of the total capital inflows respectively. The share of credit, loans and grants in the financing of the imports of the Third World countries increased from 15 % in 1960 to 19 % in 1969. (73)

Pinto and Knakal point out that this reliance was more pronounced in the case of Latin America, with loans playing as significant a role in the 1960s as did foreign investment in the 1950s. Thus, whereas the share of the region's foreign investment decreased from 64 % to 27 %, that of loans increased from 30 % to 66 %. Consequently the region's imports were financed increasingly by loans and grants at a level three times greater than that of the preceding decade. (73)

In Africa the picture is about the same. Foreign capital in Sub-Saharan Africa before the war stood at £6 billion. In the post war period another £6 billion private capital was added (to 1969). Official loans and credits in the period 1960-1969 amounted to $10 billion, almost doubling in this period. (74) Table XVI below clearly illustrates this position in regard to the Third World as a whole.

Table XVI

Composition of Capital Flows to the Third World

	Percentage		Index
			1969
	1960	1969	1960
A. *Total Private Capital*	38	42	199
1. Total investment	33	28	155
(a) direct	24	19	148
(b) portfolio	9	9	174
2. Export guarantee credits	5	14	466
B *Total Institutional Capital*	59	55	170
1. Total loans	11	27	448
(a) from government	8	22	475
(b) from multilateral agencies	3	5	361
2. Grants from governments and agencies	48	28	107
C. *Capital from Socialist Countries*	3	2	150
Total capital inflows	100	100	181

Source: UNCTAD Review of International Trade and Development 1970

European capital has had a different emphasis from that of US mono-polies. More of it, as compared with US capital, goes into agricultural production, trade and services and less into direct investment. Japanese capital, like American capital, has been directed more into energy, mining and raw material production in the Third World due to the relative scarcity of these resources in Japan.

Imperialist investment in the services and trade sector has taken on a new look, particularly in Africa. The old pattern of large companies which were part of the metropolitan string of companies operating overseas like Smith and Mackenzie, United Africa Company, African Mercantile, etc., which acted as importers of manufactures and exporters of agricultural products and raw materials, is being replaced with that of investment in manufacturing where this is found profitable. This was inevitable with the emergence of state trading corporations, marketing boards and coopera-tives in the post-independence neo-colonial period.

Thus Unilever enterprises like the United Africa Company and East African Industries went into import substitutive manufacturing. This does not mean that these companies and their like have given up import and export trade. In many cases they still act as shipping agents of state trading bodies, but sometimes operate directly on their own account where none of these bodies exist. They still maintain the exclusive agency agreements with the manufacturers in Europe and other imperialist countries and act as sole distributors of mechandise. Many of these firms entering into manufacturing are protected by high tariff barriers erected by the neo-colonial states which assure them high profits. Whatever legal barriers are created to stop them from repatriating their profits, or against movement of some of their capital, these monopolies soon find a way around them, just as they would do in the nation states of the imperialist countries, through transfer pricing, transfer accounting, etc., except that in a neo-colony such manoeuvres are easily accomplished due to relative inefficiency and corruption of the bureaucracy. In their import substitutive strategy such firms aim first at producing for the domestic market.

An example of this new strategy is the case of the United Africa Company, which was predominantly a trading company in pre-indepen-dence West Africa. It began to invest £15 million in industrial projects between 1956 and 1961. This was only 15 % of the company's annual capital expenditure. By 1961 the investment had gone up to 47 %. At the same time, the company was withdrawing from its traditional retail trade and concentrating on wholesale trade and supermarkets. It established a special department which in that period examined over 300 projects for industrial investment of which one-third were developed. In order to acquire the technical know-how, the company associated itself with firms already producing the products, mainly British firms. Similarly in East Africa, Unilever's East African Industries Ltd., is the largest producer in the region of such consumer goods as margarines, soaps, detergents, tooth-pastes and cooking oils.

Many of these companies have established assembly plants for such products as transistor radios, tyres, shoes, wigs, cameras, watches and cars. In all their investment strategies, the monopolies encourage 'runaway industries' in Third World countries in order to take advantage of cheap labour and tax incentives in these countries. It has been pointed out that cheap labour has become the only major consideration in such capital-intensive industries where technological improvements have cheapened the other components to the extent that labour costs in many of them constitute 60 % of total costs. (75) These 'runaway industries' are further assisted in their quest for cheap labour by the 'development plans' of the neo-colonial state, which use tariffs and other tariff barriers to protect the interests of these monopolies, in order to create 'a favourable climate for investment', whether this investment be private or multilateral.

The transnational corporation secures this control over the raw material ventures and manufacturing joint ventures as well as the markets in the neo-colonial world through its control of technological know-how, management skills, and marketing link-ups throughout the world. The role of a neo-colony as a preserve of the financial oligarchy is no longer in doubt. What appear as transactions between nations and separate 'national enterprises' turn out to be transactions between units of the same monopolies. The 'national bourgeoisie' and petty bourgeoisie pride themselves that they are engaged in 'bargaining' with the monopolies in order to advance 'national development'. In actual fact no such nation exists nor does any 'development' take place. To be sure, the patent and trade marks legis-lation in many of these neo-colonial Third World countries reflect this general hegemonic position of monopoly capitalism on a world scale. The legis-lations in these countries stipulate that patents issued and registered in the metropole can be registered as a matter of course in the neo-colony. Moreover, the neo-colonies upon the attainment of their formal 'political independence', as part of their 'new international status', subscribe to the objectives of the International Union for the Protection of Industrial Property under whose convention they are obliged to protect the patent rights of foreign monopolies. These patent and trade mark rights are, of course, monopoly 'rights'.

Such monopoly is only possible under imperialism. Since technology is a non-exhaustible social product whose ownership can only be attributed to the cumulative inventive achievements of man throughout his existence, it could not be owned otherwise. The cost of using and selling an already developed technology is zero for the modern 'owner' thereof. Where adaption occurs the costs are ascertainable and in many cases minimal. As Vatsos points out:

'Given market availabilities, the price between zero or tens of thousands of dollars, and millions of dollars or infinite is, in turn,

determined solely on the basis of crude relative bargaining power.
There is no price which *a priori* can be claimed to be more or less
appropriate within the two limits specified'. (76)

This apparently infinite more or less costless store of knowledge is
captured by monopoly capital and protected in order to make it secret
and a 'rare and scarce commodity', for sale at monopoly price. As
Penrose states:

'Clearly the patent system is our attempt to include the production
of other things, and to do this by creating scarcity — by limiting
the use of the invention . . . So far as inventions are concerned a
price is put on them not *because*, they are scarce but *in order* to
make them scarce to those who want to use them'. (77)

When it is realised that the export of capital, and hence of the technology
with which it is exported as a package deal, has become the preserve of the
transnational corporation, as indeed is the stated policy, then this monopoly situation accentuates the exploitative nature of monopoly capitalism
on an international scale.

Rutherford M. Poats, a one time administrator of the US Agency for
International Development (US AID) expressed the reality of the situation
when he pointed out that private or autonomous publicly owned enterprise and commerce have, and are likely to continue to have, the predominant roles in creating and transferring industrial technology. According
to him in the Third World these institutions can only make a modest
contribution. For this reason it is the multinational corporations who are
instrumental in this process; their success depends in large measure on a
global capacity to apply science and technology to production and
marketing. They are the dominant institutions for transferring industrial
technologies across national borders, which they do through the following
processes: the sale of their goods; training of workers and technicians;
technical assistance to local customers and to local suppliers of raw
materials, components, or assemblies; introduction in their locally staffed
field operations of the methodology of integrated research, development,
and engineering innovation; and through influence on or example to local
competitors and suppliers. He adds:

'Not all this makes every one happy in countries where multinational
companies have appeared on the local industrial scene, but it is one
of the new facts of international life . . .'(78)

It is therefore wrong in our view to try to show, as Alavi does, that
under the 'new' imperialism of the post-war period, exports of capital are
no longer the 'necessary condition' of production which characterised the
'Leninist model'. According to Alavi, this contemporary expansion is now
motivated by transfer of technology. Using figures of foreign investment in
India which suggest a shift in emphasis from raw material production to
manufacturing and trading he comes to the conclusion that:

'The most important new feature is the much greater expansion which has taken place in partnership with Indian big business. The key to the understanding of this new feature lies in the fact that the most profitable part of the operation is in establishing a market for goods manufactured in the metropolitan country and setting in motion a stream of payments by way of royalties and fees for "technical services", use of patents and brand names, etc. Indeed these other benefits are so large that even a quarter of the total profits earned in the corporate sector in the Indian economy is regarded as relatively unimportant by comparison'. (79)

Alavi's argument is tied up with a more basic one, which borders on underconsumptionism. According to him it is no longer 'typical of the emerging new pattern today' for imperialism to export capital in search for cheap labour to produce raw materials:

'Instead, monopoly capitalism in the advanced countries prefers to expand productive capacity at home where it is more secure and economically more advantageous. It seeks, instead, to extend its sway abroad in order to establish captive markets'. (79)

These views, as we have shown in the case of other neo-Marxists, are clearly underconsumptionist and one-sided. We have tried to show that imperialist exports of capital are tied up in a package deal with the so-called 'transfer of technology', skills, etc. We have tried to show that this technology in the majority of cases is incorporated into the machinery as well as the intermediate goods sold. To the extent that the machinery and incorporated technology act as the monopolists' objective weapon for setting in motion production from which surplus-value is extracted (in whatever form), these 'goods' and 'services' also act as capital export. The tying in of other monopoly tools such as employment of expatriate personnel, restricted markets, restricted sources of purchases, and marketing agreements all go to consolidate the grip of monopoly exploiting labour in the metropole as well as in the neo-colony.

A recent UN Report of the Group of Eminent Persons on transnational corporations referred to technology as 'an essential input for production' which is bought and sold in the following forms:

'(a) embodied in physical assets as, for example, plant, machinery equipment and sometimes intermediate products;
(b) as services of skilled and often highly specialised manpower;
(c) as information, whether of technical or commercial nature'. (80)

The encouragement of direct investment in the post-war period as a result of the multilateral strategy in which only monopolies could participate favoured vertical integration on an international scale. This integration is being re-inforced by control of technology which alone gives each monopoly an advantage against others in their capital exports. 'Technological transfer' to the Third World countries is therefore a function of monopoly exploitation and has ceased to have any beneficial effect on the former colonial countries since the monopolies real impact is to negate or retard and distort local development. Joint ventures and import substitutive industry merely anchor this exploitation more firmly, protecting the monopolies against nationalistic sentiments. Indeed import substitution first appeared with the establishment of a colonial enterprise set-up behind a colonial tariff barrier to protect 'mother' country products against other monopoly competitors. Market manipulations are also used to ensure that the monopolies' markets are not interfered with to their detriment by the neo-colonial state.

In the post-war period it has been specifically noticed as a trend that monopolies prefer *capital intensive* techniques, where this is possible. But the technical methods available in a particular case may determine the strategy. For instance in continuous process industries (e.g., chemicals, pharmaceuticals, metal refining, oil refining) and in the production of many consumer goods and intermediate goods on an assembly line, the scope for substitution is limited, except in ancillary operations, particularly metals handling, and packaging. The main types of activity in which labour intensive techniques may be utilised are road-building, irrigation, housing and construction work generally; also the production of woven fabrics, clothing, woodworking, leather, foodstuffs, bricks, tiles and simpler metal products. (81) But even in these areas capital intensive techniques may be adopted, depending on profitability and the speed with which the particular work may be required. This can significantly increase the productivity of labour and assures increased surplus-value on the project.

In Kenya, the International Labour Organisation's Report on Employment, Incomes, and Equality (the ILO Report), indicated that manufacturing was inherently capital-intensive and that foreign-owned firms appeared to be more capital-intensive than local ones. Depreciation per worker was higher in foreign firms than local ones. This was confirmed by comparisons of gross product per worker: £720 in foreign owned firms and £590 for local firms. Accordingly the share of labour in value-added was relatively lower in foreign firms (47 %) than in local ones (68 %). The report also showed that in those sectors where foreign firms and local ones co-exist, foreign firms tended to be less capital-intensive than locally owned firms. In this case depreciation was relatively lower for foreign firms than for local ones. (82)

Again, capital-intensity is sometimes chosen because of the lack of properly trained skilled labour. Thus the strategy will be influenced by the qualitative characteristics of the labour force. Arrighi classifies these as:

> (a) *unskilled labour*, versatile and less adaptable to the discipline of wage employment;
> (b) *semi-skilled* labour, specialised, regular, and identified with the job;
> (c) *skilled labour*, relatively versatile, with complex skills (e.g. carpenters, mechanics, supervisors, etc.);
> (d) *high-level manpower*, specialised by education qualification rather than on the job training (engineers, designers, cost accounting staff, production sales experts). (83)

Capital intensive techniques require not only less labour for each level of output but also a different composition of the labour force than labour intensive techniques, as they make possible the division of complex operations, which would need skilled labour, into simple operations which can be performed by semi-skilled labour. Thus labour intensive techniques are associated with a pattern of employment in which labour of types (a) and (c) predominates, whereas capital intensive techniques are associated with a pattern of employment in which labour of types (b) and (d) predominates. (83) This position is confirmed by the ILO Report on Kenya. Here it was observed by the ILO experts that there was emphasis on the need for supervisory labour as a means to labour intensity, and supervision in manufacturing seemed to be a substitute for skills. (84)

Here it can be seen that when a monopoly decides on an import substitutive industry in a neo-colony it is concerned with the need to maintain control of its raw material bases, and the market. The techniques of production are determined by the need to spread costs of research and development, but since such costs may not be large in many cases this spread assures the monopoly of maximum profits in such 'transfer' transactions. Industrialisation of this type does not therefore create an autonomous industrial base in the neo-colony but rather a mere production outpost for the monopolies, who 'put out' their capital, technology and technical know-how to exploit the cheap labour force and the natural resources available in the neo-colonies.

The idea of a joint venture is to enable the transnational corporation to exercise control in different situations. The corporation may have a majority interest in the venture, it may be a minority shareholder, or indeed it may merely participate as the owner of patents and trade marks and licensor of know-how. In its monopoly position, it can 'sell' to its exploited clients technical and managerial skills. It also 'sells' technologies already embodied in intermediate products and machinery. Other techniques of control are exercised through mechanisms like design of factory lay outs, bargaining with its monopolised markets, and even the use of its expertise in purchasing equipment and materials for the ventures from abroad (in may cases from itself). All these become vital 'assets' for sale by the monopoly to its clients and becomes the real channels for the syphoning off to the imperialist countries of the surplus-value produced by labour in the neo-colony.

A monopoly's 'clients' in the neo-colony will enter into various agreements with it. As we have seen a management and consultancy agreement will be concerned with making available or retaining for the client skills, knowledge, equipment, and facilities that it may otherwise lack for the continued operation of the enterprise. It may also include provisions for services, administrative responsibilities, technology, purchasing, sales, training of local staff, etc. Whether the transnational jointly owns the venture with a majority or a minority share, its control of management and of production processes, based on its world-wide know-how and markets, would nevertheless entail its real control of the enterprise. Management control assures the monopoly the actual running of the factory and enterprise, the organisation of marketing and the coordination of production, purchase, and installation of machinery and materials.

The question of what the joint venture enterprise 'buys' from the transnational monopoly and its implications for the neo-colonial economy cannot be understood until it is realised that the bargaining position of the monopoly is the basis for such relationship. This is assured to the monopoly through its objective power over capital and its technology as well as the market manipulations enabling its agents in the joint venture to reap great advantages, restrict exports, obtain exclusive marketing rights, and impose limits as to the sources of purchases.

Restriction of exports. In granting the licence to a joint venture, the monopoly will stipulate the geographical limits within which the licensee is permitted to sell the products from the technology. This restriction springs from the monopoly's right under the patent legislation promulgated during colonialism, through which the monopoly is enabled to have control over sale of its patents, so long as it does not restrict trade. The latter exception to the law becomes meaningless under monopoly, particularly in a neo-colony where the principal 'purchaser' is the monopoly itself. The 'majestic equality' of all before the law, here as elsewhere, works in favour of the monopoly. Vaitsos, in a study carried out in Colombia, shows that out of a sample of nationally owned firms and joint ventures in that country in the chemical, textile, and pharmaceutical sectors, 85 % of the contracts studied explicitly prohibited exports of products manufactured with the use of imported technology.

Any move by the neo-colonial state to revoke the patent laws as a defensive measure would have very limited results since the market belongs to the monopolies. This becomes quite clear when it is realised that the other markets to which such products would be exported would still have such legislation protecting the same patents, and the transnational corporation would be in a position to require compliance. The mere ownership of patents without the actual know-how which is guarded by the monopoly at its headquarters would be useless. This is the whole point about monopoly. The world imperialist monopoly market would not exist if such a system of market control were not in operation.

Exclusive marketing rights. The second type of restriction by which the foreign monopoly through joint-ventureship maintains its dominance is the exclusive reservation to itself of marketing rights. The legal terms and conditions will require the neo-colonial 'partner' to sell to the monopoly all or part of the products coming out of the use of its technology. This right may be related to the one above, but it need not be. It may be determined by the wish of the foreign monopoly to sell the product in its other market outside the immediate geographical area. But it may also be determined by the monopoly's desire to process the product further in another part of the world. This is understandable since, as we have seen, the tariff structure of the imperialist countries, and the so-called generalised schemes of preferences, clearly do not favour manufactured products being imported into their markets from the neo-colony.

Restrictions on sources of purchases. The third type of restriction concerns the source of the continuing requirements of equipment, machinery and technology after the first contracts have been concluded. This is the point at which the foreign monopoly assures itself of a continuous market in the neo-colony. It may follow naturally on the fact that the nature of technology and machinery imported may not be interchangeable with that from other sources, but this is not always the case. Thus a term and condition in the agreement for the sale of technology will require the client to buy future supplies essential to the enterprise exclusively from the monopoly. In a sample of 150 technology and licencing contracts studied by Vaitsos in diverse sectors in Bolivia, Colombia, Ecuador and Peru, more than two-thirds explicitly required the purchase of intermediates from the technology supplier or his affiliates. (85)

Apart from this type of provision in the agreement, there is usually a 'tie-in' clause, which requires that other goods specified therein shall be bought from the monopoly selling the technology, machinery and/or intermediate goods, or from the monopoly undertaking the project, or from a source approved by it. Many other types of clauses require that top personnel come from the ranks of the monopoly itself. Others are concerned with the level and structure of production, and yet others with price fixing for the sale or resale of products. Moreover, many monopolies require that technology shall only be available to the 'partner' so long as the monopoly continues to be linked in the participation of the management and equity of the enterprise. Here it becomes almost impossible to ever consider terminating the arrangement, and total dependence is assured both in terms of technology and access to the sources of equipment and machinery.

In the final analysis these manipulations are concerned with the extraction of surplus-value and its siphoning to the metropole. In transfer, management, consultancy and/or technical assistance arrangements, remuneration is on the basis of a percentage of profits after tax, plus a technical fee or a fixed fee per year for management, plus a percentage of the purchase price for the services of a purchasing agent, plus, again, royalties for technical services as a per cent of sales. In addition to the above arrangements, there will be a percentage due on capital expenditure, and a fixed sum per year plus a percentage of net profits before taxes as payment for managerial and other services. There may be a mixture of the above arrangements and percentages may be subjected to a minimum (and sometimes to a maximum) fee. The above fees, which in many cases are cumulative, are *in addition* to dividends earned on the equity share in the enterprise if the foreign monopoly is, in addition, a shareholder. These forms of extraction of surplus-value through 'transfers' of technology and skills in manufacturing are further exploitation of the neo-colony in addition to the direct exploitation of labour in raw material ventures.

Although the neo-colonial state may pass legislation to restrict foreign exchange transfers, the foreign corporation would not find it difficult, as already indicated, to transfer the surplus-value. Its transfer accounting techniques would enable the monopoly to beat the foreign exchange restrictions. The ILO Report on Kenya already cited had this to say:

> 'It is, however, widely accepted that repatriation of profits is often an inadequate measure of the total resources transferred by the foreign enterprises, particularly in the manufacturing sector. Generally speaking foreign-owned enterprises are in a position to use a number of accounting procedures falling under the heading of transfer accounting that enable them to maximise profits (by minimising their tax commitments) over the whole of their international operations, by moving resources from one country to another'. (86)

Thus the foreign corporation will through *transfer pricing, over-invoicing* or *under-invoicing* be in a position to siphon off its funds. In Kenya the ILO Report noted that a number of these firms that had made losses consistently over periods of four or five years were suspected of transfer pricing intermediate goods and accumulating outside Kenya. The over-pricing sometimes was as high as 20 to 30 % of the prices on the open market. The report concluded:

> 'If it becomes prevalent, this type of transfer pricing can have a particularly marked effect on an economy like that of Kenya, where imported intermediates comprise a very large part of gross output in the manufacturing economy. It requires only *a very small overpricing ratio to bring about transfers of resources* which can, since they are untaxed, constitute a very large proportionate addition to the resources transferred through the repatriation of profits'. (87)

In Latin America, Vaitsos cited over-pricing of imports up to 400 % in Colombia.

In addition to transfer pricing, a foreign corporation may remit its funds out of the country under the exchange control regulations themselves by duplicating heads of entitlement. The ILO Report on Kenya quotes the result of a sample of ten foreign-owned enterprises which were found to have made the following remittances abroad: £310,000 for dividends; £136,000 for management fees; £34,000 for technical services and consultation; £36,000 for royalties. Non-dividend payments amounted to 67 % of dividend remittances and 40 % of total remittances. It was also noted that the other common practice was the earning of dividends on the basis of capitalised know-how, at the same time charging royalties on the sale for technology.

All these mechanisms have ensured that neo-colonialism under multi-lateral imperialism continues under the changed circumstances of the post-war period to provide monopolies with markets, outlets for the application of capital in the production of raw materials and the application of technology and management skills for the politico-economic control of these countries.

This elaborate, octopus-like imperialist tie-up of neo-colonial economies to suit imperialism's global strategies is made possible to a great extent by the multilateral imperialist institutions set up in the post-war period to serve its interests. These bodies were examined in general perspective in terms of their broad international objectives in an earlier chapter. In order to see how these institutions have been utilised by imperialism as tools to serve it, it is necessary to see how they have operated in this period. A close examination of the operations of these institutions reveals that they are important instruments of imperialist policy in the neo-colony.

The General Agreement on Tariffs and Trade (GATT) which was established in 1947 was just such an institution for perpetuating colonial ties under multilateral imperialism. As we have observed, the colonial preferential market was to break-down gradually, giving way to an Open-Door penetration of neo-colonial markets. Under the rules of the GATT the neo-colony has to 'trade' in exactly the same way as the metropoles. Trade concessions could only be exchanged on the basis of reciprocal advantage. Since tariff reductions by a neo-colony in return for similar 'advantages' in the metropole were ruled out by its reliance on monopoly investment, it became the rule that only major suppliers could initiate tariff liberalisation. The Most-Favoured-Nation Clause in Article 1 of the GATT ensured that the neo-colony would give no special advantage to its 'own' former metropolitan power, outside the preferences allowed by the GATT itself. (88)

The use of quantitative restrictions for 'development' purposes which were allowed the neo-colony required regular reporting and in any case the neo-colony had to respond to IMF 'advice' whenever these affected transfer of payments for current transactions. Given the exclusion from the market of the metropole of any products of its 'national bourgeoisie', or even of import-substitution industries aided or jointly operated by the monopolies, the neo-colony was forced to play its true role as importer of products from the imperialist countries, to which it had to export primary products to pay for the imports. In this way the neo-colonial state economy was shaped in such a way that it perpetually acted as intermediary for the metropolitan monopoly bourgeoisie. Moreover, since the 'trade' was in products activated by finance capital, it was the monopolists who traded in these products *interse.*

Most primary products, minerals or petroleum were themselves owned by the monopolies, although in some cases peasant cash crop economy (itself generated by finance capital) might be relied on as a foreign exchange earner for a neo-colony. But soon a 'trade gap' emerged since the meagre export earnings from exploited labour of the neo-colony could not pay for monopoly products so highly priced. In these circumstances 'aid' was resorted to, to 'fill the gap'. Such 'aid' was given merely as inducement to capital exports from which earnings 'aid' would come. As the Pearson Commission showed, whereas 'aid' from the imperialist countries to the Third World increased from $1.7 billion in 1955 to $7.0 billion in 1968, private investment correspondingly increased from $1.6 billion to $5.8 billion in the same period. (89) If this were not so, the repayment of the earlier loans would be in jeopardy. It is no 'coincidence', as Barrat-Brown has shown, that in US and UK accounts, public aid and direct investment incomes 'almost exactly balance each other', (90) as Table XVII below shows

Table XVII

US and UK Direct Foreign Investment Income of Companies and Movements of Public Capital, by Regions, 1967-1969.

Region	USA ($m)		UK (£m)	
	Direct invest. income	Prov. of public funds	Direct invest. income	Prov. of public funds
all developed	2000	—	190	—
North America	900	—	130	—
Europe	900	—	90	—
Sterling area	200	—	160	—
all underdeveloped	3000	3200	170	165
Latin America	500	650	33	12
SW Asia & Korea	1500	1800	3	20
Sterling area	200	500	130	133
other	800	250	4	—
Total	5000	3200	560	165

Source: Barrat-Brown: *Economics of Imperialism, p.227.*

The UNCTAD ('poor man's club') which came in, in 1964, as a 'counter-weight' to the GATT ('rich man's club') in order to find ways of stimulating markets for neo-colonial competitive products in the metropoles has had little success. The much heralded 'break through' in the so-called Generalised Schemes of Preferences has proved to be so much verbiage. The schemes which purport to open up the markets of the 18 metropolitan countries to the processed and semi-processed products of the 77 neo-colonial territories merely reproduce the relationships of exploitation among these countries.

Indeed, the so-called 'duty-free' or 'low duty' preferences are soon cancelled out by restricted *product coverages* which exclude from the schemes the very products of 'export interest' to the neo-colony. These types of products are normally those produced by the 'national bourgeoisie' or the neo-colonial state under the 'national development plan'. Manufactures like petroleum products, leather products, and textiles are excluded from most schemes. Moreover, those products allowed in are subjected to *a priori* limitations and escape clauses so as to exclude those products from the markets. Furthermore, the rules governing 'originating products' ensure that unless the product is either wholly produced in the neo-colony or substantially transformed there with monopoly approved materials and components, they are to be excluded from entry into metropolitan markets. The 'value-added' criterion is used to exclude products containing more than 50 % value-added unless these meet with the approval of the monopoly. In addition such requirements as 'goods must be directly consigned or must have certificate of origin' help to reinforce the restrictions.

The result of the schemes are therefore neglible in advancing 'trade relationships'. The essence of the rules in the schemes is to perpetuate the production relationships based on capital exports. A neo-colony soon finds that being a market for the monopolies it cannot obtain markets of its own, nor use its own natural resources on its own account, unless such use follows within the global strategy of imperialist monopoly enterprise.

All the multilateral institutions work in a complimentary manner. As we pointed out earlier, a link between the GATT and IMF is established in the legal provisions in Articles XIV and XV of GATT. These permit the use of quantitative restrictions for balance of payments reasons only 'in manner having equivalent effect to restrictions on payments and transfers on current international transactions'. Resort to this method is possible only with the specific 'approval' of the particular restriction by the Fund. This means in effect that in every such restriction applied under GATT rules, the IMF plays a supervisory role. The IMF has not been wanting in the discharge of this duty; it has been the financial arm of the multilateral arrangement that has wielded the real big stick, enforcing monetary and financial discipline according to the dictates of monopoly capitalism. Thus although the imperialist countries comprise only one-quarter of the membership of the Fund, they hold the controlling three-quarters of the contributed quotas and two-thirds of the votes. Hence any 'advice' rendered by the IMF to the neo-colony represents monopoly interests.

With the financial backing both of the contributed quotas amounting to $29 billions, and of the investible finances of the entire imperialist camp, the Fund under the leadership of US imperialism has tremendous power over a neo-colony. Backed by the US military machine and defence pacts the institution's directives in the end have to be complied with. Thus the dubious aims and objectives of the Fund laid down in the Articles of Agreement are a necessary legal cover for enforcing measures in the Third

World countries whose objectives are to ensure free flow of private investible funds and their convertibility, a machinery which became imperative with the disappearance of the gold standard.

If the directives which the Fund gives in the form of 'advice' to the client states are not complied with the client is deprived of any further credit not only from the Fund itself but also from the other multilateral bodies like the World Bank and its affiliates (IFC and IDA). Further, such action would 'frighten' private and public sources of finance in the imperialist camp. The Fund functions as the central authority and guardian of the interests of the entire body of imperialist finance capital. This in spite of the temporary and sometimes acute contradictions among the imperialist monopolies and states themselves.

When it is considered that all the Third World countries, because of the exploitation to which they are exposed under neo-colonialism, are subject to perpetual balalnce-of-payments difficulties arising out of exploitative production relations, then the Fund's power over these countries can well be imagined. Since it was founded the Fund, in its dealings with the Third World client states, has emphasised three main policy positions which it insists have to be implemented when balance-of-payments problems arise:

(a) reduction in government spending and contraction of domestic bank credit as a means of restraining inflation;

(b) devaluation of the domestic currency in terms of the US dollar, coupled with the elimination of exchange controls on foreign exchange transactions and;

(c) encouragement of foreign investment by increasing tax benefits, guaranteeing profit remittance, and clamping down on labour strikes. (91) The aim of the Fund in emphasising these policy positions is supposed to stabilise a country's long-term credit position. But these policies in actual fact are aimed at encouraging exports, increasing imports, and giving in more to the outflows of foreign exchange which were responsible for the balance of payments problems in the first place. Moreover, to reduce government spending limits the ability of the neo-colonial state to influence those sectors of the economy which are crucial to it. This is quite deliberate, for it has the sole effect of encouraging private capital and intensifying the exploitation of labour. Furthermore, the devaluation of the currency does not result in increased exports since the demand patterns of primary products in the metropole are rather inelastic. The neo-colony cannot manipulate these to suit its own needs. If any improved exports results it may be at decreasing prices and the returns in any case end up in parasitic pockets and are remitted out of the country. The devaluation merely increases the cost of imports which under the 'advice' must be allowed to enter unrestricted.

The result of all these policies is to create a vicious circle which the neo-colonial state can never get out of so long as it operates within it. Thus, as

Payer points out, in Indonesia the Fund 'advised' a contraction of credit and liberalisation of foreign imports, in order to 'stabilise' the credit situation of Indonesia. This 'advice' led to the closure of thousands of local neo-colonial state industries, which were later taken over by US capital. In the Philippines the Fund's 'advice' given in 1962 resulted in the increased outflow of earnings (mainly profits) from $200 million in 1961 to $990 million in 1962. To ease the deficits arising out of this outflow, the Philippines was given further loans, which in turn were used for expatriation of profits. In these circumstances the vicious circle created by the GATT policies (which are intended to lead to imbalance in terms of trade) joins up the vicious circle created by the Fund. These vicious circles are at the very core of the net of neo-colonial subjugation and exploitation in this type of relationships which multilateral imperialism has woven around the world to protect its outlets for capital exports and markets.

The role of the World Bank adds another twist to the vicious circle. Under its Articles of Agreement it is a channel for private capital. (92) Moreover, it is required not to compete with private banks. As a result its interest rates are higher than commercial bank rates. This is necessary since the Bank will raise its funds from these private banks, to which it is perpetually indebted. As a result huge American banks through their finances control the Bank's policies. For this reason ever since the Bank came into being the governors of the Bank have been high ranking American executives. The five or so major imperialist powers control its operations. The US holds 28 % of the Bank's government subscriptions (and 25 % of the vote); with Britain second, holding 11 % of the subscription (and 10 % of the vote); France and West Germany each holding the equivalent of half of Britain's funds and vote. Even the US multilateral funds are channelled through the Bank, to 'drum up business competition for the private investors'. (93) By 1969, the Bank in its 23 years of existence had loaned about $13 billion mostly to Third World countries. Of this amount about 95 % was long-term loan capital at conventional interest rates terms; the other 5 % were 'soft' IDA loans which are basically from governments to governments through the Bank on approved social projects, especially agricultural and infrastructure projects. This loan capital earned the Bank and the financial oligarchies $170 million in 1969 as compared to $145 million on the average per year in the previous 5 years. (94)

In its role as a vehicle of private finance capital the Bank follows the Fund's 'advice', and itself insists on cost benefit appraisals which tend to bolster capital intensive techniques. It also advises the removal of 'inequitable and restrictive' laws in order to attract foreign investment and frowns on lending to public projects except at high interest rates.

Thus when, in 1956, India applied to the Bank for a loan, the Bank stipulated that India's public sector should be reduced, whereupon the Indian government refused the loan. Faced with a balance of payments crisis, India soon came back to the Bank on her knees, this time accepting both the loan and the conditions originally imposed. She had to accept that in future the government should not insist on 51 % majority control in the industries in which foreign capital was invested. The most profitable public enterprises were opened up to private capital, e.g., drugs, aluminium, heavy electrical engineering, fertilisers and synthetic rubber. A series of tax concessions were extended to foreign firms. (95)

The projects on which vast sums of money are spent include transportation, roads, rails, locomotives and other equipment. In the early 1960s, of the $860 million lent to African countries, 55 % were allocated to transport, 28 % to electric power, and the balance to agricultural expansion, education and mining. Vast sums were allocated to South Africa and Rhodesia. Of the $900 million lent in 1962 to Africa, over 50 % went to South Africa, Rhodesia and Zaire (for mining). In the second half of the 1960s, the Bank's funds shifted to selected targets like Sudan, Mauritania, Morocco, Tunisia and East Africa (particularly Kenya). The Bank even set up a special consultative office for East Africa in Nairobi.

As with the Fund, the Bank acts as the coordinator of world finance capital. It works closely with the Organisation for Economic Cooperation and Development (OECD), the EEC, and the various regional banks and with these institutions ensures that the interests of the financial oligarchies are preserved in the Third World neo-colonial hinterland. These measures of international monopoly capital are part and parcel of the reality of imperialism and can only be understood as a total reality. Here we see that a neo-colony under these conditions can only get out of these octopus-like exploitative production relations by revolt. No amount of policy manipulation outside the class struggle can bring about the desired end. A revolt against imperialism becomes the only basis for the national democratic revolution.

REFERENCES

1. G. Schulz, *Revolutions and Peace Treaties*, B and N, (New York, 1973), p. 89.
2. D. Horowits, op. cit. pp.27-28.
3. I.V. Stalin, *The October Revolution and the National Question*, Collected Works, Vol. IV.
4. Mao Tse Tung, *On New Democracy*, Selected Works Vol.II (Peking, 1954), pp.346-47.
5. R. Emerson, *The United States and Africa*, 1963; Edited by Walter Goldschmidt, Praeger, (New York), p.28.
6. H. Magdoff, *The Age of Imperialism*, Monthly Review, (New York, 1969), pp.173-201.
7. H. Magdoff, op. cit. p.195.
8. Bernstein, *United States Investments in Latin America*, Knopf, (New York, 1969), quoted at p.182.
9. In Bernstein, op. cit. p.184.
10. Quoted in Halliday and McCormack, *Japanese Imperialism Today*, Praeger, (New York, 1973), p.25.
11. D.K. Fieldhouse, *The Theory of Capitalist Imperialism*, Longman, (London, 1967), p.193.
12. Baran & Sweezy, *Monopoly Capital*, Penguin, (London, 1966), p.20.
13. A. Emmanuel, 'White-settler Colonialism and the Myth of Investment Imperialism', *NLR*,No.73, p.34; See also *Unequal Exchange*, NLB (London, 1972), pp.184-192.
14. A. Emmanuel, op. cit. p.35.
15. A. Emmanuel, op. cit. p.36.
16. G. Pilling, 'Imperialism, Trade and 'Unequal Exchange'; the Work of Arghiri Emmanuel', *Economy and Society*, Vol. 12, No.2, p.169.
17. G. Pilling, op. cit. p.169.
18. A. Emmanuel, *Unequal Exchange*, op. cit. p.187.
19. A. Emmanuel, op. cit. p.164.
20. A. Emmanuel, op. cit. p. 105.
21. A. Emmanuel, op. cit. p.131.
22. A. Emmanuel, op. cit. p.130.
23. A. Emmanuel, op. cit. p.82.
24. P.A. Sweezy, *Theory of Capitalist Development*, Monthly Review, (New York, 1942), p.115.
25. G. Pilling, op. cit. p.174.
26. K. Marx, *Capital*, Progress, (Moscow, 1968), Vol. I, pp.480-482, 496-525.
27. K. Marx, op. cit. p.378 and generally pp.372-380.
28. Samir Amin, *Accumulation on a World Scale*, Monthly Review, (New York, 1973), pp. 38, 87.
29. Samir Amin, op. cit. pp.146-147.

30. Samir Amin, op. cit. pp.147-148.
31. P.R. Dutt, *India Today*, Golancz, (London, 1940), p.94.
32. S. Amin, op. cit. pp.1, 38.
33. S. Amin, op. cit. pp.20-21.
34. S. Amin, op. cit. p.35.
35. S. Amin, op. cit. p.38.
36. S. Amin, op. cit. p.88.
37. S. Amin, op. cit. pp.175-176.
38. S. Amin, op. cit. p.142.
39. S. Amin, op. cit. p.59.
40. F. Engels, *Anti-Duhring*, Progress, (Moscow, 1969), Vol. I, p.178.
41. See N. Poulantzas, *Political Power and Social Classes*, New Left Books, (London, 1968), pp.13-16 for the distinction.
42. R. Luxembourg, *The Accumulation of Capital*, Allen Lane, (London, 1972), p.446.
43. Luxembourg merely touches on the question of falling profitability in a short footnote, in her *Anti-Critique*.
44. J.A. Schumpeter, *Capitalism, Socialism and Democracy*, Allen and Unwin, (London, 1970), p.18.
45. K. Marx, *Capital*, op. cit., Vol. III pp.330-331.
46. K. Marx, *Poverty of Philosophy*, Progress, (Moscow, 1973), p.133.
47. K. Marx, *Grundrisse*, Penguin, (London, 1975), pp.105-106; See also Marx, *A Contribution to the Critique of Political Economy*, Progress, (Moscow, 1970), pp.211-213.
48. V.I. Lenin, *Critical Remarks on the National Question*, Progress, (Moscow, 1974), p.129.
49. K. Marx, *Value, Price and Profit*, Progress, (Moscow, 1970), pp.53-54 (Emphasis in original).
50. V.I. Lenin, *Selected Works*, Progress, (Moscow, 1971), Volume I, p.43.
51. K. Marx, *Capital*, op. cit. Vol. III, p.193.
52. P. Anderson, see a series of three articles 'Portugal and the End of Ultra-Colonialism', in *New Left Review*, Nos. 15, 16 and 17. Issue No. 16 lists foreign interests in Portugal's colonies.
53. S. Amin, op. cit. pp.69, 60.
54. A. Emmanuel, *Unequal Exchange*, op. cit. p.267.
55. B. Warren, 'Imperialism and Industrialisation, *New Left Review*, No. 81.
56. G. Lichtheim, *Imperialism*, Penguin, (London, 1974), p.99.
57. B. Warren, op. cit.
58. See J.V. Stalin , (i) *The October Revolution and the National Question*, op. cit. (ii) *The National Question Once Again*, in *Collected Works*, Vol. VII; Mao Tse Tung, (i) *The Chinese Revolution and the Chinese Communist Party* in *Selected Works*, Vol. III (Peking 1974). (ii) *On New Democracy* in *Selected Works*, Vol. II (Peking 1974).

59.   G. Kay, *Development and Underdevelopment — A Marxist Analysis*, MacMillan, (London, 1975), p.100.

60.   G. Kay, op. cit. p.101.

61.   G. Kay, op. cit. p.102.

62.   G. Kay, op. cit. p.104.

63.   G. Kay, op. cit. p.108.

64.   G. Kay, op. cit. pp.90-93.

65.   E.A. Tarabrin, *The New Scramble for Africa*, Progress, (Moscow, 1974), p.140.

66.   P. Jalee, *Imperialism in the Seventies*, Third Press, (New York, 1974), pp.18-48.

67.   E.A. Tarabrin, op. cit. pp.145-146.

68.   H. Magdoff, *Imperialism* . . . op. cit. pp.48-49.

69.   H. Magdoff, op. cit. pp.50-51.

70.   P. Jalee, *Imperialism* . . . op. cit. pp.17, 42.

71.   P. Jalee, op. cit. p.47.

72.   R. Vernon, *Sovereignty at Bay*, Penguin, (London, 1971), p.64.

73.   A. Pinto & J. Knakal, 'The Centre-Periphery System Twenty Years Later' in N. Girvan (Ed.) 'Dependence and Underdevelopment in the New World and the Old', *ISER* Special Issue Vol. 22 No. 1, March 1973, pp.52-53.

74.   A.M. Kamarch, *The Economics of African Development*, Praeger, (New York, 1971), p.253.

75.   L. Turner, *The Multinational Company and the Third World*, Allen, (London, 1973), pp.173-209.

76.   C. Vaitsos, in Bernstein, (Ed.) *Underdevelopment and Development*, Penguin, (London, 1973), p.316.

77.   E. Penrose, *The International Patent System 1951*, p.29.

78.   R.M. Poats, *Technology for Developing Nations*, (1972) pp.63-64.

79.   H. Alavi, *Imperialism: Old and New*, in *Socialist Register*, Merlin, (London, 1964).

80.   UNO, *The Impact of Multinational Corporations on Development and International Relations*, UNO, (New York, 1974).

81.   Economic Commission for Africa, *Multinational Corporations in Africa*, (1973), p.13.

82.   ILO, *Employment, Incomes and Equality A Strategy for increasing productive employment in Kenya*, (1972), pp.446-450.

83.   G. Arrighi, in Rhodes (Ed.), *Imperialism and Underdevelopment*, (1970), Monthly Review, (New York, 1970), pp.228-229.

84.   ILO, *Employment* . . . op. cit. p.451.

85.   C. Vaitsos, in Bernstein, op. cit. p.370.

86.   ILO, *Employment* . . . op. cit. pp.453-454.

87.   ILO, op. cit. pp.455-456.

88.   Under Article 11:2 of GATT.

89.   Pearson, *Partners in Development*, Praeger, (New York, 1969), p.139.

90.   Barrat Brown, *Economics of Imperialism*, (1974), pp.226-227.

91.   C. Payer,'The IMF and the Third World', in *Monthly Review*, 1971, See also *The Debt Trap*, Penguin, (London, 1974).
92.   Article I of the *Articles of Agreement* of the World Bank.
93.   C. Payer, op. cit. p.75.
94.   Stewart Smith, *The US and Africa*, Progress, (Moscow, 1974), p.87.
95.   Haslemere Group, *Pamphlet on Aid*, 1972, p.20.

PART SIX
CONCLUSION

CHAPTER XXII

'Imperialism is the eve of the Socialist Revolution'

Lenin

Our historical survey and theoretical analysis of the phenomenon of imperialism has mainly been concerned with showing that imperialism manifests itself at various stages of development of societies. It has been shown that imperialism cannot therefore be comprehended as a general phenomenon, but has to be examined in relation to stages of development of the productive forces and their corresponding social relations and forms of organisation of production. But to do this scientifically it is necessary to establish the laws of motion specific to the various stages of development of the relevant imperialist and subordinated societies, hence the importance of historical materialism.

We have seen that in order to comprehend modern imperialism, we have to trace the historical roots of capitalism itself. Here we notice that the colonisation of the relatively backward countries, the enslavement of the peoples of Africa, and the expropriation of the peasantry in Europe were the necessary stage in the development of capital — a stage characterised by plunder and 'unequal exchange'. A number of the present day neo-colonial territories came under this form of domination which we have called 'mercantilist imperialism'. Capitalism developed under this imperialism in its 'primitive form' and formed the basis for the rise of the 'free' industrial capitalism of the era of capitalist development proper. This form of capitalism, which enabled a number of countries to develop their productive forces, gaining greatly from the earlier British development, soon gave way to a monopolistic capitalism, which is modern imperialism. The intervention of this imperialism put a stop to further development in countries still under colonial domination (e.g. India), thus converting them into a new type of colonies serving the interests of the financial oligarchy, the imperialist bourgeoisie.

This modern imperialism signalled the advent of a new division of the whole world, bringing for the first time all the uncolonised parts of the world under total domination and exploitation. The World Wars that were fought in the early half of this century were concerned with the redivision

268

and repartition of this colonised world. The rise of the socialist sector of the world in the Soviet Union spelt a new crisis for imperialism and the multilateral imperialism of the post second World War period was an attempt to stem the tide of anti-colonialism that the October Revolution intensified. This 'solution' imposed by US imperialism upon the European imperialist powers required the redivision of the world under 'Open Door' neo-colonialism, which furthered the monopolistic competition of the giant corporations.

The intensified exploitation of the working class the world over and the oppression of the peoples in the neo-colonies led increasingly to the struggle of these peoples against imperialism. The victory of the people of Indo-China gave greater inspiration and impetus to the struggling peoples of the Third World.

Thus Lenin's thesis on imperialism, based on a careful study of history, and more importantly on Marx's scientific analysis of the capitalist mode of production, still correctly explains modern imperialism and its significance for future developments of society. Lenin correctly concluded that 'imperialism is the eve of the Socialist Revolution'. This was because monopoly capitalism by socialising production on the international scale, whilst maintaining private appropriation of the product, created the material conditions for the emergence of no other system of production than a socialist one. Moreover, and as Stalin and Mao Tse-tung added, the exploitation of the colonial and semi-colonial peoples under imperialism, which ruled out their development on the basis of the old bourgeois revolution that led to capitalist development, left no other option to these colonial and semi-colonial countries but the new democratic revolution that leads to socialist development.

Our analysis has further tried to expose the bankruptcy of the neo-Marxist centre-periphery ideologists who have sought to erect a theoretical framework opposed to that of Marx and Lenin under the cover of 'Marxist analysis'. Has petty-bourgeois ideology right from the 1840s served any other purpose than that of providing support for bourgeois exploitation?

Lenin saw the danger that lay in the multiplication of the ranks of the petty-bourgeoisie after the 1880s. He noted that the petty-bourgeoisie had become the main bulwark for imperialism. This group increasingly joined the state institutions and particularly parliament, where through populism they fanned national sentiment in order to contain the working class within the confines of an imperialist policy. The split in the Second International was just such a manifestation of petty-bourgeois idealism and reformism. Lenin's castigation of the renegade Kautsky in his support of imperialism exposed the degeneration to which the revolutionary movement had been subjected by this petty-bourgeois ideology.

Much of the theorising about imperialism which is basically anti-Marxist-Leninist is provided by various groupings having their inspiration from Trotsky, Luxembourg and revisionists of the Bernstein and Kautsky period as well as their modern variants. Their theorising has produced more literature than revolutionary change. It has consisted in throwing slurs at those whose scientific analysis of concrete historical situations has led to revolutionary changes.

In our analysis we have shown that the problem of capitalist crisis was not seen by Marx as an end to capitalism *per se.* Marx clearly saw capitalist crisis as a 'danger signal' to the bourgeoisie to adjust. Marx went on to show that the bourgeoisie would restructure capitalism towards greater concentration in order to keep the system going. He was clear, however, that such options to adjust become more difficult with each passing crisis, leading to the overthrow of the system. He nowhere implied that such overthrow would occur on its own, by the 'collapse' of the system. *This was because the crisis was itself a product of the class struggle in the production process.* Any deepening crisis for capitalism also implied deepening class struggle. It did not follow that such class struggle was 'automatic'. It required organisation. So long as the class struggle remained at the trade union level without revolutionary political organisation to raise the political consciousness of the proletariat no 'collapse', 'breakdown', or overthrow of capitalism, could take place. All Marxist-Leninists thus emphasise the role of the professional revolutionary and the vanguard party.

Neo-Marxist theory condemns Marxists who are supposed to 'believe' in the collapse of capitalism 'on its own'. They do this in spite of the blunt fact that revolutions are taking place and imperialism is collapsing steadily but surely. They do this too because they have chosen to stay out of the mainstream of revolutionary practice and, being out of revolutionary practice, are incapable of seeing the reality. Being 'frustrated' by the working class in one situation or another, they end up prescribing one form of class struggle or another from the outside. Thus for example, we are told by Hamza Alavi that the theory of capitalist stagnation and not that of capitalist final crisis 'brings out the importance played by conscious struggle of the people in the establishment of socialism. The contradictions of capitalism will not necessarily do it for us', (1) as if capitalist contradiction and 'conscious struggle' are not a dialectical unity. Here capitalist crisis is counterposed to the 'conscious' class struggle.

Related to this question of capitalist crisis is the hostile attitude taken by petty-bourgeois opportunism towards the working class movement. In their theses the opportunists either argue, as the centre-periphery oppor-tunists do, that the working masses at the periphery are 'exploited' by the workers at the centre, or that because of the increasing super-profits from imperialist exploitation the workers at the centre are in a position to gain 'higher wages' than those at the periphery and that this is the basis of their political apathy and apparent defence of imperialism. For this reason, they postulate a kind of 'people's imperialism', which the working class in the centre defend against the exploited peoples in the colonies and semi-colonies. Hence they say we cannot talk of 'class solidarity' between the workers in the centre and those in the periphery. In this way the ideologue of 'unequal exchange', Emmanuel, states:

> 'The class is not a form of integration that takes precedence over the nation; this is proved by the fact that the Western working class appropriates to its own benefit part of the profits of exchange with the underdeveloped countries'. (2)

Samir Amin puts the same position in a slightly more sophisticated way. At one end of the scale he seems to suggest that because of the declining rate of profit in the centres a higher rate of surplus-value is called for, and since this is available at the periphery 'in relative terms, the proletariat of the periphery suffers an increasing degree of exploitation as compared with the proletariat at the centre'. (3) Yet at the other end of the scale it is suggested that this exploitation takes place because 'the objective mechanism which is the basis for the unity that links the bourgeoisie with its proletariat (which, it is not clear), a mechanism which limits exploitation at the centre, does not function in the extraverted periphery'. (4) As a result of the absence of this 'objective mechanism' in the periphery, the bourgeoisie at the centre although exploiting the proletariat and 'proletarianised masses' everywhere, 'exploits those of the periphery more violently and brutally'. (4) This lack of dialectical consistency in Amin's formulation leaves the whole concept of exploitation at an unscientific level, and places it in the area of morals. Mandel comes almost to the same moralising position when he suggests that the inflow of superprofits from underdeveloped countries to the metropole assists the rate of profit and 'also creates the possibility, on the basis of its monopoly of productivity, of ensuring for the workers of the metropolitan countries standards of living higher than those in the colonies'. (5)

It would be completely ahistorical to compare the 'labour aristocracy' under British free trade imperialism with the labour aristocracy under monopoly capitalism and the imperialism of monopolies, the imperialism under which the whole world except the capitalist world is colonised, an imperialism which brings the internationalisation of the class struggle nearer to reality. Under the latter imperialism, the role of the labour aristocracy becomes distinctively unique in the ideological struggle against the working class in the metropolitan country, serving to isolate that working class from the oppressed people in the colonies and to combat the proletariat's political leadership in the imperialist centre. The role of this aristocracy in all the working class movements is a real one. It disseminates bourgeois ideology with the aim of limiting the struggle of the working class by putting demands for higher wages and counterposing them to the political struggle of the working class, thus helping to de-escalate the movement towards political power. The numbers of this aristocracy have been increasing. Its chief detachments includes the *bureaucracy of the Social-Democratic Parties*, both at party level and within the state and

the *Trade Union bureaucracy*, who with the factory bourgeoisie control
the fate of individual workers. Together they decide who gets hired, who
gets fired and who gets promoted. To leave the union is tantamount to
losing the job.

In a study of the Ford Motor Industry in England, Huw Beynon shows
that the 'aristocracy' in these plants is responsible for the fact that although
the car workers have been at the centre of the class struggle, 'the struggle
has never extended beyond "guerrilla warfare". "Their battle has produced
no radical political demands. They have not been able to shift the basis
of the struggle from the effects to the causes — to an attack on causes —
to an attack upon the dominant logic of capitalist production'. (6)
Although they have fought against supervisors and the aristocracy this has
not resulted in any change:

> 'They have taken on the "bureaucrats" and they have taken on Ford.
> And they are still taking them on. For if the history of the car
> workers shows anything at all about the "new" working class it is
> that faced with the complete absence of any meaningful political
> leadership, workers will not lapse into inactivity and acquiescence.
> They will, to quote Bult again, "form their own organisations — or
> use existing ones — and fight over the issues that stare them in the
> face". For these workers experience the class struggle every day of
> their lives. If, in the way they cope with it, they would produce a
> politically confused situation that is just too bad. Radical intellec-
> tuals may put their hands to their heads in despair but that wont
> help either'. (7)

And this is the crux of the whole matter. So long as revolutionary
intellectuals turn to neo-Marxism and 'put their hands on their heads in
despair', or turn revisionist and seek to contain this struggle within a
parliamentary framework, there will be no revolutionary political movement in the imperialist centre. History demonstrates and Lenin emphasised
the point that *political consciousness* of the working class must come from
outside the working class itself, for the working class left on its own sinks
into economism. When our neo-Marxist friends 'despair', it is because they
have not grasped the central thesis of Marxism-Leninism on political
organisation of the working class, namely that a body of professional
revolutionaries who take the politics of the working class as their sole
concern must set up a party of the working class to bring it to true
consciousness of its own interests and organise it to sieze political power.
Marx, Lenin and others after them who have made revolutions and consolidated them did precisely that. As Lenin correctly emphasised:

> 'It is the task of the party to bring to the working class a true
> consciousness of its own interests, and to organise and lead the
> struggle for state power. In order to do this, the party must set
> itself the highest theoretical standards; it must wage a constant
> fight to defend the principles of Marxism and to develop an
> adequate understanding of the real conditions of society. Without
> this it will have no compass to guide its activities, but must of

necessity respond pragmatically to every new development in the
workers' movement and inevitably fall prey to bourgeois ideology'.
(8)

The petty-bourgeoisie, who constitute the bulk of neo-Marxists and
revisionists are not a new phenomenon in the mystification of reality. The
whole of Marx's polemic in *The Poverty of Philosophy*, Engels' defence
of Marxism in *Anti-Duhring* and other writings as well as Lenin's battle
against the Russian populists (Narodniks), reveal the historic role of this
'transitional' class. Marx correctly summed up their nature in *The Poverty
of Philosophy:*

> 'From head to foot M. Proudhon is the philosopher and economist
> of the petty-bourgeois. In an advanced society the petty-bourgeois is
> necessarily from his very position a socialist on the one side and an
> economist on the other; that is to say, he is dazed by the magnifi-
> cence of the big bourgeoisie and has sympathy for the sufferings of
> the people. He is at once both bourgeois and man of the people.
> Deep down in his heart he flatters himself that he is impartial and
> has found the right equillibrium, which claims to be something
> different from mediocrity. A petty-bourgeois of this type glorifies
> *contradiction* because contradiction is the basis of his existence. He
> is himself nothing but social contradiction in action'. (9)

No matter what form this sympathy takes, it is petty-bourgeois so long as
it mystifies reality, and plays the role of creating confusion in the ideology
of the working class. We are forced to conclude that neo-Marxism and
revisionism play such a role in the working class movement in the imperialist countries.

Having 'despaired' in the centre the neo-Marxists then turn to the
peasantry in the periphery in whom they now place their 'hopes'. Here the
idea is to show that since the proletariat in the centre has 'sold out', and
has joined the exploiters, the 'salvation of the revolution' lies with the
peasantry in the periphery. Jalee for a start goes as far as suggesting that
the 'acid test' of the anti-imperialist struggle is the struggle in the Third
World, since this is where the 'main contradiction' lies. (10) The centrist
neo-Marxists, Baran and Sweezy, in their 'analysis' of monopoly capital
ignore any role of the class struggle and the labour process in the centre,
on the apparent ground that the class struggle has been 'internationalised'
to the periphery:

> 'The revolutionary initiative against capitalism, which in Marx's
> day belonged to the proletariat in the advanced countries, has
> passed into the hands of the impoverished masses in the under-
> developed countries who are struggling to free themselves from
> imperialist domination and exploitation'. (11)

The peripherist neo-Marxist, Gundar Frank, also suggests that the
industrial proletariat in Latin America 'has been unionised by the (national)
bourgeoisie and has been politically tied to the same', and has become an
'ally of this bourgeoisie'. (12) Another peripherist Samir Amin, on the

basis of Lenin's statement in 1923 that the struggle in India and China, etc., in the last analysis will determine the outcome of the struggle against imperialism on account of the overwhelming majority of the population being in these countries, claims that Marx was wrong in having placed the 'essential nucleus of the proletariat at the centre'. Lenin's statement, according to Amin, 'signified that the *central nucleus of the proletariat* was henceforth no longer at the centre but in the periphery'. (13) For Amin this proletariat is not made up 'solely or even mainly of the wage-workers in large-scale modern enterprises', but included 'masses of peasants who, integrated into world exchanges, and who on that account pay, like the working class of the towns, the price of the unequal exchange that is reflected in the difference between rates of surplus-value at the centre and the periphery'. (13) Thus it can be seen that Samir Amin's 'proletariat' has nothing in common with the scientific concept of Marx and Lenin. His is a 'pure category', comprising all those who are paid 'unequally' through 'hidden transfers' perpetrated by the 'aggression' of the capitalist mode of production in the social formations of the periphery. These few examples demonstrate the eclecticism of neo-Marxism. In our view the struggles of the people in the colonial, semi-colonial and neo-colonial countries are part and parcel of the international proletarian struggle. The national democratic revolution forms part and parcel of that proletarian revolution since 1917. It is therefore of no avail to counterpose the revolutionary democratic struggles of the people of the Third World to the class struggle of the proletariat in the imperialist centres, or to subordinate the latter to the former.

To be sure, a clear understanding of the international proletarian revolution necessitates a proper characterisation of revolutionary strategies and tactics both in the imperialist countries and in the neo-colonial hinterland. Firstly what is the character of the revolution in the imperialist centres? Clearly this is a struggle between the metropolitan bourgeoisie and the proletariat in which the proletariat has first to settle accounts with its national bourgeoisie and financial oligarchy. It is therefore a revolution based on the fact that labour in these countries has established its power in production, through socialised production. Its power in production is clearly shown by the fact that labour always brings capitalist enterprise to a stop whenever it decides not to work. This power, however, is combated by the objectified power of capital by which the financial oligarchy through state power are able to subject labour to exploitation. In order for the working class to establish meaningful control over its labour, it must move to take political power to establish a socialist state.

On the other hand the struggle in the colonial, semi-colonial and neo-colonial countries, still under the domination of imperialism, requires different strategies and tactics. The true understanding of these requires a scientific study of the concrete revolutionary situations in which these struggles have been or are being waged in order to establish basic principles.

'Pure theory' will not do. Such study of concrete struggles necessitates a scientific analysis of the character of the revolution and a class analysis as well as the study of the concrete material condition in each of those countries. This is a basic Marxist/Leninist thesis.

In this manner we learn from Mao Tse-tung that the Chinese Revolution went through two phases: firstly, a bourgeois democratic revolution of a 'new type', the victory of which was to lead to the second phase, socialist revolution. This being the character of the revolution, what were the classes who pursued this revolution and against whom? These important questions of theory required a proper analysis. To Mao Tse-tung the chief targets and enemies in the first phase of the Chinese Revolution were imperialism and feudalism, the bourgeoisie of the imperialist countries and the landlord class of China. This was because China was a colonial, semi-colonial and semi-feudal country. The landlord class were enemies, being the main social base for imperialist rule in China and the class which used the feudal system to exploit and oppress the peasants. The comprador bourgeoisie, to the extent that they served imperialism and capitalists and were nurtured by them, also constituted a target of the revolution. The national bourgeoisie had a dual character. On the one hand, it was oppressed by imperialism and fettered by feudalism and hence was in contradiction with both. On the other hand, it lacked the courage to oppose imperialism and feudalism because it was 'economically and politically flabby' and still had economic ties with imperialism and feudalism. Thus, on the one hand, it was revolutionary while, on the other, it was counter-revolutionary. (14)

The main revolutionary force therefore was the proletariat whose main allies were the peasantry, who formed 80 % of the population, and sections of the petty-bourgeois, who constituted one of the motive forces of the revolution. The peasantry were subdivided into rich, middle and poor peasantry. The poor peasantry, forming with farm labourers 70 % of the rural population, constituted the 'biggest motive force . . . [the] natural and most reliable ally of the proletariat and the main contingent' (15) of the revolution. In spite of its smallness, its youth, and its low level of education, the Chinese proletariat remained 'the basic motive force' of the Chinese Revolution, since it was subjected to a three fold oppression, that of the imperialists, bourgeoisie and feudalists. (15) It is on the basis of this scientific analysis that the Chinese revolution succeeded and moved into its second phase, consolidation by the proletariat.

Another concrete situation where a revolution in a colonial, then neo-colonial, country has succeeded is Vietnam. Here the revolutionary leaders categorised the revolution in two phases as well. According to the *Political Thesis* of 1930, which was promulgated on the founding of the Vietnamese Workers' Party, it was pointed out that the Vietnamese revolution 'must go through two stages: first, the national democratic revolution; then a direct passage to socialist revolution, by-passing the stage of capitalist development'. (16) The task was to liberate the country from colonialism, thus posing the national liberation struggle as its initial stage. It was to be directed against French colonialism and imperialism. What were the classes which would take on this task? According to Le Duan, the first crucial problem of the revolution was 'correctly and fully to assert the *leading role of the working class*'. (17) President Ho Chi Minh had said: *'The working class* is the most courageous and revolutionary class which un-flinchingly and fearlessly stands up to the colonialists and imperialists'. Then the peasantry was analysed as the most active opponent of feuda-lism and imperialism. It comprised 90 % of the population. Thus the task of national liberation was essentially a task of peasant liberation from two-fold oppression of feudalism and imperialism. Though exploited, the peasantry possesses no ideology of its own to confront imperialism; therefore the worker-peasant alliance is the very basis of a National United Front.

Vietnam emerged with a 'flabby national bourgeoisie'. Restricted and dominated by imperialism, it was considered patriotic in some respects, and accordingly given a role in the struggle for national independence. The petty-bourgeoisie provided a revolutionary vanguard of intellectuals and students (though not a class) who joined in the struggle against colonia-lism and imperialism. The struggle against neo-colonialism in the south of the country established a similar alliance on the basis of which victory was won.

The situation in the other two Indo-Chinese countries of Cambodia and Laos followed a generally similar approach, although with variations in tactics. All succeeded on the basis of a two-phased struggle implying broad class alliances at first. Without a proletarian vanguard, the national democratic revolution could not be won and consolidated.

Petty-bourgeois theorising that abstracts the idea of revolution and absolutises a single historical experience in detail only serves to encourage adventurism. In the above four concrete historical experiences we note two important facts upon which a principle could be postulated. All involved an element of the *national question*, and all permitted of a *worker-peasant alliance* with a broad united front incorporating elements of the 'national bourgeoisie' and petty-bourgeoisie, at least in the first phase. The principle to be derived here is that the national question is an important element in the struggle of the colonial, semi-colonial and neo-colonial peoples against imperialism and reactionary forces of society and that because of this a broad alliance of class forces opposed to imperialism under the leadership of the proletariat is possible. This is because imperialism makes it impossible for these countries to establish independent nations. To the extent that such independence is ideologically desirable even to the bourgeoisie, the latter can be utilised at appropriate stages of the struggle. The establishment of an independent nation in these countries is also the only basis upon which socialist construction is possible. To counterpose the national democratic revolution to the socialist revolution in colonial, semi-colonial and neo-colonial countries is therefore petty-bourgeois. This is precisely what Gundar Frank does.

According to Frank, 'the immediate enemy of national liberation in Latin America is the native bourgeoisie . . . and the local bourgeoisie in . . . the countryside'. (18) This is so, according to him also in Asia and Africa 'not withstanding that strategically the principal enemy undoubtedly is imperialism'. (18) He prescribes a socialist revolution directly for these countries. Thus according to him the anti-imperialist struggle in these countries must be on the basis of 'class struggle'. This is because:

> 'Popular mobilization against the immediate class enemy on the national and local levels produces a stronger confrontation with the principal imperialist enemy than does direct anti-imperialist mobilization. Nationalist mobilization through political alliance of the broadest anti-imperialist forces does not adequately challenge the immediate class enemy, and generally it does not even result in a real confrontation of the imperialist enemy. This also applies to the neo-colonial countries of Asia and Africa and perhaps to some colonial countries, unless they are already militarily occupied by imperialism'. (19)

To support his thesis Frank then goes on to give examples from Cuba and the October Revolution as well as the 'constitutionalist struggle' in Santo Domingo, where the 'tactial' class struggle 'took precedence' over the 'strategic' anti-imperialist struggle.

Here clearly Frank reveals considerable confusion. He seems to suggest that the 'strategic' anti-imperialist struggle is not part of the class struggle! Furthermore his prescription of 'tactical' class struggle appears to be aimed merely at producing 'challenge' to the immediate enemy and 'confrontation' with imperialism, the implication being that 'strategic' anti-imperialist struggle cannot produce such confrontation but he does cite Santo Domingo's 'constitutionalist' struggle, where the initial attack against the 'immediate enemy' produced confrontation from imperialism, despite the fact that there were no initial 'military occupation by imperialism'.

We have shown throughout our analysis that since the colony, semi-colony and neo-colony has no significant 'national capital' of its own, it follows that a 'national bourgeoisie' based on this 'national capital', whether private or public, is bound to be subservient to imperialism, since their 'national industry' is objectively an integral part of monopoly enterprise in the sense that it serves it. The financial oligarchies of the imperialist countries, through exports of finance capital, have centralised the 'national capitals' to suit their global needs. To this extent the 'national bourgeoisie' and its 'national capital' serve the objective interest of the monopolies.

In fact in many African, Asian and Latin American countries the 'national bourgeoisie' is either non-existent, very 'flabby', or subservient. In many of them a *comprador* bourgeoisie exists. In others where a 'national bourgeoisie' had arisen due to favourable circumstances in the 1860s, 1930s etc., it soon became subordinated to finance capital. We assert that although this 'national bourgeoisie' *objectively* serves monopoly interests, it nevertheless has a contradiction with imperialism and finance capital, because it is precisely this domination by finance capital that makes it impossible for it to emerge fully as a national bourgeoisie. This therefore is a *subjective* contradiction, because, as we maintain, historically no conditions exist for its emergence as such a bourgeoisie. Such 'national bourgeoisies' can thus be patriotic and support the struggle against imperialism, while at the same time veering away from it, since their *objective* interest steers them towards imperialism. This is why in the second phase of the struggle this bourgeoisie becomes an enemy to the socialist order.

Our conclusion is that the struggle against imperialism in the imperialist country must be based on the correct strategy of the working class. Reformist measures based on the 'welfare state' are intended to create favourable conditions for the continued exploitation of the working class and not to benefit it. It is the role of the revolutionary vanguard to pass on the political consciousness to the proletariat. It is not the fault of the proletariat if this political consciousness is not forthcoming. The blame lies with the vanguard wherever it purportedly exists. If the vanguard fails, bourgeois ideology, as the very antithesis of proletarian political consciousness, continues to dominate.

In the colonial, semi-colonial and neo-colonial countries, a two-phased struggle historically offers the best chances of success. In this way the struggles of the working class in the imperialist centre and the colonial, semi-colonial and neo-colonial hinterland support one another. On this basis, the end of imperialism is assured, and not otherwise. In the historical unfolding of this struggle advantage must be taken of the 'weakest link' in the chain of imperialism as Stalin pointed out. Whether this weak link be in an advanced capitalist country, a backward capitalist country or in the colonial, semi-colonial and neo-colonial hinterland will depend on the concrete situation in each country; and this concrete situation is itself determined by the interplay between the objective conditions and subjective conditions. Indeed in our view such weak links exist in many countries of Southern Europe. Many 'weak moments' in these countries have been wasted by lack of political organisation and ideological vigilance. In France, 1968 was such a moment and the country is still a weak link, but what do we get from the 'vanguard' of the French proletariat? We have recently a 'new thesis' which abandons the dictatorship of the proletariat as the aim and creates a 'national party' out of the original vanguard party, thus favourably responding to the national-chauvinism of the French bourgeoisie. In Italy too a weak link exists and the incapability of the bourgeoisie to rule has been demonstrated. In Portugal revisionism and Trotskyism have clearly shown how weak links can be lost to the proletarian cause through adventurism and capitulationism. Spain, one of the weakest of the links, is crying out after Franco's death for proletarian revolution. All these countries and others in the centres do possess the objective conditions and what is lacking are the subjective conditions which a proletarian vanguard must provide.

Having regard to the fact that imperialism is in decline, the role of proletarian ideology and the struggle for political power becomes the only item on the agenda for the proletariat and those exploited by imperialist domination, whether this be in the centre or Third World; in this the ideological struggle must take precedence and organisation must assist this ideological struggle — the sole objective being the seizure of political power by the proletariat, signalling the end of imperialism.

REFERENCES

1. H. Alavi, *Imperialism: Old and New* in *Socialist Register*, Merlin, (London, 1964).
2. A. Emmanuel, *Unequal Exchange*, New Left Books, (London, 1972), p.183.
3. S. Amin, *Accumulation on World Scale*, Monthly Review, (New York, 1973), p.25.
4. S. Amin, op. cit. Vol. II p.600.
5. E. Mandel, *Marxist Economic Theory*, Merlin, (London, 1973), p.479.
6. Huw Beynon, *Working for Ford*, Penguin, (London, 1974), pp.317-8.
7. Huw Beynon, op. cit. p.319.
8. V.I. Lenin, *What Is To Be Done?* various eds.
9. K. Marx, *The Poverty of Philosophy*, op. cit. p.167.
10. P. Jalee, *Imperialism in the Seventies*, op. cit. p.
11. Baran & Sweezy, *Monopoly Capital*, op. cit. p.22.
12. Gundar Frank, 'Who Is The Immediate Enemy?', in James D. Cockcroft, Andre G. Frank, and Dale L. Johnson (Editors), *Dependence and Underdevelopment*, Penguin, (London, 1972), pp.429-30.
13. S. Amin, *Accumulation on a World Scale*, op. cit. Vol I pp.25-6. Emphasis in original.
14. Mao Tse-tung, *The Chinese Revolution and the Chinese Communist Party* in *Selected Works* Vol. II, (Peking, 1954), pp.315/320.
15. Mao Tse-tung, op. cit. pp.320/324.
16. Le Duan, *The Vietnamese Revolution — Fundamental Problems, Essential Tasks*, (Hanoi, 1973), p.21.
17. Le Duan, op. cit. p.28.
18. G. Frank, 'Who Is The Immediate Enemy?', op. cit. p.425.
19. G. Frank, op. cit. pp.425/26.

APPENDIX FOR THE SECOND EDITION

We want to take advantage of the second edition to expand the argument at certain crucial points in the text.

The following addendum is an addition to page 111 in the text as marked.

It has been suggested by some "neo-Marxists" that the increasing concentration of production enabled the resultant monopolies to develop some amount of independence from banks. One of these writers is P.A. Sweezy, who, in his book on the *Theory of Capitalist Development*, asserts that after this level of concentration of capital, the monopoly begins to rely more and more on its own reserves. He says:

> 'When this stage has been reached the position of the banks undergoes a sharp change. The function of issuing new securities, on which their power was originally founded becomes much less important. The large monopolistic corporations find themselves, in direct proportion to their resources (i.e., profitability), in possession of internal resources of funds, not only in the form of profits which can be accumulated instead of being distributed as dividends to shareholders, but also in the form of depreciation, depletion, obsolescence, and other so-called 'reserve' accounts which are to an ever increasing extent turned to the purpose of accumulation. With these internal sources of additional capital at their disposal, corporate managements are to a greater or less extent freed from dependence on the market for new securities as a source of capital, and by the same token they are freed from their dependence on bankers'.[1]

This is a misconception because not all enterprises become monopolies. The role of banks therefore continues unabated in centralising capital and putting it out. Moreover, monopolies cannot finance *all* their activities from internal sources. Finance capital implies a certain amount of coalescence of banks and industry and the oligarchy that arises is able to command larger capitals through this process of concentration and centralisation of capital. It would appear that although Sweezy is alive to the distinction between Hilferding's and Lenin's definitions of finance capital, the misconception still persists for him. The concept of 'finance capital' is important for the proper understanding of the relationship between banks and industry. In his emphasis on 'finance capital' as capital controlled by the banks and utilized by the industrialists, Hilferding tended to elevate this type of capital to a position above industrial capital. Sweezy regards this phenomenon as 'merely a passing phase from competitive capitalism to monopoly capitalism'. He states: 'Bank capital, having had its day of glory, falls back again to a position subsidiary to industrial capital, thus re-establishing the relation which existed prior to the combination movement'. And it is in this connection that Lenin criticised Hilferding's definition:

> 'This definition is incomplete insofar as it is silent on one extremely important fact — on the increase of concentration of production and

> of capital to such an extent that concentration is leading, and has led to monopoly. . . *The concentrating of production, the monopolies arising there – from, the merging and coalescence of the banks with industry – such is the history of the rise of finance capital and such is the content of that concept'.*[2]

Thus we see that this concept is much wider than Sweezy would care to accept as his is in collision with Lenin's concept of 'finance capital'. For our purposes here and specifically for this period, the role of the banks is pronounced in its power of concentration and of creating a merger of bank capital and industrial capital.

Second Addendum

The second addendum is an addition to page 180.

This evidence cited by Menshikov in Table VI on page 179 disproves once for all bourgeois and 'neo-Marxist' theories, which throw doubt on Lenin's analysis of concentration of bank capital and its relationship with industrial capital; the role of the 'financial oligarchy'; and the supremacy of finance capital over all other forms of capital in the post-war period. Pierre Jalee for instance points out that the relationship between finance capital and industrial capital has 'since the Second World War . . . undergone radical changes'[3] and concludes:

> 'The result of this is that industrial capital is now a self-starting enterprise; the hegemony of finance capital is no longer as absolute as it once was. Finance capital is defending its position. Industrial capital meanwhile, is breaking through old barriers, pushing its way into the investment business and engaging in banking and financial activities. Ultimately, the two are merging and becoming largely interdependent. The oligarchy remains and, through this pincer movement grows stronger as it unifies its functions. It begins to be a financial and industrial oligarchy'.[4]

This analysis quite clearly reveals a certain amount of confusion. It is ahistorical. It does not tell us when the battle lines between the two capitals were drawn and why the 'pincer' battles should have begun in the first place. It also misconceives Lenin's concept of 'finance capital', which has nothing to do with Hilferding's. Moreover it would appear that Jalee mistakes finance capital with bank capital. The quote is in line with Sweezy's analysis which we referred to in Chapter X, which suggests relative independence of monopoly industrial capital from finance capital. It has become characteristic of 'neo-Marxists' to quote Marx or Lenin out of context in order to argue against them and in order to show that they are making an 'original contribution'. Jalee's quote above is such an example.

To be sure, and this was the point of departure with Hilferding, Lenin pointed out that the concept of finance capital must be that in which concentration of production and capital has led to monopoly, in which banks and monopoly industry *merge and coalesce.* This concept is different from Hilferding's in which finance capital is seen as capital controlled by banks and employed by industrialists. The quote from Lenin which Jalee puts across as justifying his analysis is presented out of context. Lenin here was referring to the characteristic feature of capitalism as being one in which ownership of capital is separated from its application to production, in which the rentier who lives by clipping coupons from his money capital is separated from the entrepreneur and those directly involved in the management of capital. This analysis summarises the historical experience of competitive capitalism. He then continues:

> 'Imperialism or the domination of finance capital over all other forms of capital is that highest stage of capitalism in which this separation reaches vast proportions. The supremacy of finance capital over all other forms of capital means the predominance of the rentier and of the financial oligarchy; it means that a small number of financially 'powerful' states stand out among all the rest'.[5]

Here, by finance capital and financial oligarchy, Lenin must be understood to mean the merger and coalescence of bank capitalists and industrial capitalists. The rentiers are still many and protected by the oligarchy. The latter dominate the other capitals of small capitalists and even savings of the working population because the power to centralise these capitals belongs to them. The evidence cited by Menshikov proves this and the long report already referred to from U.S. News and World Report confirm this analysis of Lenin. This power is even more pronounced when the financial oligarchy extends its tentacles to the neo-colony. Here 'national capital' including all savings of the workers and peasants are increasingly brought under control and utilised for the production needs of monopoly, thus negating any possible development in these countries. This fact is obscured in Jalee's analysis.

Jalee in proof of his 'thesis' relies on an eclectic collection of data from Andre Piettre, B. Lelievre, J.K. Galbraith and E. Varga, etc., which he does not synthesize. For instance, he relies on the fact that whereas in the whole of the 19th century credit, savings and property advanced together in the same direction; savings were directed more readily into the capital of business enterprises; credit was extended with more frequency to the same enterprises for working capital, but that this has now changed. Savings are no longer readily directed to 'business' enterprises, instead 'business' is generating its own 'savings' and financing itself out of its own profits. He quotes figures from Piettre for the period 1962-64 as showing that the average rate of reinvested profits in the private sector was 99.3 per cent in the U.S., 109 per cent in Great Britain, 79 per cent in West Germany, and 61.8 per cent in France.[6] He also quotes Galbraith as confirming that in 1965 personal savings in the U.S. totalled 25 billion dollars, while 'business' savings, 'which include mainly the savings of big companies', rose to 83 billion dollars, or 'more than three times as much as personal savings'. Paradoxically, he then cites other evidence from the same Piettre as showing that in France in 1966 'business' financed itself to the extent of about 45 per cent from banks in short term loans, 13 per cent medium and 20 per cent long term; while reinvestments and securities were 22 per cent. While in the U.S. in 1966, 36 billion dollars were in long term loans (from banks) and 59 million re-investment. These figures are incomplete but show a sizeable amount of loan capital. Jalee further cites Varga, who in concluding that in the post-war period 'industrial monopolies have become more or less independent of the banks' was in actual fact discussing Hilferding.

Jalee then tries to show that today's mergers are of the 'conglomerate type'. He shows that 70 per cent of such mergers in the U.S. are of this type. He cites evidence from Schneider monopoly as showing that 43 per cent of the group's assets were non-industrial and invested in banks, real estate and finance; and Muchelin holding company as controlling 100 per cent of the Compagnie Financiere Michelin. In Italy he cites the Fiat holding company as managing a portfolio of which 21 per cent is in banking and finance. He then concludes that a number of these holding companies 'are taking a path diametrically opposed to the one Lenin described' for according to him, 'instead of being taken over by banks, they are becoming like banks themselves'.

> 'The result of all this is that big businesses now have their own internal, self-generating momentum, that they grow mainly through re-investment, that their undistributed profits often permit them to turn themselves into conglomerates or holding companies and even become sources of finance. In a word, industrial capital tends to free itself from finance capital'.[7]

Jalee then cites evidence from a U.S. House of Representatives committee of 1968 which shows that large U.S. banks 'are unaffected by the anti-trust legislation', and that they control 607 billion dollars in assets, 'or 60 per cent of the total institutional investment'. Insurance companies, the second largest source of investment after banks, only possess 162 billion dollars in assets. He continues:

> 'The report adds that 49 banks control 5 per cent or more capital of the 147 largest industrial companies as well as 5 per cent or more of the capital of the 17 most important merchandising companies and the 17 biggest transport companies'.[8]

He quotes the committee as concluding that because of the widespread distribution of capital, these 5 per cent interests are enough to control many boards of directors.

All this data which Jalee quotes supports Lenin's thesis of the inter-locking character and merger of bank capital and industrial capital. *Both these two monopoly situations are what Lenin calls finance capital and the financial oligarchy.* To Jalee this is a profound discovery of his. Industrial capital cannot free itself from finance capital because it is part of finance capital which is a merger of bank and industrial, both of which are under the control of the financial oligarchy.

In refutation of this 'self-finance' ideology which is widely current among both bourgeois and 'neo-Marxist' writers,[9] Menshikov [10] produces more convincing data to demonstrate that there is no 'radical change in the share of self-financing'. Giving calculations based on publications of U.S. Department of commerce, he shows that the share of long-term *external* sources of finance (among which he includes stocks, bonds, and bank credits) as amounting to 25 per cent on the average in 1949-54 and to 22 per cent in 1955-60. After a decline to 19 per cent in 1961-65, their share rose to 24 per cent in 1966. If, however, *all* external sources are taken (including commercial loans, money accumulated for payment of taxes but temporarily not spent) the share was 40 per cent in 1955-60, 32 per cent in 1961-65 and 40 per cent in 1966.[11] The above data is then compared to the data collected by W.F. Payne which show that the relationship between long-term operations on the money market (i.e., long-term debt and stocks) on the one hand, and investments on the other, from 1921 to 1956 were as follows:

Year	Per cent
1921-29	23.7
1930-39	7.3
1946-50	13.8
1951-56	19.3

This ratio shows that except for the years 1930-39, and to a lesser extent in 1946-50, external sources on long-term operations were on the average 22 per cent, a level which compares very well with the data of the U.S. Department already cited.

In order to give a more complete picture, Menshikov cites other data given by S. Kuznets which reveals that the share of external sources in the financing of large corporations in the manufacturing industry was 33 per cent in 1946-53 compared with 40 per cent in 1915-19 and 30 per cent in 1900-10. As compared to this, the share of *internal* sources in the total expenditure of all corporations was 56 per cent in 1946-56. In subsequent years it never exceeded 70 per cent and 'most often was about 60 per cent'. Mensikov concludes:

> 'Despite the difference in individual estimates, one thing is characteristic of all of them: the absence of any radical change in the share of self-financing ... Evidently, the only serious grounds for talk about a growth in self-financing was the slump of the money market in the 1930s and its incomplete recovery in the 1940s. But at the beginning of the 1950s the situation did not radically differ from that in the first third of the century. Thus, the thesis about the wane of 'external financing' does not correspond to the facts'.[12]

This irrefutably disposes of this argument. It would have been surprising for an industrial capitalist enterprise to pressure on its own resources for long-term operations, more so a monopoly. The tendency is for them as Menshikov correctly points out, to strive to break out beyond the narrow confines of its own money accumulation. It is compelled to do so by competition to renew equipment, to expand sales and to concentrate production. Moreover, the corporate form that the capitalist enterprise takes impels it to take part in operations of the money and stock markets, since its own shares would have been issued on the open market mainly through banks.

The figures which Jalee quotes from Piettre and Galbraith are inconclusive. Those from Piettre merely show the share of re-invested profits, but not the share of internal financing in relation to external sources. Moreover, this for only one year. Galbraith's figures only show the magnitudes of personal savings and retained savings of 'businesses'. Again only for one year. No comparison with any other period is made for both sets of figures. Jalee conceals the power of the financial oligarchy over these personal savings in his argument, although the evidence he cites proves this conclusively. The point he makes about holding companies and conglomerates only goes to prove Lenin. Nowhere did Lenin argue that holding companies were being taken over by the banks nor did he argue that conglomerates would not arise. On the contrary he argued that through the 'holding company' technique a handful of monopolists are able to acquire controlling interests in subsidiaries ('daughter companies'). He gives 40 per cent as sufficient to exercise control. Jalee gives evidence of 5 per cent as being sufficient to exercise control. This if anything proves the contrary of what Jalee wants to prove.

Jalee moreover makes no serious point when he plays on the distinctions between commercial banks, merchants banks, trust funds or mutual banks. Actually the manifestation of these different institutions reflect the specialisation of these various institutions and their competition for a share of the total sum of capital and savings under the concentration. The concentration of the various banking institutions into monopolies has already been alluded to and has, since Lenin wrote, further developed unabated. What this concentration and the competition between these monopolistic specialised institutions reveal is the power of the oligarchy to centralise the capitals and savings of other capitalists and working people, including pensions. This is in line with the historical trail of capitalist expropriation. It begins in embryo in the feudal womb as the expropriator of the producers and their means of production and turns them into a proletariat. Under monopoly it continues the exploitation of the proletariat but begins to expropriate the smaller capitalists who join the proletariat. As the bigger monopolies — the 'world corps' — appear, even the smaller monopolies are swallowed up. This is enabled by finance capital. The huge wealth of the oligarchy is just a small portion of the total wealth of society, but through the power of finance capital — the power to command bank and industrial capital merged or coalesced — enables this control through a '5 per cent controlling interest'. According to Menshikov; the corporate form prevailing in American industry enables the finance – capitalists to dispose of the greater part of the productive capacity in industry by holding a controlling block of shares, which as a rule comprise a small part of the total capital of corporations:

> 'Thus, the corporate form as such suggests the possibility of the conversion of the finance-capitalist into the omnipotent manager and administrator of the nation's productive forces'.[13]

In this way, in a single year 1965, the owned capital of 50 largest commercial banks in the U.S. were $10,300 million but these commanded deposits amounting to $132,200 million or 12.3 times greater than the owned capital. 'This shows that the ability of capital invested in banking to attract other people's capital and utilise it as its own is at least several times greater than the similar ability of capital invested in industry'.[14]

Menshikov goes further to show that any decrease in external financing would not be tantamount to a decline in the share of banking institutions in providing industry with free money capital. He shows that this would depend on what proportion of the securities of industrial corporations issued for sale are bought by banks, insurance companies and other financial institutions themselves and what part is resold to individual investors. He shows that in the post-war period a practice arose where new fictitious capital was formed mainly through the issue of bonds which were bought almost entirely by banking institutions themselves. With this in view it may be said that the share of external financing is rising. If to this development is added the intensive buying up of stocks by insurance and investment companies and also by pension funds, philanthropic foundations and trust departments of commercial banks, the magnitudes would increase. He quotes figures from Kuznets to show that in fact there has been fantastic growth in the 'might of finance capital', in the post-war years. The share of the banking institutions in 'external financing' is much higher than ever in the 20th century except for the 1930s. The share of banking institutions in total of industrial corporations *increased* as compared with any past period, not withstanding the fact that the share of 'self-financing in the total outlays was below the maximum registered in the 1920s'.[15] Even if it were to be maintained that there has been a considerable increase in self-financing by the large corporations it would have to be shown that this is not a quantitative phenomon but a qualitative one, which unfortunately Jalee or any other person has not been able to show.

FOOTNOTES TO THE ADDENDA

1. P.A. Sweezy, *The Theory of Capitalist Development*, Monthly Review, (New York, 1942), p.267-68.
2. V.I. Lenin, *Imperialism: The Highest Stage of Capitalism*, Progress, (Moscow, 1970), p.46.
3. P. Jalee, *Imperialism in the Seventies*, Third Press, (New York, 1974), p.122.
4. *Ibid.*, pp.134-35.
5. V.I. Lenin, *op. cit.*, p.58.
6. P. Jalee, *op. cit.*, pp.121-122.
7. *Ibid.*, p.128.
8. *Ibid.*, p.129.
9. See also P.A. Sweezy, *The Theory of Capitalist Development*, Monthly Review, (New York, 1942), p.267; and P.A. Baran and P.A. Sweezy, *Monopoly Capital*, Penguin, (Harmondsworth, 1966), pp.29-30; and also K.J. Tabruck in his Introduction at pp.35-60 to R. Luxemburg and N. Bukharin, *Imperialism and the Accumulation of Capital*, Allen Lane, (London, 1972).
10. S. Menshikov, *Millionaires and Managers*, Progress, (Moscow, 1969), pp.191-199.
11. *Ibid.*, p.191.
12. *Ibid.*, pp.192-193.
13. *Ibid.*, p.136.
14. *Ibid.*, p.138.
15. *Ibid.*, p.198.

BIBLIOGRAPHY

1. H. Alavi, 'Imperialism Old and New', in R.A. Milliband and J. Saville (eds.) 1964 *Socialist Register*, Merlin Press.
2. S. Amin, *Accumulation on a World Scale*, 1973, Monthly Review, New York.
3. P. Anderson, *Passages from Antiquity to Feudalism*, 1974, New Left Books, London.
4. P. Anderson, *Lineages of the Absolutist State*, 1974, New Left Books, London.
5. P. Anderson, 'Portugal and the End of Ultra-Colonialism', *NLR*, issues 15, 16 and 17.
6. G. Arrighi, 'International Corporations, Labour Aristocracies and Economic Development in Tropical Africa', in R.I. Rhodes (ed.), *Imperialism and Underdevelopment: A Reader*, 1970, Monthly Review Press, New York.
7. G. Bannock, *The Juggernault*, 1973, Penguin, London.
8. P. Baran, *Political Economy of Growth*, Monthly Review Press, 1957, New York.
9. P. Baran and P.M. Sweezy, *Monopoly Capital*, 1966, Penguin, London.
10. G. Barraclough, *An Introduction to Contemporary History*, 1967, Penguin, London.
11. M. Barratt Brown, *After Imperialism*, 1970, Merlin, London.
12. M. Barratt Brown, *Economics of Imperialism*, 2nd Ed. 1974, Penguin, London..
13. R.J. Barnet, *Intervention and Revolution*, 1972, Paladin, London.
14. C.B. Bastable, *The Commerce of Nations*, 9th Ed. 1923, Methuen, London.
15. J.D. Bernal, *Science in History*, 1965, Penguin, Vol. I & IV, London.
16. M.D. Bernstein, *Foreign Investments in Latin America*, (1966), 1969 reprint, Knopf, New York.
17. H. Bernstein, *Underdevelopment and Development*, 1973, Penguin, London.
18. C. Bettelheim, 'Critical Comments', in A. Emmanuel, *Unequal Exchange*, 1972, New Left Books, London.
19. H. Beynon, *Working for Ford*, 1974, Penguin, London.
20. C.R. Boxer, *The Portuguese Sea-borne Empire, 1415-1825*, 1969, Penguin, London.
21. N. Bukharin, *Imperialism and the Accumulation of Capital*, see Tarbuck (Editor) below.
22. N. Bukharin, *Imperialism and World Economy*, 1973, Monthly Review, New York.
23. Butterfield, 'The Scientific Revolution', pamphlet from an article in *Scientific American Journal*, Sept. 1960.
24. A.K. Cairncross, *Home and Foreign Investment, 1870-1913*, 1953,

Cambridge University Press, Cambridge.

25. E.H. Carr, *What is History?* Penguin, London, 1964.

26. C.M. Cipolla, (Editor) *The Fontana Economic History of Europe*, 1973, Vol. II, Penguin, London.

27. Cockcroft, Frank & Johnson (Editors). *Dependence and Underdevelopment*, 1972, Penguin, London.

28. G. Curzon, *Multilateral Commerical Diplomacy*, 1965, Michael Joseph, London.

29. M.H. Dobb, *Studies in the Development of Capitalism*, 1946, Routledge & Kegan Paul, London.

30. Dobb & Sweezy, *Transition from Feudalism to Capitalism*, 1967, Symposium, New York.

31. J.H. Dunning, (Ed.) *International Investment*, 1972, Penguin, London.

32. R.P. Dutt, *India Today*, 1940, Golancz, London.

33. W.A. Dymsza, *The Multinational Business Strategy*, 1972, McGraw Hill, New York.

34. Economic Commission for Africa: *The Multinational Corporations in 1973*, Africa.

35. Edwards, Reicn, Welsskopf, *The Capitalist System*, 1972, Prentice-Hall, Englewood Cliffs, New Jersey.

36. *European Community and the United States*, E.C. Pamphlet, 1972, New York.

37. R. Emerson, *The Unites States and Africa*, 1963, Praeger, New York.

38. A. Emmanuel, *Unequal Exchange*, 1972, New Left Books, London.

39. A. Emmanuel, 'White Settler Colonialism and the Myth of Investment Imperialism', *New Left Review*, No. 73, May-June, 1972.

40. F. Engels, *The Origin of the Family, Private Property and the State*, in Marx and Engels, Selected Works, Vol. III, 1972, Progress, Moscow.

41. F. Engels, *The Condition of the Working Class in England*, 1973, Progress, Moscow.

42. F. Engels, *Outlines of a Critique of Political Economy*, in K. Marx, *Economic and Philosophic Manuscripts of 1844*, 1974, Progress, Moscow.

43. H. Feis, *Europe the World's Banker 1870-1914*, 1964, Yale University Press, Yale.

44. D.K. Fieldhouse, *Theory of Capitalist Imperialism*, 1967, Longman, London.

45. A.G. Frank, 'The Development of Underdevelopment', *Monthly Review*, September, 1966.

46. A.G. Frank, *Capitalism and Underdevelopment in Latin America*, revised edn, 1971, Penguin, London.

47. A.G. Frank, *Latin America: Underdevelopment, or Revolution*, 1969, Monthly Review Press, New York.

47. E. Galeano, *Open Veins of Latin America*, 1973, Monthly Review, New York.

49. J. Gallagher & R.E. Robinson, *Africa and the Victorians*, 1953, MacMillan, London.

50. L.C. Gardner, *Economic Aspects of New Deal Diplomacy*, 1964, Madison, University of Wisconsin.

51. GATT, *Trends in International Trade*, 1958, Geneva.

52. GATT, *International Trade*, 1970, Geneva.

53. R.N. Gardner, *The Sterling Dollar Diplomacy*, 1969, McGraw Hill, New York.

54. GATT, *Text of the General Agreement on Tariffs & Trade*, 1969, Geneva.

55. M. Gibbs, *Feudal Order*, 1949, London.

56. N. Girvan, 'Dependence and Underdevelopment in the New World and the Old'. *ISER* Vol. 22, No. 1, 1973.

57. Felix Green, *The Enemy*, 1970, Cape, London.

58. K. Goveh, H.P. Sharma, *Imperialism in South East Asia*, 1973, Monthly Review, New York.

59. G. Haberlier, *The Theory of International Trade*, 1936, Dodge & Co, London.

60. J. Halliday & J. McCormack, *Japanese Imperialism Today*, 1973, Penguin, London.

61. A. Hamilton, *Report on Manufactures*, in H.C. Lodge (ed.), *The Works of Alexander Hamilton*, New York. 1885.

62. Hornel Hart, *The Techniques of Social Progress*, 1931, Henry Holf & Co., New York.

63. Hillary Rose & Steven Rose, *Science and Society*, 1969, Penguin, London.

64. R. Hilferding, *Finance Capital*, Vorwarts, 1923, Vienna.

65. E. Hobsbawm, *Industry and Empire*, 1969, Penguin, London.

66. J.A. Hobson, *Imperialism. A Study*, 1938, Allen & Unwin, first published 1902, London.

67. L. Huberman, *Man's Worldly Goods*, Monthly Review, 1940, New York.

68. D. Hume, *Essays and Treatise on Several Subjects*, (1793) Vol. III.

69. S. Hymer, 'Robinson Crusoe and the Secret of Primitive Accumulation', *Monthly Review*, Vol. 23, No.4, September, 1971.

70. A.H. Imlah, *Economic Elements in the Pax Britannica*, 1958, Harvard University Press, Cambridge, Mass.

71. International Labour Organisation: *Employment, Income and Equality in Kenya*, 1972, ILO.

72. P. Jalee, *Imperialism in the Seventies*, 1974, Third Press, New York.

73. L.H. Jenks, *The Migration of British Capital*, 1927, Knopf, New York.

74. A.M. Kamarch, *The Economics of African Development*, 1971, Praeger, New York.

75. E. Kaufever, *In a Few Hands*, 1966, Penguin, London.

76. G. Kay, *Development and Underdevelopment*, 1975, MacMillan, London.

77. T. Kemp, *Theories of Imperialism*, 1967, Dobson, London.

78. J.M. Keynes, *The Economic Consequences of the Peace*, 1920, MacMillan, London.

79. M. Kidron, *Western Capitalism Since the War*, 1969, Penguin, London.

80. C.P. Kindleberger, *International Economics*, 1973, Irwin, Homewood, Ill.

81. A. Kirsanov, *The USA and Western Europe*, 1975, Progress, Moscow.

82. L.C.A. Knowles, *Economic Development in the 19th Century*, Routledge & Sons, London.

83. E. Laclau, 'Feudalism and Capitalism in Latin America', *New Left Review*, No. 67, 1971, May-June.

84. Leduan, *The Vietnamese Revolution — Fundamental Problems, Essential Tasks*, 1973, Hanoi.

85. V.I. Lenin, *On the So-called Marxist Question* in *Collected Works*, Vol. I. 1970, Progress, Moscow.

86. V.I. Lenin, *Imperialism — The Highest Stage of Capitalism*, 1970, Progress, Moscow.

87. V.I. Lenin, *A Characterisation of Economic Romanticism*, in *Collected Works*, Vol. II, 1970, Progress, Moscow.

88. V.I. Lenin, *The Development of Capitalism in Russia*, 1974, Progress, Moscow.

89. V.I. Lenin, *Report on the International Situation and the Fundamental Tasks of the Communist International* in *Selected Works*, 1971, Progress, Moscow.

90. V.I. Lenin, *What Is To Be Done* in *Selected Works*, Vol. I, 1971, Progress, Moscow.

91. A. Lewis, *Economic Survey 1919-1939*, 1966, Unwin University Books, London.

92. C. Lightheim, *Imperialism*, 1971, Allen Lane and Penguin, London.

93. F. List, National System of Political Economy.

94. R. Luxembourg, *The Accumulation of Capital*, 1951, London, Routledge & Kegan Paul; first published Berlin, 1913.

95. R. Luxembourg, *The Accumulation of Capital — an Anti-Critique*, Allen Lane; first published Berlin, 1915. See under Tarbuck, K. (Ed.) below.

96. H. Magdoff, *The Age of Imperialism*, 1969, Monthly Review Press, New York.

97. H. Magdoff, '*Imperialism Without Colonies*', in R.J. Owen and R.B. Sutcliffe (eds.), *Studies in the Theory of Imperialism*, 1972, Longman, London.

98. E. Mandel, *Marxist Economic Theory*, 1973, Merlin Press, London.

99. E. Mandel, *Europe Versus America*, 1970, New Left Books, London.

first published 1968.
100. Mahotiere, *Towards One Europe*, 1974, Penguin, London.
101. Mao Tse-tung, *'The Chinese Revolution and the Chinese Communist Party'*, in *Selected Works of Mao Tse-tung*, Vol. II, 1954, Peking.
102. Mao Tse-tung, *On New Democracy*, in *Selected Works*, Vol. II, 1954, Peking.
103. K. Marx, *Capital*, Vol. I. 1968, Progress, Moscow.
104. K. Marx, *Capital*, Vol. III, 1971, Progress, Moscow.
105. K. Marx, *Capital*, Vol. III, 1971, Progress, Moscow.
106. K . Marx, *Grundrisse*, Penguin, 1975, London.
107. K. Marx, *The Poverty of Philosophy*, 1973, Progress, Moscow.
108. K. Marx, *Address on the Question of Free Trade*, in *Poverty of Philosophy*, 1973, Progress, Moscow.
109. K. Marx, *'The Future Results of British Rule in India'*, in Marx and Engels, *Articles on Britain*, 1971, Progress, Moscow.
110. K. Marx, *Theories of Surplus Value*, Parts 1-3, 1969, Progress, Moscow.
111. K. Marx, *A Contribution to the Critique of Political Economy*, 1970, Progress, Moscow.
112. K. Marx, *Value, Price and Profit*, in *Selected Works*, Vol. I, 1971, Progress, Moscow.
113. K. Marx, *'The East India Company* — Its History And Results, in Marx and Engels, *Article on Britain*, 1971, Progress, Moscow.
114. K. Marx, *Why Has the English Revolution Been Successful, A Review of Guizot's Book*, in Marx and Engels, *Articles on Britain*, 1971, Progress, Moscow.
115. Marx and Engels, *Selected Works*, 1973, Progress, Volumes I-III.
116. Marx and Engels, *The Communist Manifesto*, in *Selected Works*, Vol. I, 1970, Progress, Moscow.
117. Marx and Engels, *The German Ideology*, in *Selected Works*, Vol. I, 1970, Progress, Moscow.
118. S. Menshikov, *Managers and Millionaires*, 1969, Progress, Moscow.
119. J.S. Mill, *The Unsettled Questions of Principles of Political Economy*, Longman, London.
120. W.E. Minchiton, (Editor). *The Growth of Overseas English Trade*, 1969, Methuen, London.
121. G. Myrdal, *Economic Theory and Underdeveloped Regions*, 1954, Duckworth, London.
122. D. Neumark, *Africa and International Trade*, 1964, Stanford University Press, Stanford, Calif.
123. K. Nkrumah, *Neo-colonialism: The Last Stage of Imperialism*, 1965, Nelson, London.
124. K. Norris & J. Vaizey, *The Economics of Research and Technology*, 1973, Allen & Unwin, London.
125. R. Nurkse, *Problems of Capital Formation in Underdeveloped*

Countries and Patterns of Trade and Development, 1970, Oxford. Oxford University Press.

126. R.J. Owen & R.B. Sutcliffe, (Eds.), *Studies in the Theory of Imperialism*, 1972, Longman, London.

127. J.H. Parry, *The Spanish Seaborne Empire*, 1973, Penguin, London.

128. C. Payer, *The Debt Trap, The I.M.F. and the Third World*, 1974, Penguin, London.

129. E. Penrose, The International Patent System, 1951, London.

130. Pearson, *Partners in Development*, 1970, Praeger, New York.

131. R.M. Poats, *Technology for Developing Nations*, 1972.

132. N. Poulantzas, *Facism and Democracy*, 1974, New Left Books, London.

133. N. Poulantzas, *Political Power and Social Classes*, 1968, New Left Book, London.

134. H. Plumb, *England in the Eighteenth Century*, 1966, Pelican,London.

135. E. Praobrezhensky, *The New Economics*, 1965, Oxford University Press, Oxford.

136. W.B. Reddaway, *Effects of UK Direct Investment Overseas*, 1967, Cambridge University Press, Cambridge.

137, R.I. Rhodes, (ed.) *Imperialism and Underdevelopment: A Reader*, 1970, Monthly Review Press, New York.

138. D. Ricardo, *The Principles of Political Economy and Taxation*, 1971, Pelican, London.

139. W. Rodney, *How Europe Underdeveloped Africa*, 1973, London. Bogle L'Overture, London.

140. W.W. Rostow, *The Stages of Growth*, 1964, Cambridge University Press, Cambridge.

141. Royal Commission on the Depression of Trade and Industry, (1884), *Final Report*, HMSO.

142. S. Rungman, A History of Crusades, Vol. 1-3, 1953, Blackwell, Oxford.

143. W. Schloete, *British Overseas Trade from 1700 to the 1930s*, 1938, Blackwell, Oxford.

144. J.A. Schumpeter, *Capitalism, Socialism, Socialism and Democracy*, 1970, Allen & Unwin, London.

145. J.A. Schumpeter, *Imperialism and Social Classes*, 1972, Meridian Books.

146. Schulz, *Revolutions and Peace Treaties*, 1974, B and N, New York.

147. B. Semmell, *The Rise of Free Trade Imperialism*, 1970, Cambridge University Press, Cambridge.

148. J.J. Servan-Schreiber, The American Challenge, 1969, Penguin, London.

149. G.K. Shirokov, *Industrialisation of India*, 1973, Progress, Moscow.

150. S. Sideri, Trade and Power, 1970, Rotterdam.

151. A. Smith, *Wealth of Nations*, 1970, Penguin, London.

152. S. Smith, *The US and Africa*, 1974, Progress, Moscow.
153. J. Stalin, *The October Revolution and the National Question* in Collected Works, Vols. IV & VII.
154. H. Stephenson, *The Coming Clash*, 1972, Weidenfeld & Nicolson, London.
155. J. Strachey, *The End of Empire*, 1959, Gollancz, London.
156. P. Sweezy, *Theory of Capitalist Development*, 1942, Monthly Review, New York.
157. F. Tamas, *Studies in International Economics*, 1966, Adademiai Kiado, Budapest.
158. K. Tarbuck (ed.), *Introduction to Rosa Luxembourg and N. Bukharin, Imperialism and the Accumulation of Capital*, 1972, Allen Lane, London.
159. R.H. Tawney, *Religion and the Rise of Capitalism*, 1973, Penguin, London.
160. D. Thompson, *England in the 19th Century*, 1967, Penguin, London.
161. R. Triffin, *The Dollar Crisis*, 1960, Yale University Press, Yale.
162. C. Tugendhat, *The Multinationals*, 1971, Penguin, London.
163. L. Turner, *The Multinational Company and the Third World*, 1973, Allen, London.
164. UNO, *The Impact of Multinational Corporations on Development and International Relations*, (Summary of Hearings).
165. T. Veblen, *Economic Theory and the Business Enterprise*, 1965, Kelly, New York.
166. R. Vernon, *Sovereignty At Bay*, 1971, Penguin, London.
167. J. Viner, *International Trade and Development*, 1964, Oxford, Oxford University Press.
168. E.G. Wakefield, England and America: A Comparison of the Social and Political State of Both Nations, 1834, Kelly, New York.
169. B. Ward, *Towards a World of Plenty*, 1965, Toronto University Press, Toronto.
170. B. Warren, 'Imperialism and Capitalist Industrialization', *New Left Review*, 1973, No. 81, September.
171. S. Weissman, *The Trojan Horse*, 1974, Ramparts Press, New York.
172. E. William, *Capitalism and Slavery*, 1972, Deutsch, London.
173. C . Wilcox, *A Charter for World Trade*, 1972, Arno, New York.

MAGAZINES

1.   *Fortune Magazine*, May, 1942.
2.   *Telex Africa*, October, 1974.
3.   *International Studies Quarterly*, December, 1972.
4.   *Wall Journal*, 1971.
5.   *Economy and Society*, Vol. 2, No. 2.
6.   *Quarterly Journal of Economics*, Vol. XXIV.
7.   *US Survey of Current Business*, November, 1965.
8.   *US Survey of Current Business*, May, 1969.
9.   *Fortune Magazine*, 15, September, 1958.
10.   *ISER*, Special Issue Social and Economic Studies Vol.22. No.1, March, 1933.
11.   *Sunday Post*, Nairobi, 24, June, 1974.
12.   *Time Magazine*, 25, April, 1975.
13.   *Newsweek Magazine*, 23, April, 1975.
14.   *Japan and Africa*, London, October 1974.
15.   *United States Department of Commerce, Board of Trade Journal*, 1968.
16.   *United States Department of Commerce, Board of Trade Journal*, 23 September, 1970.

INDEX